MARIAN WENDEL
H: 817-274-7211
W: 214-767-3732

SPECULATIVE MARKETS

ROBERT A. STRONG
University of Maine

SECOND EDITION

HarperCollinsCollegePublishers

To BKKBR, once again

Acquisitions Editor: Kirsten D. Sandberg
Editorial Assistant: Kathi Kuntz
Marketing Manager: Kate Steinbacher
Project Coordination, Text and Cover Design: Proof Positive/Farrowlyne
  Associates, Inc.
Cover Illustration: Matt Walton
Production Manager: Kewal Sharma
Compositor: Black Dot Graphics
Printer and Binder: R. R. Donnelley & Sons Company
Cover Printer: The Lehigh Press, Inc.

Speculative Markets, Second Edition

Library of Congress Cataloging-in-Publication Data

Strong, Robert A.
    Speculative markets / Robert A. Strong.—2nd ed.
        p.   cm.
    Includes bibliographical references and index.
    ISBN 0-06-501249-6
        1. Options (Finance)   2. Financial futures.   3. Gold.
4. Financial engineering.   I. Title.
HG6024.3.S76   1994   93-34752
332.64'5—dc20   CIP

93 94 95 96 9 8 7 6 5 4 3 2 1

# Contents

 # Preface

The futures and options markets have changed dramatically since the first edition of this book was published in 1989. Many of those changes are reflected in academia's treatment of the subject. Just a few years ago, separate futures and options courses were relatively rare. If an educational institution did have such a course, it was often a graduate elective or an advanced undergraduate "special topics" course. The plethora of investments textbooks dealt with the trading pits in an obligatory chapter or two, relegating the topic to the backwaters of the discipline.

By 1993 there were futures and options exchanges in 40 countries. Hundreds of schools in the United States and Canada now offer courses on futures and options as part of both their undergraduate and graduate finance curriculum. What was once exotic, "nice-to-know" material has become part of the basic tool kit of fundamental knowledge.

CHANGES IN THE TEXT REFLECT CHANGES IN THE FIELD

One element of the change in the study of futures and options stems from their increasing complexity. In fact, the phrase "futures and options" is rapidly being replaced with **derivative assets** to reflect more accurately the multidimensional nature of the growing number of products both on and off the exchanges. The increasing complexity is in large part due to the emergence of the **risk management** and **financial engineering** subfields of finance, and one can find these terms prominently displayed in the organizational charts of investment houses and large commercial banks. As a consequence, I have added two new chapters to the second edition of *Speculative Markets* to provide more complete and timely coverage of these areas.

The new edition also contains two additional chapters on financial futures. I discuss **immunization strategies** in much greater detail than in the first edition and give foreign exchange futures their own chapter.

Successful application requires a good foundation in theory. For this reason, the second edition contains an additional chapter on **option pricing**, dealing with the primary *pricing model derivatives (delta, gamma, and theta)*. Colleagues have class-tested this chapter at two universities to enrich the subsequent material on financial engineering and risk management. It also provides the instructor with the option to have much snazzier *classroom examples.*

The concepts of **position risk** and **directional versus speed markets** seem to appeal to students, and these topics require a more thorough understanding of option pricing than was possible in the first edition of *Speculative Markets.* Both concepts can significantly enliven the subject of option pricing. Presented properly, the Black-Scholes derivatives provide a useful bridge from theory to practice. In fact, for some students delta, gamma, and theta seem to function as the proverbial "missing link."

BACKGROUND, PREREQUISITES, AND LEVEL

Speculative Markets is appropriate for most undergraduate futures and options courses and for application-oriented MBA courses. I assume that students taking this course have basic familiarity with time value of money principles and with equity securities. Many students who take a speculative markets course will have had a prior course in investments, although that is not a prerequisite to understanding the material presented here.

I believe that this edition of the book contains some enhancements, some changes, and some deletions, all of which will make it attractive to a great many instructors. For one thing, the level of **technical rigor** is higher in the second edition because of the evolution of the discipline. Five years ago, futures and options courses dealt largely with comparative statics. Today, a good overview of derivative assets and their use requires a **dynamic framework.** Profit and loss diagrams are still important, and I cover them in detail, but an understanding of the changing nature of the variables is increasingly important.

The added rigor, however, has not changed the focus of the book. It is intended for use in a course providing an overview of the futures and options markets, with special emphasis on the opportunities and risks associated with them. The book is especially well-suited for an *applications-oriented* course.

THE SOFTWARE PACKAGE

The software prepared for use with *Speculative Markets* is more elegant than that provided with the first edition. (The 27 programs are described at length in Chapter 1.) The disk is packaged with the Instructor's Manual and may be freely copied by *Speculative Markets* adopters for distribution to students enrolled in the course. The Lotus files, many **macro-driven,** are more user-friendly thanks to the talent of my graduate assistant, Kailash Kalantri. I appreciate his enthusiasm for this project. In many of the files, the Lotus add-in WYSIWIG, with its bells and whistles, shepherds the students away from some common mistakes.

Several new files appear in the software. The **TABLE** file generates the type of *delta table* found throughout the industry. The user inputs a starting striking price and initial values, then fires up the macro, and is presented with a table showing *put and call premiums, and delta, gamma, and theta for various striking prices*. Internal menus make amending the initial conditions easy. There are also new files to calculate *T bond conversion factors* and *bond duration*, values needed for **immunization strategies**. A separate file calculates **portfolio duration.**

The **OEX data** files, which contain daily closing levels of the Standard & Poor's 100 stock index, have been extended through most of 1993. There are now almost *twelve years of daily data* contained on the software disk, and these data provide an excellent training aid for use in investigations of "historical versus implied" volatility. To reduce personal computer memory problems, a new file is provided, **OEXWEEK,** which contains *weekly closing values of the index for the 1982–93 period*. This file can be used in the same way as the OEX files, but it runs more quickly.

ACKNOWLEDGMENTS

As usual, the book benefited from careful reviews by a number of my colleagues. They caught many errors that I missed, taught me some things about my chosen field of study, and made excellent suggestions regarding topic organization. These reviewers are listed below.

Don Chambers, Professor of Finance, Lafayette College; Andrew H. Chen, Distinguished Professor of Finance, Southern Methodist University; Yu-Min Chou, Professor of Finance, University of Michigan at Dearborn; Amy Dickinson, Assistant Professor of Finance, Florida Atlantic University; Ralph Gamble, Associate Professor of Economics and Finance, Fort Hays State University; James A. Greenleaf, Associate Professor of Finance, Lehigh University; Thomas C. Johansen, Assistant Professor of Finance, Fort Hays State University; George W. Kutner, Assistant Professor of Finance, Marquette University; Hun Y. Park, Associate Professor of Finance, University of Illinois; Elias Raad, Assistant Professor, Ithaca College; Edward J. Sullivan, Professor of Economics and Finance, Fordham University; Paul J. Swanson, Jr., Associate Professor of Finance; Jot K. Yau, Assistant Professor of Finance, George Mason University.

Kirsten Sandberg, my editor at HarperCollins, was a joy to work with and an excellent boss. I appreciate very much the energy she devoted to this project; it approached her enthusiasm for spinach salads and practical jokes. Brett Sullivan, the HarperCollins sales representative for my area, was instrumental in putting me in touch with Kirsten, and without him this book would very likely have been placed elsewhere. Gail Savage of Proof Positive/Farrowlyne Associates put the book through the copyediting and production stages faster than I would have believed possible. Her personal attention to everything greatly facilitated the process.

Robert A. Strong

Foreword

We find ourselves living in a world that is enormously complicated. In each generation the complexity seems to compound exponentially. Information multiplies at a rate most of us cannot fathom and travels at the speed of light even to remote parts of the globe. Whole new industries have emerged, employing hundreds of thousands of people completing tasks, building products, and providing services in fields nonexistent a generation ago.

Such is certainly the case in the field of financial services. The single most important reason for the fantastic numbers of new opportunities in the financial services industry has been, in my opinion, the understanding, development, and application of option pricing theory to manage risk in a world changing incredibly fast.

As Professor Strong points out, option and futures concepts have been applied in business since biblical times. It was, however, the convergence of academic theory and practical application in the early 1970s that launched virtually a whole new industry. In the late 1960s the two Chicago futures exchanges, The Chicago Board of Trade and The Chicago Mercantile Exchange, were facing a practical business problem. The agricultural markets in which they dealt were very cyclical. Member capital and trading talent were grossly underutilized much of the time. Each exchange identified a segment of the financial markets as a potential new source of member opportunity.

The Chicago Board of Trade saw great potential in the put and call option market. This was a niche market in which a handful of put and call dealers created one-of-a-kind contracts on listed stocks for a small number of investors. If The Chicago Board of Trade could figure out a way to standardize these contracts, make them fungible with each other, and trade them in an exchange environment, then it might have for its members a market whose cycles often ran counter to the agricultural cycle. The Board did. The result was the launch, in 1973, of the Chicago Board Options Exchange, Inc.

Around the same time, Leo Melamed at The Chicago Mercantile Exchange rightly guessed that there would soon be a great need for international businesses to hedge the risk of holding the various foreign currencies in which The Exchange was now dealing. Thus came standardized futures contracts on various currencies and the creation of the International Monetary Market division of The Chicago Mercantile Exchange.

Also, around the same time, the academic world was working diligently on theories and models to explain current pricing and to predict future values of these new derivative instruments. Perhaps the most significant and certainly the best known academic work to emerge from that era was from two University of Chicago professors, Fischer Black and Myron Scholes, who created the Black-Scholes Option Pricing Model.

The spectacular and immediate success of option trading at Chicago Board Options Exchange, Inc., and currency futures trading at The Chicago Mercantile Exchange created a unique market for professionals who understood and could apply mathematic principles to the trading of these new instruments. But opportunities didn't end there. As academic research expanded the universe of knowledge on option pricing theory, practitioners discovered that these principles could be applied to identifying and pricing all manner of heretofore hidden components of risk. Once the risk in holding various financial assets, as well as balance sheet assets and liabilities of corporations, could be identified and segmented, then perhaps strategists could figure out a way to hedge those risks. They did, and thus was born a whole new industry focused on financial engineering.

This may be a good place to clarify a definition. This book is entitled *Speculative Markets*. The term *speculation* has somehow taken on a pejorative context, somewhat akin to gambling. There is a rather simplistic but accurate differentiation between the two. *Gambling* is the creation of risk where none naturally exists. *Speculation* is the process by which an existing risk is transferred from the one who is holding it but doesn't want it, to a person who is willing to hold it. Needless to say, without the speculator all the incredible strides we have made in risk management techniques and strategies would be rendered moot, unable to be implemented. The speculator is absolutely essential to the process.

There is no doubt that one of the most important developments in the capital markets has been the application of derivative strategies. Those of you who come away with a basic understanding of *Speculative Markets* derived from this book will have a definite leg up in business.

William C. Floersch
Vice Chairman
Chicago Board Options Exchange

 **Introduction**

*I*t is a gloomy moment in history. Not for many years has there been so much grave and deep apprehension. Never has the future seemed so incalculable as now . . . the political cauldron seethes and bubbles. It's a solemn moment, and no one can feel an indifference. And yet, the very haste to be *rich,* which is the *occasion* of so much widespread calamity, has also tended to destroy the *moral* forces with which we are to resist and subdue the calamity!

Harper's Weekly
October 10, 1857

KEY TERMS

arbitrage
bearish
bullish
call
cash market
covered call
derivative asset
efficient
financial engineering

futures contract
hedger
immunization
implied volatility
option
put
speculator
spot market

The passage from *Harper's Weekly* is more than a century old, yet these words could easily be inserted into today's newspapers. There is world-wide interest in the financial markets and their influence on our quality of life.

The futures and options markets are very useful, perhaps essential parts of our financial system. Still, they have a long history of being misunderstood. To professionals in the field, it is a disturbing fact that many people who offer advice about the relative merits of futures and options products are ill-equipped to do so. You cannot understand these products by casual contact, by a conversation on a golf course, or by reading a few magazine articles. Futures and options require serious study if they are to be used properly. Two major objectives of this book are to illustrate their economic function and to inform the potential user so that an intelligent decision might be made regarding the role of futures and options in a particular portfolio.

USES OF DERIVATIVE ASSETS

An **option** is the *right* to either buy something (a **call** option) or sell something (a **put** option); a **futures contract** is a *promise* to buy or sell. Collectively, these are **derivative assets,** because their value is *derived* in large part from the value of another asset. While derivative assets might be useful in many different applications, these fall into three broad categories. This book covers them in much greater detail as it progresses; what follows is only a brief overview.

USES OF DERIVATIVE ASSETS: 3 BROAD CATEGORIES

1. Income Generation

The widest use of derivative assets by both individuals and institutions is the generation of additional portfolio income. **Covered calls** are the most popular means for doing so. Here a person who already owns stock gives someone else the right to buy the shares in exchange for a fee.

2. Risk Management

It is common to think that investments make money when prices rise and lose when prices fall. This is true for a simple portfolio that contains shares of stock only. Portfolios also can be constructed to benefit from a price decline. Such a portfolio will be hurt by a price rise.

Unlike a coin, the investment decision seldom has only two faces. While we speak of someone being **bullish** (they believe prices will rise) or **bearish** (they believe prices will fall), there are many intermediate points. Two people

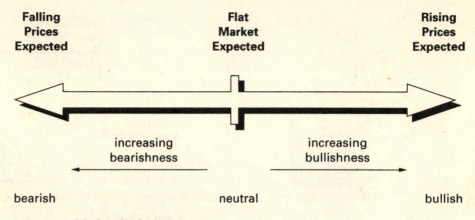

Figure 1-1 Market Outlook Continuum

may both believe that a particular stock is likely to increase in value, but one might be much more confident in his or her forecast. The use of derivative assets permits investors or portfolio managers to tailor their risk exposure to any point they choose along the bullish/bearish continuum.

Derivative assets also permit movement along this continuum at a moment's notice. A quick telephone call to your broker, adding new positions or closing out existing ones, can shift your location on the line. In fact, the passage of time will cause some portfolio components to move spontaneously along the line without the portfolio manager doing anything. So portfolios employing futures and options need periodic "maintenance" if it is necessary to keep their characteristics constant.

Financial Engineering

Financial engineering is a rapidly growing subfield of finance. Sometimes a particular combination of investment characteristics is needed, but not available in an existing exchange-traded product. By properly mixing assets, the desired combination can be created. This custom building of a portfolio is financial engineering and varies widely in the degree of sophistication required.

HEDGING AND SPECULATING

This book is primarily about the function and potential uses of the futures and options markets, where market participants either reduce the risk they face or accept risk from someone else.

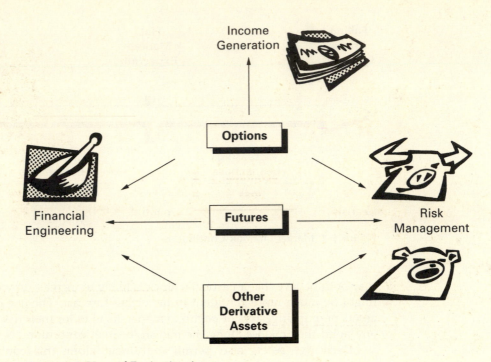

Figure 1-2 Uses of Derivative Assets

Hedgers

If someone bears an economic risk and uses these markets to reduce that risk, the person is a **hedger.** Normally the hedger understands the market well and makes an informed decision regarding if, when, and how much to hedge.

Almost everyone is familiar with the hedging concept. Homeowners hedge when they buy fire insurance on their houses. Car owners hedge by buying collision insurance. In similar fashion, you can acquire "insurance" on a portfolio to provide some protection in the event of an adverse event.

In legal circles, the courts are looking with increasing displeasure on managers who fail to properly manage risk. In a case likely to become a landmark decision, the Indiana Court of Appeals in *Brane* v *Roth*[1] found the directors of an agricultural cooperative liable for more than $400,000 in grain sale losses that might have been avoided had the cooperative hedged the inventory. The essence of the ruling is that hedging is a prudent business practice and a prudent businessperson has a legal duty to understand and use the futures market hedging mechanism.

---

[1]*Brane* v *Roth*, 52A02-9102-CV-50, Court of Appeals of Indiana, First District, April 20, 1992.

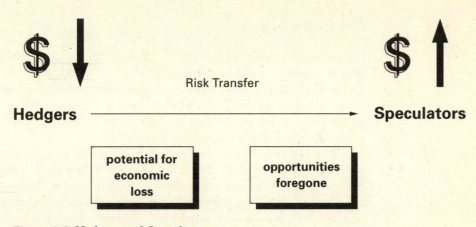

Figure 1-3 Hedgers and Speculators

In *Brane* v *Roth,* the Indiana Court of Appeals held that a prudent business-person has a legal obligation to understand and use the hedging function of the futures market.

Speculators

People who accept the risk the hedgers do not want are **speculators.** They do so because they think the potential return outweighs the risk. Insurance companies accept the risk of a house fire or auto damage because they believe the insurance premium will compensate them adequately for the risk they have chosen to bear.

The futures and options markets are widely associated with speculation, but this is not their economic function. They permit the transfer of risk between market participants as desired, and this contributes to our economic welfare.

Some speculators know what they are doing, and some do not. Those who don't are gambling in the traditional sense of the word, since they do not have sufficient knowledge to make the best decisions. In the futures and options markets, anyone who accepts risk is a speculator. Generally, a particular futures contract will not be successful unless it attracts both hedgers and speculators.[2]

---

[2]For instance, if everyone wants to buy insurance and no one wants to sell it, there will be no insurance policies created, and hence no insurance available.

Arbitrageurs

We know that well-functioning capital markets are quite **efficient,** meaning that prevailing prices accurately reflect the information available at the moment. In other words, free lunches are hard to find. In finance, a risk-free profit is **arbitrage,** and risk-free profits are difficult to find, for the same reason that you seldom find five-dollar bills on the sidewalk: They are grabbed by the first person who sees them.

This book illustrates that certain relationships must prevail among the various security, option, and futures prices. When these prices temporarily move out of line, an arbitrage situation may momentarily exist. Arbitrageurs are there to "pick up the profit" by their activities, and in so doing bring prices back into proper alignment. Option pricing theory is based on arbitrage arguments, and the theory's offspring are principal players in risk management and financial engineering applications. Widespread arbitrage would defeat most of these uses of derivatives assets and turn the market into a speculator's playground.

ORGANIZATION OF THE BOOK

The Options Market

Options give you the right, but not the obligation, to buy or sell something. The option idea has existed for centuries. We know that in the ancient seaports of Phoenicia, Rome, and Greece options traded against outgoing cargoes. Options on tulip bulbs traded in Amsterdam during the early 1600s, and stock options have traded in the United States since the early eighteenth century.

The earliest known book on "the market," *Confusion of Confusions,* was published in 1688 by Joseph de la Vega. One statement in the book sums up the attitude many people continue to hold toward speculative assets:

> Profits on the exchange are the treasures of goblins. At one time they may be carbuncle stones, then coals, then diamonds, then flint-stones, then morning dew, then tears.

The next six chapters of this book will detail how stock options can be used for a variety of purposes other than the speculation de la Vega disdains.

1. *Chapter Two: Basic Principles of Stock Options* Chapter Two begins with a discussion of why options are a good idea, how they are created, and how they are traded. It then moves into a discussion of option characteristics and terminology and shows how to read the options prices quoted in the financial pages of your newspaper.

Box 1-1

Professor Merton Miller (Nobel Laureate from the University of Chicago) tells a story of a conversation he had with the treasurer of a Chicago oil company. In the aftermath of the Persian Gulf war, the price of oil dropped sharply and the value of the firm's oil inventory declined substantially. Merton told the man that it "served him right for speculating on oil prices."

"But we didn't speculate," the man said. "We didn't use the futures markets at all."

Merton replied, "That's the point; by not hedging your inventory, you gambled that the price of oil would not drop. You guessed wrong, and you lost."

If you do not hedge, you are a de facto speculator.

Source: Conversation between the author and Merton Miller, February 7, 1992, North Miami Beach, Florida.

Put and call options can be used to make a profit from rising or falling prices. A call option gives you the right to buy something, while a put option gives you the right to sell something (even if you do not own it!). Calls are valuable if prices rise; puts are valuable if prices fall. The right to sell something is a puzzling concept to many people; you will see, however, that puts are versatile and easy to understand with a little thought.

2. *Chapter Three: Option Strategies* This chapter concentrates on ways in which options can be used as portfolio components. Specifically, options are useful risk-management tools; they can be used to alter the risk and return characteristics of an existing portfolio. When used in a portfolio, options function as a means of reducing risk, a means of generating additional income, or both.

3. *Chapter Four: Option Combinations and Spreads* Combinations and spreads are packages of options held simultaneously to create a particular combination of risk and return. Individual investors are particularly fond of spreads, while professional option traders construct option combinations daily.

4. *Chapter Five: Option Pricing* This is the most difficult but most important aspect of the study of the options markets. You will learn about one of the most consequential discoveries in modern financial management: the Black-Scholes Option Pricing Model. Practice exercises using this model will improve your understanding of options immeas-

urably. Competence with option pricing is an unusual, and marketable, skill in the investment business.

5. *Chapter Six: Delta, Gamma, and Theta* These three derivatives of the option pricing model are central to the informed use of options and futures. They measure how the option premium changes as an underlying variable in the option pricing model changes. Whether you are using derivative assets as a hedging device or for speculation, an understanding of the delta, gamma, and theta of your portfolio will improve your investment results.

6. *Chapter Seven: Stock Index Options and Overwriting Strategies* Using options to generate additional portfolio income is common, and stock index options are especially convenient for this purpose. Still, many otherwise knowledgeable options users have not considered the compelling merits of stock index options for this purpose. This chapter provides an extended example of ways these products might be used to generate income in a stock portfolio.

The Futures Market

People used to say the *commodity* futures market, because this market was concerned with agricultural goods like wheat, soybeans, and pork bellies. Today there are also futures contracts available on many different non-agricultural assets such as stock indexes, interest rates, and foreign currencies. Some people maintain that agricultural hedging applications are still the most important use of the futures market, but the financial futures are becoming more important by the minute. Chapters Eight through Twelve cover basic principles of the futures markets.

1. *Chapter Eight: Fundamentals of the Futures Market* Futures contracts are a promise to buy or sell something at a predetermined price in the future. This "promise" is an important distinction from the "right" that an option carries: A promise is an obligation.

   In this chapter we look at the hedger and speculator in detail and consider certain pricing relationships between the futures market and the **cash,** or **spot,** market. You can view the cash market like your grocery store. To get commodities there, you walk in, select the goods you want, pay for them, and take them home. Futures contracts involve trades that two parties promise to make at some point in the future; no goods are actually exchanged at the time the futures contract is bought or sold.

2. *Chapter Nine: Stock Index Futures* Stock index futures are one of the most versatile financial innovations ever to come about, and have received (wrongly) much of the blame for the October 19, 1987,

market crash. They are an extremely popular means of reducing the market risk of a portfolio, and, for many people, stock index futures will be the most important futures contract they study.

3. *Chapter Ten: Foreign Exchange Futures* Foreign exchange futures are used widely in international trade to reduce the potential for loss from fluctuating values of world currencies. Global trade and investment is common practice in the 1990s, and many international firms routinely reduce the foreign exchange risk they face via foreign exchange futures.

4. *Chapter Eleven: Interest Rate Futures* Interest rate futures are now used by most large banks to control interest rate risk. In many respects interest rate futures are the most sophisticated of the financial futures. There are many subtleties in their pricing and in the determination of the related hedge ratios. Chapter Eleven covers the basic principles of interest rate futures, with specialized applications in the following chapter.

5. *Chapter Twelve: Immunization and Spreading Strategies* Removing or reducing interest rate risk is a prime reason many financial institutions use treasury bond or treasury bill futures contracts. An **immunization** strategy is one that seeks to protect the portfolio from the effects of interest rate risk. Techniques for doing so are the primary focus of this chapter.

   Just as with options, there are ways in which several futures contracts can be combined into a position called a spread, either to reduce risk or to reduce the initial cost of the position. This chapter concludes with a review of several popular spreading strategies.

Other Derivative Assets

Futures options and other derivative assets are especially poorly understood by many people who might productively use them.

1. *Chapter Thirteen: Futures Options and Other Derivative Assets* Chapter Thirteen covers a collection of curious securities: futures options, foreign currency options, warrants, and when-issued stock. Their value is also derived from the value of other assets, so they are derivative assets, too.

Contemporary Topics

The field of finance is constantly evolving. This is particularly true of derivative assets. If finance is a major subject area, risk management and financial engineering are minors. Most developments in portfolio management stem from one of these two areas.

1. *Chapter Fourteen: Risk Management* As shown earlier, investors are seldom 100% bullish or 100% bearish. Rather, their market views lie somewhere along this market outlook continuum. The practice of risk management generally involves one of two things. Either the investor wants to occupy a specific point on the bullish/bearish spectrum, or the investor wants to reduce the damage that would be associated with an adverse price movement. There are many ways to do either of these objectives, and this is the focus of this chapter.

2. *Chapter Fifteen: Financial Engineering, GLOBEX, and Program Trading* Financial engineering is the fastest growing subfield within finance. Delta, gamma, and theta are its building blocks. By adjusting the component mix, a chemical engineer can make a plastic as hard as a bowling ball or as soft as a food wrap. Similarly, a financial manager can alter the characteristics of a portfolio by adding or subtracting delta, gamma, or theta "points" to or from the total position.

   Many financial engineering applications center on the related subfield of risk management. While risk management has always been important, this topic has developed into a sophisticated, sometimes quantitative part of the total investment problem.

   Two noteworthy trading techniques are reviewed in this chapter as well. As worldwide communication links improve in quality and increase in number, around the clock trading becomes accessible to more market participants. GLOBEX is an effort to facilitate after-hours futures trading from a computer terminal by system participants across the globe.

   Program trading is not a new topic, but one that continues to attract press, often unfavorable. There are widespread misconceptions about this practice, which is why it is included in this book. The Appendix to Chapter Fifteen discusses the market crash of 1987, its probable causes, and the marketplace's response to it.

Precious Metals and Conclusion

1. *Chapter Sixteen: Precious Metals* Globally, gold is an important investment alternative. Futures contract trade on it, and the price of gold influences many parts of the financial system. Sometimes it may have an important role to play as a portfolio risk-reducer, and is particularly important to Europeans.

   Gold traders are major players in the international marketplace, and there are a variety of ways they invest: coins, bullion, futures contracts, futures options, gold certificates, mutual funds, and mining shares. Some investment advisors feel that every portfolio should contain some gold.

2. *Chapter Seventeen: Conclusion: Hedging and Speculating in the Real World* "All book learning and no common sense" is an historic admonition of the student. The material in this book will make you knowledgeable about the futures and options markets and their products, but caveats remain about the actual conduct of trading. These closing words provide food for thought about ways to get started and pitfalls to avoid.

OTHER MATERIAL

Further Reading

The "References" section at the end of the book provides addresses where you can get further information about futures and options. The exchanges have excellent free instructional material, and you should consider acquiring some of it while you are studying these markets. The references section also includes a sample of the relevant literature from both professional and academic journals and books.

Key Terms and Points

Each chapter begins with a listing of the key terms to be discussed. In addition, sprinkled throughout the book you will find information contained in small blocks. These are major points you want to understand and remember.

Information in these small blocks stresses a key point in the text.

Software

The software packaged with this book contains Lotus 1-2-3 templates (most with macros) that help solve futures and options problems. For the programs to run properly, you must have access to Lotus 1-2-3 version 2.X or higher. The files use the Lotus add-in feature WYSIWYG, which older versions of Lotus do not have. Without WYSIWYG the computer screen may freeze up.

There are twenty-eight files on the disk. Twenty-one of these are Lotus templates (in *.WK1 format). The other seven are WYSIWYG files (in *.FMT format). The user does not interact with the FMT files.

1. *BSOPM* This file contains the Black-Scholes Option Pricing Model, the workhorse tool of many option users. Besides theoretical put and call prices, it gives you delta, gamma, and theta for an option and for the nearby in- and out-of-the-money options. Additional striking prices can be generated with two keystrokes.

2. *SIGMA* As Chapter Five will show, needed in option pricing is the one variable that cannot be directly observed: the volatility of the underlying asset. This file calculates the **implied volatility** from the current option price and enables you to find other parameters that would otherwise be elusive.

3. *TABLE* This file generates a "delta table," showing delta, gamma, and theta for three separate striking prices for a put and a call.

4. *BLACKOPM* The Black-Scholes Option Pricing Model needs modification before it will work with futures options. The BLACKOPM file is the amended version.

5. *DURATION* In some immunization strategies it is necessary to know bond duration (a technical measure of interest rate risk). This file calculates the statistic along with yield to maturity.

6. *WTDUR* This file calculates the dollar-weighted duration of a fixed income portfolio. The calculations require the individual yields to maturity as inputs, so it usually is necessary to use the DURATION file before retrieving the WTDUR file.

7. *CONVFACT* In calculating a hedge ratio with treasury bonds, it is necessary to make a technical adjustment to the number of bonds needed in the hedge. Some bonds "count more" than others. This file calculates Chicago Board of Trade conversion factors to facilitate determination of the hedge ratio.

8. *FUTURES* This is a data file containing about six months of daily opening and settlement prices on six different commodity futures contracts.

9. *OEX files* There are thirteen OEX files. Twelve of these contain daily closing values for the Standard and Poors' 100 stock index (ticker symbol OEX) from 1982–1993. They are identified as OEX82, OEX83, etc. The other file, OEXWEEK, contains weekly closing values for the index over the entire period 1982–1993.

Why Read the Book?

If you are a student, perhaps the best motivation you can draw upon as you consider this book is to recognize that people who thoroughly understand the potential uses of futures and options are scarce. If you develop a fluency with the basic principles and with hedging and speculating applications, you will have a marketable talent that makes you stand out from the crowd. All financial institutions can make some productive use of derivative assets. Investment houses use them, and so do asset-liability managers at banks,

T   DD   GTE   S
GE NYN USX UTX
IBM AIT EK ALD
F   BEL XON

State Univ. Retirement System of Illinois
Gen'l Board of Pensions – Utd Methodist Church
Tennessee Valley Authority
Annuity Board of Southern Baptist Convention
Episcopal Church Pension Fund
Army and Air Force Exchange Service
Calif. Public Employees Retirement System
Florida State Board of Administration
AND MANY, MANY OTHERS

Figure 1-4 What Pension Funds Use Derivatives?

bank trust officers, endowment fund managers, mortgage officers, pension fund managers, corporate treasurers, foreign exchange managers, multinational corporations, oil companies, ranchers, farmers, and individual investors.

In many respects, futures and options are the fastest game in the investment village. As with a competitive sport, you have to train hard to become above-average, you have to practice, and you have to keep in shape. This book provides your initial training. Reading current articles in the popular press and the financial pages will keep your memory from fading, and professional seminars, jobplace mentors, and experience will help maintain your derivative asset prowess.

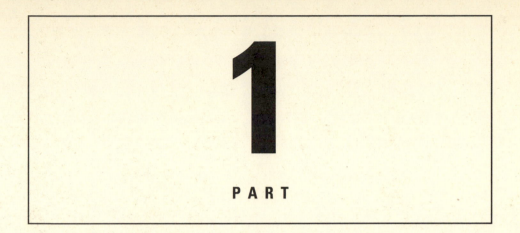

PART

1

THE OPTIONS MARKET

 **Basic Principles of Stock Options**

*T*here is an anecdote of Thales the Milesian and his financial device, which involves a principle of universal application, but is attributed to him on account of his reputation for wisdom. He was reproached for his poverty, which was supposed to show that philosophy was of no use. According to the story, he knew by his skill in the stars while it was yet winter that there would be a great harvest of olives in the coming year; so, having a little money, he gave deposits for the use of all the olive presses in Chios and Miletus, which he hired at a low price because no one bid against him. When the harvest time came, and many wanted them all at once and of a sudden, he let them out at any rate which he pleased, and made a quantity of money. Thus, he showed the world that philosophers can easily be rich if they like.

Aristotle

KEY TERMS

American option	in-the-money	Order Book Official
ask price	intrinsic value	out-of-the-money
at-the-money	limit order	premium
bid price	listed option	put option
call option	margin requirement	specialist system
closing transaction	marketmaker system	striking price
crowd	market order	time value
European option	naked call *same, p.37*	type of option
exercise	near-the-money	uncovered call
expiration date	open interest	underlying security
floor broker	opening transaction	wasting asset
fungibility	Options Clearing Corporation	write an option

This chapter covers basic principles of stock options that you must master before moving on to more advanced topics. Option traders have a language of their own, and you need to develop fluency with it quickly.

There are five major themes in this chapter:

1. What options are and where they come from;
2. Why options are a good idea;
3. Where and how options trade;
4. Components of the option premium; and
5. Where profits and losses come from with options.

WHAT OPTIONS ARE AND WHERE THEY COME FROM

There are two **types of options: call options** and **put options.** Call options are generally easier for people to understand, so these will be explained first.

Call Options

Although most people are not familiar with call options, the call option *concept* is something with which they probably *are* familiar.

Suppose you are shopping in a department store and find a leather coat on sale for $225. The sale ends today, and you do not have enough money with you to pay for it. You might find the store manager and ask if you could put the coat on 30-day layaway at the sale price. Suppose the manager agrees, provided you pay a $5 nonrefundable layaway processing fee. If you accept these terms, the store has created a call option: You have the right (but not the obligation) to buy one coat at a predetermined price ($225) anytime in the next 30 days, when your option expires. The store charged $5 for the option. With any option, the amount you pay for it is the **premium.**

The option premium is the amount you pay for the option.

See p.173

It is important to recognize that you have not *promised* to buy the coat. If you should find an identical coat at a lower price in another store, you can simply abandon your option with the original store and buy the coat in the cheaper location.

The owner of a call option has the *right to buy* within a specified time period. In exchange for this right, the owner of the option has paid a cash premium to the option seller.

A call option gives its owner the *right* to buy; it is not a promise to buy.

Put Options

A call gives you the right to *buy;* a put gives you the right to *sell.* Put options are conceptually difficult for many people because the right to sell something is not as intuitively comfortable as the right to buy.

A put option gives its owner the right to *sell.*

One large real estate agency gives a free put option to homeowners who list their homes for sale with the agency. After the real estate agent and the homeowner agree on a reasonable listing price for the house, the agent makes the usual attempts to sell the house. In the event that a buyer is not found, the homeowner has the right to sell the house *to the agency* at 70 percent of the original listing price. Again, the homeowner is not obliged to sell the house to the agency at this price; but if circumstances warrant, the homeowner can exercise the right to do so.

Where Options Come From

If I buy an option, someone has to sell it to me; there must be two parties to the trade. Unlike more familiar securities such as shares of stock, there is no set number of put or call options. In fact, the number in existence changes every day. Options can be created, and they can be destroyed. This unusual fact is crucial to understanding the options market.

There is no set number of put and call options on a given underlying security.

Opening and Closing Transactions   The first trade someone makes in a particular option is an **opening transaction** for that person. When the individual subsequently closes that position out with a second trade, this latter trade is a **closing transaction.** Purchases and sales can be either type of transaction.[1] Retail stockbrokers should routinely ask their option customers if a particular trade is *to open* or *to close.*

The owner of an option will ultimately do one of three things with it:

1. sell it to someone else;

---

[1] At the exchange, anyone making a trade has the right to ask who is taking the other side of their order, and if the trade is "to open" or "to close." To the professional option trader, every bit of information helps, and all traders are interested in the activities of the "big players." A large trade to open, for instance, must eventually be closed. A large trade to close, however, does not necessitate another trade at a later time.

2. let it expire; or
3. exercise it.

This is easy to explain using tickets to a university athletic event. Suppose you buy two tickets for a *premium* of $12 each. This is analogous to an *opening transaction*. The ticket gives you the right, but not the obligation, to go to the game. If you choose, you can (1) sell your tickets to someone else before the game. Or you could (2) decide to watch the game on television and leave the tickets in your desk drawer where they will "expire"—they will be worthless. Finally, you could (3) **exercise** the tickets and go to the game. No matter which of these courses of action you choose, it is analogous to a *closing transaction*. Game day is analogous to *expiration day*, and once it passes the tickets are worthless.[2]

Buying something as an opening transaction is perhaps easier to understand than *selling* something as an opening transaction. The university created the tickets and sold them; this was an opening transaction for the university. When an option is sold as an opening transaction, this is called **writing the option**.

Selling an option as an opening transaction is called *writing the option*.

No matter what the owner of an option does, the writer of the option keeps the option premium that he or she received when it was sold. Returning to the athletic event example, the university keeps the $24 you paid for the two tickets, regardless of whether you go to the game or not.[3]

The option writer keeps the option premium no matter what happens in the future.

Exchange-traded options have an important characteristic called **fungibility.** This means that, for a given company, all options of the same type with the same expiration and striking price are identical.[4] The **striking price**

---

[2]Note that options are routinely created or canceled in the market, unlike stocks and bonds, which already exist and which are generally fixed in number.

[3]Sport tickets are usually an imperfect example of a call option, as there is no middle outcome between going to the game and not going. In general, the option holder gains or loses depending on some underlying event (such as the stock price going up). One reviewer of this book has a 1964 Phillies world series ticket, which would have given him the option to go to a game if the Phillies made it to the series that year. They didn't, and the ticket "expired worthless."

[4]There is a vast over-the-counter market for options, too. These are not fungible. Rather, they are customized arrangements between investment houses and institutional investors (although an individual could also use them). Prior to the advent of the options exchanges in 1973, no options were fungible, and this impediment to trading was a prime reason the exchanges began to list options.

of an option is its predetermined transaction price. Fungibility is particularly important to the option writer. I may write an option and receive a premium for doing so. If market conditions change a week later, I can *buy* an option on the same company with the same contract terms, and this gets me out of the market: writing an option and buying a similar one are two transactions that cancel in my brokerage account. I have to pay for the option I buy, and the amount I pay may be more or less than the amount I received when I wrote it. The important point is that I do not have to buy the option back from the specific person to whom I sold it, because the options are fungible. Note that football tickets, in general, are *not* fungible, because all seats are not equally desirable.

The Role of the Options Clearing Corporation   The **Options Clearing Corporation** (OCC) is an important aspect of the options market. This organization positions itself between every buyer and seller and acts as a guarantor of all option trades. When someone buys or sells an option, that person is actually buying it from or selling it to the OCC. The OCC also regulates the trading activity of members of the various options exchanges, setting minimum capital requirements and providing for the efficient transfer of funds among members as gains or losses occur. The OCC publishes a

Figure 2-1 Buying a Call Option

BUYING A CALL OPTION

is like buying a ticket to a University of Maine
hockey game:

Having bought the ticket, I can
either:

- Exercise it and go to the game;

- Sell it;

- Abandon it and let it expire.

The University   *wrote*   the option and gets
to keep the premium (the ticket cost) no matter
which alternative I choose.

All Sales are actually to the OCC; all purchases are actually from the OCC.

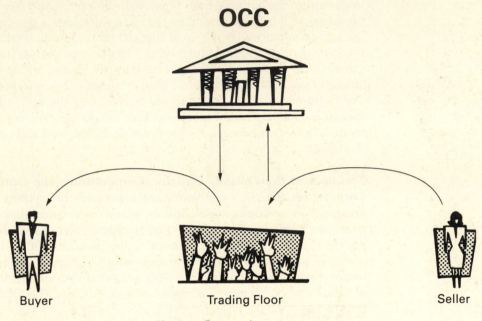

Figure 2-2 The Options Clearing Corporation

booklet entitled *Characteristics and Risks of Standardized Options,* which every potential option user receives upon opening an options account. These materials are available from any brokerage firm.

WHY OPTIONS ARE A GOOD IDEA

In the early days of our country, security investors faced a relatively simple set of choices. First, they chose between stocks and bonds. Second, they selected which stocks or which bonds.

Today's financial world is complicated. We face many sources of risk that were not present in the mid-nineteenth century. Today's communication technology provides us almost instantaneous information about events such as the Persian Gulf war, corporate announcements, world trade balances, inflation estimates, or industrial accidents like those at Bhopal, Chernobyl, or Three Mile Island. Each bit of news can impact on investment value.

Experienced investors are seldom 100 percent bullish or 100 percent bearish.[5] Our decision trees have many branches and decision nodes. The constant arrival of new information that can affect our investments means that for many people the investment process is dynamic: Positions need to be constantly reassessed and portfolios adjusted.

Portfolio Risk Management

We also know much more now about the behavior of security prices and the interaction of the security markets. This knowledge makes it possible and prudent for us to "fine tune" our investment strategy to deal with the many possible future states of the world.

Stock options are widely used in portfolio risk management. Options are much more convenient (and less expensive) to use than wholesale purchases or sales of shares of stock each time an adjustment is appropriate. This topic will be discussed in considerable detail later in the book.

Risk Transfer

Options also provide a means for risk to be transferred from one person to the next. I may own a portfolio of stock and face some potential risk that I find unacceptable. Using options, I can transfer that risk to another market participant, who is willing to bear it.

Financial Leverage

Options provide financial leverage, and this is one primary reason many speculators buy them. For example, I may feel that XYZ Corporation is an excellent takeover candidate, and I suspect that the price of the common stock (currently $65) is likely to rise sharply in value. If I were to buy 100 shares of this stock, it would cost me $6500. As an alternative, I could speculate on the takeover rumors using a stock option selling for perhaps $300. With this position, I would benefit from a sharp, immediate increase in the stock price, because a rise in the stock price would necessarily cause the option premium to rise as well. However, I would have only a modest amount of money at risk. The worst that could happen to me is that I would lose all $300; if I bought the stock, I could lose much more than that—as much as the entire $6500—if the stock plummeted.

---

[5]A person who is *bullish* believes that prices are going to rise; a *bearish* person believes the opposite.

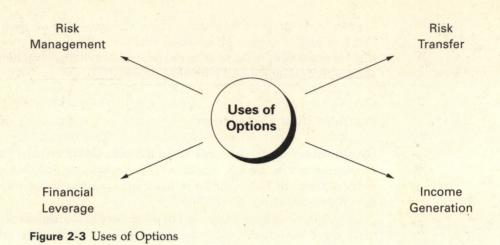

Figure 2-3 Uses of Options

Income Generation

Some people use options for generating additional income from their investment portfolio. Options are widely used for this purpose in the portfolios of endowment funds, pension funds, and individual portfolios.

The important point to remember is that options give investors and speculators opportunities to adjust risk or alter income streams that would otherwise not be available. An economist would say that options provide enhanced "spanning" of the market, or more investment substitutes.

WHERE AND HOW OPTIONS TRADE

Exchanges

In the United States, most options trade on one of four exchanges: the Chicago Board Options Exchange (CBOE), the American Stock Exchange (AMEX), the Philadelphia Stock Exchange (Philly), or the Pacific Stock Exchange (PSE). A very limited amount of trading also occurs at the New York Stock Exchange (NYSE).

In 1993, well-regulated options exchanges similar to the CBOE existed in Australia, Sao Paulo, Canada, Amsterdam, Hong Kong, Osaka, Manila, Singapore, Sydney, and the United Kingdom.

Over-the-Counter Options

Besides trading options on the exchanges, it is also possible to enter into "private" option arrangements with brokerage firms or other dealers. Institutions sometimes do this when they need a product with characteristics that are not available in an exchange-traded product. The striking price, life of the option, and premium are negotiated between the parties involved.

Because of their unique characteristics, these options are generally *not* fungible. They also might not be liquid; that is, an owner of an over-the-counter option might not be able to sell it quickly at a reasonable price. A **listed option** is traded on an options exchange, and such an option can always be quickly sold.

Standardized Option Characteristics

All options have standardized **expiration dates.** For most options, this is the Saturday following the third Friday of certain designated months. Individual investors typically view the third Friday of the month as the expiration date, because the exchanges are closed to public trading Saturday. Saturday is reserved for bookkeeping operations among the brokerage firms whose clients have dealt in the just-expiring options.

The **striking price** of an option is the predetermined transaction price. These are at multiples of $2.50 or $5, depending on the current stock price. Stocks priced at $25 or below have the lower multiple, while higher priced stocks have the $5 multiple. Shifts in the price of a stock result in the creation of new striking prices. As a matter of OCC policy, there is always at least one striking price above and at least one below the current stock price to increase

Figure 2-4 Identifying an Option

Expiration
(3rd Friday in March)

Type of
Option

Boeing Mar 45 Call

Underlying Asset
(Boeing common stock)

Striking Price
($45 per share)

Box 2-1   **OPTION TICKER SYMBOLS**

Option ticker symbols have three parts, one each for the underlying asset, the expiration month, and the striking price, expressed in that order. A Boeing March 45 call is BACJ:

BA	C	J
company	expiration	striking price

The code for the underlying asset is its stock ticker symbol, BA for Boeing. Examples of striking price and expiration codes are shown below.

Striking Prices

A	B	C	D	E	F	G	H	I	J
$ 5	$ 10	$ 15	$ 20	$ 25	$ 30	$ 35	$ 40	$ 45	$ 50
105	110	115	120	125	130	135	140	145	150
205	210	215	220	225	230	235	240	245	250

K	L	M	N	O	P	Q	R	S	T
$ 55	$ 60	$ 65	$ 70	$ 75	$ 80	$ 85	$ 90	$ 95	$100
155	160	165	170	175	180	185	190	195	200
255	260	265	270	275	280	285	290	295	300

$2½ Interval Codes

U	V	W	X
7½	12½	17½	22½

Note that striking price codes correspond to more than one number. "A" represents a striking price of $5, $105, or $205. Normally, a single security will have options with only one of these striking prices at a time.

Expirations

	Call/Put		Call/Put		Call/Put
Jan	A/M	May	E/Q	Sep	I/U
Feb	B/N	Jun	F/R	Oct	J/V
Mar	C/O	Jul	G/S	Nov	K/W
Apr	D/P	Aug	H/T	Dec	L/X

the potential usefulness of the options to a variety of potential users. The merits of different striking prices will become apparent as the text progresses.

Both puts and calls are based on 100 shares of the **underlying security,** which is the security the option gives you the right to buy or sell. If I buy a call option on the stock of a particular company, I am purchasing the right to buy *100 shares* of stock. It is not possible to buy or sell "odd lots" of options. A stock option is identified by company, expiration, striking price, and type of option (generally in that order).

Trading Mechanics

Bid Price and Ask Price   In both the specialist and marketmaker systems, there are actually *two* prices for an option at any given time: a **bid price** and an **asked price.** The bid price is the highest price anyone is willing to pay for a particular option, while the asked price is the lowest price at which anyone is willing to sell. By definition, at any moment there is only one bid price and one asked price, as only one price can be the "highest" or the "lowest."

Types of Orders   When someone wants to make an options trade, he or she must specify precisely what the broker is supposed to do, and this is done by specifying the type of order to be submitted. *Market orders* and *limit orders* are the two most important types.

See p. 177-180

A **market order** expresses a wish to buy or sell immediately, at the current price. A **limit order**, in contrast, specifies a particular price (or better) beyond which no trade is desired. A person who wanted to buy 3 IBM March 100 calls at the current price would tell the broker, "Buy 3 IBM March 100 calls at the market." The phrase "at the market" shows that the order is a market order.

Figure 2-5 The BID Price and the ASK Price

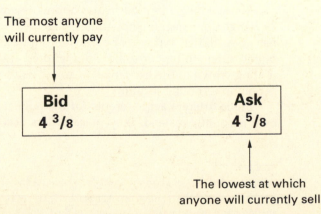

The most anyone
will currently pay

Bid	Ask
$4\,^3/_8$	$4\,^5/_8$

The lowest at which
anyone will currently sell

Another person might say "Buy 3 IBM March 100 calls at $2½, good until canceled." This indicates a limit order, as a price was specified. Limit orders also require a time limit, which is usually either "for the day" or "good 'til canceled (GTC)." Day orders are canceled at the end of the day if they are not executed.

Trading Floor Functions   Under the **specialist system** (used at the Philadelphia and American Stock Exchanges), there is a single individual through whom all orders to buy or sell a particular security must pass. The specialist keeps an *order book* with limit orders[6] from all over the country, and tries to ensure that the market in these securities is maintained in a fair and orderly fashion. If no private individual has placed an order to buy the option you want to sell, the specialist *must* buy the option from you at a price close to the current price. This is part of the specialist's job, and it helps contribute to the ease of entry and exit from the marketplace.

Under the **marketmaker system** (used at the CBOE and Pacific Exchange), the specialist's activities are divided among three groups of people: *marketmakers*, *floor brokers*, and the *order book official*. Instead of a single specialist, competing marketmakers trade in a specific location much like the trading pits discussed in Chapter 8 (Fundamentals of the Futures Market). The number of marketmakers can range from a small handful to sometimes over 500. These people compete against each other for the public's business by attempting to *be there first* with the best price to take your order.

Marketmakers must be quick to react to arriving orders if they want any business. Their bread and butter is buying options at the bid price and then selling at the asked price to someone else as quickly as possible. If, for instance, a particular marketmaker buys 10 option contracts (options on 1000 shares) at $4 each and sells them 30 seconds later for $4⅛, this is a profit of $125. The result of this constant competition for the public business is that you can be confident that you will get a market-determined price for your valuable option.[7]

Marketmakers in a particular option assemble in a specified part of the exchange floor, near an individual called the Order Book Official. This person has many duties, but one of particular importance is making sure that small public orders to buy or sell are not ignored and, in fact, *get priority* from the trading **crowd** at the exchange. "Crowd" is the colloquial term used for the people in a trading location.

Floor brokers act as agents for the public. They may not trade for their own accounts; instead, they place orders according to the wishes of their

---

[6]Market orders do not go in the specialist's book, as they are executed immediately.

[7]This is true barring another market crash. There were some scattered problems with the specialist and marketmaker systems during the October 19, 1987, market crash.

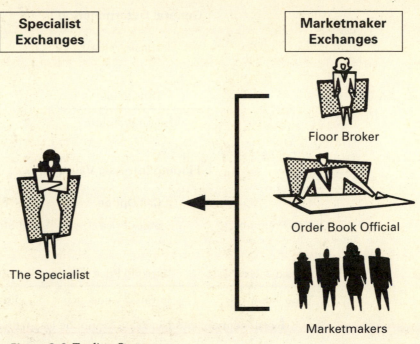

Figure 2-6 Trading Systems

customers. An order that an individual placed with a broker at Kidder, Peabody will eventually be transmitted to a floor broker at the appropriate exchange.

Order book officials are employees of the exchange and, like floor brokers, may not trade for their own account. They are responsible for ensuring that public limit orders get priority from the trading crowd when the limit price is reached. The order book official literally stops the trading among the marketmakers until the requirements of the public limit order book are satisfied. A marketmaker can be censured by the exchange for failure to pay attention to the price information quoted by the Order Book Official or for making a trade with another individual on the exchange floor when a public order was "on the book" at the identical price.

THE OPTION PREMIUM

Intrinsic Value and Time Value

The price of an option is called the *premium*, which has two components: **intrinsic value** and **time value.** For a call option, intrinsic value is equal to

General Determination

Intrinsic Value

+

Time Value

_____

Option Premium

Finding Intrinsic Value

	Call Option	**Put Option**
Option Premium	Stock Price (s)	Striking Price
−	−	−
Intrinsic Value	Striking Price (k)	Stock Price
Time Value	Intrinsic Value	Intrinsic Value

(By convention, intrinsic value cannot be less than zero.)

Figure 2-7 Intrinsic Value and Time Value

stock price minus the striking price; for a put, intrinsic value is striking price minus stock price. By convention, intrinsic value cannot be less than zero. Time value is equal to the premium minus the intrinsic value.

An option is **out-of-the-money** if it lacks intrinsic value—in other words, if its intrinsic value is zero. If it does have intrinsic value, it is **in-the-money.** In the special case where an option's striking price is exactly equal to the price of the underlying security, the option is **at-the-money.** Options that are "almost" at-the-money are **near-the-money.**

Option Price Quotations

Figure 2-8 is an extract from the financial press illustrating some of the basic characteristics of stock options. This listing shows selected prices from the CBOE. In the right section of the extract, find the listing for Boeing, which will be used for many examples that follow.

The number 46 listed below the company name is the current price of a share of Boeing common stock. The next column lists striking prices from 40 to 55. (Note that the stock price of $46 is repeated on each row.) The next six columns are actually two sets of three columns: three for calls and three for

C14 THE WALL STREET JOURNAL THURSDAY, FEBRUARY 20, 1992

Wednesday, February 19, 1992

Options closing prices. Sales unit usually is 100 shares.
Stock close is New York or American exchange final price.

CHICAGO BOARD

Option & NY Close	Strike Price	Calls-Last Feb	Mar	Apr	Puts-Last Feb	Mar	Apr
Alcoa	60	r	r	14	r	r	3/8
71 5/8	65	7	8 1/2	8 1/2	r	3/8	1 1/8
71 5/8	70	2	3 3/8	4 1/2	3/16	1 11/16	2 1/8
71 5/8	75	1/8	1 1/4	1 3/4	4 7/8	r	r
AmGenl	40	r	r	r	r	r	1 3/8
AmStrs	30	r	r	6 3/8	r	r	r
35 7/8	35	1 3/8	2 3/8	3 1/4	r	1 1/8	1 5/8
35 7/8	40	s	1/2	1	s	r	r
AT&T	35	3 3/8	3 7/8	3 3/4	r	r	5/8
38	40	1/16	3/8	11/16	1 3/4	2 1/16	r
AmTlvC	55	2 3/4	r	r	r	r	r
58	60	r	r	1/4	r	r	r
Atl R	100	r	5	r	3/16	1 11/16	r
102 3/4	105	1/2	2 1/2	3 1/2	2	3 7/8	r
102 3/4	110	1/8	1	2	6 1/2	7 3/4	r
Avon	45	3/8	1 5/8	2 1/2	5/8	1 1/2	2
44 3/4	50	r	1/4	r	r	5 1/2	5 3/4
BankNY	25	r	s	r	r	s	1/16
40	30	r	s	10 1/4	r	s	r
40	35	r	r	5 7/8	r	r	r
40	40	7/16	r	r	r	1 1/4	r
BankAm	35	r	r	5 7/8	r	1/4	7/16
40 1/8	40	5/8	1 13/16	2 3/8	1/4	1 3/8	2 1/16
BattlM	5	r	r	3 1/4	r	r	r
8 1/4	7 1/2	3/4	7/8	1	r	3/16	r
8 1/4	10	r	r	1/8	r	r	r
BearSt	15	r	s	4 1/4	r	s	r
Bear o	16 5/8	s	s	2 7/8	s	s	r
BearSt	17 1/2	1 3/4	r	2 3/8	r	3/8	r
19 1/4	20	1/16	3/4	1 1/8	1	1 1/2	1 5/8
BeckIn	20	r	1	r	r	9/16	r
BellAtl	40	r	4	4 1/2	r	r	7/16
44 1/4	45	1/16	5/8	1	3/4	r	2 1/8
44 1/4	50	r	r	r	6	r	r
Beth S	12 1/2	2 1/2	r	2 3/4	r	3/16	5/16
15	15	5/16	3/4	1	r	1 1/16	r
15	17 1/2	r	r	7/16	r	r	r
15	20	r	r	1/16	r	r	5
Biogen	25	r	r	6	r	9/16	1 1/8
29 1/4	30	3/8	2 1/4	3	3/4	2 3/8	r
29 1/4	35	r	5/8	1 3/8	5 1/2	5 7/8	6 1/2
29 1/4	40	1/16	1/4	5/8	r	r	r
29 1/4	45	r	r	1/4	r	r	r
29 1/4	50	s	s	1/4	s	s	r
Biomet	17 1/2	s	r	6	s	r	r
23	20	s	3	3 1/2	s	11/16	7/8
23	22 1/2	5/8	1 7/8	2 3/4	3/8	2 3/8	3 1/4
23	25	1/8	7/8	1 7/8	2 11/16	r	3 5/8
23	27 1/2	s	s	7/8	s	s	r
23	30	r	1/8	r	7	r	7 3/4
Bolar	10	s	r	1 5/8	s	1/2	r
10 5/8	15	s	1/8	1/4	s	r	r
BorInd	50	s	s	20 1/2	s	s	r
71	60	s	s	12 7/8	s	s	2 1/8
71	65	r	r	r	r	r	3 3/8
71	70	1 11/16	5	r	3/4	3 7/8	5 3/8
71	75	1/4	2 15/16	4 1/2	4 5/8	6 5/8	8
71	80	1/16	1 5/16	2 1/2	9	10 1/2	r
71	85	1/16	1/2	1 7/8	14 1/8	r	14 7/8
71	90	r	s	7/8	r	s	r
BurlN	40	2	r	r	r	r	r
CarnCr	35	s	5/8	r	s	r	r
Cntocr	30	r	r	6 1/4	r	r	2 5/8
33 1/8	35	r	r	3 3/8	r	r	4 7/8
33 1/8	40	r	1 1/16	1 3/4	r	7 1/2	8 1/4
33 1/8	45	1/16	3/4	1 1/8	11	12 1/8	12 1/4
33 1/8	50	1/16	3/8	7/8	16 3/4	17	17 1/2
33 1/8	55	1/16	1/4	5/8	21 3/4	21 3/4	21 5/8
33 1/8	60	1/16	1/8	7/16	27 1/8	26 1/4	25 1/8
33 1/8	65	1/16	s	7/16	r	s	r
ChamDv	30	r	2 3/16	r	1/8	r	r
Chiron	50	2 1/4	3 1/4	5 1/8	15/16	3 3/8	3 3/8
51 3/8	55	1/8	1 5/16	3	4 1/2	r	r
51 3/8	60	r	r	1 9/16	10 1/2	r	r

Option & NY Close	Strike Price	Calls-Last Feb	Mar	Apr	Puts-Last Feb	Mar	Apr
37 1/2	40	1/16	7/8	1 1/4	r	r	r
Upjohn	35	r	5 1/2	r	r	1/4	r
40 1/8	40	1/2	1 1/2	2 1/8	3/8	1 1/4	1 7/8
40 1/8	45	1/16	5/16	11/16	4 7/8	5	5 3/8
40 1/8	50	1/16	r	3/16	r	r	r
VLSI	10	r	r	7/8	r	r	r
Weyerh	25	r	r	8	r	r	r
33 3/4	30	3 3/4	3 7/8	3 1/2	r	r	r
33 3/4	35	r	1/2	1	r	r	r
WinDix	40	4 1/2	r	r	r	r	r
44 1/4	45	1/4	r	r	r	r	r
Xerox	70	8 3/4	r	r	r	r	1
79 1/4	75	3	4	5 5/8	1/8	1 1/4	2
79 1/4	80	11/16	1 5/8	2 1/2	1 1/4	3 1/2	r
79 1/4	85	s	13/16	1 3/8	s	r	r
		Feb	Mar	May	Feb	Mar	May
AirbFr	30	r	1/2	r	r	r	r
AlexAl	20	1 7/16	r	r	r	r	r
21 1/8	22 1/2	r	r	5/8	r	r	r
AlianP	25	r	10 1/8	11	r	r	15/16
35 3/4	30	3	5 7/8	r	3/16	1 1/8	3
35 3/4	35	5/8	3 1/4	5 1/8	13/16	3	4 7/8
35 3/4	40	3/16	1 5/16	3	5	7 5/8	r
35 3/4	45	r	5/8	2 1/2	r	r	r
Amdahl	15	2 7/8	r	3 1/8	r	r	r
17 1/2	17 1/2	9/16	1 1/16	1 5/8	1/4	r	1 3/8
A E P	30	r	r	1 3/4	r	r	r
AlnGrp	80	8 1/4	s	r	r	s	r
86 1/2	85	2 1/16	4 3/8	5 3/8	3/8	r	r
86 1/2	90	1/16	r	3 7/8	2 1/8	3 3/8	5 3/8
86 1/2	95	r	r	1 13/16	7 1/4	r	8 1/2
Amoco	45	r	r	r	1/8	1/2	1 1/4
46 1/4	50	1/8	r	11/16	r	3 1/2	4
A M P	60	2 3/4	r	r	r	r	r
Anadrk	20	r	r	1 3/8	r	r	r
BMC Sft	55	9 7/8	s	r	r	s	r
65 3/4	60	r	r	r	1/4	r	r
65 3/4	65	1 11/16	r	r	1 7/8	4 1/8	r
65 3/4	70	1/2	r	r	r	r	r
65 3/4	75	1/4	1 7/16	r	r	r	r
Baxter	30	r	r	5	r	r	r
34 5/8	35	1/2	1 1/8	1 5/8	3/4	1 3/8	1 7/8
34 5/8	40	r	1/4	9/16	5 5/8	r	5 3/8
BioTcG	10	1/8	1/2	1	1/2	1 1/16	r
9	12 1/2	r	r	1/2	r	r	r
Blk Dk	17 1/2	9	r	9	r	r	r
26 1/8	20	6 1/4	6 1/2	6 1/4	r	r	r
26 1/8	22 1/2	r	4	4 1/8	r	r	3/4
26 1/8	25	1 3/8	2	2 5/8	1/4	r	1 1/4
26 1/8	30	s	r	15/16	s	r	r
Boeing	40	6 1/4	s	7 1/8	r	s	1/2
46	45	1 1/4	2 1/2	3 1/2	1/8	1 1/16	1 3/4
46	50	1/16	7/16	1 1/4	4 1/8	4 1/4	4 3/4
46	55	r	r	1/2	r	r	r
Bois C	17 1/2	r	s	6 7/8	r	s	r
25	20	r	r	5	r	r	r
25	22 1/2	1 1/2	r	2 7/8	r	r	1/2
25	25	1/2	1 3/16	1 3/4	1/2	r	r
Brunos	12 1/2	r	r	3	r	r	r
C B S	135	13 1/2	r	r	r	r	3 1/8
148 3/8	140	8	r	r	r	1 3/8	4 5/8
148 3/8	145	3 1/2	6 3/4	10 1/4	r	3 1/2	r
148 3/8	150	3/4	4 1/8	7 3/8	3 5/8	r	r
148 3/8	155	1/16	2 1/2	5 1/8	7 1/8	r	r
148 3/8	160	r	1 3/8	4 1/4	r	r	r
148 3/8	165	r	s	2 5/8	r	s	r
148 3/8	175	1/16	s	s	r	s	s
CamBio	10	1 5/16	r	2 9/16	r	r	r
11 1/8	12 1/2	r	1/2	r	r	r	1 15/16
11 1/8	15	s	r	1/2	s	r	r
CapCit	110	16 1/2	s	s	r	s	s
427 1/4	380	r	s	r	r	s	5 1/8
427 1/4	410	s	r	r	s	4 3/4	r
427 1/4	430	3 5/8	14 1/2	r	r	r	r
427 1/4	460	1/8	r	r	r	r	r
427 1/4	480	r	2	r	r	r	r
Coke	55	22 1/4	s	s	r	s	s

Figure 2-8 Sample of Stock Options Listings, *WSJ* 2/20/92

Option & NY Close	Strike Price	Calls-Last Feb	Calls-Last Mar	Calls-Last Apr	Puts-Last Feb	Puts-Last Mar	Puts-Last Apr
65 3/4	70	1/2	r	r	r	r	r
65 3/4	75	1/4	1 7/16	r	r	r	r
Baxter	30	r	r	5	r	r	r
34 5/8	35	1/2	1 1/8	1 5/8	3/4	1 3/8	1 7/8
34 5/8	40	r	1/4	9/16	5 5/8	r	5 3/8
BioTcG	10	1/8	1/2	1	1/2	1 1/16	r
9	12 1/2	r	r	1/2	r	r	r
Blk Dk	17 1/2	9	r	9	r	r	r
26 1/8	20	6 1/4	6 1/2	6 1/4	r	r	r
26 1/8	22 1/2	r	4	4 1/8	r	r	3/4
26 1/8	25	1 3/8	2	2 5/8	1/4	r	1 1/4
26 1/8	30	s	r	15/16	s	r	r
Boeing	40	6 1/4	s	7 1/8	r	s	1/2
46	45	1 1/4	2 1/2	3 1/2	1/8	1 1/16	1 3/4
46	50	1/16	7/16	1 1/4	4 1/8	4 1/4	4 3/4
46	55	r	r	1/2	r	r	r
Bois C	17 1/2	r	s	6 7/8	r	s	r
25	20	r	r	5	r	r	r
25	22 1/2	1 1/2	r	2 7/8	r	r	1/2
25	25	1/2	1 3/16	1 3/4	1/2	r	r
Brunos	12 1/2	r	r	3	r	r	r
C B S	135	13 1/2	r	r	r	r	3 1/8
148 3/8	140	8	r	r	r	1 3/8	4 5/8

Intrinsic Value of Mar 45 Call Option

$46 – 45 = $1.00

Time Value of Mar 45 Call Option

$2 1/2 - $1 = $1 1/2

Intrinsic Value of Mar 45 Put Option

$45 – $46 = $0

Time Value of Mar 45 Put Option

$1 1/16 – $0 = $1 1/16

Figure 2-9 Determining Intrinsic Value

puts. At the top of each of these columns is the expiration month. The numbers below the expiration months are the option premiums.

You need to become proficient at quickly determining an option premium from the paper. As two quick examples, Figure 2-8 (p. 31) shows that the premium for a Boeing March 45 *call* is $2½; the premium for a Boeing March 45 *put* is $1 1/16.

The financial pages list the price for an option on a single share. Because "one option" really means an option on 100 shares, an individual who buys one Boeing MAR 45 call @ $2½ would actually pay $2½ per share × 100 shares, or $250.

The Boeing MAR 45 call is in-the-money, because the right to buy at $45 is valuable when the stock price is $46. For a call option, intrinsic value is the stock price minus the striking price: in this case, $46 − $45 = $1. We know the option premium and we know the intrinsic value, so we can solve for the time value: time value = premium − intrinsic value, or $2½ − $1 = $1½.

The Boeing MAR 45 *put* is out-of-the-money, because there is no incentive to sell at $45 when the market price of the stock is more than this. Though this option has no intrinsic value, it *does* have time value: $1 1/16. This helps illustrate an important point: Before their expiration, out-of-the-money options *are not worthless.*

LISTED OPTIONS QUOTATIONS

Option/Strike				Vol	Exch	Last	Net Chg	a-Close	Open Int
Fluor	Apr	45		101	CB	1 7/16	+ ⅛	44½	1,840
Foodmk	May	10		100	CB	9/16	+ ⅜	9	89
Ford	Mar	45		124	CB	4⅛	– ⅝	49	4,339
Ford	Mar	45	p	120	CB	1/16	...	49	2,980
Ford	Mar	50		138	CB	7/16	– 5/16	49	5,537
Ford	Mar	50	p	517	CB	1⅛	+ 5/16	49	1,268
Ford	Apr	50		92	CB	1⅜	– ¼	49	2,476
Ford	Jun	50		65	CB	2⅜	– ⅜	49	6,739
Ford	Jun	55		64	CB	¾	– ¼	49	693
FostWh	Jul	35		250	PC	¾	...	31⅛	85
FounHl	Mar	30		476	AM	1⅛	+ ½	30⅛	626
FounHl	Mar	30	p	163	AM	1	– 2½	30⅛	280
FruitL	Mar	50	p	215	NY	3⅞	– 1⅜	46	706
FstChi	Apr	45		110	CB	1½	+ ⅛	44½	325
FstChi	Jul	45		590	CB	2 13/16	+ 1/16	44½	2,260
-G-H-I-									
G M	Mar	35		405	CB	3⅝	– 1⅜	38½	8,800
G M	Mar	35	p	288	CB	1/16	...	38½	7,774
G M	Apr	35	p	329	CB	⅜	+ ⅛	38½	1,277
G M	Jun	35		143	CB	4⅞	– 1	38½	5,084
G M	Jun	35	p	78	CB	15/16	+ 3/16	38½	3,574
G M	Mar	40		1,530	CB	¼	– ½	38½	19,158
G M	Mar	40	p	439	CB	1⅝	+ 1	38½	4,127
G M	Apr	40		717	CB	15/16	– ⅝	38½	5,348
G M	Apr	40	p	98	CB	2¼	+ ⅞	38½	688
G M	Jun	40		239	CB	1⅞	– 11/16	38½	8,299
G M	Jun	40	p	341	CB	3⅛	+ ¾	38½	1,316
G M	Sep	40	p	64	CB	3¾	+ ⅜	38½	856
G M	Apr	45		153	CB	⅛	– ⅛	38½	359
G M	Jun	45		270	CB	9/16	– ¼	38½	1,392
G M	Sep	45		62	CB	1⅜	– 3/16	38½	1,124
G T E	Mar	35		60	AM	1¾	+ ⅜	36¾	7,151
GMills	Apr	75		75	PC	1⅛	...	73⅛	368
GPU	Aug	30		60	NY	1 3/16	+ ⅝	29¾	488
GaGulf	Apr	20		60	PB	1	– ¼	20	85
GaPac	Jul	60	p	317	PB	2¼	+ 7/16	64⅝	296
GaPac	Mar	65		98	PB	1 5/16	– 15/16	64⅝	429
GaPac	Mar	65	p	206	PB	1¼	+ ¾	64⅝	406
GaPac	Apr	65		134	PB	2⅝	– 1¼	64⅝	2,591
GaPac	Apr	65	p	61	PB	2¼	+ ⅝	64⅝	657
GaPac	Jul	65		615	PB	4⅝	– 2⅜	64⅝	468
GaPac	Mar	70	p	68	PB	5¼	+ 2	64⅝	453
GaPac	Apr	70		218	PB	13/16	– 9/16	64⅝	836
GaPac	Apr	70	p	100	PB	5⅞	+ 2¼	64⅝	126
Gap	Mar	30		156	CB	4⅜	+ ⅜	34⅛	924
Gap	Jun	30		156	CB	5¼	+ ⅝	34⅛	439
Gap	Mar	35		439	CB	7/16	+ 1/16	34⅛	4,260
Gap	Jun	35		83	CB	2	– ⅛	34⅛	1,924
Gen El	Mar	55		140	CB	33	+ ¼	87½	172
Gen El	Apr	80	p	82	CB	5/16	...	87½	619
Gen El	Jun	80	p	135	CB	1	...	87½	4,181
Gen El	Sep	80	p	66	CB	1⅝	– ⅛	87½	422
Gen El	Mar	85		1,378	CB	2⅞	– ⅛	87½	5,406
Gen El	Apr	85		155	CB	3⅝	– ⅜	87½	404
Gen El	Jun	85		168	CB	5	+ ¼	87½	4,825
Gen El	Jun	85	p	121	CB	2	+ ⅛	87½	1,099
Gen El	Mar	90		77	CB	¼	+ 1/16	87½	3,218
Gen El	Apr	90		519	CB	15/16	– 1/16	87½	863
Gen El	Jun	90		1,199	CB	2¼	– ¼	87½	3,401
Gen El	Sep	90		82	CB	3½	...	87½	1,340
Gencp	Mar	12½		85	CB	9/16	– 3/16	13	295
Gensia	Mar	20		60	CB	2½	– 3/16	21	356
Gensia	Mar	20	p	181	CB	15/16	– 5/16	21	944
Gensia	Apr	20		125	CB	3¾	+ ⅜	21	439
Gensia	Mar	22½		150	CB	1 5/16	+ ⅛	21	470
Gensia	Apr	22½		67	CB	2⅝	+ ¼	21	188
Gensia	Mar	25		98	CB	7/16	...	21	1,171
Gensia	Apr	25		79	CB	1 7/16	– 1/16	21	320
Gensia	Apr	30		115	CB	¼	– ¼	21	53
Gentch	Oct	30		660	PC	7¼	– ¾	34¾	139
Gentch	Oct	30	p	764	PC	1 15/16	+ 3/16	34¾	1,618
Gentch	Apr	40		60	PC	⅜	– ⅛	34¾	1,718
Genzym	Mar	35		70	CB	5/16	– ⅛	33	2,302
Genzym	Mar	35	p	174	CB	1⅞	– 1⅝	33	801
Genzym	Apr	35		155	CB	1 9/16	+ 1/16	33	444
Genzym	Mar	40	p	100	CB	6⅝	– 1	33	953
Genzym	Apr	40		61	CB	⅝	+ 1/16	33	954
Genzym	Oct	40		100	NY	3⅜	+ 3⅜	33	178
Genzym	Jul	45		75	NY	1⅜	+ ½	33	518
GerbPd	Jul	30	p	250	AM	1¼	...	31⅞	168
Gillet	Mar	60		147	AM	1¾	+ 3/16	60¾	1,722
Gillet	Jun	60		89	AM	3¼	– ¼	60¾	843
Glaxo	Mar	17½		120	AM	1½	– 15/16	18⅞	527
Glaxo	Apr	17½		234	AM	2⅛	– ½	18⅞	244

Option/Strike				Vol	Exch	Last	Net Chg	a-Close	Open Int
JohnJn	Apr	45	p	236	CB	2 1/16	+ 3/16	44⅛	1,722
JohnJn	Jul	45		71	CB	2⅜	– ⅜	44⅛	3,624
JohnJn	Jul	50		140	CB	⅞	– 1/16	44⅛	1,765
K mart	Jun	22½		150	CB	3½	+ ½	25⅛	747
K mart	Mar	25		513	CB	⅜	– ¼	25⅛	6,271
K mart	Apr	25		471	CB	1	– ⅛	25⅛	1,064
K mart	Jun	25		348	CB	1⅜	– ⅛	25⅛	3,576
K mart	Jun	30		160	CB	¼	...	25⅛	1,210
Kellog	Jun	60		84	AM	8¼	+ ¾	67¼	840
Kellog	Mar	65		143	AM	2⅝	+ ⅝	67¼	485
Kellog	Sep	65		129	AM	6	+ ⅝	67¼	19
Kellog	Apr	70		141	AM	1	+ ¼	67¼	56
Kemper	Apr	35		134	PB	9/16	...	32	594
L S I	Apr	12½		145	CB	1½	+ ¼	13⅜	1,799
LDDS	Apr	35	p	210	PC	1¾	– 3/16	35⅞	303
LDDS	Jun	35		62	PC	3¾	+ ⅜	35⅞	187
LaPac	Aug	60	p	82	AM	1⅜	– ¼	70⅞	11
LaPac	Aug	65	p	66	AM	2⅞	+ 1	70⅞	7
LaPac	Mar	75		145	AM	¼	– 1½	70⅞	1,813
LaPac	Apr	75		108	AM	1¾	– 2½	70⅞	42
LandsE	Mar	25		129	CB	2½	+ 1 9/16	27⅜	127
Lennar	Apr	30		73	AM	4⅜	+ ¼	34	40
LibMdA	Jul	30		60	CB	6⅝	...	33¾	64
LibMdA	Jul	35		205	CB	3⅞	+ ⅜	33¾	228
LibMdA	Oct	35		65	CB	4¾	...	33¾	70
Lilly	Mar	55		143	AM	3/16	– ⅛	52¾	728
Lilly	Mar	55	p	450	AM	2¼	+ 7/16	52¾	1,809
Lilly	Apr	55	p	410	AM	3	+ ⅝	52¾	1,192
Lilly	Jul	55		184	AM	1 13/16	– ½	52¾	899
Lilly	Apr	60		147	AM	3/16	...	52¾	4,078
Limitd	May	22½	p	150	CB	⅝	+ ⅛	24¾	1,462
LinB	May	90		60	PB	1¼	– ¼	83⅝	260
Litton	Mar	50		76	CB	2¾	+ ⅜	52⅝	660
LizClab	Jul	40		83	CB	1	– ⅜	36⅛	801
LongvF	Mar	15		115	CB	3¼	– ⅜	18½	145
Lotus	Mar	25		69	AM	1¾	– ½	26½	945
-M-N-O-									
M C I	Apr	40		89	CB	3	– ⅞	42¾	2,816
M C I	Apr	45		132	CB	11/16	– 3/16	42¾	1,606
M C I	Jul	45		377	CB	1 13/16	+ 1/16	42¾	745
M M M	Apr	105	p	105	CB	1¼	...	109	232
MBNA	Mar	20		200	AM	6¼	– ¾	26⅞	65
MBNA	Mar	22½		202	AM	4⅛	– ½	26⅞	1,797
MBNA	Mar	25		98	CB	⅞	– ⅞	26⅞	1,286
MBNA	Jun	25	p	100	CB	1⅛	– 15/16	26⅞	1,165
MTC El	May	7½	p	140	CB	1 1/16	– 3/16	9	102
MTC El	Mar	10		240	CB	5/16	– 1/16	9	1,085
MTC El	May	10	p	135	CB	2⅜	– ⅝	9	170
Magnal	May	30		112	CB	2½	...	30⅝	251
Marion	Apr	25		135	PC	¼	– 1/16	23	227
Marriot	Mar	25	p	150	PB	1/16	– 3/16	26½	225
Marriot	Apr	25		497	PB	1 13/16	+ 9/16	26½	2,314
Marriot	Jul	25		101	PB	2½	+ 3/16	26½	149
Marvel	Mar	22½		75	AM	9/16	+ 1/16	21⅞	728
Mattel	Mar	25		128	AM	1/16	...	21⅛	361
Mattel	Apr	25		228	AM	¼	– ⅛	21⅛	696
Maxtor	Mar	7½		90	CB	⅛	– ⅛	7	641
Maxtor	Jul	10		122	CB	½	...	7	2,023
Maxus	Apr	7½		269	PC	1½	– ⅛	8¾	6,612
Maxus	Apr	10		609	PC	½	– ⅛	8¾	6,716
MayDS	Mar	60		125	CB	17½	+ ⅞	76⅝	113
MayDS	Mar	60	p	125	CB	⅛	...	76⅝	409
Maytag	Jul	15		140	NY	1	+ ⅛	14¾	638
MblTel	Mar	12½		100	CB	4	+ ¼	16¾	485
MblTel	Jun	12½		110	CB	4½	+ ¾	16¾	285
McCawC	Apr	30	p	125	AM	¼	– 1/16	36½	450
McCawC	Apr	35	p	100	AM	13/16	– 3/16	36½	300
McCawC	Apr	40		103	AM	½	– 1/16	36½	278
McCawC	Jun	45		100	AM	½	...	36½	95
Mead	Apr	50	p	60	CB	6¾	+ 6¾	43⅛	...
MedCrA	Jul	17½		75	PC	4½	+ 1	20⅛	157
MedCrA	Apr	20	p	75	PC	1 15/16	– 9/16	20⅛	745
MedcoC	Mar	30	p	85	PC	⅛	– ¼	34	322
MedcoC	Apr	35		67	PC	1½	+ ½	34	1,039
Medeva	May	12½	p	166	CB	11/16	– 9/16	13½	2
Medtrn	Mar	75		85	CB	4	– ¼	78	418
Medtrn	Apr	75	p	118	CB	2	– ⅜	78	162
Medtrn	Mar	80		248	CB	1½	+ ¼	78	435
Merck	Mar	35	p	275	CB	1/16	...	39⅛	3,868
Merck	Apr	35		145	CB	4¾	– ⅝	39⅛	2,046
Merck	Apr	35	p	119	CB	⅜	+ ⅛	39⅛	4,248
Merck	Jul	35		113	CB	5¾	– ¼	39⅛	1,263
Merck	Jul	35	p	270	CB	15/16	...	39⅛	3,896

Figure 2-10 Sample Options Listing, *WSJ* 3/12/93

Stock prices can change every day, and consequently so can the option premium. Even if stock prices do not change, the option premium can still change. Why? The longer the option has until expiration, the more it is worth, because the stock price has more time to fluctuate and therefore has a greater potential to rise or fall. If you look again at the premiums shown in Figure 2-8 (p. 31), you will see that for a given striking price, option premiums increase for more distant expirations.

See p. 78

As an option moves closer to expiration, its time value decreases. Option traders refer to this phenomenon as *time value decay.* Everything else being equal (i.e., the stock price does not change), the value of an option will decline over time. This fact makes an option a **wasting asset,** which is an often misunderstood term. Football tickets are also wasting assets, because there is a time when they cease to have any value. Anyone who has ever observed activities around a football stadium knows that the price that scalpers get for tickets begins to decline when kickoff occurs. By the end of the first half, the price has fallen substantially. However, just because something is a wasting asset does not mean that it is not useful.

Figure 2-8 shows prices from the *Wall Street Journal* on February 20, 1992. This format continues to be used by major newspapers such as *The New York Times,* but the *WSJ* recently changed its reporting format to save space. Figure 2-10 is an example. All options are listed alphabetically, and grouped by striking price and expiration. Puts are identified by the small letter "p" after the striking price, with a blank representing a call option. This new listing format also shows the **open interest** in the option, which is the number of option contracts that currently exist.

PROFITS AND LOSSES WITH OPTIONS

Understanding the Exercise of an Option

American vs. European Options   Options give you the right to buy or sell. With an **American option,** this right can be exercised anytime prior to the expiration of the option. **European options,** on the other hand, can only be exercised at expiration.

Although they can be exercised anytime, there are very few situations in which it is advantageous to exercise an American option early. Doing so essentially amounts to abandoning any time value remaining in the option. Consider the Boeing MAR 45 call selling for $2½, while the underlying stock sells for $46. If this option were exercised, stock would be purchased for $1 less than its market price: The option has intrinsic value of $1. If you exercise it, you recover this intrinsic value, but you would throw away the remaining $1½ of option premium.

Exercise Procedures   If I decide to exercise any option (put or call), I must notify my broker of my desire to do so. My broker, in turn, notifies the Options Clearing Corporation, which selects a contraparty to receive the exercise notice. As all trades are through the clearing corporation, neither the option exerciser nor the option writer knows the identity of the opposite party.

The option premium is *not* a downpayment on the option terms. A person who exercises a call option with a striking price of $25 must put up $25/share × 100 shares, or $2500. Remember that the option premium is the option writer's to keep, no matter what happens. Similarly, I must either already own or buy 100 shares of stock for each put I want to exercise. The premium I paid for the put does not "count" toward the cost of the stock.

▌The option premium is not a downpayment of the purchase of the stock.

The *writer* of a call option must be prepared to sell 100 shares of the underlying stock to the call owner if the call owner decides to exercise. If the writer owns these shares, the writer delivers the share certificate to the broker, who will deliver it to the Options Clearing Corporation. The OCC will then arrange to have a new share certificate transferred to the exerciser of the call, will collect the striking price proceeds from the exerciser's brokerage account, and also will have the striking price proceeds transferred into the writer's account. If the writer does not own any shares of the stock, then the writer must first purchase the shares in the open market at the current price. The writer of a put option must be prepared to *buy* shares of stock if the put holder decides to exercise and sell them.

An important point to note out of this discussion is the fact that the ball is in the option holder's court; the option writer sits back and waits. The option holder decides when and if to exercise, not the option writer. The standardization of exchange traded options conveys the characteristic of fungibility to these instruments. Because options are fungible, the option writer can reverse (or offset) a position if it is profitable to do so. Then the consequences of exercise are someone else's concern.

▌The option *holder* decides when and if to exercise, not the option writer.

There is another fundamental fact of options trading that is initially surprising to many people. This is the general rule that you should seldom buy an option with the intent of exercising it: you should sell it instead.

▌In general, you should not buy an option with the intent of exercising it.

We have already seen that options are not normally exercised until just before they expire, because earlier exercise amounts to discarding the remaining time value. If I exercise a call near the end of its life, I must come up with the money to pay for the stock, which might be inconvenient. I also would have to pay my broker a commission to exercise the call. When I sold the stock, I would pay another commission.

The same thing is true with puts. Unless I already owned the stock, I would have to buy shares in the open market (paying a commission), and would pay another commission when I exercised the put.

I can recover the value contained in any option by simply selling it. This way I do not have to come up with any more money, I pay a single, relatively low commission, and I am out of the market.

Profit and Loss Diagrams

A convenient way to envision what happens with option strategies as the value of the underlying security changes is with the use of a profit and loss diagram. These are used in this chapter and the next two as an aid in analyzing option positions.

The vertical axis of the diagram reflects profits or losses on option expiration day resulting from a particular strategy, while the horizontal axis reflects the stock price on option expiration day. At expiration, there is no time value left, so the option will sell for its intrinsic value. By convention, the diagrams ignore the effect of commissions you have to pay.

Intrinsic value
call : S - k
put : k - S

Buying a Call Option   Figure 2-11 is a profit/loss diagram for a person who *buys* a Boeing MAR 45 call for $2½. A colloquial term for buying something is "going long." When the option expires, it is worthless if the price of Boeing stock is $45 or less. Note that the maximum loss is $2½. An important point to remember with options is that when you buy an option, the most you can lose is the option premium. You will never be required to put up more money.[8] It is true that you can lose 100 percent of your money, but 100 percent of the option premium amounts to fewer dollars than 100 percent of an investment in 100 shares of stock.

> When you buy an option, the most you can lose is the premium you paid when the option was purchased.

At any price above the striking price of $45, the option will have intrinsic value. The diagram shows that in this situation the option buyer breaks even

---

[8]There is an exception to this rule with index options. It is discussed in Chapter 7. *p. 150-151*

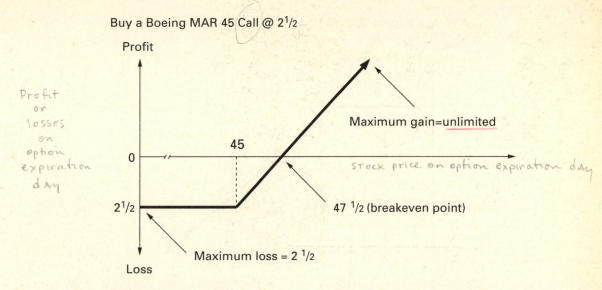

Buy a Boeing MAR 45 Call @ $2\frac{1}{2}$

Profit or losses on option expiration day

m: slope = +1

Maximum gain=unlimited

45

0

STOCK PRICE on option expiration day

$2\frac{1}{2}$

47 $\frac{1}{2}$ (breakeven point)

Maximum loss = 2 $\frac{1}{2}$

Loss

Figure 2-11 Long Call

(before commissions) at a stock price of $47½. At this price, the option will be intrinsically worth $47½ minus $45, or $2.50. This is exactly what it cost, and it can be sold for this amount.

Once the stock price reaches the breakeven point of $47½, the option holder earns a dollar for every dollar rise in the price of the stock. Because the stock price can rise to any level, profits are theoretically unlimited.

It is very important to keep in mind that these profit and loss diagrams apply to option expiration only. Before expiration day, an option has time value. Consequently, its premium will be greater than that shown in the typical expiration day diagram; profits and losses will logically differ as well.

Writing a Call Option   What about the option writer? This person is on the "other side of the market" from the option buyer. Ignoring commissions, the options market is a zero sum game; aggregate gains and losses will always net to zero. If the call buyer makes money, the call writer is going to lose money, and vice versa.

Figure 2-12 (p. 38) shows this situation from the perspective of the person who has *written* the call. A written option is also colloquially called a short option. If I write a call and do not own the underlying shares, this is called writing a **naked call.** Naked calls are also called **uncovered calls.**

You will note that the profit and loss diagram from Figure 2-8 (p. 31) has simply been rotated about the horizontal axis. The option writer's maximum profit is always equal to the option buyer's maximum loss.

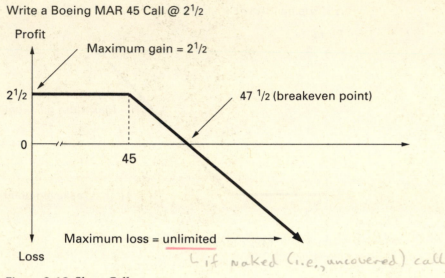

Write a Boeing MAR 45 Call @ 2½

Figure 2-12 Short Call

▌The most an option writer can make is the option premium.

The thought-provoking part of Figure 2-12 is the potential for unlimited losses. If the stock price rises sharply from its current level of $46, the naked call writer can lose a lot of money.

Buying a Put Option   People who buy puts generally do so because they anticipate a decline in the price of the underlying security. Suppose I believe that Boeing common stock is overpriced and about to fall. From Figure 2-8 (p. 31), I see that the premium for a Boeing MAR 45 put is $1¹⁄₁₆. It costs me 100 times this, or $106.25 to buy such a put. Remember that a principle of options trading is that when an option is purchased, the maximum loss is the option premium. This means my maximum loss from the purchase of this put is $106.25. Figure 2-13 shows the profit/loss possibilities.

The figure shows that the maximum loss will occur at all stock prices at or above the option striking price of $45. If the stock price at option expiration is $50, for instance, my option would be worthless, because it would not make sense to exercise the right to sell at $45 when the market price is $50.

If stock prices fall, then I can benefit from my put. The best thing that could happen to the put buyer is for the stock price to fall to zero. Then the put would permit the sale of 100 shares of worthless stock for $45 per share, for a profit of $4500 on the stock. My net gain would be $4500 minus the $106.25 paid for the put, or $4393.75.

Buy

Write a Boeing MAR 45 Put @ $1^1/16$

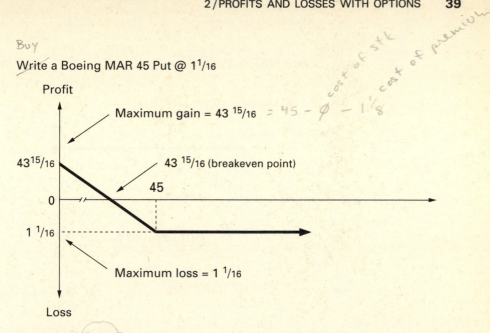

Figure 2-13 Long Put

Note that in the diagram the bend in the profit/loss plot occurs at the striking price of $45. This set-up is a general rule with such diagrams and will be particularly helpful with more advanced strategies.

In profit and loss diagrams, any bend(s) in the diagram occurs at the striking price(s).

Writing a Put Option   Writing put options is without doubt the least used of the simple option strategies. This is not because writing puts is a bad idea; it is because very few people, brokers included, understand this strategy very well. Put options are conceptually awkward for many people. The right to sell something is not something we encounter very often. If I *write* a put and sell it to you, I have created the right for you to sell me something you might not even own. This explanation can easily furrow brows.

If I *own* a put, I have the right to sell. But where did the put come from? It came from the put writer, who is agreeing to buy your shares if you exercise the put. The put holder has the right to sell, while the put writer has the obligation to buy if the put is exercised. The colloquial term "put it to him" probably has its roots in the options market. When I write a put, I may discover that I am obliged to purchase shares of stock because of falling stock prices. The put holder can "put shares in my account" anytime before the option expires. If the put holder chooses to do so, I must pay the striking price for each share I buy.

Write a Boeing MAR 45 Put @ $1^1/_{16}$

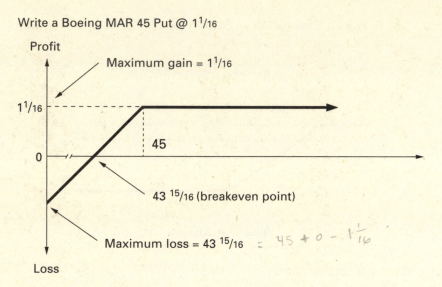

Figure 2-14 text within diagram:
Profit
Maximum gain = $1^1/_{16}$
$1^1/_{16}$
0
45
$43^{15}/_{16}$ (breakeven point)
Maximum loss = $43^{15}/_{16}$ = $45 + 0 - 1\frac{1}{16}$
Loss

Figure 2-14 Short Put

A put writer may have to involuntarily purchase shares of stock if the put owner decides to exercise.

Suppose I write a MAR 45 put on Boeing for a premium of $1¹⁄₁₆. The $106.25 is mine to keep no matter what happens. The person who buys the put wants stock prices to go down, because this is how the buyer makes a profit. I, on the other hand, having written the put want prices to go up, or at least to remain above the striking price. If this happens, the put will expire worthless, and I, as writer, will not have to buy any shares.

Figure 2-14 is a diagram of the profit and loss possibilities if I write a MAR 45 put on Boeing. My maximum profit is $1¹⁄₁₆: This is the option premium I receive for writing the put. The maximum loss occurs if Boeing stock falls to zero. Here, the holder of the put could exercise the option, and as the put writer, I would be obliged to buy 100 shares at $45 each, even though they are worthless. I still get to keep the $1¹⁄₁₆ per share premium, though, so my net loss is $43¹⁵⁄₁₆ per share ($4393.75).

A Note on Margin Requirements[9]

See p. 90, cf. Some option transactions have a **margin requirement.** This is analogous to posting collateral and can be satisfied by a deposit of cash or other securities

---

[9]Margin requirements will be discussed in more detail in Chapter 4.

into your brokerage account. If you *write* an option, the loss associated with an adverse price movement can be large. The margin system is to reduce the likelihood that option writers will be unable to fulfill their obligations under the option terms.

If the posting of margin were not necessary, someone could always generate additional cash by writing more options. Losses from unfavorable price movements could always be covered by writing more options. If carried to the extreme, this process obviously could bankrupt the OCC system.

SUMMARY

There are two types of options: puts and calls. Calls give you the right to buy; puts give you the right to sell. All options have a predetermined buying/selling price called the striking price, and a predetermined expiration date.

In-the-money options have both intrinsic value and time value. Intrinsic value changes every time the value of the underlying security changes, and time value declines as the expiration date approaches.

The first trade an individual makes in a particular option is an opening transaction; when the position is closed out, the trade is a closing transaction. When options are sold as an opening transaction, this is called writing the option.

QUESTIONS

1. In general, does a person who buys a call option want prices to go up or down? *p. 7*
2. True or false: "Buying a call is exactly the same as writing a put." Explain your answer. *F. Call: unlim gain ; put : max gain = premium*
3. Why are options considered wasting assets?
4. True or false: "If there are 1000 people who own Boeing put options, then there have to be 1000 people who wrote Boeing puts." Explain your answer. *T. p.19*
5. Why do most people sell their valuable options rather than exercising them?
6. Explain why it is possible for an options contract to *disappear* without expiring or being exercised.
7. Suppose you are bullish on a stock. What are the relative advantages and disadvantages of (a) buying a call, versus (b) writing a put?
8. Refer to Figure 2-8. Give an example of an option that is *at-the-money*.

9. Refer to Figure 2-8 (p. 31), and look at the section pertaining to CBS. Using the striking prices listed as a clue, do you think the price of CBS common stock has (a) risen or (b) fallen in the weeks prior to these prices?

10. Why do you think some options have more striking prices listed than others?

11. Would you expect an American option on a particular stock to always sell for at least as much as a European option with the same exercise terms? Why or why not?

12. Comment on the following statement: "An option that is out-of-the-money must have time value prior to expiration." *NO INTRINSIC value, p.30*

13. Comment on the following statement: "An option that is in-the-money must have intrinsic value." *Intrinsic value = S-k for call; k-S for put p.30*

14. Comment on the following statement: "Options are nothing more than a side bet on the direction stock prices are going to move."

15. Briefly explain why the following statement is *wrong*: If you buy an XYZ JUN 25 call option in March, the only way you can make a profit is if the price of XYZ closes above 25 on expiration day in June."

16. True or false: "An at-the-money option has time value equal to its intrinsic value prior to expiration." *F. No intrinsic value bec S = k*

17. Briefly explain how it is possible for an out-of-the-money put option on XYZ to sell for *more* than an in-the-money put option on XYZ. *Time value*

18. True or false: "If I sell an option as an opening transaction, this is called writing the option. But just because I wrote an option does not mean it was an opening transaction."

19. True or false: "The quantity of XYZ call options in existence at any time is always a constant." *F. Quantity changes as positions are opened + closed.*

20. Why are typical profit and loss diagrams such as those discussed in this chapter only valid at option expiration?

21. How is the option premium different from a downpayment?

PROBLEMS

Note: Use Figure 2-8 (p. 31) as needed. $5\frac{7}{8} - (40-35) = 5\frac{7}{8} - 5 = \frac{7}{8}$

1. How much time value is in a Bank of New York APR 35 call option?

2. What is the intrinsic value of a BankAmerica FEB 35 call? $40\frac{1}{8} - 40 = \frac{1}{8}$

3. What is the intrinsic value of a BankAmerica FEB 35 put? $\varnothing$

4. Suppose you write a Boise Cascade (Bois C) MAR 25 call. What is your maximum profit? *$1\frac{3}{16}$ option premium*

5. Suppose you buy a Boeing MAR 45 put for the price listed. At expiration, Boeing stock sells for $41⅜. What is your profit or loss? *option*

Profit: $45 - 41\frac{3}{8} - 2\frac{1}{2} = \frac{3}{8}$

6. What is your maximum profit if you buy a Xerox MAR 80 call? *unlimited if stk prices ↑, p.37*

7. Construct a profit/loss diagram for the purchase of a Boeing MAY 50 call.

8. Construct a profit/loss diagram for the writing of a naked MAR 35 call on Biogen.

9. Construct a profit/loss diagram for the purchase of a Bell Atlantic APR 45 put.

10. Construct a profit/loss diagram for the writing of a Boise Cascade FEB 25 put.

11. How much time value is in a Bank of New York APR 30 call option?

12. What is the intrinsic value of a BankAmerica FEB 40 call?

13. What is the intrinsic value of a BankAmerica FEB 25 put?

14. Suppose you write a Bethlehem Steel (Beth S) MAR 15 call. What is your maximum profit? *option premium*

15. Suppose you buy a Boeing MAY 45 put for the price listed. At expiration, Boeing stock sells for $41⅜. What is your profit or loss? *#5 is similar*

16. What is your maximum profit if you buy a Xerox MAR 70 call? *#6 is similar*

17. Construct a profit/loss diagram for the purchase of a Boeing MAY 45 call.

18. Construct a profit/loss diagram for the writing of a naked APR 40 call on Biogen.

19. Construct a profit/loss diagram for the purchase of a Bell Atlantic FEB 45 put.

20. Construct a profit/loss diagram for the writing of a Boise Cascade MAY 22½ put.

21. What is the ticker symbol for a Boeing FEB 40 call?

22. What is the ticker symbol for a Boeing FEB 40 put?

23. What is the ticker symbol for a Boise Cascade (BCC) MAR 17½ call?

24. What is the ticker symbol for a Boise Cascade (BCC) MAR 22½ put?

Note: Refer to Figure 2–10 (p. 33) for problems 25–30.

25. What is the premium for a Georgia Pacific MAR 65 put?

26. What is the premium for a Georgia Pacific MAR 65 call?

27. How many Kellog JUN 60 calls exist?

28. On which exchange do Marriott options trade?

29. What is the stock price for The Gap?

30. What is the most you can lose if you write a MMM APR 105 put? *105 — option premium*

3 Basic Option Strategies

*T*he value of a perpetual European put option is zero.

Robert Merton

KEY TERMS

covered call
covered put
deep in-the-money
improve on the market
long position
naked put

protective put
put overwriting
short call
short put
short sale
synthetic option

The previous chapter dealt with basic option principles and terminology. You should now be fluent with the key terms listed at the front of Chapter 2, and with the concepts in the chapter summary.

This chapter concentrates on ways in which options can be used as a portfolio component rather than as an isolated security. People using options as a portfolio component usually do so either to provide "insurance" against adverse price movements or to generate additional portfolio income.

USING OPTIONS AS A HEDGE

A homeowner is uncomfortable bearing the full risk of a house fire. The consequences of a total loss of an uninsured home can be devastating, and this is why most homeowners transfer part or all this risk to an insurance company. The insurance company accepts the risk that the homeowner does not want and receives the homeowner's insurance premium for doing so. While the analogy is not perfect, the homeowner hedges by buying insurance, and the insurance company speculates that the house will not burn. It is important to note that neither party wants the house to burn.

Hedgers transfer unwanted risk to speculators who are willing to bear it.

At the end of the policy year, the insurance ends. The insurance company keeps the premium paid by the homeowner, who must get a new policy (or renew the old one) to continue coverage against economic loss. It does not mean that the insurance was a waste of money if the house did not burn; the fact that the home was insured provided peace of mind to the family. Still, many people subconsciously view the money spent for "unused" insurance as unproductive.

Students often find themselves choosing between hedging and speculating when they begin to study for an exam. Perhaps the class has been provided a list of ten essay questions, of which the instructor will select three to be answered. As a student, you might have a strong suspicion regarding which three will be selected. If you were a fearless (and stupid) speculator, you might study only those three and use the rest of your time to party. Most students would choose to hedge, though, by spending time reviewing all ten. There are degrees of hedging/speculating that could obviously occur in this example as you allocate your study time to the ten questions. You may study four questions thoroughly, and spend less time on the other six. With these thoughts in mind, we now look at options as portfolio components.

Ex. 1, Q. 6
see p. 47

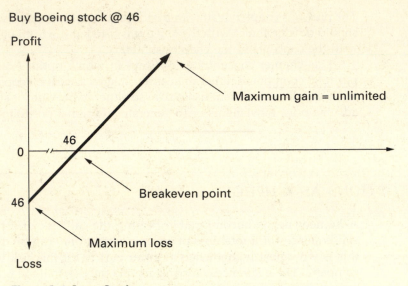

Figure 3-1 Long Stock

Protective Puts

Someone who owns shares of stock has a **long position** in the security. In the investment business, the term "long" simply means that you own something. It has nothing to do with time span.

Figure 3-1 is a profit/loss diagram for the purchase of Boeing common stock at $46 per share. The maximum loss occurs if the stock declines to zero, while the potential profit is unlimited. Ignoring commissions, dividends, and opportunity costs, the strategy "breaks even" if the stock price is unchanged at a specific future time. In this diagram no options are involved, but the stock price can be noted on option expiration day (the X axis value).

There are often situations in which an investor anticipates a decline in the value of an investment, but does not want to sell it because of tax considerations or other reasons. In such a situation the investor might consider using a **protective put.**[1]

A protective put is not a special kind of put option; it is a descriptive term given to a long stock position combined with a long put position. If someone owns shares of Boeing and buys a Boeing put (regardless of striking price or expiration), the put is a protective put.[2]

[1]This term was probably coined by Robert C. Pozen in an article entitled "The Purchase of Protective Puts by Financial Institutions," *Financial Analysts Journal* (Jul/Aug, 1978): 47–60.

[2]The more it is out of the money, though, the less protection the put provides.

TABLE 3-1 PROFIT/LOSS WORKSHEET FOR A BOEING MAR 45 PROTECTIVE PUT

	Stock Price at Option Expiration			
	$0	$25	$45	$65
buy stock @ $46	−46	−21	−1	+19
buy put @ 1¹⁄₁₆	+43¹⁵⁄₁₆	+18¹⁵⁄₁₆	−1¹⁄₁₆	− 1¹⁄₁₆
net	− 2¹⁄₁₆	− 2¹⁄₁₆	−2¹⁄₁₆	+17¹⁵⁄₁₆

A protective put is not a special kind of option; it is the simultaneous holding of a long stock position and a put option on that stock.

Figure 2-13 (p. 39) shows the profits and losses resulting from various stock prices when a Boeing MAR 45 put is purchased; Figure 3-1 shows profits and losses for a long position in Boeing stock. What happens if these two diagrams are combined graphically?

In time you can quickly sketch the profit/loss diagrams for complex option strategies. Getting to that point, however, takes practice. At first it is helpful to prepare worksheets like the one in Table 3-1.

The worksheet shows that the maximum loss is $2¹⁄₁₆, occurring if the stock becomes worthless. Further investigation reveals that the maximum loss also occurs at all stock prices of $45 or below. The strategy appears to break even at a stock price somewhere between $45 and $65. If you check a few more prices, you will find that the break-even point is $47¹⁄₁₆. At this price, the value of the stock has risen $1¹⁄₁₆. The put expires out-of-the-money, so it is worthless. But the stock rose exactly enough to offset the put premium paid. The maximum gain is unlimited, because the stock can rise to any value. Figure 3-2 (p. 48) shows the combined positions graphically.

In many respects, a protective put is like a collision insurance policy on an automobile. A car is valuable, and its owner suffers if it is damaged in an accident. To protect against this potential for loss, people buy insurance, fully expecting to "lose" all the money they pay for it. A person should not feel discouraged if an accident-free year goes by without the necessity of filing a claim with the insurance company.

When you choose your insurance policy, you can choose how much protection you want. If you want coverage for the first dollar of auto body damage, the insurance policy will be expensive. On the other hand, if you are willing to assume the risk of the first $250 in damage and just buy insurance against a major loss, the insurance premium is much lower. Larger deductibles mean a lower premium, and this is also true in the options market.

Selecting the striking price for a protective put is analogous to selecting the deductible you want for stock insurance. The more protection you want,

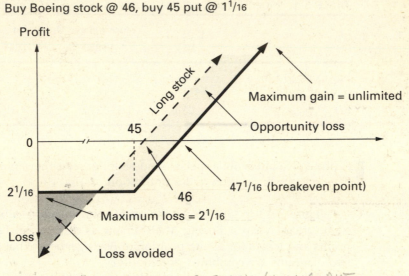

Buy Boeing stock @ 46, buy 45 put @ $1^1/_{16}$

Figure 3-2 Protective Put   LONG STOCK / LONG PUT

the higher the premium you are going to pay. Returning to the example, you might decide to buy a Boeing March 45 put to protect your long stock position of 100 shares. You pay the option premium of $106.25 to the person who wrote the put and hope that the stock continues to rise. In other words, you *fully expect to lose all the money paid for the protective put.* It may seem odd that you would ever buy a security expecting to lose money in your investment, but remember the motivation for buying fire insurance on your home or collision insurance on your car. The situations are similar. Table 3-2 shows analogies between a protective put and an insurance policy.

The shape of Figure 3-2 is generally the same as Figure 2-11 (p. 37), "Buying a Call." This illustrates an important result with options. Certain

TABLE 3-2   ANALOGIES BETWEEN AN INSURANCE POLICY AND A PROTECTIVE PUT

Insurance Policy	Put Option
Premium	Time Premium
Value of Asset	Price of Stock
Face Value	Strike Price
Amount of Deductible	Stock Price Less Strike Price
Duration	Time Until Expiration
Likelihood of Loss	Volatility of Stock

From "Portfolio Insurance," by Nicholas Hanson, in *Institutional Options Update* (July/August, 1986).

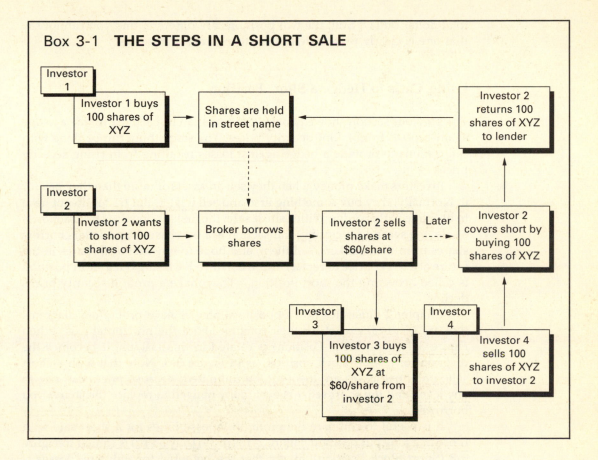

Box 3-1 **THE STEPS IN A SHORT SALE**

combinations of securities are equivalent to certain others. Here, buying a protective put is very similar to the outright purchase of a call option. The term **synthetic option** describes a collection of financial instruments that are equivalent to an option position.

long stock + long put = long call
        P. 48   P. 37

This does not mean that someone should always buy calls and should never buy stock. Many institutions and individuals need the long-term benefits of a stock portfolio. For these people, put options are a convenient way to obtain temporary "insurance" against declining prices of stock already owned. It is fair to say though, that a person should seriously consider the purchase of a call rather than the *simultaneous* purchase of shares of stock and a put. It will certainly be cheaper in terms of commissions and total dollar outlay. Still, the two positions are different, and you cannot say that one is clearly preferable to the other in every instance.

Using Calls to Hedge a Short Position

[handwritten annotation: LONG ... STOCK]

The previous section showed how put options can be used to provide a hedge against losses from falling security prices. The same thing can be done with call options to provide a hedge against losses resulting from rising security prices.

Investors make money when they sell an asset for more than they pay for it. Normally, they buy something first, and sell it later. But trades do not have to be made in this order. With a **short sale,** the first (or opening) transaction is a sale; the second (or closing) transaction is a purchase. Short sellers borrow shares from their brokers, sell them, and hope to buy identical shares in the future at a lower price to replace those borrowed. Closing out a short position is called "covering the short position." They make a profit if security prices decline.

Chapter 2 illustrates how opposite strategies have profit/loss diagrams that are identical except for their rotation about the horizontal axis. When Figure 3-1 (Long Stock Position) is rotated in this fashion, it becomes the diagram for a short stock position, as in Figure 3-3. Note that with a short sale, potential losses are theoretically unlimited, because prices can rise to any level, and the short seller is eventually obliged to replace the shares you borrowed.

It is useful to compare the profit/loss possibilities for a short sale with those of a long put position. Figure 2-13 (p. 39) (Buy a Put) is similar to Figure 3-3 (Short Stock Position), except that the potential for unlimited losses is eliminated. In buying a put, the most that can be lost is the amount paid for the option, yet the profit potential is very similar to the more risky strategy of selling short. Most informed individual investors who are bearish find the purchase of a put vastly preferable to a short sale of the stock for this reason.[3] In addition, buying a put requires less capital than the hefty margin requirements necessary to open a short account with a brokerage firm.[4]

In general, an individual investor should not sell a stock short if there is a put option available on it.

---

[3]Note, however, that puts have a finite lifetime, while a short position may remain open indefinitely. If the investor's timing is off, the put may expire before the anticipated price movement occurs. Also, there is no premium to recover if you sell short; profits begin as soon as commissions are recouped.

[4]Margin refers to the amount of collateral required to be on deposit with a brokerage firm before an investor is permitted to engage in certain types of security transactions.

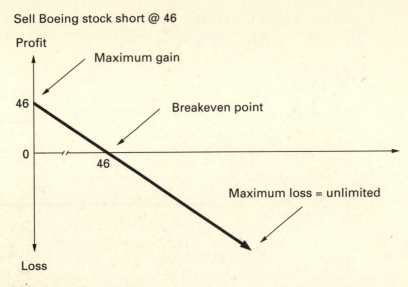

Figure 3-3 Short Stock

Although short positions are dangerous for the typical investor, they are often used by professional traders and brokerage firm portfolio managers. On the exchange floor, members often "day trade" using short sales, meaning that they close out the short position that same day before the market closes. Margin requirements are avoided because the position is not held overnight, and the risk of adverse price movements stemming from overnight news is eliminated. Even for such well-financed people positioned on the front lines of the marketplace, however, the potential for large losses is uncomfortable.

One way to hedge this risk is to combine a long position in a call option with the short stock position. If you graphically combine Figure 2-11 (Long Call, p. 37) and Figure 3-3 (Short Stock), you arrive at Figure 3-4 (p. 52). This represents being short stock and simultaneously being long a call option on the same stock. The important feature of Figure 3-4 is that the potential for unlimited losses has been eliminated. The most that the short seller can lose in this situation is $4\frac{7}{16}$. While the stock price can keep rising (resulting in increasing losses on the short position), for every dollar the stock rises above $50 the call becomes worth a dollar more. The dollar gain on the call exactly cancels the dollar loss on the short position.

short stock + long call = long put

Another way to look at a situation like this is via a profit and loss display like Table 3-3. This presents the same information as the graph.

SHORT STOCK / LONG CALL

Short stock @ 46, buy ⑤⓪ call @ $^7/_{16}$

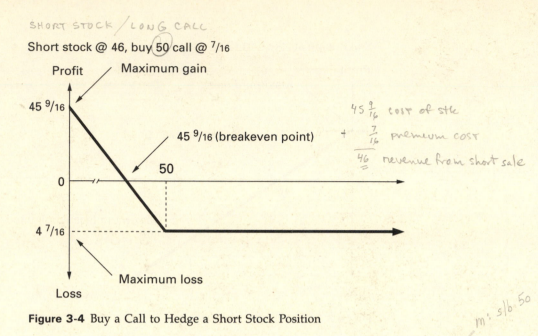

handwritten, right side:

$45\frac{9}{16}$ cost of stk

$+ \quad \frac{7}{16}$ premium cost

46 revenue from short sale

handwritten, far right: m: s/b 50

Figure 3-4 Buy a Call to Hedge a Short Stock Position

At a stock price of zero, the speculator gains \$46 on the short stock position. The expiring call is out-of-the-money, so it is worthless, and the premium of \$7⁄16 is lost. The net gain is \$45⁹⁄16. At a stock price of \$45, the option is at-the-money; at any higher stock price the option will be in-the-money. The loss in the short position and the gain in the long call position exactly cancel if there is any stock price rise above \$50, so the maximum loss on the combined positions occurs at \$50 and above.

Note that the shape of Figure 3-4 is similar to that of Figure 2-13 (Long Put, p. 39). If you are simultaneously short stock and long a call on that same stock, your combined position is equivalent to a long put.

Writing Covered Calls to Protect Against Market Downturns

handwritten: m: Appears that the "cushion" is the premium received, see p. 54

A final motivation for writing covered calls is to protect yourself against downturns in the market. Sometimes an investor is long shares of stock, suspects that the market will soon turn down, but really does not want to sell the shares now. This person might consider using covered calls to provide some cushion against losses from a falling market.

Returning to the newspaper prices for Boeing, someone might decide to hedge against the risk of a declining market by writing a MAY 50 call. The \$1¼ premium received means that no actual cash loss occurs until Boeing falls below the current price (\$46) minus the premium received (\$1¼), or

TABLE 3-3 PROFIT/LOSS POSSIBILITIES FROM A SHORT STOCK POSITION AND LONG CALL OPTION

	Stock Price at Option Expiration				
	0	25	35	45	65
short stock @ $46	+46	+21	+11	+1	−19
long 50 call @ $ 7/16	− 7/16	− 7/16	− 7/16	− 7/16	+14 9/16
net	+45 9/16	+20 9/16	+10 9/16	+ 9/16	− 4 7/16

$44¾. Of course, if the investor's feeling about the market is wrong, and Boeing continues to advance above $46, there is the risk of the stock being called until you make a closing transaction to get rid of your option position.

While this strategy provides some downside protection, this is not a particularly effective hedge. In general, an individual who needs protection against falling stock prices is better off buying put options. *i.e., protective put p. 46*

USING OPTIONS TO GENERATE INCOME

A very popular use of options by individual investors is to generate additional portfolio income. This can be done by writing either puts or calls, although calls are used far more often than puts.

Some people familiar with the options markets are uncomfortable associating the word "income" with the option premium. While it is true that the option writer gets to keep the premium no matter what happens, the premium is really compensation for bearing added risk or for foregoing future price appreciation. It is not income in the sense of cash dividends or bond interest. Still, income is a term commonly used with regard to the receipt of option premiums.

Writing Calls to Generate Income

Writing calls to generate income can be either very conservative or very risky, depending on the composition of the rest of the portfolio.

Writing Covered Calls   When a call is written against stock already owned, the call is a **covered call.** A covered call is the same as any other call option, except that you simultaneously are long the stock. Figure 3-5 shows the profit/loss possibilities for a MAY 50 covered call on Boeing. This graph

LONG STOCK / SHORT CALL

Buy stock @ 46, write APR 50 call @ 1¼

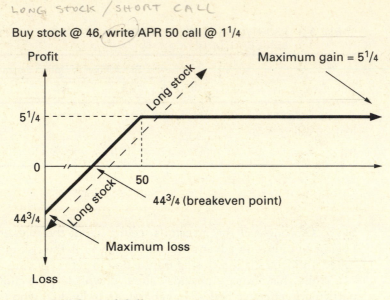

Figure 3-5 Covered Call : LONG STOCK , SHORT CALL

incorporates the profit and loss diagram for a long position in the stock and a short position[5] in the MAY 50 call.

P. 52

Option writers get the premium right away, and it is theirs to keep no matter what happens to the stock price. Figure 3-5 shows that if the stock price were to decline, the call premium cushions the loss. Even if the stock were to drop to zero, you still keep the option premium, so your net loss is "only" $44¾ (rather than $46 as in Figure 3-1, p. 46).

Writing covered calls is a very popular activity with individual investors. Brokers find the idea easy to sell to their clients. Consider another example. Suppose you are a new stockholder in Boeing, having just bought 300 shares at $46 on February 19. Your broker points out that a MAY 50 call on Boeing sells for $1¼, or $125.00 on 100 shares. Writing three of these calls results in a credit of $375.00 into your account (ignoring commissions), and you could use the money to buy another security or you could take the cash and spend it elsewhere. The worst thing that could happen to you would be for the stock of Boeing to fall to zero; this, of course, could have happened even if you had not written the options.

If prices advance above the striking price of $50, your stock will be "called away," and you must sell it to the owner of the call option for $50 per

---

[5]It is common practice to say that you are "short" an option when you have written it. Therefore, a covered call is also a **short call.** Unlike selling stock short, though, you have not borrowed anything. When you buy back a call you have written, you are "covering the call." Conceivably, then, you could "cover" a "covered call." These semantics may seem awkward, but they are part of the options lingo. There are really two entirely different meanings to the term "covered."

Feb to MAy = 3 mos

$$\frac{400 + 125}{4600} \times 4 = 45.7\%$$

share, despite the current stock price. You should not feel too upset about this, though, because you made a good profit. The stock rose from $46 to $50[6] for a gain of $400, plus you received the $125 premium when you sold the option. This is an annualized rate of return of about 46 percent. Writing covered calls is an attractive way to generate income, especially with foundations, pension funds, and other portfolios that need to produce periodic cash payments.

▌Writing covered calls is the most popular use of stock options by both individual and institutional investors.

There is an interesting paradox here. Writing covered calls is without doubt the most common option strategy by small investors; writing *puts* is without doubt the least common. Yet if we compare Figure 3-5 (Writing a Covered Call) with Figure 2-14 (Writing a Put, p. 40), we see the profit/loss plots have the same characteristic shape.

covered call

▌long stock + short call = **short put**

P. 54   P. 40

In terms of commission costs and capital required, writing puts is certainly cheaper. Ignorance about the merits of this strategy is responsible for its absence from many portfolios.

▌Writing puts has risk and return characteristics very similar to writing covered calls.

While writing covered calls is a very popular option activity, there are times when writing calls is not appropriate. One such time is when option premiums are low. This can occur for several reasons, the most important being when volatility in the market is expected to be low also. It also is usually not best to write very long-term options as a means of generating income. As will be seen in the option pricing material to come, more income is earned by writing a series of short-term options rather than a single long-term option.

Writing Naked Calls We have previously seen that writing naked calls is risky business because of the potential for unlimited losses. Despite this, there are many market participants who engage in continuous call writing as a means of generating income.

p. 38

---

[6]From your perspective, $50 is the ceiling on the stock price because you will have to sell it for $50 at any market price above that.

In Figure 2-8 (p. 31), the premium for a FEB 75 call on BMC Software is listed as ¼, while BMC Software's stock is $65¾. These prices are from the February 20th issue of the *Wall Street Journal*; February 22nd was the third Friday of the month (expiration day). A brokerage firm might feel it is extremely unlikely that BMC Software stock will rise to $75 per share in 2 days, and the firm may decide to write 100 of these call options (options on 10,000 shares). If they can do this at the listed premium of ¼, this results in a cash inflow of $0.250/share × 10,000 shares, or $2,500. The firm receives the money now, and, provided the stock price stays below $75, nothing else happens. If the stock were to rise dramatically, the firm could sustain a large loss. Brokerage firms monitor the market carefully, and if BMC Software stock began to move up, the firm would close its option positions by buying them back at a higher price (incurring a loss).

Individual investors can write naked options, too, but brokerage firms discourage small investors from doing so by enforcing certain minimum account balance requirements before permitting this type of speculative activity.[7]

Writing Puts to Generate Income

Naked vs Covered Puts   The previous section indicates that writing puts is equivalent to writing covered calls. The terms **naked put** and **covered put** are not used very often, and they probably have ambiguous meanings. When these terms are used, a naked put usually means a short put by itself, while a covered put is the combination of a short put and a short stock position.

Anytime you write an option you generate income, but you create a contingent liability on your personal balance sheet. When you write a call, you must sell stock if asked to do so. When you write a put, you must buy stock if asked to do so. A naked option position is one where you do not have another related security position that would cushion losses from price movements that adversely affect your short option position. With a covered option position, you *do* have some way of cushioning losses. We have seen that a long stock position cushions losses from a short call, and therefore the call is a covered call.

Similarly, a short stock position would cushion losses from a short put, since the shares you get from the exercise of the put could be used to close out the short stock position. For this reason, some people refer to this latter situation as a *covered put.* The term is not common.

short stock + short put = short call
covered put   p.38

---

[7]For margin purposes, most brokerage firms treat naked calls as if they were short stock positions.

TABLE 3-4 PUT OVERWRITING WORKSHEET
(Buy stock at $46, write $50 put @ $4¾)

	Stock Price at Option Expiration				
	0	20	40	45	60
long stock	−46	−26	− 6	−1	+14
short put	−45¼	−25¼	− 5¼	− ¼	+ 4¾
	−91¼	−51¼	−11¼	−1¼	+18¾

(handwritten: 45-46= −1)
(handwritten: 45 − 50 + 4¾ = −¼)

Put Overwriting   There is another important option strategy involving puts that has not yet been discussed. **Put overwriting** (sometimes called *overriding*) involves owning shares of stock and simultaneously writing *put* options against these shares. While this strategy is not common, there are many investors who could logically use it.

Put overwriting involves being simultaneously long stock and short puts on the same stock.

Because owning shares and writing puts are both bullish strategies, put overwriting must also be a bullish strategy. Remember that anytime an investor writes an option, the largest possible gain is the option premium, but losses can be large if prices move against you.
Suppose an investor simultaneously buys shares of Boeing at $46 and writes a $50 Boeing put. Table 3-4 is a profit and loss worksheet for this strategy, and Figure 3-6 is the associated profit/loss diagram.

Figure 3-6 Put Overwriting
(handwritten: LONG STOCK / SHORT PUT)
Buy stock @ 46, write 50 put @ 4³/4

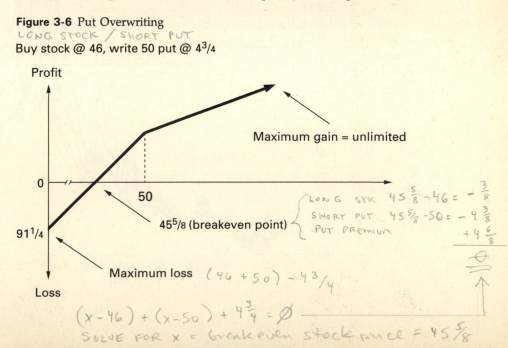

(handwritten annotations:
LONG STK 45 5/8 − 46 = − 3/8
SHORT PUT 45 5/8 − 50 = − 4 3/8
PUT PREMIUM + 4 6/8
Maximum loss (46 + 50) − 4³/4
(x − 46) + (x − 50) + 4 3/4 = ∅
SOLVE FOR x = breakeven stock price = 45 5/8)

The diagram shows that if prices rise above the option striking price, the put will expire worthless and dollar for dollar profits are enjoyed on the stock rise. If prices fall, the position loses twice because the stock is depreciating and progressively larger liabilities are being incurred on the short put position.

Put overwriting may be appropriate for a portfolio manager who needs to generate additional income from the portfolio but does not want to write calls for fear of opportunity losses in a bull market. If the portfolio does continue to increase in value, the puts will expire worthless, the portfolio will benefit from the premium income received, and the portfolio will remain intact. On the other hand, if stock prices turn down and the portfolio manager does not trade out of the put positions quickly, the overall effect on the portfolio could be disastrous.

Figure 3-7 shows the results of a strategy of continuous put overwriting on a 25 security portfolio over a 239-week period from 1977–82. An equal dollar amount was invested in each of the original 25 common stocks on which put options were available. The portfolio value was initially indexed at $10,000 for ease in interpretation over the period.

Figure 3-7 25 Security Portfolio

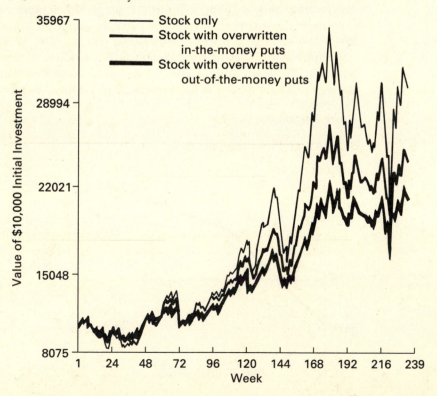

When a portfolio is overwritten with put options that are in-the-money, the portfolio must increase in value in order for the puts to expire worthless. With out-of-the-money puts, the value of the stock in the portfolio could actually decline without the risk of exercise by the put holder. Writing in-the-money puts is a riskier strategy, and Figure 3-7 shows that over long term, the riskiest strategy showed a higher realized return than the other two (as expected by finance theory). During some intermediate periods, though, writing in-the-money puts resulted in major portfolio losses.

The evaluation of any investment strategy must be done cautiously, because it is crucial to consider total market behavior during the period of investigation. Over the five-year period shown in Figure 3-7, though, it is apparent that put overwriting would have significantly improved the returns of this portfolio.

IMPROVING ON THE MARKET

There are two important strategies that have both hedging and income generation aspects. These methods are not the best means of hedging nor the best means of generating income, but may serve certain purposes well.

Writing Calls to Improve on the Market

Occasionally someone decides to sell shares of stock, but is not in any immediate need of the cash proceeds from the sale. This person can sometimes increase the amount they receive from the sale of their stock by writing **deep-in-the-money** calls against their stock position. The term *deep-in-the-money* is subjective and cannot be precisely defined. This description applies to any option that has "substantial" intrinsic value.

Suppose that on December 15th an institution holds 10,000 shares of Boeing and has decided to liquidate the entire position. Figure 3-8 (p. 60, again from the *Wall Street Journal* of 2/20/92) shows that the premium for a FEB 40 call on Boeing is $6¼; the current market price of Boeing stock is $46. The institution could simply sell their shares outright and receive $46/share × 10,000 shares, or $460,000. The institution would receive this money, minus selling commissions, on the fifth business day after the sale.

Alternatively, the portfolio manager might consider writing 100 FEB 40 calls on Boeing. If these could be sold for the newspaper price of $6¼ each, the institution would receive $62,500 in premium income the next day. These calls are in-the-money by a substantial amount. If Boeing is above $40 per share on expiration Friday, the holder of the call options will exercise them. Then the portfolio manager would have to sell 10,000 shares of Boeing for

Option & NY Close	Strike Price	Calls-Last			Puts-Last		
		Feb	Mar	Apr	Feb	Mar	Apr
Boeing	40	6¼	s	7⅛	r	s	½
46	45	1¼	2½	3½	⅛	1¹/₁₆	1¾
46	50	¹/₁₆	⁷/₁₆	1¼	4⅛	4¼	4¾
46	55	r	r	½	r	r	r

Figure 3-8 Boeing Listing, *WSJ* 2/20/92

Reprinted by permission of *Wall Street Journal,* © 1992 Dow Jones & Co., Inc. All Rights Reserved Worldwide.

$40 each, receiving $400,000. The total received by the institution here is $62,500 + $400,000, or $462,500. This is $2500 more than would have been received had the stock simply been sold. Two commissions are involved with this strategy, one to write the calls and one to sell the stock. Almost certainly the firm ends with more money than if options had not been used.

While the deep-in-the-money strategy may look attractive, there are several things to consider before embracing it. First, there is some risk with this strategy that you would not incur if you sold the stock outright. Selling stock results in cash in hand. While it may be unlikely, it is certainly possible that Boeing could fall below the striking price of $40/share, in which case the options would not be exercised. The option premium received means this improving-on-the-market strategy would "break even" at a stock price of $39¾. At this price, the stock has fallen in value by $6.25, but you still have the option premium you received for writing the call. The two amounts exactly cancel each other. If the stock falls below that, you would have fared better had you disposed of your shares in traditional fashion.

Also, experienced option traders know that you need to be careful about relying on option prices listed in the financial pages. It may not be possible for you to actually trade at the stated premium of $6¼; the current market price may be less than this. Still, there is usually some time value associated with these deep in-the-money options, and you can often capture it with a strategy like the one described here.

Writing Puts to Improve on the Market

An institution might write deep-in-the-money calls when it wishes to sell stock. Similarly, an institution might write deep-in-the-money puts when it wishes to buy stock.

Option & Strike NY Close	Price	Calls-Last			Puts-Last		
		Feb	Mar	Apr	Feb	Mar	Apr
BorInd	50	s	s	20½	s	s	r
71	60	s	s	12⅞	s	s	2⅛
71	65	r	r	r	r	r	3⅜
71	70	$1^{11}/_{16}$	5	r	¾	3⅞	5⅜
71	75	¼	$2^{15}/_{16}$	4½	4⅝	6⅝	8
71	80	1/16	$1^5/_{16}$	2½	9	10½	r
71	85	1/16	½	1⅞	14⅛	r	14⅞
71	90	r	s	⅞	r	s	r

Figure 3-9 Borland Listing, *WSJ* 2/20/92

Suppose a decision is made to buy 1000 shares of Borland International (abbreviated BorInd in Figure 3-9). Rather than buying the shares outright at $71 each (for a total investment of $71,000), the fund manager could write 10 MAR 80 puts @ $10½ and receive total premium income of $10,500. If Borland International stock remains below the striking price of $80, the puts will be exercised and the fund manager will be required to buy 1000 shares at $80 each. The cash outlay would be $80,000 from the exercise minus the premium income of $10,500 for a total of $69,500. In this example, improving on the market by writing these in-of-the-money puts enables the institution to acquire the stock at an effective price of $69½ rather than the current price of $71.

As with selling stock this way, there is some risk involved. If Borland International rises above the striking price of $80, the puts will not be exercised and the institution will not obtain the shares. Even so, the premium income is the institution's to keep.

SUMMARY

Hedging is the act of transferring unwanted risk to a speculator who is willing to bear it. Options can be used to hedge against losses resulting from adverse price movements, to provide additional portfolio income, or a combination of these two motives.

A protective put is a long put position held in conjunction with a long position in the underlying stock. This is like an insurance policy on stock. The investor selects the deductible, the policy term, and pays a premium for the insurance.

Certain combinations of securities are equivalent to others:

PROTECTIVE PUT

covered call

COVERED PUT

LONG STK + SHORT PUT
P. 57

✓**1** long stock + long put = long call   p. 48   p. 37
 2 short stock + long call = long put   p. 52   p. 39
✓**3** long stock + short call = short put   p. 54   p. 40
 4 short stock + short put = short call   p. 56   p. 38

The most common use of stock options by both individuals and institutions is writing covered calls, which involves writing call options against stock already owned. This strategy has risk and return characteristics similar to that of writing put options, which is a strategy much less frequently used.

Writing puts against a portfolio is called put overwriting. This strategy generates additional portfolio income, but involves substantial added risk if stock prices decline. Writing deep in-the-money calls can be an effective way to sell stock at a slightly higher than current price. Writing deep in-the-money puts can be an effective way to buy stock at an effective price below the current market price. Both strategies are often called improving on the market.

QUESTIONS

p. 50

1. Explain the difference between the terms *covered call* and *covering a call*.

2. Why do many people feel that buying a put is preferable to selling short shares of the underlying stock?

3. Explain the statement from Robert Merton at the beginning of the chapter. Would you agree with a similar statement about American call options?

4. What should a portfolio manager consider before embarking on a put overwriting program during a bear market?

5. Suppose you were the portfolio manager for a church's endowment fund. How would you justify buying protective puts, where you fully expected to lose your entire investment in these options?

6. Suppose you held 10,000 shares of CBS in your pension fund. Refer to Figure 3-10. Based on current market conditions given there, which striking price would you choose for a protective put? Explain your answer.

7. In question 6, which striking price would you choose for a covered call? Why?

8. Give an example of **(a)** *hedging* by buying a call, and **(b)** *speculating* by buying a call.

9. Refer to Figure 3-10. You are considering improving on the market by writing covered calls with a March expiration against shares of Black &

Option & NY Close	Strike Price	Calls-Last Feb	Mar	Apr	Puts-Last Feb	Mar	Apr
Alcoa	60	r	r	14	r	r	3/8
71 5/8	65	7	8½	8½	r	3/8	1⅛
71 5/8	70	2	3⅜	4½	3/16	11/16	2⅛
71 5/8	75	1/8	1¼	1¾	4⅞	r	r
Biogen	25	r	r	6	r	9/16	1⅛
29¼	30	3/8	2¼	3	3/4	2⅜	r
29¼	35	r	5/8	1⅜	5½	5⅞	6½
29¼	40	1/16	1/4	5/8	r	r	r
29¼	45	r	r	1/4	r	r	r
29¼	50	s	s	1/4	s	s	r
Bois C	17½	r	s	6⅞	r	s	r
25	20	r	r	5	r	r	r
25	22½	1½	r	2⅞	r	r	½
25	25	½	1 3/16	1¾	½	r	r
Blk Dk	17½	9	r	9	r	r	r
26⅛	20	6¼	6½	6¼	r	r	r
26⅛	22½	r	4	4⅛	r	r	3/4
26⅛	25	1⅜	2	2⅝	1/4	r	1¼
26⅛	30	s	r	15/16	s	r	r
C B S	135	13½	r	r	r	r	3⅛
148⅜	140	8	r	r	r	1⅜	4⅝
148⅜	145	3½	6¾	10¼	r	3½	r
148⅜	150	3/4	4⅛	7⅜	3⅝	r	r
148⅜	155	1/16	2½	5⅛	7⅛	r	r
148⅜	160	r	1⅜	4¼	r	r	r
148⅜	165	r	s	2⅝	r	s	r
148⅜	175	1/16	s	s	r	s	s
Coke	55	22¼	s	s	r	s	s
77	60	16½	s	r	r	s	r
77	65	11¼	s	r	r	s	5/8
77	70	7⅛	6⅞	7¾	r	3/8	1⅛
77	75	2⅜	3	4½	3/16	1⅝	3⅛
77	80	1/8	1	2¾	3⅝	4½	6¼
77	85	r	r	1 3/16	r	r	r
Xerox	70	8¾	r	r	r	r	1
79¼	75	3	4	5⅝	1/8	1¼	2
79¼	80	11/16	1⅝	2½	1¼	3½	r
79¼	85	s	13/16	1⅜	s	r	r

Figure 3-10 Listings for Questions and Problems, *WSJ* 2/20/92

Decker you own. Is there any relative advantage of the MAR 20 call over the MAR 22½ call?

10. If a short seller wants to generate additional income by writing options, does it matter which type of option is chosen?

11. Compare the risk of writing a covered put with the risk of writing a covered call.

12. If you buy a protective put, you can "cancel" your insurance policy by selling your put. Is it possible for you to cancel your insurance and realize a *profit*?

13. Comment on the relative merits of protecting against a market downturn by **(a)** buying puts and **(b)** writing covered calls.

14. Why is writing an in-the-money put more risky than writing an out-of-the-money put?

15. Suppose someone owns 1000 shares of XYZ (current price: $40) and buys 5 XYZ APR 40 puts and also buys 5 XYZ APR 30 puts. Is this the same as buying 10 XYZ APR 35 puts?

16. Refer to Figure 3-1. What does it mean to say "ignoring opportunity costs," the strategy breaks even if the stock price is unchanged at a future time? p. 46

17. Does the term "improving on the market" imply a pricing inefficiency in the options market?

PROBLEMS

Refer to Figure 3–10 (p. 63) as necessary.

1. Draw a profit/loss diagram for writing a Xerox MAR 75 put option.

2. Suppose you simultaneously buy 400 shares of Alcoa and write two APR 70 puts. What is your gain or loss if, at option expiration, the common stock of Alcoa sells for $74?

3. Draw a profit/loss diagram for the simultaneous purchase of 100 shares of Coca Cola at $77 and the writing of a MAY 80 call at 2¾.

4. Suppose you bought 200 shares of Biogen at $29¼, and simultaneously bought 2 MAR 30 puts @ $2¾ as a hedge against a declining market. At option expiration, Biogen stock sold for $25. Were your protective puts a good idea?

5. Draw a profit/loss diagram for the simultaneous purchase of 100 shares of Boise Cascade and the writing of a MAY 22½ put.

6. Suppose an investor engages in *three* simultaneous transactions: **(1)** she buys 100 shares of CBS common stock, **(2)** she *writes* a MAR

145 put, and **(3)** she *buys* a MAR 140 put. Does this strategy make any sense?

7. In problem 6, what is her profit or loss if CBS is unchanged at option expiration?

8. Draw a profit/loss diagram for the simultaneous positions of short 100 shares of CBS and short one MAR 145 CBS put. What other option strategy is similar to this?

9. Draw a profit/loss diagram for writing a Xerox APR 75 put option. See #1

10. Suppose you simultaneously buy 300 shares of Alcoa and write one MAR 70 put. What is your gain or loss if, at option expiration, the common stock of Alcoa sells for $72? See # 2

11. Draw a profit/loss diagram for the simultaneous purchase of 100 shares of Coca Cola at $77 and the writing of a MAR 80 call at 1. See # 3

12. Suppose you bought 200 shares of Biogen at $29¼, and simultaneously bought 2 APR 25 puts at $1⅛ as a hedge against a declining market. At option expiration, Biogen stock sold for $23. Were your protective puts a good idea? See # 4

13. Draw a profit/loss diagram for the simultaneous purchase of 100 shares of Boise Cascade and the writing of a FEB 25 put. See # 5

 **Option Combinations and Spreads**

*R*isk Not Thy Whole Wad

Chicago Mercantile Exchange

KEY TERMS

backspread	diagonal spread
bearspread	hedge wrapper
bullspread	horizontal spread
butterfly spread	margin
calendar spread	ratio spread
combination	spread
combined call writing	straddle
condor	strangle
credit	time decay
cross company spread	time spread
debit	vertical spread

The previous two chapters focused on fundamental principles of options, showing how options can be used to generate income, to speculate, or to provide protection against adverse price movements. This chapter covers strategies that have the distinguishing characteristic of <u>seeking a trading profit rather than hedging or income generation.</u>

COMBINATIONS

Combinations are strategies in which you are simultaneously long or short options of different types. Technically, there are many different option combinations. This chapter covers the most popular ones.

An <u>option combination is a strategy in which you are simultaneously long *or* short puts *and* calls.</u>

Straddles

PUT + CALL
ONE striking price
ONE expiration date

Straddles are probably the best-known option combination. <u>If you own both a put and a call</u> with the same striking price, the same expiration date, on the same underlying security, you are *long* a straddle. If you are short these options, you have *written* a straddle. Let's look at the motivation behind each of these strategies.

Buying a Straddle It may seem illogical to simultaneously buy a put and a call on the same stock. <u>A long call is bullish, and a long put is bearish.</u> Buying both seems to violate the fundamental need to "take a stand" on the direction of the market.

Suppose a speculator buys a MAY 45 straddle on Boeing. According to the figures in Figure 2-8 (p. 31), it costs $350 to buy the call and $175 to buy the put, for a total investment of $525. Table 4-1 is a profit and loss table for various stock prices at option expiration. <u>A long straddle becomes</u>

TABLE 4-1 LONG STRADDLE WORKSHEET

		Stock Price at Option Expiration			
		$0	$45	$65	$85
buy MAY 45 call @	$3½	− 3½	−3½	+16½	+36½
buy MAY 45 put @	$1¾	+43¼	−1¾	− 1¾	− 1¾
net cost	$5¼	+39¾	−5¼	+14¾	+34¾

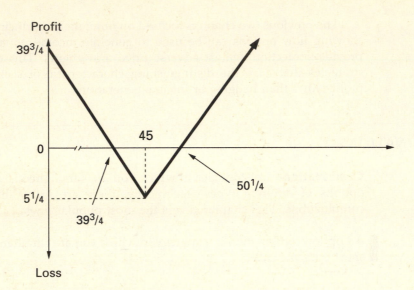

Figure 4-1 Long Straddle

profitable if prices rise *or* fall, provided they rise or fall substantially. Figure 4-1 shows this.

The profit and loss diagram for a long straddle is simply the graphic combination of a long call and a long put. The worst outcome for the straddle buyer is when both options expire worthless. In this example, if Boeing is exactly at $45 on expiration day, both options expire worthless. At any other price, one of the options will have some intrinsic value.

The straddle buyer will still lose money if Boeing closes near the striking price of $45. In fact, the stock must rise or fall by enough to recover the initial cost of the position, $5¼. If the stock rises, the put expires worthless, but the call becomes valuable. Conversely, if the stock falls, the put is valuable, but the call expires worthless. From the diagram, it is apparent that there will be two breakeven points with the straddle, one corresponding to a price rise and one for a price decline. Each breakeven point is $5¼ away from the $45 striking price.

When might someone buy a straddle? The answer is anytime a situation develops when it is likely that a stock will move sharply one way or the other. Perhaps a company is involved in takeover talks and is awaiting a Federal Trade Commission decision regarding antitrust rules. If the merger is approved, the stock to be acquired probably will rise sharply. If the merger is disallowed, then the stock might drop just as sharply. Another situation lending itself to the purchase of a straddle is when a court decision is imminent. Perhaps a firm is involved in a class action suit because of alleged corporate negligence or product liability resulting in some personal injury claims against the company. If the firm is found liable, the stock will almost

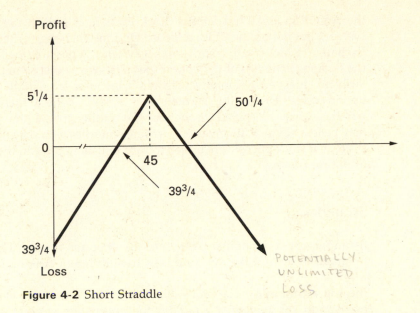

Figure 4-2 Short Straddle

certainly fall in value. If the firm is exonerated, the uncertainty has been largely resolved and the stock may recover to a higher level.

Writing a Straddle   The straddle buyer wants the stock price to move significantly in one direction or the other. The straddle writer wants just the opposite: little movement in the stock price. Figure 4-2 is the diagram of a short straddle. The maximum gain in this strategy occurs when the options finish at-the-money, and therefore expire worthless. Losses are potentially unlimited on the upside, because the short call is uncovered.

Although the potential profit may seem out of line with the risk of such a strategy, it is popular with some speculators. Some experienced option players refer to the "convergence phenomenon" on expiration, in which it is alleged that stock prices show an unusual tendency to close exactly at a striking price if the stock price was close to that value a few days before option expiration. For example, a stock might close at $24¾ Wednesday of expiration week. The convergence phenomenon means that there is a statistically significant likelihood that the stock will move toward the striking price of $25 as expiration approaches. Similarly, if the stock price Wednesday were $25⅜, the alleged phenomenon predicts a price decline toward $25 from Wednesday to Friday.

Strong and Andrew tested this hypothesis.[1] Using various control groups, they found evidence in support of the convergence phenomenon on

----

[1]Robert A. Strong and William P. Andrew, "Further Evidence of the Influence of Option Expiration on Stock Prices," *Journal of Business Research* (August, 1987): 291–302.

the American and Philadelphia Stock Exchanges (which use the specialist system), but not on the Chicago Board Options Exchange or the Pacific Stock Exchange (which use the marketmaker system). A possible explanation lies in the hedging activities of the option specialist, who must sometimes involuntarily buy inexpensive options with a little intrinsic value in the last days of an option cycle. Under the marketmaker system, where these involuntary purchases may be spread throughout the trading crowd, the need to hedge may be less obvious. In any event, writing straddles would be the appropriate strategy if stock prices were biased toward a striking price in the last few days of option trading.

Strangles   *Put and call / 2 striking prices / one expiration date*

Strangles are very popular with professional option traders. They are similar to straddles, except the puts and calls have different striking prices.

Buying a Strangle   The motivation for buying a strangle is similar to the motivation for buying a straddle: the speculator expects a sharp price movement either up or down in the underlying security.

There are two striking prices involved with a strangle. With *long strangles*, the most popular version involves buying a put with a lower striking price than the call you buy. Done this way, the profit and loss characteristics are similar to those of the long straddle, but the maximum loss is reduced.

Figure 4-3 Long Strangle

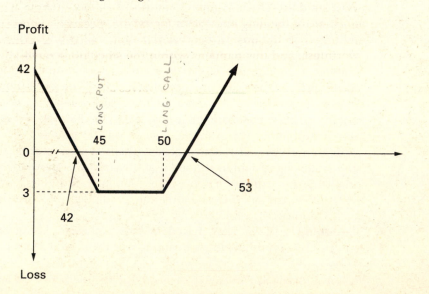

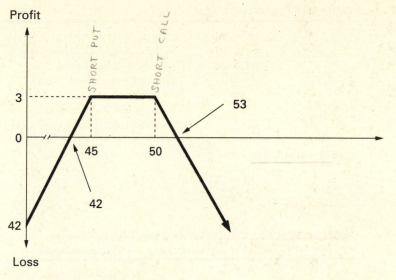

Figure 4-4 Short Strangle

Figure 4-3 shows the characteristics of a long strangle constructed by buying a Boeing MAY $45 put and buying a Boeing MAY $50 call. The maximum loss occurs over the price range $45 to $50, because between these values both options expire worthless. Once outside the range, one option has intrinsic value. The position costs $1¾ + $1¼ = $3, and to break even, this much intrinsic value must be recovered.

Writing a Strangle   Figure 4-4 shows the short strangle. This is exactly the opposite of the long strangle in Figure 4-3. Because a short strangle involves writing the options, the maximum gain occurs if both options expire worthless, and this happens within the stock price range of $45–$50.

In the short straddle, the maximum profit occurs at a single point, the striking price. The short strangle involves a slightly reduced maximum profit, but it is earned over a broader price range.

The term *strangle* probably originated during April, 1978, when stock in International Business Machines was experiencing wide price swings. Many professional options traders routinely write options on active stocks like IBM, and many were wiped out on short IBM strangles during this infamous month.

Puts + calls / all calls / all puts

Condors
4 striking prices
one expiration date

Condors are a less risky version of the strangle, involving *four* different striking prices.

TABLE 4-2 CREATING A LONG CONDOR

calls only:	long A and D; short B and C
puts only:	long A and D; short B and C
puts and calls:	long call A; short call B; short put C; long put D
	or
	long put A; short put B; short call C; long call D

Note: (B − A) = (C − B) = (D − C) in all cases

$$B - A = C - B = D - C$$
$$45 - 40 = 50 - 45 = 55 - 50$$

TABLE 4-3 LONG CONDOR WORKSHEET FOR BOEING (using MAY 40/45 puts and MAY 50/55 calls)

			Stock Price at Option Expiration				
			$0	$40	$45	$50	$55
A	buy 40 put @	− ½	+39½	− ½	− ½	− ½	− ½
B	write 45 put @	+ 1¾	−43¼	−3¼	+1¾	+1¾	+1¾
C	write 50 call @	+ 1¼	+ 1¼	+1¼	+1¼	+1¼	−3¾
D	buy 55 call @	− ½	− ½	− ½	− ½	− ½	− ½
	cost	+3 credit	−3	−3	+2	+2	−3

Net premium income

Buying a Condor   A long condor can be constructed in various ways. Suppose we have striking prices A, B, C, and D, where A < B < C < D. Table 4-2 shows the various ways in which a long condor can be constructed. Figure 4-5 shows the characteristic shape of a long condor.

The condor buyer hopes that stock prices remain in the B through C range, because this is where maximum profits occur. However, outside this range at least one option will have intrinsic value.[2]

Let's look at an example of a long condor using *WSJ* prices on Boeing using both puts and calls. Table 4-3 is a worksheet to calculate the profit/loss characteristics.

---

[2]Commissions have been ignored in these examples. However, with multiple option strategies like condors, commissions can become material. Many brokerage firms have a minimum commission of $35 per trade. Establishing a condor involves four trades, or $140. Outside the B to C price range there will be another trade when the option or options with intrinsic value are either sold or exercised.

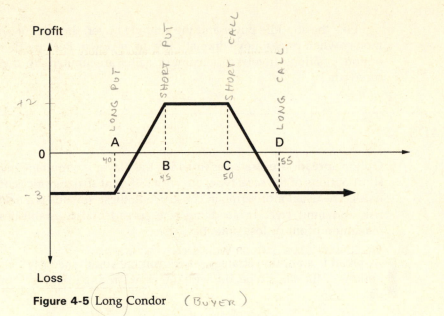

See
butterfly, p.80

Figure 4-5 Long Condor   (BUYER)

Writing a Condor   Figure 4-6 is a profit and loss diagram for a short condor position using the options listed in Table 4-3. The diagram is easily constructed by reversing the signs from the long condor worksheet. A quick glance is all that is necessary to understand the positive and negative outcomes associated with a position like this.

Figure 4-6 Short Condor   (WRITER/SELLER)

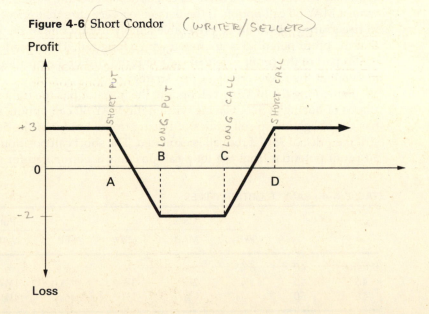

Like the straddle buyer and the strangle buyer, the condor writer makes money when prices move dramatically up or down. Because there are short option positions involved, maximum gains are limited by the premiums received.

SPREADS

Option **spreads** are strategies in which the player is simultaneously long *and* short options of the *same* type, but with different striking prices or expiration dates. The usual motivation in constructing these spreads is a need to reduce risk and limit cost. In so doing, the spreader also establishes a known maximum profit or loss potential.

A spread is an option strategy where you are simultaneously long and short options of the same type, but with different striking prices and/or expiration dates.

Types of Spreads

Vertical Spreads   In a **vertical spread,** options are selected vertically from the financial pages. Table 4-4 below is an extract from Figure 2-8 (p. 31).

A person who believes that Boeing common stock is going to appreciate soon may choose to buy a MAY 45 call option on Boeing, and simultaneously write a MAY 50 call option. If the person felt very sure that prices were going to rise sharply, it would be preferable simply to buy one of the calls. Recall that the profit potential is unlimited with a long call. The spreader, however, trades part of the profit potential for a reduced cost of the position. Let's look in detail at the implications of this strategy.

Being long the MAY 45 call option, the investor has the right to purchase shares of Boeing at $45. Having written the MAY 50 call option, the investor has the obligation to sell shares of Boeing to the holder of the 50 call at the striking price of $50, if the call is exercised. The short call position means that all profit potential from the long call position is eliminated for stock prices

TABLE 4-4   SAMPLE OPTION PRICES

		Calls				Puts		
		FEB	MAR	MAY		FEB	MAR	MAY
Boeing	40	6¼	s	7⅛		r	s	½
46	45	1¼	2½	3½		⅛	1¹⁄₁₆	1¾
46	50	¹⁄₁₆	⁷⁄₁₆	1¼		4⅛	4¼	4¾

LONG CALL (lower strike price)
SHORT CALL (higher strike price)
DIFFERENT STRIKING PRICES
SAME EXPIRATION

TABLE 4-5 A VERTICAL CALL WORKSHEET (BULLSPREAD)

		\$0	\$40	\$45	\$50	\$55
		Stock Price at Option Expiration				
buy MAY 45 @	\$3½	−3½	−3½	−3½	+1½	+6½
write MAY 50 @	1¼	+1¼	+6¼	+1¼	+1¼	−3¾
net cost	\$2¼	−2¼	−2¼	−2¼	+2¾	+2¾

vertical bullspread

greater than \$50. Looking at the situation another way, if stock prices rise to \$60, I have a profit on the MAY 45 call, but I have lost on the MAY 50 call that I wrote. As stock prices rise above \$50, the added loss in the short call exactly cancels the added gain in my long call. Table 4-5 presents the profit and loss components for this strategy.

Buying the MAY 45 requires a cash outlay of \$350; writing the MAY 50 brings in \$125, which reduces the actual cost of the spread to \$225. This is the maximum loss, which, as Table 4-5 shows, occurs at stock prices of \$45 and below. The maximum gain occurs when the stock price is \$50 or higher. At prices above this, the spreader will receive an exercise notice on the 50 call, and, therefore will lose any further gains from the long 45 call. Figure 4-7 shows the profit and loss possibilities.

Remember that a fundamental rule of preparing these profit/loss diagrams is that bends in the plot occur at striking prices. A vertical call spread has two striking prices, and therefore has two bends in the diagram.

Figure 4-7 Bullspread

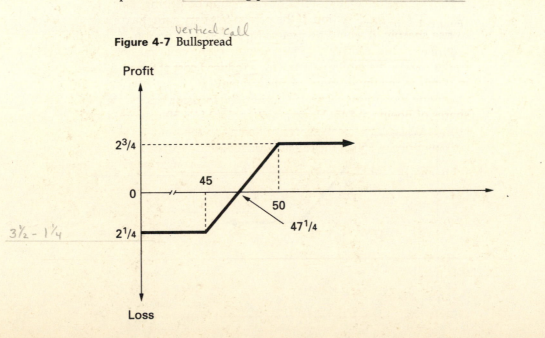

3½ − 1¼

SHORT CALL (lower strike price)
LONG CALL (higher strike price)
DIFFERENT STRIKING PRICES
SAME EXPIRATION

TABLE 4-6 A VERTICAL CALL WORKSHEET (BEARSPREAD)

Vertical
bearspread

		Stock Price at Option Expiration				
		$0	$40	$45	$50	$55
write MAY 45 @	$3½	+3½	+3½	+3½	−1½	−6½
buy MAY 50 @	1¼	−1¼	−1¼	−1¼	−1¼	+3¾
credit	$2¼	+2¼	+2¼	+2¼	−2¾	−2¾

The strategy depicted in Figure 4-7 (p. 75) commonly is called a **bullspread,** because the maximum profit occurs when prices rise. Another type of vertical call spread is a **bearspread,** where just the reverse occurs: the maximum profit occurs with falling prices.

In setting up a bullspread, the investor buys the option with the lower striking price and writes the option with the higher striking price. The opposite occurs with a bearspread; the call option with the high striking price is purchased and the call with the low striking price is written. Table 4-6 uses the same options as Table 4-5 (p. 75) in constructing a bearspread.

Figure 4-8 shows the profit and loss possibilities at various stock prices at option expiration.

Individual investors typically set up spreads using call options. They also can be done using puts, and in some circumstances the use of puts is preferable.

Figure 4-8 Bearspread

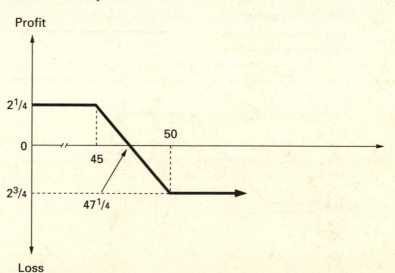

LONG PUT (lower striking price)
SHORT PUT (higher striking price)   4/SPREADS   **77**
DIFFERENT STRIKING PRICES
SAME EXPIRATION

TABLE 4-7   VERTICAL PUT WORKSHEET (BULLSPREAD)

		Stock Price at Option Expiration			
		$0	$45	$50	$55
buy MAY 45 @	1¾	+43¼	−1¾	−1¾	−1¾
write MAY 50 @	4¾	−45¼	− ¼	+4¾	+4¾
credit	$3	−2	−2	+3	+3

In Table 4-5 (p. 75) the spread is constructed using the MAY 45/50 calls; this requires a net cash outlay of $225 (before commissions). An alternative strategy is to set up a similar bullspread using the MAY 45/50 puts. This is done the same way as with calls: buy the option with the lower striking price and write the option with the higher one.

A primary difference in these two approaches is that the put spread results in a **credit** to the spreaders' account (meaning money comes in) while the call spread results in a **debit** (meaning money goes out). Table 4-7 is a worksheet for the put bullspread.

In this example, the profit and loss payoffs for the put spread are approximately the same as with the call spread, and this is a general characteristic of the two methods of constructing the spreads. The maximum profit occurs at all stock prices above the higher striking price, while the maximum loss occurs at stock prices below the lower striking price. With vertical spreads, the spreader is concerned only with the range of stock prices between the two striking prices. If the stock price closes outside this range, the spreader incurs either the maximum gain or loss as determined at the extremes of the range.

These examples of vertical spreads used options that were a single striking price apart (45 and 50). This does not have to be the case. I could, for instance, buy the MAY 45 call and write the MAY 55 call. This is still a vertical bullspread, but it involves a different package of risk and return.

Calendar Spreads   Vertical spreads employ options listed vertically in the financial pages; with **calendar spreads,** options are chosen *horizontally.* In fact, they are also called **horizontal spreads,** or **time spreads.** Because they are chosen horizontally from the listing, they necessarily involve options with the same striking price. They are also either bullspreads or bearspreads, depending on the options purchased and the options written.

As an example, a speculator might be bullish on Boeing and buy a MAY 50 call for $1¼ (refer to Table 4-4, p. 74). If the speculator believes there is little likelihood that Boeing will rise to $50 by option expiration in March, he or

BULLISH CALENDAR SPREAD
WRITE MAR 50 CALL
BUY   MAY 50 CALL

she also might choose to write a MAR 50 call for 7/16. This latter action results in a cash inflow to the spreader's options account, and provided Boeing remains below $50 per share until the third Friday in March, the option will expire unexercised. The speculator still owns the MAY 50 call and continues to hope for stock price appreciation. With any calendar spread, an element of timing is superimposed on the bullish or bearish attitude toward the underlying stock. A bullish speculator will buy a call option with a distant expiration and write one that is near expiration. A bearish speculator will do the opposite.

BEARISH CALENDAR SPREAD
BUY MAR 45 CALL
WRITE MAY 45 CALL

As an example of a bearish calendar spread, suppose I buy the MAR 45 call and write the MAY 45 call from Table 4-4 (p. 74). I expect Boeing to decline, so I expect to lose all my money on the March option. I expect the expensive option I wrote (the MAY 45) to decline in value, yielding a profit to me. My motivation in buying the cheap call is to reduce risk. If I simply wrote a call when I expected the stock to fall, the call would be uncovered, and we have previously seen that potential losses with naked calls are unlimited.[3] If I am right in my assessment and the stock falls, the call I bought will expire worthless, and I will most likely buy another call in the May series to "cover" the call I am short. At the March expiration, the price of a MAY 45 also will have fallen if the stock has gone down, and this may be the option I choose to buy.

See p. 34

Calendar spreaders are concerned with an important option phenomenon called **time decay.** Options are worth more the longer they have until expiration. As time passes, options decline in value if the price of the underlying asset does not change. This is advantageous to the option writer, who hopes that the options written expire worthless or at least decline in value.

Figure 4-9 shows how the value of a call option declines over time if other things remain equal. When there is a "significant" amount of time remaining in the option's life, time value decay is approximately linear. In the last few weeks of an option's life, its time value begins to drop sharply. The calendar spreader hopes to capture this time value by writing options that deteriorate in value.

Calendar spreads cannot be conveniently graphed, nor can a profit and loss table be constructed in the traditional manner. This is because the strategy involves more than one expiration date.

---

[3]One inconvenience with calendar spreads involves those situations where you write the option with a more distant expiration and buy the near one. For margin purposes, the distant option will probably be considered uncovered by your brokerage firm, subjecting you to more strict capital requirements. Margin is discussed later in this chapter.

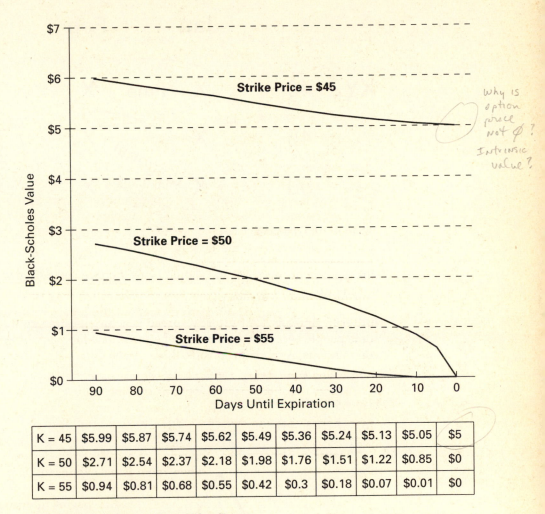

Why is option price not ∅? Intrinsic value?

	90	80	70	60	50	40	30	20	10	0
K = 45	$5.99	$5.87	$5.74	$5.62	$5.49	$5.36	$5.24	$5.13	$5.05	$5
K = 50	$2.71	$2.54	$2.37	$2.18	$1.98	$1.76	$1.51	$1.22	$0.85	$0
K = 55	$0.94	$0.81	$0.68	$0.55	$0.42	$0.3	$0.18	$0.07	$0.01	$0

Figure 4-9 Call Option Time Value Decay

Diagonal Spreads A **diagonal spread** involves options from different expiration months and with different striking prices: they are chosen diagonally from the financial pages. One example with Boeing would be the purchase of a MAY 40 call and the sale of a MAR 45 call. Diagonal spreads also can be bullish or bearish, but it is less clear what an investor has in mind with certain diagonal spreads. Someone might buy the Boeing MAR 45 call for $2½ and write the MAY 40 call for 7⅛. This would be unusual; it seems that the investor wants Boeing to skyrocket before the March option series expires, then nosedive so that the May option expires worthless. Spreads of

DIFFERENT STRIKE PRICE
DIFFERENT EXPIRATION

WRITE MAR 45
BUY MAY 40

BUY MAR 45
WRITE MAY 40

MAR   MAY
45   40

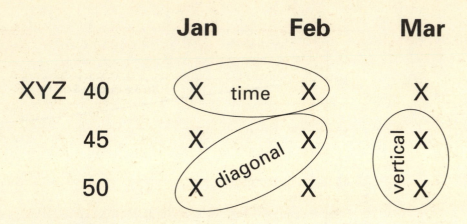

Figure 4-10 Types of Spreads

this type are uncommon, and should be well-conceived before you choose to set one up.

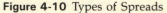

Butterfly Spreads   A **butterfly spread** is a curious strategy that appeals to some people because they can often be constructed for very little cost beyond commissions. As with all spreads, these can be done with either puts or calls.

m: straddle is to butterfly spread as a strangle is to a condor regarding shape of profit diagram

Figure 4-11 Butterfly Spread

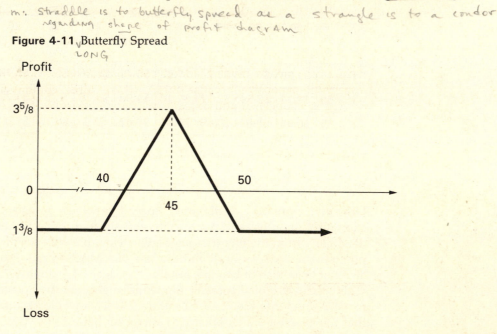

[handwritten: condor has 4 strike prices (p.72)
Butterfly has 3 strike prices.]

TABLE 4-8 METHODS OF BUILDING A BUTTERFLY SPREAD*

1. long call A, short 2 calls B, long call C;
2. long put A, short 2 puts B, long put C;
3. long put A, short put B, short call B, long call C;
4. long call A, short call B, short put B, long put C.

*The quantity (B − A) = (C − B) in each version.

[handwritten: condor]

Unlike spreads discussed thus far, this strategy also can be constructed using puts *and* calls.

As an example, suppose the options on XYZ have striking prices at $40, 45, and 50. For simplicity call these A, B, and C, respectively. There are four ways in which a butterfly spread could be constructed, as Table 4-8 shows.

Using the May Boeing option prices from Table 4-4, we can prepare a worksheet for a long butterfly spread using approach #1 from above. Table 4-9 shows that with this strategy, very little money is at risk. If prices rise or drop dramatically, losses occur, but the maximum loss is only 1⅜. The largest profit occurs if the middle options are at-the-money when they expire. Figure 4-11 is a profit and loss diagram of this long butterfly spread.

These spreads look attractive, but the potential spreader should recognize that it is difficult to establish any option spread at the exact prices published in the financial pages.

While all spreads involve added commission costs, butterfly spreads are especially expensive because they involve three commissions when the spread is established and at least one at option expiration. *[handwritten: i.e., 4 commissions]*

TABLE 4-9 LONG BUTTERFLY SPREAD

		Stock Price at Option Expiration			
		$0	$40	$45	$50
A	buy one 40 call @	7⅛	−7⅛	−7⅛	−2⅛	+2⅞
B	write two 45 calls @	3½	+7	+7	+7	−3
C	buy one 50 call @	1¼	−1¼	−1¼	−1¼	−1¼
	cost	1⅜	−1⅜	−1⅜	+3⅝	−1⅜

Box 4-1   **THE METAMORPHOSIS OF BUTTERFLIES INTO ALLIGATORS**

Butterfly spreads sometimes appear to be costless, but there is usually more than meets the eye from the financial pages. Suppose the newspaper lists one-month calls on XYZ as follows.

Striking Price	Premium
45	5
50	3
55	1

Buying one contract each of the 45s and 55s costs $600; writing two contracts of the 50s brings in $600, for an apparent net outlay of zero. The broker's computer screen, however, provides added information:

Striking Price	Bid	Ask
45	4⅞	5⅛
50	2⅞	3⅛
55	⅞	1⅛

The actual cost of the butterfly spread, then, is

buy $45 call	$5⅛ × 100 =	$512.50 outlay
write 2 $50 calls	$2⅞ × 200 =	575.00 inflow
buy $55 call	$1⅛ × 100 =	112.50 outflow
	net	50.00 outflow

In addition, your brokerage firm has a $35 minimum commission per transaction. The butterfly spread involves 3 transactions, so this adds $105 to the cost. The total cost of the "free" butterfly spread is therefore $165.00. The unseen costs of bid/ask spreads and commissions are the reason some people prefer to call these alligator spreads.

NONSTANDARD SPREADS

The strategies considered so far are well-known and constitute a fundamental part of the options game. Market conditions change, and sometimes an investor finds it advisable to alter an existing position by removing part of it or adding to it. Several examples of how this might be done are discussed here.

Ratio Spreads

Ratio spreads are variations on the bullspreads and bearspreads just discussed. Instead of a simple "long one, short one" strategy, ratio spreads involve an unequal number of long and short options.

Call Ratio Spread   A call bullspread can be transformed into a call ratio spread by writing more than one call at the higher striking price. The result is a profit/loss diagram like Figure 4-12.

   A person might be inclined to use this type of spread when the market is near the lower striking price, and the investor anticipates a modest rise in prices, but also feels that there is potential for a near term downturn. If prices

[handwritten margin notes: EG. BUY MAY 45 WRITE MAY 50 WRITE MAY 50 ; mi vertical — p. 75 ; Sparvero]

Figure 4-12 Call Ratio Spread

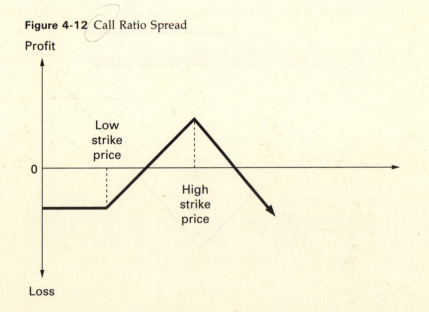

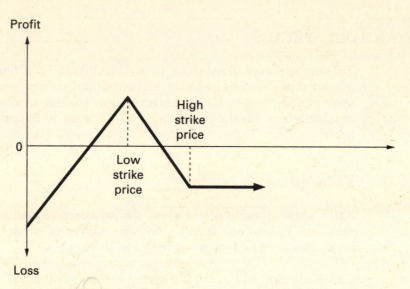

Profit

0

High strike price

Low strike price

Loss

Figure 4-13 Put Ratio Spread

behave as expected, the extra short option provides added income and lowers the cost of the spread.

Put Ratio Spread   A bearspread with puts becomes a put ratio spread by the addition of extra short put positions. Figure 4-13 illustrates this strategy; it is

WRITE MAY 45
BUY MAY 50
BUY MAY 50

vertical put

Figure 4-14 Call Ratio Backspread

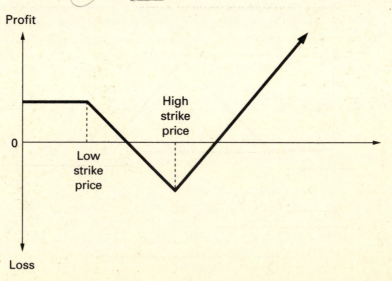

Profit

0

High strike price

Low strike price

Loss

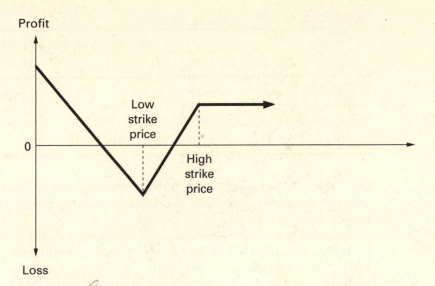

Figure 4-15 Put Ratio Backspread

appropriate when a bearish speculator also feels there is a significant risk of a sharp rise in prices.

!! A bear expects this!

Ratio Backspreads

Backspreads are constructed exactly the opposite as the ratio spreads described above. Backspreads can generate a credit to your account, while ordinary ratio spreads result in a debit. Call bearspreads are transformed into call ratio backspreads by adding to the long call position, and put bullspreads become put ratio backspreads by adding more long puts. These strategies are diagramed in Figures 4-14 and 4-15.

Building a Hedge Wrapper[4]   *Also called a collar.*

Suppose an investor owns a stock that has risen in value since its purchase, and for which the outlook continues to be bullish, but with added risk of a significant price decline. What can be done? One alternative would be to sell

---

[4]My good friend Gary Gastineau, author of the excellent *Options Manual* and the fascinating reference book *Dictionary of Financial Risk Management,* points out that hedge wrappers are also called collars, fences, fence spreads, cylinders, spread conversions, conversion spreads, range forwards, tunnel options, and cap and floors.

(handwritten margin notes:)
call bearspread, p. 76
put bullspread p. 77

Call Ratio backspread
WRITE MAY 45
BUY MAY 50
BUY MAY 50

Put ratio backspread
Buy MAY 45
write MAY 50
BUY MAY 50

TABLE 4-10 BUILDING A HEDGE WRAPPER

	Stock Price at Option Expiration			
	0	45	50	55
buy stock @ 38	−38	+7	+12	+17
write 50 call @ 1¼	+ 1¼	+1¼	+ 1¼	− 3¾
buy 45 put @ 1¾	+43¼	−1¾	− 1¾	− 1¾
net	+ 6½	+6½	+11½	+11½

covered call (handwritten note)

the stock; another would be to buy a protective put. A third would be to create a **hedge wrapper,** which involves writing a covered call and also buying a put.

Assume you bought Boeing when the stock price was $38 and the current price is $46 as Table 4-4 (p. 74) shows. If Boeing continues to rise, the long stock position appreciates. But, Table 4-10 works out the net effect of an alternative—simultaneously buying a MAY 45 put (for $1¾) and writing a MAY 50 covered call (for $1¼).

The table shows that no matter what happens, you have locked in a profit! Buying the put protects the unrealized gains in the stock position.[5] Figure 4-16 is a diagram of the original long stock position, and your combined position after completion of the hedge wrapper.

The maximum profit with a hedge wrapper occurs once the stock price rises to the striking price of the call, while the lowest return is realized if the stock falls to the striking price of the put or below. The fundamental result is that the hedge wrapper transforms the profitable stock position into a certain winner, although with reduced potential for further gain.

A hedge wrapper can be used to transform a profitable long position into a riskless profit; the strategy reduces the possibility for further gain from stock price increases.

Combined Call Writing

Suppose an investor owns 1000 shares of Boeing. This investor continues to be bullish on Boeing, but finds it necessary to generate some extra income. The investor could write 10 MAY 45 calls for $3½ each. This would yield a total of $3500 in immediate income, but because the calls are currently

[5]The same thing can happen if you buy a protective put *after* you have a paper gain in the underlying stock.

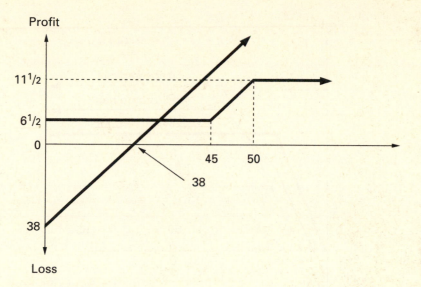

Figure 4-16 Hedge Wrapper

in-the-money, they stand a good chance of being exercised. Another tactic would be to write 10 MAY 50 calls at $1¼. This generates $1250, less income with less chance of exercise.

In **combined call writing,** the investor writes calls using more than one striking price. Consider the portfolio of 1000 shares of Boeing, 5 short MAY 45 calls, and 5 short MAY 50 calls. Table 4-11 is a profit and loss worksheet for this strategy.

In Figure 4-17 (p. 89), this strategy (using two different striking prices) is compared with two more traditional covered call strategies: (a) writing ten in-the-money calls, and (b) writing ten out-of-the-money calls.

The highest gain is possible when the calls with the highest striking price are written. But this strategy also generates the least income to the portfolio

2 STRIKE PRICES
SAME EXPIRATION

TABLE 4-11   BOEING COMBINED 45/50 COVERED CALL WRITING

	Stock Price at Option Expiration*			
	$0	$45	$50	$55
long 1000 stock @ $46	−46.00	−1.00	+9.00	+19.00
short 5 $45 calls @ 3½	+ 1.75	+1.65	−0.75	− 3.25
short 5 $50 calls @ 1¼	+ 0.625	+0.75	+0.75	− 1.875
net	−43.625	+1.40	+9.00	+13.875

*profits and losses in thousands

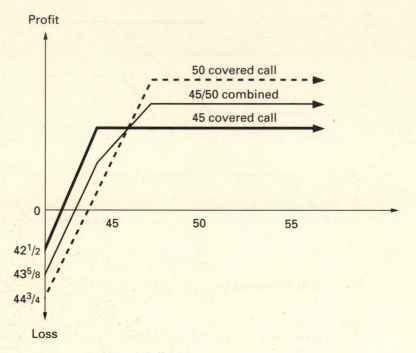

Figure 4-17 Combined Call Writing

manager. The combined write is a compromise between income and potential for further price appreciation.

> A combined write position is a covered call strategy using more than one striking price, and is a compromise between income and the potential for further price appreciation.

Cross-Company Spreading

Sometimes speculative situations develop in which an attractive investment strategy involves *more than one company*. An actual example from a few years ago will illustrate.

During most of 1986 the common stock of Squibb and Merck (both pharmaceutical companies) sold for approximately the same price. In late summer, rumors in the marketplace caused the price of Merck to fall relative to the price of Squibb. One day the price gap widened to $99⅝ for Merck and $114½ for Squibb. Perhaps you felt that a difference of this magnitude was unwarranted and believed that the price gap was likely to narrow in the near future. How could you have taken advantage of this situation?

One way would be to buy calls on Merck (the low-priced security) and buy puts on Squibb (the higher-priced security). This strategy, however, would require a substantial cash outlay. A better approach would be concurrent spreads on the two companies: a bull spread on Merck and a bear spread on Squibb. This strategy is called a **cross-company spread.** Suppose you observed the following price information.

Squibb:	OCT 105 call = $13⅛	OCT 120 call = $5¾
Merck:	OCT 95 call = $ 8¼	OCT 110 call = $2

Because there are two underlying securities, and consequently more than one "stock price at option expiration," it is not possible to construct a typical profit and loss diagram. You *can* calculate maximum profit and loss figures from the combined positions. Table 4-12 does this.

The table shows that the combined maximum loss from this strategy is $13⅞, or $1387.50 per 100 shares. This occurs if you are completely wrong in your assessment of the situation and the spread between the price of MRK

TABLE 4-12 SQUIBB/MERCK CROSS-COMPANY SPREAD

		Stock Price at Option Expiration		
		$95	$99⅝	$110
Merck:				
Buy OCT 95 call @	8¼	−8¼	−3⅝	+6¾
Write OCT 110 call @	2	+2	+2	+2
net cost	$6¼	−6¼	−1⅝	+8¾

		Stock Price at Option Expiration		
		105	114½	120
Squibb:				
Write OCT 105 call @	13⅛	+13⅛	+3⅝	−1⅞
Buy OCT 120 call @	5¾	− 5¾	−5¾	−5¾
credit	7⅜	+ 7⅜	−2⅛	−7⅝

	Max Loss	Max Gain	Result If Stock Unchanged
Combined:			
MRK spread	− 6¼	+ 8¾	−1⅝
SQB spread	− 7⅝	+ 7⅜	−2⅛
total	−13⅞	+16⅛	−3¾

and SQB widens rather than narrows. The maximum gain occurs if Merck rises above $110 and Squibb falls below $105. If both securities remain unchanged at option expiration, your combined loss is a modest $375.

MARGIN CONSIDERATIONS

See p. 40

An important consideration in option spreading is the necessity to post **margin** with certain strategies. If you buy an option, the most you can lose is the option premium you paid. If you write an option, you run the risk of losses far more than the option premium received. The requirement to post margin simply means that a speculator in short options must have sufficient equity in his or her brokerage account before the option positions can be assumed.

> Posting margin refers to the "extra" cash requirement associated with certain option strategies.

This is necessary to help ensure the integrity of option contracts. The Options Clearing Corporation interposes itself between the option buyer and seller and guarantees these trades. At the end of every trading day, some accounts have made money and some have lost. From the OCC's perspective, these gains and losses net to zero. On the books of a given brokerage firm, however, the collective gains and losses of its customers *do not* net to zero every day. Brokerage firms are unwilling to assume the entire risk of investor default in the event of unfavorable price movements. Writing a naked call, for instance, can result in catastrophic losses to the writer if stock prices advance sharply. Before writing an uncovered call, an options trader will be required to show an ability to withstand such a loss. This is done by depositing and maintaining equity in the option account until the uncovered option position is closed.

Imagine the situations that could develop if such an escrow account were not required. Investors short on pocket change near the end of the month could merely call their brokers and write some options, generating immediate cash that could be spent for whatever purpose the investors chose. If the initial options ultimately became unprofitable, no problem: simply write more options to generate enough cash to satisfy your cash requirements in closing the unprofitable position.

It is important to make a distinction between this use of the term *margin* and the practice of borrowing part of the cost of securities from your stockbroker. An investor in the stock market who buys shares on margin is actually borrowing money and paying interest on it. When you post margin with an option strategy, you *are not* borrowing money, and you pay no interest. This seems unclear to many investors, and may be one reason some attractive option strategies are not used more often.[6]

Margin Requirements on Long Puts or Calls

When you buy an option, there is no requirement for you to advance any sum of money other than the option premium and the commission required to make the trade. You simply pay for the option in full; no other cash need be deposited.

Margin Requirements on Short Puts or Calls

If you write an uncovered call or put on shares of common stock, the initial margin requirement is the greater of these two amounts:

$$\text{Premium} + 0.20 (\text{Stock Price}) - (\text{Out-of-Money Amount})$$
or
$$\text{Premium} + 0.10 (\text{Stock Price})$$

As an example, suppose you write a call with a $125 striking price for a premium of 4⅝ while the stock price is $116. You must deposit the greater of these two:

$$\$462.50 + 0.20(\$11,600) - [(\$125 - \$116)(100)] = \$1882.50$$
or
$$\$462.50 + 0.10(\$11,600) = \$1622.50$$

Your minimum deposit is therefore $1882.50.

Under current rules, each account is "marked to market" every day. This means each day additional funds are required or excess funds are released as the relative profitability of a position changes. If you write naked calls and the stock price rises, you must add cash to your account. On the other hand, if the stock price falls, you may be able to withdraw funds from the account.

The computer system your brokerage firm uses will continually monitor the status of your account, and transfer money within your account as needed. If you do not have sufficient funds to meet a margin requirement, your brokerage firm must close out your position.

Brokerage firms are careful about encouraging or even permitting clients to write uncovered options. As we have seen, losses from such a strategy can be substantial. Besides the margin rules discussed here, most brokerage firms

---

[6]Option traders on the exchanges often borrow money from their bank to post the margin requirement. In a sense, these people do pay interest on the margin they post.

have in-house rules on minimum customer account equity requirements before permitting uncovered option writing. A minimum equity requirement of $20,000 is a general rule at many brokerage firms.

Margin Requirements on Spreads

Spread requirements are more lenient than those for uncovered options. All spreads must be done in a margin account, though with certain spreads there is no margin requirement. To receive the more lenient spread margin, the long option must not expire before the written option. Therefore, certain calendar or diagonal spreads would be treated as separate option positions.

olc

vertical spreads
butterfly

bullish calendar spread
some call ratio spreads

All spreads must be done in a margin account.

For spreads, the rule is this: You must pay for the long side in full, and you must deposit the amount by which the long put (or short call) exercise price is below the short put (or long call) exercise price, and the initial spread requirement must be maintained during the life of the position. This may seem complicated, so let's look at a few examples.

Suppose you want to establish the vertical call bullspread evaluated in Table 4-5 (p. 75). These options expire at the same time, so the spread rules are in effect. The short call exercise price is *not* below that of the long call, so the only requirement is that the long side be paid for in full. This is accomplished by depositing $1 from your pocket and $1¼ from the sale of the short option.

Instead of using calls for the bullspread, an investor might choose to use the puts. Suppose someone buys a MAY 45 put on Boeing and writes a MAY *p. 77* 50 put. The long put exercise price is $5 below that of the short put, so the rules require the investor to put up $500. This amount must remain in your account for as long as the spread is in place. If the investor had written the 55 put instead of the 50, the margin requirement would have been 10 points ($1000) instead of $500, since this is the difference between the striking prices.

A General Margin Rule with Spreads:

If the spread results in a debit to your account, you must deposit the net cost of the spread.

If the spread results in a credit to your account, you must deposit the difference between the option striking prices.

Margin Requirements on Covered Calls

There is no margin requirement when writing covered calls, because you can cover any loss in the short option by delivering the shares of stock. Your brokerage firm will, however, restrict your ability to sell your shares of the underlying stock while you have calls written against it unless you are approved for uncovered call writing.

In a call bullspread, the call option that you write is considered covered by the other call option. While you do not own shares of stock, you own the right to obtain them at an advantageous price if the stock moves up sharply. That is why there are no stiff margin requirements on the short call.

EVALUATING SPREADS

What determines a "good" spread? This is a question that option traders continually ponder. If you can predict the future, there is always another strategy that will dominate a profitable spread strategy. A 100 percent bullish speculator should buy calls and write puts; if bearish, he or she should buy puts and write calls.

It is important to remember that to be successful with your speculative activities you *must take a stand* on the direction of the market. You may anticipate an advance or a decline, or you may expect the market to trade in a relatively flat range for a period of time. You cannot cover all the bases such that you make money no matter what happens. Spreads and combinations are bullish, bearish, or neutral. You must decide on your outlook for the market before searching for an appropriate strategy.

The Debit/Credit Issue

If a strategy requires an outlay of funds from your account, it requires a debit. If the strategy generates income, it yields a credit. There are usually several competing option strategies that may serve a particular end, and some will involve a debit and others a credit. Consider bullspreads: they can be done with calls (at a debit) or with puts (at a credit). Tables 4-5 and 4-7 (pp. 75, 77) are examples of bullspreads using both types of options. If you were to do the spread using calls, you would have a net cash outlay of $225, plus commissions. With puts, your account would be credited with $300, minus commissions. In this example, your maximum gain or loss is about the same in either situation. This is not always the case, but the differences will normally be small.

With bear spreads, the option with the lower striking price is written. This means that a debit balance will result from a bearspread with puts and a credit balance from a spread with calls. Everything else being equal, one rule of thumb is to use puts for bullspreads and calls for bearspreads.

One Spreader's Point of View: To get credit to your account, Bullspreads should be done with puts. Bearspreads should be done with calls.

The Reward/Risk Ratio

Another consideration in looking at spreads is the maximum gain relative to the maximum loss. Gains are good and losses are bad, so we want this ratio to be high.

In Table 4-5 (p. 75), the Boeing call bullspread has a maximum gain of $275, which occurs at all stock prices at or above $50. The maximum loss of $225 occurs at or below $45. The reward/risk ratio is then $275/$225, or 122 percent. Table 4-7 (p. 77) is a bullspread using puts, with a reward/risk ratio of 3/2, or 150 percent, which (everything else being equal) is preferable to a ratio of 122 percent.

It is not common to use the reward/risk ratio as a stand-alone decision criterion, but it can provide useful information about a particular spread. A CBS FEB 140/145 call bullspread (see Figure 3-10, p. 64) has a maximum gain of ½ and a maximum loss of 4½ for a ratio of 11.1 percent, which is not particularly attractive. 8 - 3½ = 4½ net cost of position

Buy Feb 140 call
Write Feb 145 call

The "Movement to Loss" Issue

A third piece of information that can be useful in evaluating spreads is the magnitude of stock price movement that is necessary for a position to become unprofitable. In the CBS spread above, the reward/risk ratio is low. In order for *any* loss to occur with this strategy, the stock price would have to fall from its current level of $148⅜ to $144¼ in the next two days. If you consider this unlikely, the CBS spread may seem reasonable.

Breakeven @ 144½
cost to buy (140)
Net premium (4½)

After learning about principles of option pricing in Chapter Five, you will see that estimating the probability of "movement to loss" is not difficult if a reasonable estimate of the volatility of the underlying asset is available.

Specify a Limit Price

Spreads involve at least two options: You want to obtain a high price for the options you sell and want to pay a low price for the options you buy. Suppose you want to establish a bullspread like the one pictured in Figure 4-7 (p. 75).

In analyzing this strategy, we assumed that you could establish the spread for a net cost of $225. However, if you simply give your broker two separate market orders, one to buy a call and a second to sell a different call, you run a significant risk of winding up with a net cost higher than the $2¼ price you extracted from the newspaper.

You can deal with this kind of uncertainty by specifying a dollar amount for the debit or credit at which you are willing to trade. In the bullspread example in Figure 4-7, you could give your broker an order to establish the spread at $2¼ debit. Then the two components of your order are considered simultaneously on the exchange floor, and you can avoid the awkward situation of finding that you didn't complete part of the spread. If your specified price is "away from the market," meaning that you are unable to trade at as good a price as you want, then neither order is executed.

DETERMINING THE APPROPRIATE STRATEGY: SOME FINAL THOUGHTS

The basic steps in any decision making process are simple:

1. learn the fundamentals;
2. gather information;
3. evaluate alternatives;
4. make a decision.

You should be at the point now where you can do an above-average job of tackling the first three steps. Making a decision (taking a stand on the market) can be the toughest part. As you consider your involvement with stock options, you might consider the "Rules for Options Survival," presented in Table 4-13.

TABLE 4-13   TEN RULES FOR OPTION SURVIVAL FOR THE BEGINNER

Rule 1:	You should seldom, if ever, go naked.
Rule 2:	Don't put all your eggs in one basket.
Rule 3:	Make some money during quieting markets. Use credit spreads.
Rule 4:	Don't be afraid to cash in early. You don't need to hold every valuable option until its expiration.
Rule 5:	Know where you stand. Monitor your positions.
Rule 6:	Don't press your entry. ("Don't try to get the last eighth.")
Rule 7:	Don't place market orders.
Rule 8:	Know the markets.
Rule 9:	Use a brokerage house whose people comprehend options.
Rule 10:	Have fun!

From "How to Survive the First Few Months of Options Trading," by William Degler. *Futures* (August, 1986): 52–53.

This chapter and the previous one have illustrated some ways in which options can be combined to suit the particular purpose of an investor or speculator. We have seen how some portfolios of options are equivalent to other collections. Options trading can be exciting and rewarding, but it also can be expensive if you fail to pay attention to basic principles or if you do not respect the risk of your positions. Remember the old Wall Street expression: "There is room in the market for bulls and for bears, but not for hogs." Greed can be your worst enemy.

SUMMARY

Option combinations are strategies in which you are simultaneously long or short options of different types. The best known combination is a straddle, which is a long call position and a long put position on the same underlying asset, where the two options have the same striking price. Buying straddles is appropriate when a major price move in the underlying security is anticipated in either direction. Writing straddles is appropriate if little price change is expected.

Other well-known combinations are strangles and condors. Strangles are like straddles except the two options have different striking prices. A condor is a less risky version of a strangle. There is almost no limit to the number of option combinations that might be constructed on a particular stock.

Option spreads are strategies in which someone is simultaneously long and short options of the same type, but with different striking prices or expiration dates. The motivation in constructing spreads usually involves some desire to hedge.

There are many different types of spreads. Popular types include vertical spreads, calendar (or time or horizontal) spreads, diagonal spreads, backspreads, butterfly spreads, and ratio spreads.

QUESTIONS

1. Suppose an investor feels that a stock price is likely to remain stable over the next few months. What are the advantages and disadvantages of writing a *straddle* versus a *strangle*?

2. In Figure 4-16, the plot of the hedge wrapper is similar to that of a bullspread. How are these two strategies different?

3. An investor who is long 100 shares of a stock might write *two* calls on this stock: one would be covered, the other uncovered. What strategy discussed in this chapter has risk and return characteristics similar to this? (You may want to construct a profit/loss diagram for the "covered call + a naked call" strategy to see what it looks like.)

4. What is the significance of the point in Figure 4-17, where all three plots cross? What stock price corresponds to this point? In a combined write, will there *always* be a common point of intersection for competing strategies such as these?

5. What do you think the quotation at the beginning of the chapter means?

6. "Bullish diagonal spreads should always have the long option position in the most distant expiration month available, and the short side in the closest. This way you only have to buy once, and you can write options three times (one for each expiration) against your long position." Do you agree with this statement?

7. In a call option bullspread, why is the short option position considered covered?

8. Comment on the following statement. "If you own 100 shares of stock and write two calls against it, you have, for all practical purposes, written a straddle."

9. Why must a long straddle always have some intrinsic value if it is not at-the-money?

10. What is the speculator's motivation for a call ratio spread?

11. What is the speculator's motivation for a call ratio backspread?

12. What is the speculator's motivation for a put ratio spread?

13. What is the speculator's motivation for a put ratio backspread?

14. Comment on the following statement: "Hedge wrappers transform risky positions into riskless positions."

15. Using current economic events, make up an example of a cross-company spread.

PROBLEMS

Refer to Figure 4–18 (p. 98) as needed. Unless the problem states otherwise, assume any shares of stock are purchased at the price shown there.

1. Construct a profit and loss diagram for an Alcoa MAR 70/75 call bullspread.

2. Construct a profit and loss diagram for an Alcoa MAR 70/75 call bearspread.

3. Construct a profit and loss diagram for an Alcoa APR 60/65 put bullspread.

4. Construct a profit and loss diagram for an Alcoa APR 60/65 put bearspread.

5. Construct a profit and loss diagram for a Coca-Cola MAY 70/80 call bullspread.

Option & NY Close	Strike Price	Calls-Last Feb	Calls-Last Mar	Calls-Last Apr	Puts-Last Feb	Puts-Last Mar	Puts-Last Apr
Alcoa	60	r	r	14	r	r	3/8
71 5/8	65	7	8 1/2	8 1/2	r	3/8	1 1/8
71 5/8	70	2	3 3/8	4 1/2	3/16	1 11/16	2 1/8
71 5/8	75	1/8	1 1/4	1 3/4	4 7/8	r	r
Biogen	25	r	r	6	r	9/16	1 1/8
29 1/4	30	3/8	2 1/4	3	3/4	2 3/8	r
29 1/4	35	r	5/8	1 3/8	5 1/2	5 7/8	6 1/2
29 1/4	40	1/16	1/4	5/8	r	r	r
29 1/4	45	r	r	1/4	r	r	r
29 1/4	50	s	s	1/4	s	s	r
Blk Dk	17 1/2	9	r	9	r	r	r
26 1/8	20	6 1/4	6 1/2	6 1/4	r	r	r
26 1/8	22 1/2	r	4	4 1/8	r	r	3/4
26 1/8	25	1 3/8	2	2 5/8	1/4	r	1 1/4
26 1/8	30	s	r	15/16	s	r	r
Boeing	40	6 1/4	s	7 1/8	r	s	1/2
46	45	1 1/4	2 1/2	3 1/2	1/8	1 1/16	1 3/4
46	50	1/16	7/16	1 1/4	4 1/8	4 1/4	4 3/4
46	55	r	r	1/2	r	r	r
C B S	135	13 1/2	r	r	r	r	3 1/8
148 3/8	140	8	r	r	r	1 3/8	4 5/8
148 3/8	145	3 1/2	6 3/4	10 1/4	r	3 1/2	r
148 3/8	150	3/4	4 1/8	7 3/8	3 5/8	r	r
148 3/8	155	1/16	2 1/2	5 1/8	7 1/8	r	r
148 3/8	160	r	1 3/8	4 1/4	r	r	r
148 3/8	165	r	s	2 5/8	r	s	r
148 3/8	175	1/16	s	s	r	s	s
Coke	55	22 1/4	s	s	r	s	s
77	60	16 1/2	s	r	r	s	r
77	65	11 1/4	s	r	r	s	5/8
77	70	7 1/8	6 7/8	7 3/4	r	3/8	1 1/8
77	75	2 3/8	3	4 1/2	3/16	1 5/8	3 1/8
77	80	1/8	1	2 3/4	3 5/8	4 1/2	6 1/4
77	85	r	r	1 3/16	r	r	r
Delta	65	r	r	r	1/8	r	1 5/8
69 3/8	70	1/2	2 3/8	3 1/8	1	2 1/2	3 1/2
69 3/8	75	r	5/8	1 5/8	r	r	r
Xerox	70	8 3/4	r	r	r	r	1
79 1/4	75	3	4	5 5/8	1/8	1 1/4	2
79 1/4	80	11/16	1 5/8	2 1/2	1 1/4	3 1/2	r
79 1/4	85	s	13/16	1 3/8	s	r	r

Figure 4-18 Listings for Problems, *WSJ* 2/20/92

6. Construct a profit and loss diagram for a Coca-Cola MAY 70/80 put bullspread.

7. Construct a profit and loss diagram for a Coca-Cola MAY 70/80 put bearspread.

8. Construct a profit and loss diagram for a Coca-Cola MAY 70/80 call bearspread.

9. Construct a profit and loss diagram for a long condor on CBS using MAY 145/150/155/160 calls.

10. Construct a profit and loss diagram for a long condor on Coca-Cola using MAY 65/70/75/80 puts.

11. Construct a long butterfly spread on CBS using MAY 155/145/150 calls.

12. Suppose a speculator establishes a calendar spread by writing a Xerox MAR 80 call and buying a Xerox APR 80 call. What does the speculator want to happen to the stock price of Xerox?

13. Suppose you establish a butterfly spread on Boeing using the MAY 40/45/50 calls. What is your profit or loss if, at option expiration, the stock price remains at $46?

14. Repeat problem 13 using puts.

15. Suppose you previously bought 200 shares of Black and Decker at $20. Show how you can use a hedge wrapper to lock in a profit.

16. Draw a profit and loss diagram for a long APR 70/75 strangle on Delta Airlines.

17. Draw a profit and loss diagram for a long APR 65/75 strangle on Delta Airlines. How do the risk/return characteristics of this combination differ from those of the strangle in problem 16?

18. An investor buys 1000 shares of Xerox and does a combined write using 5 contracts each of the APR 80 and 85 calls. Draw a profit and loss diagram.

19. An investor buys 600 shares of Biogen and does a combined write using 3 contracts each of the MAR 30 and 35 calls. Draw a profit and loss diagram.

20. In problem 19, what is the person's profit or loss if, at option expiration, the price of Biogen stock is $32½?

5 Option Pricing

We sent the first draft of our paper to the *Journal of Political Economy* and promptly got back a rejection letter. We then sent it to the *Review of Economics and Statistics* where it also was rejected.

Merton Miller and Eugene Fama at the University of Chicago then took an interest in the paper and gave us extensive comments on it. They suggested to the *JPE* that perhaps the paper was worth more serious consideration. The journal then accepted the paper . . .

Fischer Black, on his journal article with Myron Scholes that gave birth to the Black-Scholes options pricing model

.... **KEY TERMS** ....
arbitrage
historical volatility
implied volatility
law of one price
put/call parity

A very good argument can be made that discoveries about option pricing have been the single most important development in the field of finance during the last 20 years. Many professional students of the marketplace spend a good deal of their time investigating the relationship between option prices and other economic and psychological variables.

A BRIEF HISTORY OF OPTION PRICING

The Early Work[1]

In 1877, Charles Castelli wrote *The Theory of Options in Stocks and Shares*, published in London. This practical, 177-page exposition sought to explain to the public the hedging and speculation aspects of options. Castelli's work was generally unremarkable at the time and lacks a theoretical base.

Louis Bachelier defended his mathematics dissertation *Théorie de la Spéculation* on March 19, 1900. This is now a classic, but, sharing Castelli's fate, his research attracted little initial attention. Benoit Mandelbrot, the famous mathematician, feels that Bachelier's chairman, Henri Poincaré, did not understand the importance of Bachelier's work. In fact, *Théorie de la Spéculation* contains the first profit and loss diagrams, which are now standard textbook fare. Fifty years passed before Bachelier began to receive the attention his work deserved. One person who did notice it was Paul Samuelson.

The Middle Years

During the 1950s and 1960s, option pricing research was reborn. In 1955 Samuelson wrote an unpublished paper entitled "Brownian Motion in the Stock Market" that referred to Bachelier's earlier work. That same year one of Samuelson's M.I.T. students, Richard Kruizenga, completed his dissertation *Put and Call Options: A Theoretical and Market Analysis*, citing Bachelier.

In 1962 A. James Boness finished his Ph.D. dissertation (*A Theory and Measurement of Stock Option Value*) at the University of Chicago under the famous economist Lawrence Fisher. The pricing model he developed constitutes a significant theoretical jump from Bachelier's work and is a precursor to that of Fischer Black and Myron Scholes.

---

[1] I am grateful to Edward J. Sullivan of Fordham University for his generous help in educating me about the early days of option pricing.

The following year Boness translated Bachelier's dissertation into English; it subsequently appeared in Paul Cootner's now famous work *The Random Character of Stock Market Prices*, inspiring many research papers and graduate theses.

The Present

The cornerstone of modern option pricing is the Black-Scholes option pricing model (hereafter BS or OPM), developed in 1973. Extensive empirical testing proves this model to be an excellent representation of reality. The Black-Scholes model is really an improved version of the Boness model, with the most substantial changes being the Black-Scholes proof of the risk-free interest rate as the correct discount factor and the absence of assumptions about investors' risk preferences. While there are other pricing models in use today, most are modest variations of Black-Scholes. This chapter covers the fundamentals of the Black-Scholes model. It is based on arbitrage arguments, so let's review this topic before moving on.

ARBITRAGE

Finance is sometimes called "the study of arbitrage." **Arbitrage** is the existence of a riskless profit. A central precept of the theory of finance is that risk and expected return are proportional, so we would not expect to find riskless profit opportunities very often. If for some reason such a situation does develop, we would expect it to be exploited very quickly. This is exactly what happens in practice.

Here is an actual example of an arbitrage situation that occurred on a major university campus several years ago. In the university community, there were two competing bookstores dealing in textbooks. One bookstore had a major sale, offering a particular paperback title for $10.00. At the other bookstore, two blocks away, its buy-back offer for that same book was $10.50. Students somehow discovered the arbitrage and exploited it by buying books at $10.00 and selling them at $10.50. The arbitrage did not last long, as the $10.00 books quickly sold out and were transported to the other store.

Sometimes the apparent mispricing is so small that it is not worth the effort to investigate it. We see this in everyday life. You do not find $5 bills on the sidewalk very often; if you should see one, you would pick it up. But you can find pennies on the ground in any parking lot. We have all seen them, and many of us just let them stay there. They are not worth the trouble to pick up.

Modern option pricing techniques are based on arbitrage principles. Certain packages of securities are equivalent to other packages. In a well-functioning marketplace, equivalent packages should sell for the same price. Given the required information, we can solve for what an option price must be for arbitrage to be absent. The classic study[2] of arbitrage in option pricing gave birth to the term **put/call parity**, the subject of the next section.

The Theory of Put/Call Parity

We have seen that the shape of the profit/loss diagram for a covered call position is essentially the same as that of a short put. (Refer to Figures 2-14, p. 40 and 3-5, p. 54 if you need to verify this.) What happens if you combine a covered call with a *long* put?

The diagram for a long put is obtained by rotating the short put about the horizontal axis: a long put is exactly the opposite of a short put. We can then prove that with European options and a non-dividend paying stock, an investor who combines a long stock position with a short call and a long put has a riskless position. The combination of a short put, a short stock position, and a long call also yields a riskless position, and riskless investments should earn the riskless rate of interest, if the riskless position requires you to advance funds.[3]

Suppose an investor borrows money to buy stock, and simultaneously writes a call and buys a put (assume that both options are at-the-money). The investor then holds this position until option expiration. This results in a perfect hedge, and, in theory, a bank should be willing to lend money at r, the riskless rate of interest for the period until expiration. If an investor can establish these three positions and make a profit, arbitrage is present. Arbitrage profits should equal zero, so I anticipate that

$$C - P - \frac{Sr}{(1 + r)} = 0$$

where C = call premium
P = put premium
S = value of 100 shares of stock
r = riskless interest rate

(5-1)

---

[2]Hans Stoll, ''The Relationship Between Put and Call Option Prices,'' *Journal of Finance* (December 1969): 801–24.

[3]An ''investment'' requires that money be invested. A simultaneous long position in stock and short position in the same stock involves no outlay of funds, is therefore not an investment, and does not earn the riskless rate of interest.

Profit/loss contingency table

TABLE 5-1 PUT/CALL PARITY ARBITRAGE TABLE

Activity	Cash Flow	Stock Price at Option Expiration Value	
		$S_1 \leq K$	$S_1 > K$
Write call	$+ C$	0	$K - S_1$
+ buy stock	$- S_0$	S_1	S_1
+ buy put	$- P$	$K - S_1$	0
+ borrow	$K(1 + r)^t$	$- K$	$- K$
= sum	$C - P - S_0 + K/(1 + r)^t$	0	0

This equation comes from the following logic. After establishing the three positions, there is one cash *inflow* (from writing the call) and two cash *outflows* (paying for the put and paying the interest on the bank loan). I can ignore the principal of the loan, because I spend it when I receive it. The interest on the bank loan is paid in the future: it needs to be discounted to a present value. That is why the interest charge (Sr) is divided by the quantity $(1 + r)$.

I can rearrange the equation as follows.

$$C - P = \frac{Sr}{(1 + r)} \tag{5-2}$$

Dividing both sides of the equation by the value of the stock (S), we get

$$\frac{C}{S} - \frac{P}{S} = \frac{r}{(1 + r)} \approx r \tag{5-3}$$

The quantity $r/(1 + r)$ is approximately equal to r. The point is that relative put and call prices differ by about the riskless rate of interest. In other words, the call premium should exceed the put premium, and the difference will be greater as the price of the stock goes up.

A simple example will show the implications of this. First let's expand our list of variables:

C	=	call premium
P	=	put premium
S_0	=	stock price now
S_1	=	stock price at option expiration
K	=	striking price
r	=	risk-free interest rate
t	=	time until option expiration

Suppose we do as before: write the call, buy the put (with the same striking price as the call), and buy stock, but instead of borrowing the current stock value we borrow the *present value* of the *striking price* of the options, discounted from the option expiration date. If the options are at-the-money, the stock price is equal to the option striking price. It is necessary to discount the striking price, because this amount is paid in the future, and dollars today are not the same as dollars tomorrow. This yields a profit/loss contingency table for the combined positions as Table 5-1 shows.

Regardless of whether the stock price at option expiration is above or below the exercise price, the net value of the combined positions is zero. This results in the put-call parity relationship.

The Put/Call Parity Model

$$C - P = S_0 - K/(1 + r)^t \qquad (5\text{-}4)$$

This table tells you that call prices, put prices, the stock price, and the riskless interest rate form an interrelated securities complex. If you know the value of three of these components, you can solve for the equilibrium value of the fourth. The relationship assumes that the options can only be exercised at expiration and that the underlying stock does not pay any dividends during the life of the options.

A simple example will show why the put/call parity model must hold true. Without arbitrage, equivalent financial claims should sell for the same price. Suppose we have stock and option prices like those in Table 5-2 (p. 106). No matter what the stock price at option expiration, the activities described yield a certain profit. Conversely, if the put price is too high relative to the call price, the arbitrageur could write the put, buy the call, sell a share of the stock short, and invest the proceeds from the short sale at the 6 percent interest rate.

The theory of put-call parity indicates that, *when the options are at-the-money and the stock pays no dividends,* relative call prices should exceed relative put prices by about the riskless rate of interest.

The Binomial Option Pricing Model

The Black-Scholes option pricing model is conceptually an appealing model once it is understood. It is based on arbitrage relationships like the put/call parity model. An important finance principle is the **law of one price,** which requires that equivalent assets sell for the same price. For many people, the binomial options pricing model provides some useful intuition into the more complex Black-Scholes model.

TABLE 5-2   ARBITRAGE VIA OPTION MISPRICING

Basic Values:

Stock Price (S_0)	=	$50
Option Striking Price (K)	=	$50
Time Until Expiration	=	6 months
Annual T Bill Interest Rate	=	6%
Call Premium	=	$4¾
Put Premium	=	$3

Present value of the striking price

Theoretical Put Value (given the call value):

$$P = \$4.75 - \$50 + \$50/1.06^{0.5}$$
$$= \$4.75 - \$48.56$$
$$= \$3.31$$

This means that the actual call price ($4¾) is *too high* or that the put price ($3) is *too low.*

To Exploit the Arbitrage:

Write 1 call @	$4¾
Buy 1 put @	$3
Buy 1 share @	$50
Borrow $48.56 @	6% for six months

Stock Price at Option Expiration

Profit/(Loss)	$0	$50	$100
from call	4.75	4.75	($42.25)
from put	47.00	(3.00)	(3.00)
from loan	(1.44)	(1.44)	(1.44)
from stock	(50.00)	0.00	50.00
Total	$0.31	$0.31	$0.31

Suppose (1) that a share of stock currently sells for S_0 and (2) that in one period it must sell for one of two prices: S^+ if the stock goes up, or S^- if the stock goes down. These are the only two possible future prices.

The premium for a call option that expires in one period is C. At expiration, the call will be worth either C^+ if the stock goes up, or C^- if the stock goes down. If K is the striking price of the call, then we also know

$$C^+ = \text{the greater of} \begin{cases} S^+ - K \\ \text{zero} \end{cases} \tag{5-5}$$

$$C^- = \text{the greater of} \begin{cases} S^- - K \\ \text{zero} \end{cases} \tag{5-6}$$

Now suppose we construct a portfolio by borrowing $\$L$ at the riskless rate r and buying N shares of stock. The value of this portfolio is

$$V_0 = NS_0 - L \tag{5-7}$$

When the options expire, the portfolio will be worth

$$V^+ = NS^+ - L(1 + r) \quad \text{if the stock goes up}$$
$$\text{or} \tag{5-8}$$
$$V^- = NS^- - L(1 + r) \quad \text{if the stock goes down}$$

We can select a quantity of stock and an amount to borrow such that in one period the value of the portfolio is exactly equal to the value of the call:

$$C^+ = NS^+ - L(1 + r)$$
$$C^- = NS^- - L(1 + r) \tag{5-9}$$

Solving these two equations simultaneously, we can solve for an equilibrium value of N and of L. Call these values N_e and L_e:

$$N_e = \frac{(C^+ - C^-)}{(S^+ - S^-)} \tag{5-10}$$

$$L_e = \frac{(C^+ S^- - C^- S^+)}{(S^+ - S^-)(1 + r)} \tag{5-11}$$

This means that if we buy N_e shares of stock and borrow L_e dollars, we have a portfolio that exactly replicates the payoff to the call option. By the law of one price, the equilibrium call price C_e must be

$$C_e = N_e S_0 - L_e \tag{5-12}$$

This is the binomial options pricing model. Let's use it in an example.

Suppose we have the following known information.

$$S_0 = \$100$$
$$S^+ = \$105$$
$$S^- = \$\ 95$$
$$K = \$100$$
$$r = 6.5\%$$

If the stock goes up to $\$105$, the call will be worth $\$5$; if the stock goes down, the call will expire worthless. Therefore $C^+ = \$5$ and $C^- = \$0$.

Then $\quad N_e \quad = \quad \dfrac{\$5 - \$0}{\$105 - \$95} \quad = \quad 0.5 \text{ shares}$

And $\quad L_e \quad = \quad \dfrac{\$5(\$95) - 0}{(\$105 - \$95)(1.065)} \quad = \quad \$44.60$

So $\quad C_e \quad = \quad 0.5(\$100) - \$44.60 \quad = \quad \$\ 5.40$

TABLE 5-3 ARBITRAGE WITH BINOMIAL PRICING MODEL

Activity Now	Cash Flow Now	Portfolio Value in 1 Period If Stock Price Equals:	
		$105	$95
Buy 1/2 share of stock @ $100	−$50.00	+$52.50	+$47.50
Borrow $44.60	+ 44.60	− 47.50	− 47.50
Write 1 call	+ 6.00	− 5.00	0.00
Total	+$ 0.60	$ 0.00	$ 0.00

The call should sell for $5.40. If it does not, then an arbitrage opportunity is present.[4]

If, for instance, the call sells for $6.00, how do we take advantage of this alleged arbitrage situation? The answer is simple: sell the overvalued asset and hedge your position appropriately with the other securities.

Equation 5-11 is the key. We now know the value of each entry in this equation. We can lock in the arbitrage profit by purchasing 0.5 shares of stock at the current price of $100, borrowing $44.60 at 6.5%, and writing one call at $6.00. The details are in Table 5-3.

This shows that by buying N_e shares, borrowing L_e dollars, and writing one call, the arbitrageur receives an immediate cash inflow of sixty cents and that the portfolio will have a net value of zero in one period, regardless of whether stock prices move up or down. There is a riskless profit, which is the definition of arbitrage.

THE BLACK-SCHOLES OPTION PRICING MODEL

The Model

This pricing model has been one of the most path-breaking developments in finance in this century. While listed options are popular with a growing number of individual investors, institutional investors have used them productively for many years. Most option analysts use some form of the Black-Scholes Option pricing model to help them in their decision making. There are several suppliers of computer software that generate theoretical

---

[4]Of course, it is not possible to buy half a share of stock. But everything can be scaled upward with no loss of generality. You could, for instance, buy 500 shares, and borrow $44,600.

TABLE 5-4   THE BLACK-SCHOLES OPTION PRICING MODEL

$C = SN(d_1) - Ke^{-Rt} N(d_2)$

where
- C = theoretical call premium
- S = current stock price
- t = time until option expiration
- K = option striking price
- r = risk-free interest rate
- N = cumulative standard normal distribution
- e = exponential function (2.7183)

and

$$d_1 = \frac{ln\ (S/K) + (r + \sigma^2/2)^t}{\sigma\sqrt{t}}$$

$d_2 = d_1 - \sigma\sqrt{t}$
- σ = standard deviation of stock returns
- ln = natural logarithm

OPM values, and some firms provide hourly printouts of computed option prices to floor traders on the option exchanges.

Table 5-4 presents this famous model. It looks forbidding, but with a little practice you can become comfortable with it. Let's walk through the model using an example. Suppose we have the information given below:

- S = \$30
- K = \$25
- t = 3 months = 0.25 year
- r = 5% per year = 0.05
- σ = 45% per year = 0.45; sigma is the estimate of future volatility of the underlying asset.

The first thing we need to do is calculate d_1 and d_2, the arguments for the standard normal functions, $N(\cdot)$.

$$d_1 = \frac{ln\ (S/K) + (r + \sigma^2/2)t}{\sigma\sqrt{t}}$$

$$= \frac{ln\ (30/25) + (0.05 + 0.45^2/2)0.25}{0.45\sqrt{0.25}}$$

$$= \frac{0.1823 + (0.1513)0.25}{0.2250}$$

$$= 0.978$$

$$d_2 = d_1 - \sigma\sqrt{t}$$

$$= 0.978 - 0.45\sqrt{0.25}$$

$$= 0.753$$

Now that we have the two arguments d_1 and d_2, we can determine the values for the normal probability functions $N(d_1)$ and $N(d_2)$. To do this we

TABLE 5-5   CUMULATIVE NORMAL PROBABILITY DISTRIBUTION

	0.00	0.01	0.02	0.03	0.04	0.05	0.06	0.07	0.08	0.09
-3.00	0.0014	0.0013	0.0013	0.0012	0.0012	0.0011	0.0011	0.0011	0.0010	0.0010
-2.90	0.0019	0.0018	0.0018	0.0017	0.0016	0.0016	0.0015	0.0015	0.0014	0.0014
-2.80	0.0026	0.0025	0.0024	0.0023	0.0023	0.0022	0.0021	0.0021	0.0020	0.0019
-2.70	0.0035	0.0034	0.0033	0.0032	0.0031	0.0030	0.0029	0.0028	0.0027	0.0026
-2.60	0.0047	0.0045	0.0044	0.0043	0.0041	0.0040	0.0039	0.0038	0.0037	0.0036
-2.50	0.0062	0.0060	0.0059	0.0057	0.0055	0.0054	0.0052	0.0051	0.0049	0.0048
-2.40	0.0082	0.0080	0.0078	0.0075	0.0073	0.0071	0.0069	0.0068	0.0066	0.0064
-2.30	0.0107	0.0104	0.0102	0.0099	0.0096	0.0094	0.0091	0.0089	0.0087	0.0084
-2.20	0.0139	0.0136	0.0132	0.0129	0.0125	0.0122	0.0119	0.0116	0.0113	0.0110
-2.10	0.0179	0.0174	0.0170	0.0166	0.0162	0.0158	0.0154	0.0150	0.0146	0.0143
-2.00	0.0228	0.0222	0.0217	0.0212	0.0207	0.0202	0.0197	0.0192	0.0188	0.0183
-1.90	0.0287	0.0281	0.0274	0.0268	0.0262	0.0256	0.0250	0.0244	0.0239	0.0233
-1.80	0.0359	0.0351	0.0344	0.0336	0.0329	0.0322	0.0314	0.0307	0.0301	0.0294
-1.70	0.0446	0.0436	0.0427	0.0418	0.0409	0.0401	0.0392	0.0384	0.0375	0.0367
-1.60	0.0548	0.0537	0.0526	0.0516	0.0505	0.0495	0.0485	0.0475	0.0465	0.0455
-1.50	0.0668	0.0655	0.0643	0.0630	0.0618	0.0606	0.0594	0.0582	0.0571	0.0559
-1.40	0.0808	0.0793	0.0778	0.0764	0.0749	0.0735	0.0721	0.0708	0.0694	0.0681
-1.30	0.0968	0.0951	0.0934	0.0918	0.0901	0.0885	0.0869	0.0853	0.0838	0.0823
-1.20	0.1151	0.1131	0.1112	0.1094	0.1075	0.1057	0.1038	0.1020	0.1003	0.0985
-1.10	0.1357	0.1335	0.1314	0.1292	0.1271	0.1251	0.1230	0.1210	0.1190	0.1170
-1.00	0.1587	0.1563	0.1539	0.1515	0.1492	0.1469	0.1446	0.1423	0.1401	0.1379
-0.90	0.1841	0.1814	0.1788	0.1762	0.1736	0.1711	0.1685	0.1660	0.1635	0.1611
-0.80	0.2119	0.2090	0.2061	0.2033	0.2005	0.1977	0.1949	0.1922	0.1894	0.1867
-0.70	0.2420	0.2389	0.2358	0.2327	0.2297	0.2266	0.2236	0.2207	0.2177	0.2148
-0.60	0.2743	0.2709	0.2676	0.2644	0.2611	0.2579	0.2546	0.2514	0.2483	0.2451
-0.50	0.3085	0.3050	0.3015	0.2981	0.2946	0.2912	0.2877	0.2843	0.2810	0.2776
-0.40	0.3446	0.3409	0.3372	0.3336	0.3300	0.3264	0.3228	0.3192	0.3156	0.3121
-0.30	0.3821	0.3783	0.3745	0.3707	0.3669	0.3632	0.3594	0.3557	0.3520	0.3483
-0.20	0.4207	0.4168	0.4129	0.4091	0.4052	0.4013	0.3974	0.3936	0.3897	0.3859
-0.10	0.4602	0.4562	0.4522	0.4483	0.4443	0.4404	0.4364	0.4325	0.4286	0.4247
-0.00	0.5000	0.4960	0.4920	0.4880	0.4841	0.4801	0.4761	0.4721	0.4681	0.4642

Choose units and tenths vertically; select hundredths horizontally.

must look up the appropriate values from a probability table like Table 5-5. Read down the columns in the table until you find a value of x that corresponds to the value you want. You may not find the exact number needed; if this is the case, you can either interpolate or you can use the closest entry.

It can make a significant difference in the theoretical value you find if you approximate rather than interpolate. In our example, the value for $N(0.978)$ is approximately 0.836. $N(d_2) = N(0.753)$, and the corresponding function value is about 0.773.

TABLE 5-5   CUMULATIVE NORMAL PROBABILITY DISTRIBUTION (continued)

	0.00	0.01	0.02	0.03	0.04	0.05	0.06	0.07	0.08	0.09
+0.00	0.5000	0.5040	0.5080	0.5121	0.5159	0.5199	0.5239	0.5279	0.5319	0.5358
0.10	0.5398	0.5438	0.5478	0.5517	0.5557	0.5596	0.5636	0.5675	0.5714	0.5753
0.20	0.5793	0.5832	0.5871	0.5909	0.5948	0.5987	0.6026	0.6064	0.6103	0.6141
0.30	0.6179	0.6217	0.6255	0.6293	0.6331	0.6368	0.6406	0.6443	0.6480	0.6517
0.40	0.6554	0.6591	0.6628	0.6664	0.6700	0.6736	0.6772	0.6808	0.6844	0.6879
0.50	0.6915	0.6950	0.6985	0.7019	0.7054	0.7088	0.7123	0.7157	0.7190	0.7224
0.60	0.7257	0.7291	0.7324	0.7356	0.7389	0.7421	0.7454	0.7486	0.7517	0.7549
0.70	0.7580	0.7611	0.7642	0.7673	0.7703	0.7734	0.7764	0.7793	0.7823	0.7852
0.80	0.7881	0.7910	0.7939	0.7967	0.7995	0.8023	0.8051	0.8078	0.8106	0.8133
0.90	0.8159	0.8186	0.8212	0.8238	0.8264	0.8289	0.8315	0.8340	0.8365	0.8389
1.00	0.8413	0.8437	0.8461	0.8485	0.8508	0.8531	0.8554	0.8577	0.8599	0.8621
1.10	0.8643	0.8665	0.8686	0.8708	0.8729	0.8749	0.8770	0.8790	0.8810	0.8830
1.20	0.8849	0.8869	0.8888	0.8906	0.8925	0.8943	0.8962	0.8980	0.8997	0.9015
1.30	0.9032	0.9049	0.9066	0.9082	0.9099	0.9115	0.9131	0.9147	0.9162	0.9177
1.40	0.9192	0.9207	0.9222	0.9236	0.9251	0.9265	0.9279	0.9292	0.9306	0.9319
1.50	0.9332	0.9345	0.9357	0.9370	0.9382	0.9394	0.9406	0.9418	0.9429	0.9441
1.60	0.9452	0.9463	0.9474	0.9484	0.9495	0.9505	0.9515	0.9525	0.9535	0.9545
1.70	0.9554	0.9564	0.9573	0.9582	0.9591	0.9599	0.9608	0.9616	0.9625	0.9633
1.80	0.9641	0.9649	0.9656	0.9664	0.9671	0.9678	0.9686	0.9693	0.9699	0.9706
1.90	0.9713	0.9719	0.9726	0.9732	0.9738	0.9744	0.9750	0.9756	0.9761	0.9767
2.00	0.9772	0.9778	0.9783	0.9788	0.9793	0.9798	0.9803	0.9808	0.9812	0.9817
2.10	0.9821	0.9826	0.9830	0.9834	0.9838	0.9842	0.9846	0.9850	0.9854	0.9857
2.20	0.9861	0.9864	0.9868	0.9871	0.9875	0.9878	0.9881	0.9884	0.9887	0.9890
2.30	0.9893	0.9896	0.9898	0.9901	0.9904	0.9906	0.9909	0.9911	0.9913	0.9916
2.40	0.9918	0.9920	0.9922	0.9925	0.9927	0.9929	0.9931	0.9932	0.9934	0.9936
2.50	0.9938	0.9940	0.9941	0.9943	0.9945	0.9946	0.9948	0.9949	0.9951	0.9952
2.60	0.9953	0.9955	0.9956	0.9957	0.9959	0.9960	0.9961	0.9962	0.9963	0.9964
2.70	0.9965	0.9966	0.9967	0.9968	0.9969	0.9970	0.9971	0.9972	0.9973	0.9974
2.80	0.9974	0.9975	0.9976	0.9977	0.9977	0.9978	0.9979	0.9979	0.9980	0.9981
2.90	0.9981	0.9982	0.9982	0.9983	0.9984	0.9984	0.9985	0.9985	0.9986	0.9986
3.00	0.9986	0.9987	0.9987	0.9988	0.9988	0.9989	0.9989	0.9989	0.9990	0.9990

Choose units and tenths vertically; select hundredths horizontally.

Now we can continue with our efforts to find a theoretical Black-Scholes value for this call option. Returning to the formula, we can plug in the values we just determined:

$$C = \$30(0.836) - \$25e^{-(.05 \times .25)}(0.773)$$
$$= \$25.08 - \$24.69(0.773)$$
$$= \$25.08 - \$19.08$$
$$= \$6.00$$

Given our assumptions, according to the Black-Scholes option pricing model, a three-month call option on this stock should sell for very close to $6.00.

Development and Assumptions of the Model

The actual development of this model is complicated. Many steps used in building it come from physics, from mathematical short cuts, and from arbitrage arguments like those presented earlier. Fischer Black had been working on a valuation model for stock warrants, a type of security closely related to call options. After taking a derivative to measure how the discount rate of a warrant varies with time and the stock price, the resulting differential equation was very similar to a well-known heat transfer equation from physics. Myron Scholes joined Fischer Black in working on the problem, and the result is the model used throughout finance today.

While for many option professionals the Black-Scholes model has become a trusted navigational aid, there are some things about the model that you should keep in mind as you use it. The more you understand about these equations, the better you will be in options work.

1. *The Stock Pays No Dividends During the Option's Life.* The Black-Scholes model assumes that the underlying security pays no dividends during the life of the option. If you try the model on securities that have different dividend yields but that are similar in every other respect, the model will predict the same price, because the OPM does not consider dividends. As you will see, the higher the dividend yield, the lower the call premium, and the financial pages would most likely not reflect the same premium for these two options.

    Most stocks do pay dividends, however. This does not mean the OPM is useless for these securities. It is possible to make an adjustment that helps account for the effect of the dividend payment. A common way of doing this is to *subtract the discounted value* of a future dividend *from the stock price* used as an input to the model. For instance, if a 50 cent cash dividend will be earned on our stock 82 days from today, you can turn this future value into a present value equivalent, in the same way as in other financial applications. The use of the natural logarithm in the OPM assumes continuous compounding of interest. We should be consistent in our dividend adjustment, so

---

[5]It is common practice to discount the dividend from the ex-dividend date rather than from the date of payment. This is because the stock that the call gives you the right to buy materially changes on the ex-dividend date. Before that date, the stock comes with the dividend; on that date and after, you are not entitled to the dividend.

we will discount the 50 cents continuously as well. Eighty-two days is $82/365$ of a year, or 0.2247. The present value of the dividend payment is then[5]

EXP (−.05 x .2247) on calculator

$$= e^{-(0.05)(.2247)} (\$0.50)$$
$$= 0.989 (0.50)$$
$$= \$0.49$$

The adjusted stock price is then $\$30.00 - \$0.49$, or $\$29.51$, and the adjusted call premium is $\$5.44$.

2. *European Exercise Terms Are Used.* Another assumption of the OPM is that the option is European. Unlike American options, which can be exercised anytime before their expiration, a European option can only be exercised on the expiration date. American options are more valuable than European options, because the flexibility of exercise is valuable. This is not a major pricing consideration, however, because very few calls are ever exercised before the last few days of their life. A person who exercises a call early is essentially throwing away the time value remaining on the call. When you exercise, you recover the intrinsic value, but that is all. Right before the expiration date, the remaining time value is minuscule.

3. *Markets Are Efficient.* The Black-Scholes option pricing model also assumes that the stock market is informationally efficient, meaning that people cannot, as a rule, predict the direction of the market or of an individual stock. The theory of put-call parity, for instance, implies that regardless of whether you are bullish or bearish, you and everyone else will agree on the option premium. You might be absolutely convinced that the market is about to crash, yet theoretically you and the bulls will still agree on the call premium. If this were not so, there would be an arbitrage profit for someone to pick up.

▎Bulls and bears both agree on the equilibrium call premium.

Many option traders have trouble with this statement. This assumption does *not* say that everyone is equally ready to buy puts or to buy calls. If you are bullish, you will not be interested in buying puts as a speculation. But there remains a relationship between the value of puts and calls that we have shown must be true for arbitrage to be absent.[6]

---

[6]This statement assumes that accurate market information is available; e.g., it is not lunchtime on Black Monday II.

Market efficiency is a central paradigm in modern investment theory. There are concerns about this, though, and market efficiency should always be taken with a grain of salt. What good, for instance, would Black-Scholes prices have been on October 19, 1987, the day the market crashed? To paraphrase a famous quotation about democracy, market efficiency may not be a very good explanation of investor behavior, but it is head and shoulders above any other theory we have.

4. *No Commissions Are Charged.* Another important assumption of Black-Scholes is that market participants do not have to pay any commissions to buy or sell. We know this is not true. Even floor traders pay fees, which finance the administration and self-regulation of the exchanges. The commissions paid by individual investors are more substantial and can significantly affect the true cost of an option position. These trading fee differentials cause slightly different "effective" option prices for different market participants. We can return to the example of pennies in the parking lot. For some egos, the "loss of face" from bending over to pick them up is too expensive a commission.

5. *Interest Rates Remain Constant.* Another assumption is that the interest rate (r) in the model is constant and known. The "risk-free rate" is a common term in finance, but there actually is no such interest rate. It is common to use the discount rate on a U.S. Government Treasury Bill that has 30 days left until maturity as a proxy for this important interest rate, but even this figure can change daily. During a period of rapidly changing interest rates, the use of a 30-day rate to calculate the value of, for instance, a six-month option would not be advisable. There are many people who spend much time looking for ways to value options when the parameters of the traditional Black-Scholes model are not known or are changing.

6. *Returns Are Lognormally Distributed.* The model also assumes that the logarithms of the returns of the underlying security are normally distributed. This is a reasonable assumption for most assets on which options are available.

Intuition into the Black-Scholes Model

We can partition the Black-Scholes OPM into two parts as follows.

$$C = \left| \begin{array}{c} \text{Part A} \\ SN(d_1) \end{array} \right| - \left| \begin{array}{c} \text{Part B} \\ Ke^{-rt} N(d_2) \end{array} \right|$$

In Part A of the OPM equation, S is the current stock price, which by finance theory is also the discounted value of the expected stock price at any future point. (If this were not so, the markets would not be in equilibrium.) $N(d_1)$ is the probability that, at expiration, the stock price will be greater than the option exercise price. Part B of the equation can be viewed as the present value of having to pay the exercise price on expiration day. The value of a call option, then, is the difference between the expected benefit from acquiring the stock outright and paying the exercise price on expiration day.

We know that at expiration calls are valuable if the stock price is higher than the option striking price. We also know that the higher the volatility of the underlying security, the greater the likelihood that the security will reach a distant striking price. This is the primary reason that option models are so sensitive to the estimate of volatility used in the model and the reason why many analysts in the securities business make a career of studying volatilities.

Notes, p. 25

Calculating Implied Volatility *Skip this section (pp. 115-116) for exam #1*

Using the Black-Scholes Model   The BS model is very sensitive to the volatility of the underlying asset. Professional option traders spend a good deal of time revising estimates of volatility as market conditions change. An important first step in this process is calculating the volatility that is implied in the BS call premium. In other words, instead of solving for the call premium, *assume the market-determined call premium is correct* and solve for the volatility that makes the equation hold. This value is called the **implied volatility.**

If you refer to Table 5-4 (p. 109), you will note that sigma (the standard deviation estimate) enters the equation several times. Unfortunately, sigma cannot be conveniently isolated in the equation such that we can solve for it. We have to solve for sigma using a trial and error, or iterative, process. Taking the other variables (stock price, striking price, interest rate, and time until expiration) as given, we estimate a value for sigma and see what call premium the model gives us. We then compare this premium with the market-determined premium. If the BS model gives us a premium that is too high, we know that the implied volatility is lower than our estimate, so we reduce our estimate and try again. We continue revising our estimate until we arrive at a BS call premium that equals the current price. Once we find this value, it is the implied volatility.

When the market becomes more volatile, option premiums increase substantially. As an example, consider the Standard and Poors 100 index. This is a broad measure of market activity on which very popular put and call options trade. One month before the stock market crash in October 1987, 30-day, near-the-money calls on this index had an implied annual volatility of 23.27 percent. One month after the crash, similar calls had an implied annual volatility of 41.36 percent. A change in volatility of this magnitude translates into about a 70 percent increase in the premium for a one-month, at-the-money option.

An Implied Volatility Heuristic   For an exactly at-the-money call option, high level mathematics[7] proves that implied volatility can be determined via equation 5-13, with all variables as previously defined.

$$\sigma = \frac{0.5(C + P) \sqrt{(2\pi/t)}}{K/(1 + R)^t} \tag{5-13}$$

Suppose an at-the-money call option has sixty days until expiration, a striking price of $50, the riskfree interest rate is 5 percent, and volatility is 0.20. Theoretical Black-Scholes premiums are $1.82 for the call and $1.42 for the put. The volatility implied in these premiums is naturally 0.20, the input value.

Substituting in equation 5-13, we find the same result:

$$\sigma = \frac{0.5(1.82 + 1.42) \sqrt{[2\pi/(60/365)]}}{50/(1.05)^{60/365}}$$

$$= \frac{1.62 \sqrt{(38.22)}}{49.60} = 0.20$$

Historical versus Implied Volatility   The volatility solved for by using a past series of prices is an **historical volatility.** This statistic is very useful, and most option traders will follow it. It cannot, however, capture recent developments that may portend major changes in market conditions. Implied volatility gives some indication of what the market thinks about likely volatility in the future.

MORE ON THE DETERMINANTS OF THE OPTION PREMIUM

Market Factors

As shown in the Black-Scholes model, options research has discovered six variables that significantly influence the option premium. Because a call option lets you buy at a predetermined price, it seems logical that the lower the *striking price* for a given stock price, the more the option should be worth. This is exactly what we observe in the financial pages. Figure 2-8 (p. 31) shows that as the striking price gets lower for a given company's options, the option premium goes up.

---

[7] A Taylor series expansion

We have also seen that the more *time* the option has until expiration, the more it is worth. Figure 2-8 shows that for both puts and calls, the option premium increases for more distant expirations.

A third factor influencing the call premium is also easy to understand: the current *stock price*. The higher the stock price, the more a given call option is going to be worth. Remember that a primary reason many people buy call options is to benefit from a rise in the price of the stock. If the stock price goes up, so will the value of the call option.

The other three factors influencing the call premium may be less obvious. They are the *volatility* of the underlying stock, the current level of *interest rates* in the economy, and the *dividend yield* on the underlying security.

Assets that show price volatility lend themselves to option trading.[8] The greater the price volatility of an asset, the greater its option premium. In the Black-Scholes model, volatility is the annualized standard deviation of returns anticipated in the underlying asset over the remaining term of the option. As elsewhere in finance, what happened in the past is not as important as what is expected to happen in the future. Past volatility can be measured, but future volatility must be estimated. A volatility estimate is called *sigma*, and it is the one variable that cannot be directly observed.

In option pricing, a volatility estimate is called sigma.

It is not uncommon to look in the financial pages and find options on two different companies where the current stock prices are equal and where both companies have, for instance, APR 40 calls. But, these two options might sell for very different premiums. Why? Because the intrinsic value of an option is a calculated value that does not depend on anything other than the current stock price and the option striking price, differences in the premium for these two options must be because of differences in the *time value* of the option. More time means a greater chance of a price change in the underlying asset.

The more volatile a security, the higher its option premium.

m: i.e., The 2 companies differ in the volatility of their stk.

A fifth factor that influences the call option premium is the *dividend yield on the underlying common stock*. This makes sense when you think about it, although it is often forgotten by typical investors. There is a precise series of events after a corporation announces a dividend to be paid on its stock. The Board of Directors of the company announces that a certain dollar amount of dividend will be paid on a certain date (the date of payment) to the

---

[8]They may also lend themselves to trading in the futures market.

stockholders as of a certain cut-off date (the date of record). To eliminate uncertainty due to processing time, mail delays, etc. in determining exactly who is on the company's shareholder list on the date of record, the brokerage industry uses the *ex-dividend date convention.* The ex-dividend date is four business days before the date of record, and you must buy stock before the ex-dividend date to qualify for the dividend that is about to be paid. People who buy the stock *on* the ex-dividend date do not receive the dividend, and this provides downward pressure on the price of the stock. If it were possible to hold all the other factors influencing stock prices constant, we would expect the value of a share of stock to fall by about the amount of the dividend on the ex-dividend date.

A person who buys a call option does not want the price of the stock to fall, yet the payment of a dividend will necessarily cause the price to fall. The higher the dividend, the more the price will fall. Modern stock options are not adjusted for the payment of a cash dividend. Companies that pay large dividends will have a smaller option premium than companies with low dividend yields. This is easy to understand if we consider an extreme example where a firm announces its intent to pay a liquidating dividend and go out of business. After payment of this dividend, shares in the firm will be worthless, and so will the associated call options. Anyone who owns these calls and does not exercise them before the last ex-dividend date will lose 100 percent of their investment. Therefore, option holders are interested in corporate dividend announcements and in some circumstances will find it profitable to exercise their options before the ex-dividend date.

The sixth factor that influences option premiums is the *risk-free interest rate.* The higher this interest rate, the higher the option premium, everything else being equal. If you review the section on put-call parity you will see why this is the case. A higher "discount rate" applied to the striking price, with all other variables held constant, means that the call premium must rise for the equation to hold.

$$\overset{+\ -\ +\ +\ -\ +}{\text{Call premium} = f(S,\ K,\ t,\ \sigma,\ D,\ r)}$$

where
S = current stock price
K = option striking price
t = time until option expiration
σ = stock volatility
D = stock dividend yield
r = current risk-free interest rate

Accounting Factors

Put and call options that trade on options exchanges are adjusted for stock splits or stock dividends. The most common event requiring an adjustment is

$100 \times \frac{3}{2} = 150$

when a firm splits its common stock shares. Two-for-one splits are common; this means that a shareholder who owns 100 shares of stock before the split will own 200 afterward. Similarly, a 4-for-1 split would mean the holder of 100 pre-split shares would have 400 post-split shares. Sometimes the split ratio is not a whole number like 2 or 4. In a 3 for 2 split, the holder of 100 shares would have 150 after the split. Splits of this type are often called *odd-lot generating,* because they result in many people holding shares that are no longer in multiples of 100. Adjustments to the option terms differ, depending on whether the split is odd-lot generating.

It is important to recognize that a stock split does not inherently increase the shareholders' wealth. The firm is worth some specific dollar amount, and it does not matter into how many pieces the pie is cut. If I eat one piece of a pie that is cut into four pieces, I have eaten exactly the same amount of pie that I would get had I been given two pieces of a pie cut into eighths. The stock market is not fooled by stock splits. If I own 100 shares of stock worth $50 each, and the firm splits 2 for 1, after the split I will have 200 shares each worth about $25. My total wealth has not changed.

$100 \times \frac{2}{1} = 200$

$\$50 \times \frac{1}{2} = 25$

Suppose you own 1 Boeing MAR 45 call, and Boeing then splits two for one. The Options Clearing Corporation will dictate the following adjustment to all outstanding options on Boeing: the striking price would be reduced by the split ratio, and the number of options you own would be increased by the split ratio. Here, I would discover on my monthly brokerage account statement that I now own 2 Boeing MAR 22½ calls. The dollar amount represented by these two calls is the same as the dollar amount represented by my original single call option.

If Boeing were to have an odd-lot generating split, say 3 for 2, the adjustment is different. Listed options are only written on multiples of 100 shares; I cannot have an option to buy 50 shares. In this case, the striking price of the option would be reduced by the split ratio (as with the first example). Instead of increasing the number of options you own, the number of shares *covered* by your option would be increased by the split ratio. This means that after the 3 for 2 split you would own 1 Boeing MAR *30* call, and that 1 call would give you the right to buy *150* shares. As before, the dollar amount represented by the call is the same before and after the split.

$\$45 \times \frac{2}{3} = 30$

$100 \times \frac{3}{2} = 150$

CALCULATING BLACK-SCHOLES PRICES FROM THE *WSJ*

This section to end of chapt. not on exam!

Call Values

As we have seen, to calculate the theoretical value of a call option using the Black-Scholes option pricing model, we need to know the following: the stock price, the option striking price, the time until option expiration, the

TABLE 5-6 RECENT STOCK PRICES FOR XYZ

DEC 31 1991	$34	DEC 31 1992	$39¼
JAN 31 1992	34½	JAN 31 1993	40⅛
FEB 28 1992	35¾	FEB 28 1993	39½
MAR 31 1992	34	MAR 31 1993	42⅜
APR 30 1992	35⅞	APR 30 1993	41½
MAY 31 1992	36¼	MAY 31 1993	40⅞
JUN 30 1992	37⅜	JUN 30 1993	39⅞
JUL 31 1992	37	JUL 31 1993	38½
AUG 31 1992	38½	AUG 31 1993	39
SEP 30 1992	37⅝	SEP 30 1993	37½
OCT 31 1992	37⅛	OCT 31 1993	38¼
NOV 30 1992	38⅜	NOV 30 1993	39¼

riskless interest rate, and the volatility of the stock as measured by the standard deviation (or variance) of return on the stock.

Suppose in December 1993 we are interested in the theoretical value of a call on a non-dividend paying stock with a $40 striking price and 36 days until expiration. The current stock price is $39¼, and we also have the stock price information in Table 5-6.

We have the current stock price (39¼), the striking price (40), and the time until expiration (36 days, or $^{36}/_{365} = 0.0986$ year). We still need the interest rate and the stock volatility. The interest rate we can obtain from the "Money Rate" section of the *WSJ*. This column shows current interest rates on securities of varying maturities and risk. We want to extract the US Treasury Bill rate for a maturity that is close to the remaining life of the option, so we would select the 30-day rate. Suppose it is listed as 5.88%.

Determining the volatility is the most involved part of the exercise. To do this, we need historical data like that of Table 5-6, and we also need to prepare some preliminary calculations. Because it is volatility of *returns* that interest us, we must take the stock price data and compute the returns. One assumption of the Black-Scholes model is that the natural logarithms of these returns are normally distributed. This means that once we have the returns, we need to take their logarithms and look at the standard deviation of this revised series of numbers. We can prepare a worksheet like Table 5-7 to aid in this chore.

Return relatives on a non-dividend paying stock are calculated by simply dividing the price on each date by the preceding price; subtracting one gives the return. We have monthly price observations for 24 months, and since it takes two price observations to yield one return, we have 23 monthly returns. The mean of these logreturns is simply the sum of them divided by 23.

We could go through the exercise of calculating the variance by hand, but almost certainly the option analyst is going to let a computer spreadsheet software package do that. A computer or a handheld calculator will show that

TABLE 5-7 STOCK RETURN WORKSHEET

Date	Stock Price	Return Relative	LN Return
DEC 31 1991	34	—	—
JAN 31 1992	34½	1.0147	0.0146
FEB 28 1992	35¾	1.0362	0.0356
MAR 31 1992	34	0.9510	−0.0502
APR 30 1992	35⅞	1.0551	0.0537
MAY 31 1992	36¼	1.0105	0.0104
JUN 30 1992	37⅜	1.0310	0.0306
JUL 31 1992	37	0.9900	−0.0100
AUG 31 1992	38½	1.0405	0.0397
SEP 30 1992	37⅝	0.9773	−0.0230
OCT 31 1992	37⅛	0.9867	−0.0134
NOV 30 1992	38⅜	1.0337	0.0331
DEC 31 1992	39¼	1.0228	0.0225
JAN 31 1993	40⅛	1.0223	0.0220
FEB 28 1993	39½	0.9844	−0.0157
MAR 31 1993	42⅜	1.0728	0.0703
APR 30 1993	41½	0.9794	−0.0209
MAY 31 1993	40⅞	0.9939	−0.0061
JUN 30 1993	39⅞	0.9755	−0.0248
JUL 31 1993	38½	0.9655	−0.0351
AUG 31 1993	39	1.0130	0.0129
SEP 30 1993	37½	0.9615	−0.0392
OCT 31 1993	38¼	1.0200	0.0198
NOV 30 1993	39¼	1.0261	0.0258

mean of return logarithms = 0.00660

variance of return logarithms = 0.00094

the variance of these logreturns is 0.00094. At this point there is an easy mistake to make. Annual variance is different from daily, weekly, or monthly variance. The use of natural logarithms assumes continuous compounding over one year, and the raw stock prices are taken monthly. The estimate of variance from Table 5-7 needs to be multiplied by 12 to convert our monthly estimate into an annual estimate. The annual variance of return is then 12 × 0.00094, or 0.01128. The square root of this is 0.10621, and this is the variable we need for the Black-Scholes OPM. Now we are ready to solve for the value of the call. Here again is the model:

$$C = SN(d_1) - Ke^{-rt} N(d_2)$$

$$d_1 = \frac{ln\ (S/K) + [r + \sigma^2/2]t}{\sigma\sqrt{t}}$$

$$d_2 = \quad\quad d_1 - \sigma\sqrt{t}$$

As before, we solve for the arguments d_1 and d_2 first:

$$d_1 = \frac{ln\ (39.25/40) + [.0588 + .1062^2/2].0986}{0.1062\sqrt{.0986}}$$

$$= -0.377$$

$$d_2 = -0.377 - 0.1062\sqrt{.0986}$$

$$= -0.410$$

Using Table 5-5, $N(-0.377) = 0.351$ and $N(-0.410) = 0.339$. Now we have all the input necessary for the final calculation:

$$C = \$39.25(0.351) - \$40e^{-(0.0986)(.0588)} (0.339)$$

$$= \$13.78 - \$13.48$$

$$= \$0.30$$

These call options should sell for about ⁵⁄₁₆.

Put Values

Once the call premium is known, the corresponding put option is accurately valued using the put-call parity model. It is common practice for option analysts to calculate a theoretical call value using the Black-Scholes OPM, and to use the result to find the put value that must exist without arbitrage profits.

The Black-Scholes model can be combined with the put/call parity model to yield the put valuation model shown in Table 5-8. Note that interest rates enter the valuation model with a different sign than in the call valuation model. This means that higher interest rates will *reduce* put values, everything else being equal. If the general level of interest rates falls and everything else is held constant, we would expect put values to climb and call values to fall.

See notes, p. 26

Let's calculate a BS put value using the same initial data as we did in Table 5-4: striking price = \$25, stock price = \$30, time remaining = ¼ year, interest rate = 5%, annual standard deviation = 45%.

$$d_1 = \frac{ln\ (30/25) + [.05 + (.45)^2/2].25}{.45\sqrt{.25}}$$

$$= 0.978$$

$$N(-d_1) = 0.163$$

$$d_2 = 0.978 - .45\sqrt{.25}$$

$$= 0.753$$

$$N(-d_2) = 0.227$$

TABLE 5-8 BLACK-SCHOLES PUT VALUATION MODEL

$P = Ke^{-rt} N(-d_2) - SN(-d_1)$
with all variables are as defined in Table 5-4.

then

$$P = 25e^{-(.05|.25)}(.227) - 30 \ (.163)$$
$$= \$0.71$$

The put should sell for about $11/16$.

Problems Using the Black-Scholes Model

The Black-Scholes option pricing model does not work well with options that are deep-in-the-money or substantially out-of-the-money. Research also shows that it produces biased values for very low or very high volatility stocks. Both mispricings increase as the time until expiration increases.

Also, under certain circumstances, the model may yield unreasonable values when an option has only a few days of life remaining. The value of either type of option is a strictly decreasing function of time: everything else being equal, the value of an option cannot go up as time passes. Occasionally the OPM will show that the price of a call rises a few cents in the last few days of trading.

For options that are near the money, and usually for options with the next striking price on either side of the stock price, the model works well. The point to remember is that you should always make sure your OPM value is reasonable. Do not use it blindly as a black box.

SUMMARY

Option pricing is based on arbitrage arguments. We can show that the price of an asset, puts and calls on that asset, and the riskless rate of interest form an interrelated securities complex. If we know the value of three of these factors, we can solve for the value of the fourth. The basic relationship between put and call option prices is called put/call parity, and related logic leads to the Black-Scholes option pricing model.

Research into option pricing shows that there are six important factors determining the value of an option: the stock price, the striking price, the time remaining until the option expires, the volatility of the underlying asset, the dividend yield of the underlying asset, and the level of interest rates.

The Black-Scholes OPM may not yield reasonable values for options that are substantially out-of-the-money, for options that are deep in-the-money, or when there are only a few days remaining until option expiration. In these extreme cases it is important to make sure that the indicated option value is reasonable before accepting it.

QUESTIONS

1. Suppose you look in the newspaper and see that an option has changed price since yesterday, but the stock price has remained the same. Explain three factors that could cause the option premium to change while the stock price remains unchanged.

2. Suppose the general level of interest rates in the economy rises. What affect would this have on call premiums? Why do interest rates matter at all in option pricing?

3. Which do you think is more important to an option trader: historical volatility or implied volatility?

4. Briefly explain why stock splits do not adversely affect the holder of a stock option.

5. Why do changes in interest rates affect call premiums and put premiums differently?

6. In your words, explain the "law of one price."

7. Why does the dividend yield adversely affect the value of a call option?

8. Suppose a company *cut* its dividend. Would you expect this to increase the value of a call?

9. Why is the value of a perpetual European put option zero?

PROBLEMS

Note: ◉ indicates the software disk can be used for this problem

1. Suppose a call option sells for $2⅝, a put option sells for $2, both options have a $25 striking price, the current stock price is $25½, and the options both expire in 46 days. Using the put/call parity model, calculate the implicit rate of interest contained in these numbers.

◉ 2. A stock currently sells for $43½ and pays no dividends. There is a call option (striking price = $45) on this security that expires in 67 days. At present, US Treasury bills are yielding 5.3% per year. You estimate the volatility of the stock returns to be 44%. According to the Black-Scholes Option pricing model, what is the value of this call?

3. Using the information in problem 2, what is the value of the corresponding put option?

4. A stock currently sells for $56 and pays no dividends. There is a call option (striking price = $65) on this security that expires in 200 days. At present, US Treasury bills are yielding 4.3% per year. You estimate the volatility of the stock returns to be 24%. According to the Black-Scholes option pricing model, what is the value of this call?

5. Using the information in problem 4, what is the value of the corresponding put?

6. Calculate the Black-Scholes put value using the following information: stock price = $45½, striking price = $40, time until expiration = 123 days, riskfree interest rate = 5.9%, stock variance of return = 34% per year.

7. Suppose you own 10 APR 60 puts on XYA, and the company splits the stock 3 for 2. What are your option holdings after the split adjustments are made to the contract terms?

8. A stock currently sells for $75, and in one period will sell for either $77 or $73. If interest rates are 6%, what should an at-the-money call option sell for, according to the binomial option pricing model?

9. Repeat problem 8 using a striking price of **(a)** $70 and **(b)** $80.

10. You look at the options on XYZ stock. A six-month $45 call sells for $4½, while a six-month $45 put sells for $4. Interest rates are 6%, and the stock price is $44. There is an arbitrage opportunity present. Show how to take advantage of it.

11. From the financial pages, select three companies in the same industry, and calculate the volatility implied in their options. What do you conclude from the results?

12. A stock sells for $45. At-the-money, 90 day calls sell for $1.56, puts for $1.13. If T-bills yield 4% per year, what is the implied volatility of these options? Use the implied volatility heuristic.

13. A stock sells for $65. At-the-money, 60 day calls sell for $3.36, puts for $2.94. If T bills yield 4% per year, what is the implied volatility of these options? Use the implied volatility heuristic.

6 Delta, Gamma, and Theta

*T*actics not mated to strategy lead to consequences unintended.

Gary Kasparov
World Chess Champion

126

The previous chapter showed how the Black-Scholes option pricing model (OPM) is useful in determining the value of a put or call option. Delta, gamma, and theta are partial derivatives of the OPM, each with respect to a different variable. These values are central to modern portfolio risk management. Delta is the best-known and most useful of them and will be discussed first.

DEFINITIONS

Delta

When option traders or analysts get together, you will almost certainly hear someone use the term "Delta" during the conversation. **Deltas** are an important by-product of the Black-Scholes model, and they provide particularly useful information to those people who use options in portfolios. There are three definitions of delta. Each of them focuses on a different use of this statistic.

Measure of Option Volatility   One definition of delta is the change in option premium expected from a small change in the stock price, *ceteris paribus*. Symbolically, for a call option,

$$\Delta_c = \frac{\delta C}{\delta S} \tag{6-1}$$

where $\delta C/\delta S$ is the partial derivative of the call premium (C) with respect to the stock price (S). Similarly, the put delta is the partial derivative of the put premium (P) with respect to the stock price (S), or

$$\Delta_p = \frac{\delta P}{\delta S} \tag{6-2}$$

This value is useful because it allows us to find how many options are needed to mimic the returns of the underlying stock. A call delta of 0.75, for instance, means that if the stock price rises by $1.00, the call option will advance by 75 cents. A put delta of −0.75 means that the put option will decline by 75 cents if the stock rises by a dollar.

Fortunately, the Black-Scholes OPM makes determination of the call delta a simple task: it is exactly equal to $N(d_1)$.[1] Delta for a call option will always be less than one and greater than zero, because $N(d_1)$, the area under

---

[1] With a basic understanding of calculus, this can be seen readily from the Black-Scholes model. The stock price occurs in the model only once, and its coefficient is $N(d_1)$. When you take the derivative, the "constants" drop out and you are left with just $N(d_1)$.

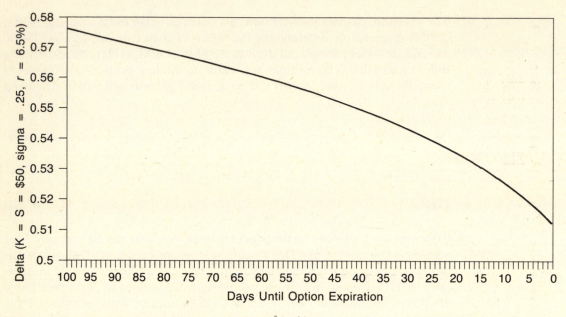

Figure 6-1 <u>Call Option Delta Decay (K = S)</u>   *At-the-money*

the normal curve, ranges from 0 to 100 percent. In the example following Table 5-5 (p. 109), we determined a <u>value of 0.836 for $N(d_1)$</u>, the option delta. This means that for a <u>very small unit change in the price of the underlying</u> <u>stock price, the option would change about 84 percent as much.</u>

Figure 6-2 <u>Call Option Delta Decay (K > S)</u>   *OUT-OF-THE-MONEY*

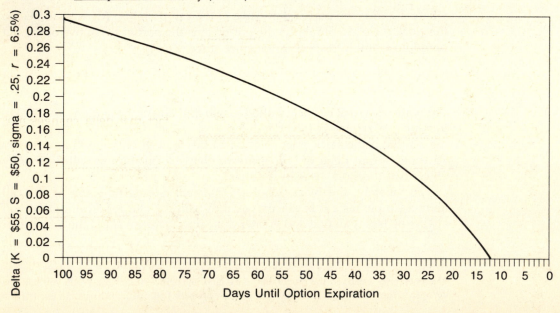

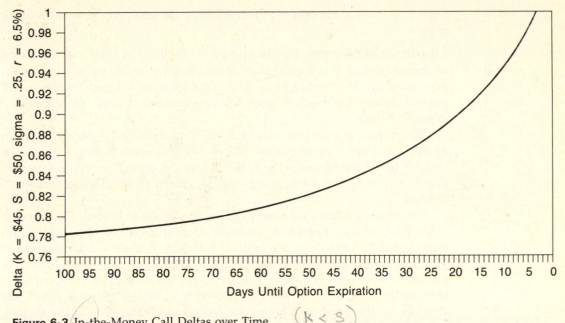

Figure 6-3 In-the-Money Call Deltas over Time $(K < S)$

Figures 6-1 through 6-3 show how an option's delta changes over time for an at-the-money option, an out-of-the-money option, and an in-the-money option, respectively. For an at-the-money option (Figure 6-1), the decline in delta is approximately linear in time until the last month or so of the option's life, with delta approaching 0.50 at expiration. The delta of an out-of-the-money option (Figure 6-2) approaches 0.0 as time passes, with delta declining more rapidly as time passes. Less time means it is less likely that the option will wind up in-the-money. The option premium eventually drops to zero and doesn't change, giving a delta of zero. In-the-money options (Figure 6-3) act more and more like the stock itself as expiration approaches. Their delta rises as time passes, approaching 1.0 on expiration day.

An important mathematical result is the fact that delta changes most rapidly for options that are near-the-money.

▌ Delta changes most rapidly for options that are near-the-money.

Hedge Ratio   Another definition of delta stems from its use as a **hedge ratio.** This indicates how many of a particular option are necessary to mimic the returns of the underlying asset, or another related asset. Suppose a particular XYZ call option has a delta of 0.250. A short option position (a written option) has a delta opposite in sign to a long option position. This means that if someone owned 100 shares of XYZ, writing four of the above call contracts would result in a theoretically perfect hedge for small changes in the stock price.[2]

Likelihood of Becoming In-the-Money   A final use of delta is as a measure of the likelihood that a particular option will be in the money on option expiration day. If an option has a delta of 0.445, there is approximately a 44.5 percent chance that the stock price will be above the option striking price on expiration day.

This aspect of delta can be very useful in evaluating the merits of certain option strategies. Suppose a speculator is considering a long straddle on Upjohn (UPJ) and observes the following information: $S = \$40\frac{1}{8}$, $K = \$40$, $C = \$2\frac{1}{8}$, $P = \$1\frac{3}{4}$, $r = 4\%$, and $t = 58$ days, with all variables as previously defined.

To calculate a delta we need to know the option volatility, and, because volatility is initially unknown, we must extract it from the option premium information by calculating the implied volatility. Using the call premium of $\$2\frac{1}{8}$ and the SIGMA file[3] gives an implied volatility of 0.3045. With this information we can figure out the likelihood of the stock price rising or falling sufficiently to result in a profit. It costs $\$2\frac{1}{8} + \$1\frac{7}{8} = \$4$ to establish this straddle, so the breakeven points are four points either side of the striking price of $40, or $36 and $44.

Using these two values as "imaginary" striking prices and inputting them one at a time into the OPM, we find "deltas" of 0.843 (for $36) and 0.259 (for $44). Given a volatility of 0.3045, 84.3 percent of the time the stock will be above $36 at expiration. Logically, then, 15.7 percent of the time it will be below $36, in which case the straddle will be profitable. With the higher breakeven price, 25.9 percent of the time the stock will finish above this level, resulting in a profit. Figure 6-4 is a traditional profit and loss diagram annotated with the likelihood of the position being profitable. Some spreaders and users of option combinations are especially fond of gathering this information about potential positions before establishing them.

Theta

Theta is a measure of the sensitivity of a call option to the time remaining until its expiration. Options become less valuable as they approach expiration day. Because time until expiration can only get shorter, theta usually is defined as the negative of the partial derivative, shown for a call.

---

[2]The hedge is only perfect for small movements in the stock price. Gamma becomes important for larger changes, as we shall see shortly.

[3]This file is on the computer disk available with the book, and facilitates the calculation of implied volatility.

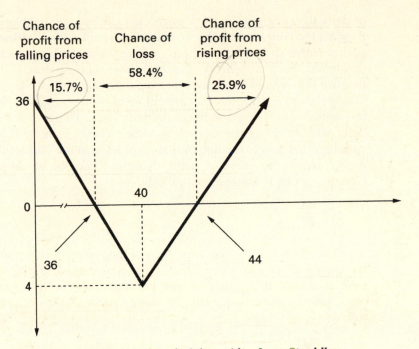

Figure 6-4 Likelihood of Profitability with a Long Straddle

$$\Theta = -\frac{\delta C}{\delta t} \qquad (6\text{-}3)$$

Theta can be calculated as follows:

for a call, $\quad -\dfrac{S\sigma e^{d_1^2}}{2\sqrt{(2\pi t)}} + Kr^{-t}\,(ln\ r)\,N(d_2)$ $\qquad (6\text{-}4)$

for a put, $\quad -\dfrac{S\sigma e^{d_1^2}}{2\sqrt{(2\pi t)}} + Kr^{-t}\,(ln\ r)\,N[(d_2) - 1]$ $\qquad (6\text{-}5)$

with all variables as defined in the OPM.

The passage of time hurts the holder of a long option position, so theta for a long call or a long put is negative. Conversely, the passage of time is to the benefit of the option writer, so theta is positive for a short call or short put.

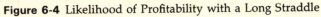

Gamma

Gamma (sometimes called **lambda**) is the second derivative of the option premium with respect to the stock price. Logically, it is also the first derivative of delta to change in the stock price. As calls become further in-the-money, they act increasingly like the stock itself. Consider the limiting case of a call option with a striking price of zero, where the underlying stock does not pay dividends. Such a security should behave almost exactly like the stock because they would be equivalent claims (this ignores trivial factors such as voting rights.) For options that are out-of-the-money, option prices are much less sensitive to changes in the underlying stock. This means that an option's delta *will change* as the underlying stock price changes. If you recall the variables that go into the determination of $N(d_1)$ in the OPM, this relationship makes sense; the value of delta changes when the stock price changes. Gamma can be expressed symbolically as

$$\gamma = \frac{\delta \Delta}{\delta S} \qquad (6\text{-}6)$$

One use of gamma is as a measure of how often option portfolios need to be "repaired" as stock prices change and time passes. Options with gammas near zero have deltas that are not particularly sensitive to changes in the stock price, and consequently are more "robust." Gamma is calculated as follows:

$$\gamma = \frac{e^{-0.5\,d_1^{\,2}}}{S d_2 \sqrt{2}} \qquad (6\text{-}7)$$

where S, d_1, and d_2 are as defined in the Black-Scholes OPM.

The easiest way to remember the sign of gamma is to learn that, for a given option position, the sign of gamma is always opposite to the sign of theta.

The sign of gamma is always opposite to the sign of theta.

A positive gamma comes from long option positions. A portfolio with a positive gamma becomes more bullish as prices rise (i.e., delta increases) or

TABLE 6-1 SIGN RELATIONSHIPS

	delta	theta	gamma
long call	+	−	+
long put	−	−	+
short call	−	+	−
short put	+	+	−

more bearish as prices decline (delta declines). Negative gammas, conversely, come from short options.

Sign Relationships

It is very helpful to determine quickly the sign for delta, gamma, or theta of a particular option position. Table 6-1 summarizes these relationships.

└ p. 132

Position Derivatives

Often a portfolio contains a few different options in addition to shares of the underlying stock. A manager might, for instance, have written calls to provide income and also have purchased puts for downside protection. Each portfolio component has its own delta, theta, and gamma. The sum of the deltas for a particular security is the **position delta.** Similarly, the sum of the gammas is the **position gamma** and the sum of the thetas is the **position theta.**[4]

└ i.e., security and related options

An Example

Figure 6-5 (p. 134) illustrates the position derivative concept. Here we see a portfolio containing 10,000 shares of stock, against which 100 call option contracts have been written and combined with 50 protective puts. The resulting position delta of 7320 suggests that the total portfolio is equivalent in market risk to 7320 shares of stock, or 73.2 percent of the risk of the unoptioned portfolio. The position theta of 70 means that if all other variables remain unchanged, the passage of one day will result in an increase of $70 in the value of the portfolio. This is because the decline in the value of the options written (which is good from your perspective) will exceed the decline in time value of the puts purchased. The meaning of a position gamma of −180 is less obvious, and will be discussed later in the chapter.

Caveats About Position Derivatives

Option derivatives are dynamic; they change with the passage of time or any other of the underlying variables. This means that position derivatives

---

[4]The term "position delta" is not generally used to refer to the sum of the deltas on different assets. That is, you would not normally combine deltas on Exxon and General Motors options.

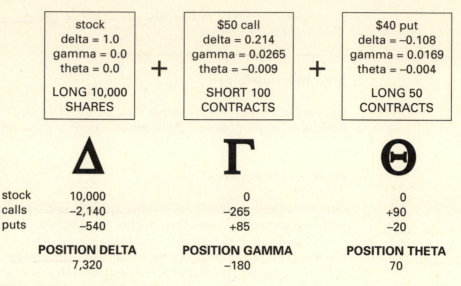

Figure 6-5 Position Derivatives

change every day (and sometimes every minute). A portfolio that is bullish ($\Delta > 0$) can suddenly become bearish ($\Delta < 0$) if stock prices change sufficiently. The need to monitor position derivatives is especially important when many different option positions are in the same portfolio.

DELTA NEUTRALITY

We have previously seen that as the price of the underlying security changes, options on that security do not all change in value by the same percentage. Delta measures the extent to which an option premium will change for a given small change in the price of the underlying security.

Certain option strategies are predicated on initial **delta neutrality** of the portfolio of options, meaning the combined deltas of the options involved net out to zero. Delta neutrality is an important issue to institutional traders who make large trades using straddles, strangles, and ratio spreads.[5]

A speculator who buys a straddle, for instance, makes money if the price of the underlying asset moves sharply up or down. A straddle is a neutral strategy: it is neither bullish nor bearish. It is unlikely, however, that the deltas of the put and of the call making up the straddle are equal in absolute value. Consequently, a given percentage rise in the value of the underlying

---

[5]Theoretical option pricing models, in fact, assume you are market direction neutral.

asset will not yield precisely the same result as an equal percentage decline. This means that unless you "weight" the relative proportion of the two classes of options appropriately, your straddle position may *not* actually be neutral. Your option position may be unintentionally slightly bullish or bearish. A quick example will help illustrate the situation.

Calculating Delta Hedge Ratios

EXAMPLE

- STRANGLE

- DELTA
NEUTRALITY

Suppose stock XYZ is currently trading at $44, the annual volatility of the stock is estimated at 15 percent, Treasury bills yield 6%, and an options trader has decided to write six-month strangles using $40 puts and $50 calls. *SHORT PUT SHORT CALL* The two options will have different deltas, and so the trader will not write an equal number of puts and calls. To find the proper number to use, it is necessary to calculate the deltas of each option and consider their ratio.

Delta for a call is $N(d_1)$ from the Black-Scholes option pricing model (Table 5-4); for a put, delta is $-N(-d_1)$. The expression for d_1 is repeated below.

$$d_1 = \frac{ln\ (S/K) + [r + \sigma^2/2]t}{\sigma\sqrt{t}}$$

We can now calculate each delta.

SHORT
$50 Call:

$$d_1 = \frac{ln\ (44/50) + [.06 + .15^2/2]0.5}{.15\sqrt{0.5}}$$

$$= -0.87$$

$$N(-0.87) = 0.19 \quad \text{Per p. 132, sign s/b negative}$$

SHORT
$40 Put:

$$d_1 = \frac{ln\ (44/40) + [.06 + .15^2/2]0.5}{.15\sqrt{0.5}}$$

$$-N(-1.23) = -0.11 \quad \text{Per p. 132, sign s/b positive}$$

The ratio of these two deltas is $-0.11/0.19 = -0.5789$. This means that delta neutrality is achieved by writing 0.5789 calls for each put written. One approximately delta neutral combination would be to write 261 put contracts and 151 call contracts. To check this, simply observe that

$$(-261)(100)(-0.11) + (-151)(100)(0.19) = 2.00$$

This is not materially different from zero.

Why Delta Neutrality Matters

The reason for maintaining delta neutrality is simple: strategies calling for delta neutrality are strategies in which you are *neutral about the future prospects for the market.* You do not want to have either a bullish or a bearish position.

▮ Neutral option strategies should be established such that they are approximately delta neutral.

EXAMPLE

Consider another example. In the XYZ strangle example, the position was established with $40 calls and $50 puts. Suppose that 100 options of each type were written. If we use the Black-Scholes model to estimate the prices of the options, we find that the $40 calls would sell for $0.48 each and the $50 puts would sell for $0.31. Writing 100 contracts of each of these would generate immediate income of ($48 × 100) + ($31 × 100) = $7900.

Now suppose XYZ rises by 1% to $44.44 per share. The predicted BS prices would be $0.29 for the puts and $0.57 for the calls, for a total of ($29 × 100) + ($57 × 100) = $8600. Because you wrote the options, your position has *deteriorated* by $700.

If XYZ instead *falls* by 1% to $43.56, the predicted BS prices are $0.35 for the puts and $0.42 for the calls, for a total value of ($35 × 100) + ($42 × 100) = $7700. This means your short option positions have *appreciated* in value by $200. (After you write options, you want their value to decline.)

Notice that a 1% rise in the stock price did not result in the same dollar change in your portfolio value as a 1% fall. The reason for this is that the original position, short 100 calls and short 100 puts, was *not delta neutral.* For this strangle, the position delta is

(# calls × call delta) + (# puts × put delta)
= (100 × 0.1896) + (100 × −0.1075)
= 0.0821

vs bearish position on p.

Thus, the combination of 100 $40 puts on XYZ and 100 $50 calls on XYZ is a slightly bullish position, since the position delta is greater than zero. We note that when the stock rises by 1%, the dollar change in the value of the portfolio is larger than the dollar change if the stock falls by a similar percentage.

Options, of course, can only be written on multiples of 100 shares. This means that it may not be possible to achieve exact delta neutrality. For large institutional investors or arbitrageurs, you can come very close. For these XYZ options, one approximately delta neutral combination is 75 calls and 132 puts. The position delta is (75 × 0.1896) + (132 × −0.1075) = 0.03.

Had we written puts and calls in these quantities, we would have received (75 × $48) + (132 × $31) = $7692. A 1% rise in the stock price would have caused the portfolio value to change to (75 × $57) + (132 × $29) = $8103. A 1% fall would result in a value of (75 × $42) + (132 × $35) = $7770. The dollar changes are not exactly equal, but they are closer than when 100 options each were written.

We have seen that an option's delta changes as its expiration date approaches, the stock price changes, volatility estimates are revised, or interest rates change. The sophisticated options trader will need to revise option positions continually if it is necessary to maintain a delta neutral position. This usually is done by closing a few contracts each day as necessary to keep the position even. The lower *gamma* is, the less often this needs to be done.

A gamma near zero means that the option position is robust to changes in market factors.

TWO MARKETS: DIRECTIONAL AND SPEED

Our attitudes toward "the market" usually focus on whether we are bullish or bearish. This is the **directional market.** In options applications, however, there is another consideration: how quickly we expect the anticipated move to occur. This is the **speed market.**

Directional Market

Delta measures exposure in the directional market. A bullish investor wants to have a positive position delta, because this means that a rise in the value of the underlying asset will result in an increase in the value of the option position. A long position in the underlying asset has a positive delta, as do long calls and short puts. A bearish speculator wants a negative position delta. Negative deltas come from short positions in the underlying asset, from long puts, and from short calls.

Speed Market

The speed market is not a particular concern to the stock investor, but it can be important to the option speculator. Writing calls and buying puts, for instance, are both bearish strategies; they have negative deltas. If you anticipate a major decline in the value of a particular stock, however, you would stand to earn larger profits from buying puts than from writing calls,

p. 132

because your maximum profit from writing calls is limited to the option premium.

Similarly, in a rapidly advancing market you would benefit from either owning calls or writing puts. Again, your maximum profit is limited to the option income if you write puts. In a fast market you want to buy calls or buy puts (referring to Table 6-1, p. 132); notice that both strategies have positive gammas. This is the fundamental rule: In fast markets you want positive gammas. By the same logic, in slow markets you want negative gammas.

In a fast market, profits are greatest with positive gammas. In a slow market, profits are greatest with negative gammas.

Combining Directional and Speed Markets

Ideally, option positions are established within a framework that considers both the anticipated direction of the market and the rapidity with which the move is anticipated. Suppose, for instance, that someone is bullish on the market but does not expect any sudden price jumps. Rather, he or she expects gradually increasing prices for the foreseeable future. This person is bullish, so the appropriate option position will have a positive delta. A slow market is expected, so gamma should be negative. What option strategies fit this bill?

Table 6-1 shows that positive deltas come from long calls and short puts, and that negative gammas come from short calls and short puts. So writing puts may be the most appropriate strategy. Table 6-2 shows the appropriate strategy under the various scenarios one might envision.

While a table like Table 6-2 is useful, it should not be taken as gospel. Writing options involves potentially significant risk, and this fact should always be considered before embarking on such a strategy. Simply buying options will not always generate a profit, either. One can choose from

TABLE 6-2 DIRECTIONAL AND SPEED MARKETS

| | | Directional Market | | |
		down $\Delta < 0$	neutral $\Delta = 0$	up $\Delta > 0$
Speed Market	slow $\gamma < 0$	write calls	write straddles	write puts
	neutral $\gamma = 0$	write calls; buy puts	spreads	buy calls; write puts
	fast $\gamma > 0$	buy puts	buy straddles	buy calls

many different striking prices and expiration dates, and their relative merits may vary considerably.

DYNAMIC HEDGING

One fact of options life is that with derivative assets as risk management tools, the level of protection they provide or the technical characteristics associated with them routinely change. Delta depends on the other variables that determine the option premium. Consequently, a position delta also will change as interest rates change, as stock prices change, as volatility expectations change, or as portfolio components change. This means that portfolios need periodic tune-ups.

As an example, suppose that a portfolio contains 10,000 shares of XYZ stock, which sells for $55 per share. Interest rates are 5%, XYZ's volatility is 0.24, and a $50 put expires in 88 days. Such a put has a delta of −0.167. Suppose that 150 of these put contracts are combined with the stock to provide some protection against a fall in the price of XYZ stock. After these puts are purchased, the position delta is

$$(10,000 \text{ shares} \times 1.0) + (15,000 \text{ puts} \times -0.167) = 7495$$

The following day, XYZ stock has fallen to $53. The new Black-Scholes delta for the put is −0.256, so the position delta has changed to

$$(10,000 \text{ shares} \times 1.0) + (15,000 \text{ puts} \times -0.256) = 6160$$

Figure 6-6 Portfolios Need Periodic "Tune-Ups"

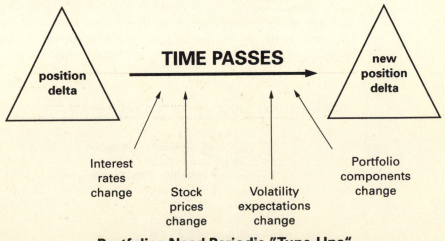

Portfolios Need Periodic "Tune-Ups"

Overnight, the portfolio has become substantially less bullish because of the changing delta of the put. If the manager wanted to maintain the original delta exposure of about 7500, it would be necessary to sell some puts, as selling them would remove negative deltas from the portfolio. The number of puts that must be sold is equal to the number of deltas we want to eliminate divided by the delta of one option: $(7500 - 6160)/0.256 = 5234$. So about 52 put contracts should be sold to maintain the original market exposure.

With a cash or futures position, you can be confident your position will remain the same until you do something to change it. But, with options, your price and volatility bets can change in size and even in direction, even when you don't do anything.

Clark Heston
Futures Magazine

Minimizing the Cost of Delta Adjustments

Writing options brings income in, but potentially involves large losses if prices move adversely. Purchasing options requires a cash outlay, which is a disadvantage, but also results in a known and limited maximum loss to the option buyer. It is possible (and common practice) to adjust a portfolio's delta by using *both* puts and calls to minimize the cash requirements associated with the adjustment.

EX

Suppose that in July a portfolio contains 10,000 shares of XYZ and that the portfolio manager decides to reduce the XYZ market exposure by half, to a position delta of 5000. Assume we have the information shown in Table 6-3. Using algebra, we can set up a series of simultaneous equations to achieve the position delta we want and have a net cash outlay of zero. The portfolio manager decides to write calls in sufficient quantity to pay for the needed puts. Table 6-4 shows the necessary steps.

TABLE 6-3 XYZ STOCK AND OPTION INFORMATION

stock price	=	$33
days until September expiration	=	66
riskfree interest rate	=	5%
implied volatility of XYZ stock	=	0.31
price of SEP 35 call	=	$ 1.06
delta of SEP 35 call	=	0.377
price of SEP 30 put	=	$ 0.50
delta of SEP 30 put	=	−0.196

short *long*

TABLE 6-4 SIMULTANEOUS EQUATIONS

Key: Let C = number of calls
      P = number of puts

Stock delta − call delta + put delta = 5000	(1)
10,000 − 0.377C − 0.196P = 5000	
Price of puts − income from calls = \$0	(2)
\$0.50P − \$1.06C = \$0	
Solve for P in terms of C in (2):	
0.50P = 1.06C	(3)
P = 1.06C/0.50 = 2.12C	(4)
Substitute (4) into (1):	
5000 − 0.377C − 0.196(2.12C) = 0	(5)
5000 − 0.377C − 0.416C = 0	(6)
5000 − 0.793C = 0	(7)
5000 = 0.793C	(8)
C = 5000/0.793 = 6305.17 ÷ 100 SH/contract = 63	(9)
Substitute for C in (4):	
P = 2.12(6305.17)	(10)
P = 13366.94 ÷ 100 SH/contract = 134	(11)
Rounding to whole contracts:	
P = 134 contracts (buy -- i.e., long)	
C = 63 contracts (write -- i.e., short)	

Table 6-5 (p. 142) shows the resulting position delta and net position cost. The position delta of 4998.5 is close to the target figure of 5000; the income from writing the calls is sufficient to pay for all but \$22 of the cost of the puts.

Position Risk

Position risk is an important, but often overlooked, aspect of the riskiness of portfolio management with options. Suppose an options speculator holds the positions shown in Table 6-6 (p. 142).

This portfolio has a "grand total" position delta of −155, so it is slightly bearish. This does not mean, however, that the speculator wants the market to fall precipitously. Delta is a first derivative, and first derivatives become less useful as the magnitude of the change in variables increases.

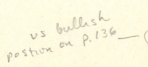
vs bullish position on p. 136

EX

Consider first what happens if the market advances very sharply, such as a "market crash in reverse." All the puts will go to zero, as the stock price rises above the put striking prices. You are short twenty calls and long fifteen others, for a net call holding of short five contracts. Also, you are long 10 lots of stock, or 1000 shares. The calls will be exercised, leaving you with 500 shares of stock. During a major market advance, this is an acceptable position.

short call
normal sign
for long put
is negative

TABLE 6-5   POSITION DELTA AND POSITION COST

<u>Resulting Position Delta</u>

$$10{,}000 \text{ shares of stock} \times \frac{1.0 \text{ deltas}}{\text{share}} = 10{,}000.0$$

short calls

$$63 \text{ call contracts} \times \frac{-0.377 \text{ deltas}}{\text{call}} \times \frac{100 \text{ calls}}{\text{contract}} = -2{,}375.1$$

long puts

$$134 \text{ put contracts} \times \frac{-0.196 \text{ deltas}}{\text{put}} \times \frac{100 \text{ puts}}{\text{contract}} = -2{,}626.4$$

$$\text{Position Delta} = 4{,}998.5$$

<u>Cost of Position</u>

long
$$\text{cost of puts: } 134 \text{ contracts} \times \frac{\$0.50}{\text{put}} \times \frac{100 \text{ puts}}{\text{contract}} = \$6{,}700$$

short
$$\text{income from calls: } 63 \text{ contracts} \times \frac{\$1.06}{\text{call}} \times \frac{100 \text{ calls}}{\text{contract}} = \$6{,}678$$

$$\text{Net Cost} = \$\quad 22$$

Ex

What if the market crashes? Then the <u>calls will go to zero</u>, and you will be left with a <u>net put position of five long contracts.</u> These will provide protection against 500 of your shares, but the other 500 will be unprotected. This is <u>no good.</u> Despite your position delta being negative, you will be hurt if <u>the market free falls.</u> Table 6-7 shows the portfolio value at various stock

TABLE 6-6   DETERMINING POSITION RISK

Initial Conditions: $\sigma = 0.22$ $S = 38$ $R = 5\%$ $T = 116$ days

option	contracts	pos. Δ	pos. γ	pos Θ
35 call	−15	−1203.0	−33.6	+13.5
40 call	+15	615.0	47.1	−15.0
45 call	− 5	− 60.0	− 8.1	+ 2.5
Call Total	− 5	− 648.0	5.4	+ 1.0
30 put	+10	− 18.0	+ 3.6	− 1.0
35 put	−20	+ 396.0	−44.8	+20.0
40 put	+15	− 885.0	+47.1	−10.0
Put Total	+ 5	− 507.0	+ 5.9	+ 9.0
Stock	+10	+1000.0	0.0	0.0
Grand Total		− 155.0	+11.3	+14.5

TABLE 6-7 PORTFOLIO VALUES AT VARIOUS STOCK PRICES
(Theoretical Black-Scholes Values)

position	0	30	32	33	34	36	38 (current)	40	42	50
short 15 $35 calls	0	−390	−1,050	−1,560	−2,205	−3,930	−6,135	−8,700	−11,475	−22,500
long 15 $40 calls	0	30	135	225	390	960	1,950	3,435	5,370	16,005
short 5 $45 calls	0	0	−5	−5	−15	−50	−130	−300	−590	−3,100
long 10 $30 puts	30,000	1,250	600	390	250	90	30	10	0	0
short 20 $35 puts	−70,000	−9,460	−6,320	−5,000	−3,860	−2,160	−1,100	−520	−220	0
long 15 $40 puts	60,000	15,000	12,000	10,500	9,000	6,030	4,020	2,505	1,455	90
long 1000 stock	−38,000	−8,000	−6,000	−5,000	−4,000	−2,000	0	2,000	4,000	12,000
portfolio value	−18,000	−1,960	−640	−450	−440	−1,060	−1,365	−1,570	−1,460	2,495
profit or loss	−16,635	−595	725	915	925	305	0	−205	−95	3,860

Note: r = 5%, sigma = .22, t = 116 days, S = 38

prices. (These are Black-Scholes theoretical prices with the assumption that prices change instantaneously with no passage of time.)

Figure 6-7 shows the general form of the profit and loss relationship. Assuming the options are all priced exactly as they should be according to the Black-Scholes model, the initial situation is at the zero profit mark corresponding to a stock price of $38. The negative position delta means that profits accrue if prices fall, so the curve moves into profitable territory if the stock price declines. If the stock price declines too far, however, the curve will turn down, indicating that large losses are possible. On the upside, losses occur if the stock price advances a modest amount, but if it really runs up then the position delta turns positive and profits accrue to the position.

A useful rule to remember is that, away from the extremes where the stock falls to zero or rises infinitely, the "intermediate" maximum profits occur if the underlying asset changes by a percentage amount approximately equal to the position delta divided by the position gamma. In this example, the figure is −155.0/11.3 = −13.7%. A 13.7% decline from the current stock price of $38 gives a new stock price of $32.8. Table 6-7 and Figure 6-7 show that the intermediate maximum profit is around this point. The percentage amount is a non-exact rule of thumb, but a useful one. (Note that in the extreme, maximum profits are unlimited as the underlying stock price rises.)

INTERMEDIATE
Maximum profits occur if the underlying asset changes by a percentage approximately equal to the position delta divided by the position gamma.

Negative position delta of −155

Figure 6-7 Position Risk
GENERAL FORM OF THE PROFIT AND LOSS RELATIONSHIP

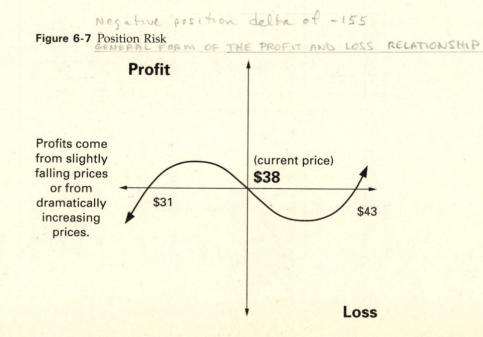

The point behind the position risk idea is that Black-Scholes derivatives are not particularly useful for major movements in the price of the underlying asset. An options expert needs to be aware of the doomsday scenario associated with any position.

OTHER DERIVATIVES: VEGA AND RHO

Delta, gamma, and theta are by far the most important of the derivatives of the OPM. There are others, however, and an options professional should be familiar with them, even if they seldom influence decisions.

Vega

Vega is the first partial derivative of the OPM with respect to the volatility of the underlying asset. For a call,

$$\text{Vega} = \frac{\delta C}{\delta \sigma} \tag{6-8}$$

To my knowledge no one knows where the term *vega*[6] originated. Vega is one of the twenty brightest stars (Alpha in the constellation Lyra), but vega is not a Greek letter (though many options folks think it is), and finance people have always had a penchant for Greek letters. Perhaps for this reason, vega is also called **kappa,** which *is* a Greek letter.

Vega is positive for both long calls and long puts. The higher the anticipated volatility of the underlying asset, the higher the value of the option, everything else being equal. If an option has a vega of 0.30, it will gain 0.30 percent in value for each percentage point increase in the anticipated volatility of the underlying asset.

Vega is calculated as follows:

$$V = \frac{S\sqrt{t}\, e^{-d_1^2/2}}{\sqrt{(2\pi)}} \tag{6-9}$$

Rho

Rho is the first partial derivative of the OPM with respect to the riskfree interest rate:

---

[6]It means "falling vulture" in Arabic, not "soaring eagle" as some people believe.

$$p = \frac{\delta C}{\delta r} \qquad\qquad (6\text{-}10)$$

$$= tKr^{-(t+1)} N(d_2) \qquad\qquad (6\text{-}11)$$

Rho is the least important of the derivatives. Unless an option has an exceptionally long life, its value is only modestly affected by changes in interest rates. As shown by the math in Chapter 5, rho is positive for call options and negative for puts.

Others

It is also possible to take a derivative of the OPM with respect to the striking price, or of the modified OPM with respect to a dividend yield. In practice, these statistics are not useful and are very seldom calculated.

SUMMARY

Delta is a measure of how the price of an option changes in response to small changes in the value of the underlying asset. Many options strategies are based on delta neutrality, meaning that options are combined in unequal numbers such that the weighted average of their deltas is zero. Straddles and strangles are important delta-neutral option packages. Delta changes with the passage of time, necessitating frequent adjustments to maintain delta neutrality.

Theta is a measure of how the value of an option changes with the passage of time. Long option positions have a negative theta, because options are wasting assets. Short option positions have a positive theta, as the passage of time is beneficial to the option writer, who wants the option to expire worthless.

Gamma is a measure of how delta changes as the price of the underlying asset changes. Negative gammas are potentially consequential, because a major market movement can seriously hurt an options position with a negative gamma. Gamma is always opposite in sign to theta.

The sum of the deltas in a portfolio is the position delta. Similarly, you can calculate the portfolio position theta or position gamma.

All option derivatives can change rapidly as the underlying conditions change. For this reason, it is necessary to "tune up" options positions as time passes and the value of the underlying asset changes.

First derivatives are only useful for relatively small movements in the underlying asset. Options traders, therefore, are especially concerned with position risk, which is a measure of the consequences of a "doomsday" move, where the market advances or declines sharply.

Vega and rho are relatively unimportant derivatives of the OPM that seldom influence managerial decisions.

QUESTIONS

1. What are the three definitions of delta?

2. As time passes, does the delta of an in-the-money call rise or fall? Why?

3. Suppose that a call option had a striking price of zero. What would its delta be?

4. Why are some strategies (like straddles) constructed to be delta neutral by many professional option traders?

5. Suppose you establish a delta neutral straddle that is exactly at-the-money. As time passes (and assuming everything else remains unchanged), will the position delta change? If so, in what direction?

6. How is delta useful in determining the potential profitability of an options strategy?

7. A long option position, by convention, has a negative theta. More time, however, means more option value. Doesn't this mean that theta should be positive, because premium goes up as time goes up?

8. Suppose you construct a bull spread with calls using one option at each striking price. Is the resulting position delta positive, negative, or indeterminable?

9. Refer to Figures 6-1, 6-2, and 6-3. Why do you think that the delta of an in-the-money call *rises* over time while the delta of an out-of-the-money call *falls*?

10. Why is it not possible for the delta of a call option to be greater than one or less than zero? Explain this using intuition rather than mathematics.

11. Why is delta neutrality an important issue with some option strategies?

12. Why is a gamma near zero often desirable?

13. Why is a negative gamma generally undesirable?

14. Does the concept of delta neutrality have any meaning for an option *spreader*?

15. Is there any added risk associated with establishing delta neutrality?

16. Suppose interest rates rise. Will an option's delta change if the stock price remains unchanged?

17. Why is gamma neutrality a convenience for an options portfolio manager?

18. Explain the difference between the directional market and the speed market.

19. Suppose you were bullish but expected a slow market. What strategy is particularly appropriate?

20. Briefly explain the idea of position risk.

21. Are any of the OPM derivatives more important than the others? If so, why?

PROBLEMS

Note: Use the following information for all problems:

$$t = 100 \text{ days} \qquad r = 5\% \qquad S = \$45 \qquad \sigma = .26$$

◉1. Calculate the delta of a $45 call option.

◉2. Suppose you own 5,000 shares of stock. How many $45 calls would you need to write to be approximately delta neutral?

◉3. If you wrote 15 $50 calls while holding 5,000 shares of stock, what percentage of the market risk of the position have you eliminated?

◉4. You are asked to determine the number of $45 calls and $45 puts that must be purchased to have a delta neutral straddle that costs about $4,000. Find the number of contracts of each type of option that satisfies these requirements.

◉5. Use your answer to problem 4, and assume the following: Twenty days have passed, and the stock price has changed to $48. What must you do to return to delta neutrality?

◉6. Suppose you own 10,000 shares of this stock. You want to write $50 calls and buy $45 puts to be delta neutral and have as little cash outflow as possible. Solve this using simultaneous equations.

◉7. Using the initial data at the start of this problem section, find the position delta, position gamma, and position theta of the following portfolio.

Short 15 $40 calls	Long 10 $40 puts
Short 25 $45 calls	Long 50 $35 puts

◉8. Suppose an investor owns 4,000 shares of this stock. How many $40 puts are necessary to hedge half the position?

◉9. Refer to the portfolio in problem 7. Suppose the portfolio also contains 800 shares of stock. Comment on the position risk of the portfolio.

Stock Index Options and Overwriting Strategies

What's a good way to raise the blood pressure of an Investor Relations Manager? Answer, talk about the pros and cons of stock options.

Eilene H. Kirrane
1983 Chairperson, Boston Chapter
National Investor Relations Institute

KEY TERMS

cash-secured put   margin
cash settlement   OEX
fiduciary put   overwriting
index option

Stock index options are one of the most successful innovations in the history of organized options exchanges. These put and call options have almost the same characteristics as options on common stock, but to an institutional investor are far more useful. The principal difference is that the underlying security is an index representing the current level of some set of asset prices.

Option overwriting is an increasingly popular portfolio activity, especially with index options. Overwriting refers to the creation and sale of stock options in conjunction with a stock portfolio.

STOCK INDEX OPTIONS

Characteristics

Index options are very similar to the traditional stock options discussed in the early chapters of this book. A significant difference is that there is no delivery mechanism with index options; they are **cash-settled.** It is not practical to deliver share certificates for each component of the index. With stock options, the option holder knows exactly how much money must be paid (with calls) or will be received (with puts). This is not necessarily so with index options.

Index options are cash-settled.

Investors who choose to exercise an index option must notify their brokers before a certain cut-off time established by their brokerage firm. Under current exchange policy, it is the closing price on expiration day that determines the actual dollar amount due or to be received from option exercise. Because the cut-off time may fall before determination of the closing price, it is not possible to be certain that an option will be in-the-money at the closing bell. Many index option users choose to avoid dealing with expirations, trading out of their long positions instead. A good argument can be made that a rational investor would never exercise such an option without knowing the price of the underlying financial instrument.

The booklet "Characteristics and Risks of Standardized Options," published by the Options Clearing Corporation, notes the special exercise risk of index options:

> A holder of an index option who exercises it before the closing index value for that day is available runs the risk that the level of the underlying index may subsequently change. If such a change causes the exercised option to fall

out-of-the-money, the exercising holder will be required to pay the difference between the closing index value and the exercise price of the option (times the applicable multiplier) to the assigned writer.

Suppose I own a call option with a striking price of 300, give my broker notice that I want to exercise it when the index level is 305.17, and find that at the end of the day the index has fallen to 299.00. In this case, I would not receive any money; I would have to *pay* $100.

Index options that are exercised are almost always in-the-money. The normal circumstance, then, is for option exercisers to receive a credit into their brokerage accounts.

Popular Index Contracts

Three especially popular index options are those on the S&P 100 index and the S&P 500 index, both of which trade at the Chicago Board Options Exchange, and the Major Market Index, trading at the American Stock Exchange. Ticker symbols for these indexes are **OEX,** SPX, and XMI, respectively, and this is how traders know these options. Less actively traded options are available on other indexes as well.

The OEX is the most popular of these. It began trading at the CBOE in March, 1983, and was an immediate success. Individual investors and

Figure 7-1 Two Popular Index Options

institutions alike discovered how useful these options can be, and in 12 months more than one half all options trading volume was in index options. Eighteen months after opening, the OEX pit at the CBOE was second only to the New York Stock Exchange in trading volume. Table 7-1 lists characteristics of the OEX option contract.

The most popular index options are those on the S&P 100 stock index, known by the ticker symbol OEX.

Since 1983 the other exchanges have followed the CBOE's lead, and index options now trade on the American, New York, Philadelphia, and Pacific Stock Exchange as well as the CBOE. Still, over 90 percent of index option trading occurs in Chicago. Figure 7-2 shows the history of the S&P 100 index.

TABLE 7-1   S&P 100 (OEX) CONTRACT SPECIFICATIONS

Underlying Asset

The S&P 100 index is a capitalization-weighted index of 100 stocks from a broad range of industries. The price of each component stock is multiplied by the number of shares outstanding; these are summed for all 100 stocks and divided by a predetermined base value. Base values for the index are adjusted to reflect changes in capitalization resulting from mergers, acquisitions, stock rights, or substitutions.

Contract Size

$100 times the index level

Premium Quotation

Stated in points and fractions. One point equals $100. Minimum tick for series trading below 3 is 1/16 ($6.25) and for all other series, 1/8 ($12.50).

Strike Price Intervals

5-point intervals; 10-point intervals in the far-term month

Expiration Date

Saturday immediately following the third Friday of the expiration month

Expiration Months

Four near-term months

Exercise Style

American: option contract may be exercised on any business day before the expiration date.

Settlement of Option Exercise

Exercise notices tendered will result in the delivery of cash on the business day following the day on which the exercise notice was tendered. The amount is equal to the difference between the closing value of the index on the trading day on which the exercise notice was tendered and the exercise price of the option, times $100 (the multiplier).

Trading Hours

8:30 a.m.–3:15 p.m. Central Time

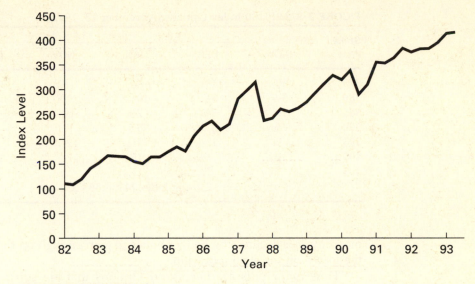

Figure 7-2 S&P 100 Index

Hedging with Index Options

One advantage of index options is that they have little unsystematic risk. There are 100 securities making up the OEX index, a number that obviously provides diversification benefits. This characteristic is one reason so many institutional investors favor them.

Index options have little unsystematic risk.

Figure 7-3 (p. 154) shows actual OEX information from November 13, 1992. On this day the closing value of the index was 383.33; this is analogous to the closing price for a share of stock. Striking prices are at $5 intervals from 375 to 405. The expirations are consecutive months: November, December, and January.

Consider the OEX DEC 380 put, listed at 4⅝. The buyer of one of these contracts pays 100 × $4.625, or $462.50. This is the maximum money at risk unless the option holder exercises it; then it could be more for the reason discussed above. People buy index puts for the same reasons they buy any other put: perhaps they expect the market to decline or want to protect a long position in stock.

Suppose the motivation for buying an index put is the latter: protecting a diversified portfolio of common stock against an anticipated market downturn. The same principles applicable to stock index futures are at work here. If

FIGURE 7-3 S&P 100 Index Options (November 13, 1992)

Strike Price	CALL			PUT		
	NOV	DEC	JAN	NOV	DEC	JAN
375	9¼	11½	....	11⁄16	3¼	6⅞
380	5⅛	8¼	10¾	1⁷⁄16	4⅝	9⅛
385	1⅞	5¼	7⅞	3⅜	6¾	12
390	7⁄16	3	5⅜	7	9½	16
395	⅛	1⁹⁄16	3⅛	12¾	....	19¾
400	1⁄16	13⁄16	1⅞	17	17½	....
405	1⁄16	7⁄16	1³⁄16	....	....	....

Closing Index Value 383.33

How do they behave?

market prices decline, the hedger hopes to gain enough on the puts to offset the losses on the stock portfolio.

How many puts are necessary? Options that are substantially in-the-money behave differently than options that are out-of-the-money. How does a hedger decide which striking price to pick? In principle, any of the puts could be used, although the relative cost of using them would differ markedly. The key to determining the appropriate number comes from delta. Delta measures how an option price changes for a given small change in the underlying stock (or index) value. Table 7-2 is a delta table[1] for the options shown in Figure 7-3.

Delta is necessary to determine a proper option hedge. *-- i.e., the number of puts.*

Suppose the delta for the DEC 380 put[2] is −0.368. This means for each point (or dollar) decline in the S&P 100 index, the value of this put will increase by about 37 cents. Delta must be recalculated every time the index changes to be strictly accurate.

With this information, you calculate a hedge ratio, using the following formula:

HEDGE RATIO =

$$HR = \frac{\text{portfolio value}}{\text{contract value}} \times \text{portfolio beta} \times \frac{1}{|\text{delta}|}$$

---

[1]Table 7-2 is prepared on the basis of a single option. Some delta tables are based on one contract; if this were done in Table 7-2, each value would be multiplied by 100.

[2]On November 13, 1992 T-bills yielded about 3%. There were 35 days until the December expiration. Using the near-the-money DEC 385 call, the implied volatility is 0.1167. With these data, the delta of the DEC 380 put is −0.368.

Check this calculation, if possible.

TABLE 7-2 OPTION DELTAS *BASED ON ONE OPTION*

Strike Price	CALL			PUT		
	NOV	DEC	JAN	NOV	DEC	JAN
375	.920	.759	.720	− .080	−.241	−.280
380	.720	.632	.622	− .280	−.368	−.378
385	.411	.491	.516	− .589	−.509	−.484
390	.153	.352	.410	− .847	−.648	−.590
395	.035	.232	.312	− .965	−.768	−.688
400	.005	.140	.227	− .995	−.860	−.773
405	0	.077	.158	−1.00	−.923	−.842

Suppose the portfolio has market value of $125,000 and a beta of 1.10. The number of puts we need to buy to hedge is then

contract value

$$\frac{\$125,000}{380 \times \$100} \times 1.10 \times \frac{1}{0.368} = 9.83$$

The investor would buy ten OEX DEC 380 puts to hedge this portfolio.

OVERWRITING

Forty percent of employee benefit plans with assets over $1 billion use options in their portfolios. Oppenheimer Capital is the largest U.S. manager of options programs for institutional investors, with responsibility for about $3 billion. Its most popular offering is an options overwriting program that is independent of a client's equity holdings, so the option trades do not affect the underlying portfolio. **Overwriting** refers to an option writing program in conjunction with an existing portfolio, usually with different managers for the stock portfolio and the options program. Audited financial statements show that since 1977 Oppenheimer's program has added 120 basis points annually to average client returns.[3]

1 basis pt = .01% = .001
120 basis pts = 120 × .001 = .12

The most common motivation for option overwriting is the generation of income.

One mutual fund, Gateway Index Plus, has followed a policy of continuous option overwriting since 1977. The principal investment strategy of this very successful mutual fund is maintaining a stock portfolio similar to

---

[3]See "Overwriting Options," *Institutional Investor* (November 1990), pp. 145–46.

the S&P 100 index and writing OEX calls against it. Peter Thayer, the fund manager, lists four things an option overwriting program should be expected to do:[4]

1. significantly lower the risk of investing in the stock market;
2. create steady, predictable returns;
3. achieve competitive returns during an extended bull market;
4. dramatically outperform the stock market during an extended bear market.

Using Index Options to Generate Income

Consider the case of a manager who has a $5 million, well-diversified stock portfolio, containing 50 individual securities. If it becomes necessary to generate more income from this portfolio, one possibility is to write call options against the individual components in the portfolio. If the portfolio contains 5000 shares of IBM, you could write 50 covered IBM calls. If there are 10,000 shares of General Motors, you could write 100 GM covered calls.

Each option transaction involves a commission. If you write calls against all fifty stocks in the portfolio, you will pay fifty commissions. You also run the risk that one or more of the stocks will get called away because of a takeover, unexpected good news, or another "company specific" event.

Another solution is to write index calls instead of traditional equity calls. Figure 7-3 (p. 154) shows that on November 13, 1992, the OEX index stood at 383.33. DEC 400 calls sold for 13/16, or $81.25 per contract of 100 "shares." The call options will become in-the-money once the OEX index rises above 400; this amounts to a 4.3 percent increase in the market in one month.

Writing index calls removes the risk of specific securities being called away.

With equity options, it is clear how many options can be written and still be covered by your stock: you can write one option contract for each 100 shares you own. What about index options? How many DEC 400 calls can you write? The next section discusses the somewhat complicated answer.

Margin Considerations in Writing Index Call Options The term **margin** has caused innumerable problems for fund managers. Many individual investors are familiar with margin accounts as a means of getting leverage in

---

[4]From "Options Overwriting: Seven Reasons to Choose Index Options," by Peter W. Thayer. Paper presented at the 1992 Chicago Board of Trade/Chicago Board Options Exchange Risk Management Conference.

their investments by borrowing money to buy securities. Tax-exempt funds generally cannot borrow money to invest without incurring some tax liability, so they seldom choose to use a margin account for this purpose.

The use of a margin account is not *prima facie* evidence of borrowing money. In fact, many charitable funds or fiduciary accounts have employed margin accounts for years and have *never* used them to borrow; their purpose is to provide the fund manager with added flexibility in managing the account.

Use of a margin account does not necessarily involve borrowing money or paying any interest.

With the OEX index at 383.33, the value of one contract is 383.33 × $100 = $38,333. Assume we have a stock portfolio worth $5 million. Despite what you might expect,

> *Regulation T and exchange margin rules do not permit short index calls in a cash account to be covered by a deposit of the underlying components with the broker.* Market index covered call writing on a cash account basis can only be effected if a custodian bank were to issue to the broker an Options Clearing Corporation ("OCC") index option escrow receipt.[5]

See Figure 7-4 (p. 158) for a sample Index Option Escrow Receipt. In this escrow receipt a bank certifies that it holds collateral sufficient to cover the writing of "X" number of index call options. The necessary collateral can be provided by the deposit of cash, cash equivalents, marginable stock, or any combination of the above. The collateral must total the full closing value of the underlying index on the trade date.

This means that a $5 million portfolio could be used to provide the collateral for writing 130 DEC 400 OEX index calls in a cash account, as calculated below.

$$\frac{\$5 \text{ million}}{\$38,333 \text{ per contract}} = 130.44 \text{ contracts}$$

Writing 130 DEC 400 contracts would generate immediate cash of 130 × $81.25, or $10,562.50. For more income, a lower striking price or a longer time until maturity could be used. Alternatively, you could use a margin account, enabling you to write more calls, as we will see next.

If index calls are written in a margin account, the funds required equal *the market value of the options plus 15% of the index value times the index multiplier less any out-of-the-money amount.* The margin requirement is also subject to a minimum amount equal to the market value of the options plus 10% of the market value of the index value times the index multiplier.

[5]Chicago Board Options Exchange, *Options Reference Manual*, p. M-2.

THE OPTIONS CLEARING CORPORATION   IOE **1069**

Index Option Escrow Receipt   Date _____

To: (Clearing Member name) _____ and (Broker name) _____
and The Options Clearing Corporation:

The undersigned (the "Bank") having an office at _____ hereby represents and warrants that (a) it is a bank or trust company organized under the laws of the United States or a state thereof and supervised and examined by state or federal authority having supervision over banks or trust companies, (b) the equity attributable to all outstanding shares of capital stock issued by the Bank is not less than $20,000,000 and (c) the total amount of cash and securities (at current market value) held by it pursuant to outstanding escrow receipts and guarantee letters collateralizing put and call options does not exceed a dollar amount equal to 25% of the equity attributable to all outstanding shares of capital stock issued by the Bank.

The Bank certifies that it holds the cash and/or securities hereinafter described (the "Deposit") in the United States of America as custodian for the account of _____ (the "Customer") and that the Customer or its agent has specifically authorized the Bank to file this Escrow Receipt with you and to hold the Deposit as an escrow deposit pursuant to the Rules of The Options Clearing Corporation (the "Corporation") in respect of the Customer's position ("short position") as a writer of the following index call option contracts:

Trade Date		Underlying Index:	
		Option Series	
Number of Contracts	Aggregate Closing Index Value Per Contract at Trade Date	Expiration Month/Year	Aggregate Exercise Price Per Contract

The Bank further certifies that:

(i) The Deposit consists of (a) cash, (b) cash equivalents meeting the requirements of §220.8(a)(3)(ii) of Regulation T of the Board of Governors of the Federal Reserve System (the "FRB"), (c) common stocks listed on a national securities exchange or included in the current List of OTC Margin Stocks published by the FRB, or (d) any combination thereof.

(ii) The total market value of the Deposit as of the trade date indicated above (valuing cash equivalents and common stocks at their closing sale prices, if subject to last sale reporting, or at their most recent bid prices, if not subject to last sale reporting) was not less than the product of (a) the number of contracts indicated above and (b) the aggregate closing index value per contract at trade date indicated above (such product being hereinafter referred to as the "Initial Position Value").

(iii) To the extent that the Deposit includes securities, the Bank has by book entry or otherwise identified as being included within the Deposit (a) specific certificates for such securities in the Bank's possession, (b) a quantity of such securities that constitutes or is part of a fungible bulk of securities in the Bank's possession, (c) a quantity of such securities that constitutes or is part of a fungible bulk of securities credited to the account of the Bank on the books of a financial intermediary (as defined in §8-313(4) of the Delaware Uniform Commercial Code), or (d) any combination thereof;

(iv) To the extent that the Deposit includes securities described in clause (iii)(a) or (iii)(b) above, such securities are in good deliverable form (or the Bank has the unrestricted power to put such securities into good deliverable form) in accordance with the requirements of the primary market for such securities.

(v) The Customer or its agent has duly authorized the Bank to liquidate any securities included in the Deposit to the extent necessary to perform the Bank's obligations hereunder;

(vi) The Bank will not subject nor permit the Customer to subject the Deposit or any portion thereof to any lien or encumbrance, or cause or permit the Deposit or any portion thereof to be applied to or used in satisfaction of any claim of the Bank (in any capacity whatsoever) against the Customer or any other person or entity or used by the Bank as an offset in whole or in part in any manner whatsoever and the Bank will promptly notify the Corporation (the Clearing Member named above (the "Clearing Member") and the Broker, if any, named above (the "Broker") if any notice of lien, levy, court order or other process which may or purports to affect the Deposit or any portion thereof is served upon it.

(vii) The Bank maintains a written affirmation from the Customer or its agent stating that all index options written for the Customer's account and covered by escrow receipts issued by the Bank are written against a diversified stock portfolio.

Upon the instructions of the Customer or its agent, the Bank may from time to time substitute cash, cash equivalents described in clause (i)(b) above, or common stocks described in clause (i)(c) above for any property theretofore included in the Deposit, provided that (a) the current market value of the substituted property is at least equal to that of the property for which it is substituted, and (b) the representations made in clauses (iii), (iv) and (v) above remain true and correct after giving effect to such substitution.

Upon the request of the Corporation, the Clearing Member or the Broker (collectively the "Beneficiaries") at any time while this Escrow Receipt remains outstanding, the Bank will promptly provide such Beneficiary with a written listing of the cash, cash equivalents and/or common stocks then included within the Deposit. If the total market value of the Deposit shall at any time be less than 55% of the product of (a) the number of contracts indicated above and (b) the aggregate current index value of the underlying index (as defined in article XVII of the By-Laws of the Corporation), the Bank shall promptly notify the Customer or its agent thereof and request that the Deposit be supplemented. If the total market value of the Deposit shall at any time be less than 50% of said product (whether or not a request to the Customer for supplementation is then pending), the Bank will immediately advise the Beneficiaries in writing thereof. If any cash equivalent included in the Deposit shall cease to meet the requirements of clause (i)(b) above, or if any common stock included in the Deposit shall cease to meet the requirements of clause (i)(c) above, such cash equivalent or stock shall be assigned a value of zero for the purpose of any computation of total market value hereunder.

The Bank agrees that it will hold the Deposit in accordance with the terms hereof until this Escrow Receipt is released or the Bank is directed to make payment as hereinafter provided. Upon presentation of this Escrow Receipt with the Endorsement of Release below duly executed on behalf of each of the Beneficiaries, the Bank will release the Deposit to the Customer or its agent. Upon presentation of this Escrow Receipt (i) by the Corporation with the Payment Order below duly executed on its behalf, (ii) by the Clearing Member with the Payment Order below duly executed on its behalf and the Endorsement of Release below duly executed on behalf of the Corporation, or (iii) by the Broker with the Payment Order below duly executed on its behalf and the Endorsement of Release below duly executed on behalf of the Corporation and the Clearing Member, the Bank will promptly pay to the order of the party presenting this Escrow Receipt, out of the Deposit or the proceeds thereof, an amount in cash equal to the aggregate exercise settlement amount of the number of index option contracts indicated above or such lesser number of contracts as shall be specified in the Payment Order, plus all applicable commissions and other charges. As used herein, the term "exercise settlement amount" means the amount [illegible] index value of the underlying index (as defined in Article XVII of the By-Laws of the Corporation) on the date of exercise [illegible] receipt [illegible] indicated above.

In the event that the Bank is presented with a Payment Order for a lesser number of index option contracts than the number indicated above, the Bank will issue to the party presenting the Payment Order, in exchange for this Escrow Receipt, an identical Escrow Receipt for the number of contracts indicated above minus the number of contracts covered by the Payment Order.

The Bank has been authorized by the Customer or its agent to confirm the Customer's understanding that (i) the index option described [illegible] closed out, it is the Customer's responsibility to ensure that this Escrow Receipt is released, and until this Escrow Receipt is [illegible] drawn from the Corporation, the Corporation will retain the right to demand payment in accordance herewith upon the assignment of an exercise notice to any short [illegible] agrees of an option contract identified above carried in the Clearing Member's customers' account with the Corporation, and (ii) exercise notices assigned by the Corporation to short positions [illegible] which escrow receipts have been deposited with the Clearing Member are allocated to particular customers by the Clearing Member or by their respective brokers, and if the Clearing Member is suspended by the Corporation and the Corporation cannot promptly determine the identities of the assigned customers, the Corporation will reallocate such exercise notices and such reallocation shall be binding on the Customer, notwithstanding any contrary notice or confirmation which the Customer may have received from the Clearing Member or the Customer's broker.

If the Customer is the Bank acting in a fiduciary or similar capacity, or a trust or custodial or similar account maintained with the Bank, it is nonetheless understood that in issuing this Escrow Receipt and functioning as escrowee and bailee of the Deposit hereunder, the Bank is acting in a wholly separate capacity, and not in any particular capacity set forth above. Nothing herein shall be deemed to require the Bank to make payment in contravention of any court order or judgment binding on the Bank in its capacity as escrowee and bailee hereunder, which on its face affects the Deposit or the proceeds thereof.

(Bank) _____

By: _____

Endorsement of Release

The undersigned hereby releases all rights with respect to this Escrow Receipt:

The Options Clearing Corporation

By _____ Date _____

Clearing Member

By _____ Date _____

Broker

By _____ Date _____

Payment Order

The undersigned hereby certifies to the above-named Bank that an exercise notice for _____ index call option contracts of the series indicated below filed with The Options Clearing Corporation on _____ 19____ has been assigned to the short position of the above-named Clearing Member which includes the above option contract(s), and demands payment of the amount indicated below, which constitutes the aggregate exercise settlement amount for the contracts comprising the assigned short position plus all applicable commissions and other charges.

Assigned Series _____ $ _____
   (Index Exp Mo Ex Price)   Amount payable

☐ The Options Clearing Corporation   ☐ Clearing Member   ☐ Broker

By _____ Date _____

Figure 7-4 Index Option Escrow Receipt Form

TABLE 7-3 MARGIN EQUIVALENTS

Cash:	100%
U.S. Treasury Securities:	96%
Non-convertible corporate debt trading at par:	80%
Stock:	50%

The funds required can be provided in various forms, and some forms "count more" than others. While the precise rules can change, the information in Table 7-3 is a general guideline.

We can now calculate the maximum number of index calls that can be written using the alternate forms of providing margin. See Table 7-4.

The margin account alternatives obviously provide you with the opportunity to generate much more income using index calls than in a cash

TABLE 7-4 MAXIMUM NUMBER OF INDEX CALLS THAT COULD BE WRITTEN AGAINST A $5 MILLION STOCK PORTFOLIO

(Using DEC 400 OEX calls @ $^{13}/_{16}$; OEX = 383.33)

Note: N = maximum permissible number of contracts

Using Cash

15% of index value:	15% × $383.33 × 100 × N	=	$5,749.95N
	PLUS		
market value of options:	N × $0.8125 × 100	=	81.25N
	MINUS		
out-of-the-money amount:	($400 − 383.33) × 100 × N	=	($1,667.00N)
		Total	4,164.20N

$5 million = 4,164.20N

N = 1,200 contracts

Using Treasury Bonds

(96% of cash level)

1,200 contracts × 96% = 1,152 contracts

Using Corporate Bonds

(80% of cash level)

1,200 contracts × 80% = 960 contracts

Using Stock

(50% of cash level)

1,200 contracts × 50% = 600 contracts

account. Using cash in a margin account, writing the maximum number of 1200 contracts enables you to generate 1200 contracts × $81.25 per contract, or $67,500 in income.[6] This is over six times as much as in a cash account.

The Risk of Index Calls   The risk here is that the index will rise above the striking price you select. The lower the striking price you select, the more income you will receive, but the greater the likelihood that the option will end in-the-money.

If the index calls you write do end in-the-money, it is no great inconvenience because of the cash-settlement feature. There is no delivery mechanism with these securities. The call writer owes the call holder the intrinsic value of the call at option expiration. If you write 130 DEC 400 OEX calls and the index is at 401.00 on expiration day, you must pay (401.00 − 400.00) × $100 × 130 contracts = $13,000 to the holder(s) of the call options.

Presumably the value of your stock portfolio has risen as well, so that gain will partially (or fully) offset the option liability. In any event, you also get to keep the proceeds from writing the options.

If index options expire in-the-money, the option writer pays the option buyer the intrinsic value.

Under current rules the composition of your portfolio makes no difference in determining the equity requirement for covered index-call writing. Conceivably you could own $1 million in a *single security*, and use this as "collateral" for the index options you wrote.

What's Best?   Is index option writing preferable to writing calls on the portfolio components? Many people think so, but there is no universal consensus on this point. It is a fact that many managers of large funds use index options almost exclusively. They have several clear advantages.

1. The portfolio manager needs only a single option position instead of many.
2. Aggregate commission costs are lower.
3. There is much less company-specific risk associated with index options.
4. There is less disruption of the portfolio when calls expire in-the-money and are exercised.

There is obvious potential here for regulatory confusion regarding covered call writing using index options. Options are a difficult enough idea

---

[6]Even though the rules permit writing this many option contracts, this action probably involves more leverage and consequently more risk than many portfolio managers acting as a fiduciary would be willing to bear.

for many people, and an option on an "imaginary" asset like an index will give these people even more difficulty.

Also, the saying that "a little knowledge is a dangerous thing" is especially relevant here. It is not hard to imagine someone who knows a little about options questioning the prudence of "writing naked index options" in a fiduciary account. The portfolio manager is going to have to explain why the index option writing strategy is *covered,* is *appropriate,* and is *preferable* to traditional equity call writing.

cash settlem't

No one strategy has been proven appropriate for all market conditions, yet no market scenario has developed for which the prudent use of options could not improve the likelihood of realizing one's investment objective.

Chicago Board Options Exchange

A Comparative Example: Covered Call Writing, Covered Index Call Writing, Writing Fiduciary Puts, and Put Overwriting

The following example illustrates the gains or losses associated with each of the above four strategies under three market scenarios: an advance of 5%, no change, and a decline of 5%. (In all instances, commission costs are not included.) It is important to recognize that these four strategies are *not substitutes* for each other. Writing fiduciary puts and put overwriting are bullish strategies, for instance, while writing covered calls is less so and may even be done in anticipation of declining prices.

Assume we have a portfolio of five stocks as shown in Table 7-5.

Covered Equity Call Writing   In this first strategy, individual equity call options will be written against each of the five securities in the portfolio. Various striking prices and expirations could be chosen, depending on the

TABLE 7-5 STOCK PORTFOLIO

Stock	Price	Shares	Value	Beta
Atl. Richfield	61⅛	500	$ 30,563	1.10
Bell Atlantic	70	400	28,000	0.80
Int. Paper	76⅝	400	30,650	1.10
Upjohn	93⅞	300	28,163	1.00
Federal Express	63½	500	31,750	1.20
Total			$149,126	1.05

manager's intent. Table 7-6 shows the manager's selection of options and the performance of the portfolio under each of the three scenarios.

The portfolio makes money in each of these scenarios. Greatest profits occur when the market advances, but each of the five securities is called and

TABLE 7-6 WRITING COVERED EQUITY CALLS

Write 5 ARC APR 60 calls	@ 3¼	=	$1625	income
Write 4 BEL APR 70 calls	@ 2¾	=	$1100	income
Write 4 IP APR 75 calls	@ 5¼	=	$2100	income
Write 3 UPJ APR 95 calls	@ 7	=	$2100	income
Write 5 FDX APR 65 calls	@ 4	=	$2000	income
	Total		$8925	income

Market Up 5%

Stock	Price	Gain	Income	Total
ARC	64.5*	−563	$1625	$1062
BEL	72.8*	0	$1100	1100
IP	80.8*	−650	$2100	1450
UPJ	98.6*	338	$2100	2438
FDX	67.3*	750	$2000	2750
			Total	$8800

Market Unchanged

Stock	Price	Gain	Income	Total
ARC	61⅛*	−563	$1625	$1062
BEL	70	0	1100	1100
IP	76⅝*	−650	2100	1450
UPJ	93⅞	0	2100	2100
FDX	63½	0	2000	2000
			Total	$7712

Market Down 5%

Stock	Price	Gain	Income	Total
ARC	57.8	−$1663	$1625	−$ 38
BEL	67.2	− 1120	1100	− 20
IP	72.4	− 1690	2100	410
UPJ	89.2	− 1403	2100	697
FDX	59.7	− 1900	2000	100
			Total	$1149

*Indicates that the stock would be called because the call option expires in-the-money

TABLE 7-7   WRITING COVERED INDEX CALLS

Write 3 DEC 385 OEX calls at $5¼ = $1575 income
initial value of OEX index = 383.33

Market Up 5% (index = 402.50)

Stock	Price	Gain	Options:	
ARC	64.5	$1688	Loss on cash settlement =	
BEL	72.8	1120	(385 − 402.50) × 300 =	$5250
IP	80.8	1670		
UPJ	98.6	1418	Income received =	1575
FDX	67.3	1900		
	Stock gain	$7796	Net option loss	−$3675

→ Net gain = $4121 ←

Market Unchanged (index = 383.33)

Stock	Price	Gain	Options:	
ARC	61⅛	$0	Cash settlement:	
BEL	70	0	Options expire worthless	
IP	76⅝	0		
UPJ	93⅞	0	Income received =	1575
FDX	63½	0		
	Stock gain	$0	Net option gain	$1575

→ Net gain = $1575 ←

Market Down 5% (index = 364.16)

Stock	Price	Gain	Options:	
ARC	57.8	−$1663	Cash settlement:	
BEL	67.2	−1120	Options expire worthless	
IP	72.4	−1690		
UPJ	89.2	−1403	Income received = $1575	
FDX	59.7	−1900		
	Stock loss	−$7776	Net option gain $1575	

→ Net loss = −$6201 ←

must be sold to the holders of the call options. All the options are in-the-money at expiration, so they will be exercised.

Two securities, ARC and IP, are also called under the "no change" scenario. The options on these securities were initially in-the-money.

No securities are called in the "down 5%" scenario. The option income of $8,925 mitigates the effect of the decline in market value of the five stocks, resulting in an overall modest gain.

TABLE 7-8 WRITING FIDUCIARY INDEX PUTS

Write 3 DEC 380 OEX puts @ $4⅝ = $1387 income

Note: Assume $149,126 invested in cash at 5% for 3 months, yielding $1864 in interest.

Market Up 5% (Index = 402.50)

Options expire out-of-the-money:
Options premium received	= $1387	
Interest received	= 1864	
	Total	$3251

Market Unchanged (Index = 383.33)

Options expire out-of-the-money:
Options premium received	= 1387	
Interest received	= 1864	
	Total	$3251

Market Down 5% (Index = 364.16)

Options expire in-the-money:
Options loss is (364.16 − 380.00) × 300	= −$4752	
Options premium received	= 1387	
	Total	−$3365
	Interest received	1864
	Total	−$1501

Covered Index Call Writing[7]   In this strategy, DEC 385 S&P 100 index calls are written rather than individual equity call options. In Table 7-7 (p. 163) you see the results of this strategy under the same three scenarios.

Index options are settled in cash at expiration day, so none of the stocks in the portfolio are called. Instead, the portfolio manager is responsible for paying the value of the options to the option holder on expiration day.

---

[7]Three calls are written in a *cash account* in this example. With the OEX index at 383.33, three contracts are the most that can be written against a portfolio worth $149,126: $149,126/ 383.33 = 3.89, rounded down to 3.

In a *margin account*, the maximum permissable number is

$$.5 \times \frac{149,126}{.15(38333) + 525} = 11$$

TABLE 7-9 PUT OVERWRITING

Write 5 ARC APR 65 puts	@ 5¼	=	$2625	income
Write 4 BEL APR 70 puts	@ 2½	=	$1000	income
Write 4 IP APR 75 puts	@ 5¼	=	$1100	income
Write 3 UPJ APR 95 puts	@ 7	=	$1650	income
Write 5 FDX APR 65 puts	@ 4⅛	=	$2063	income
		Total	$8438	income

Market Up 5%

Stock	Price	Gain	Income	Total
ARC	64.5	$1688	$2375*	$ 4063
BEL	72.8	1120	$1000	2120
IP	80.8	1670	$1100	2770
UPJ	98.6	1418	$1650	3068
FDX	67.3	1900	$2063	3963
			Total	$15,984

Market Unchanged

Stock	Price	Gain	Income	Option Loss	Total
ARC	61⅛	0	$2625	−1938	$ 687
BEL	70	0	1000	0	1000
IP	76⅝	0	1100	0	1100
UPJ	93⅞	0	1650	− 338	1312
FDX	63½	0	2063	− 750	1313
				Total	$5412

Market Down 5%

Stock	Price	Gain	Income	Option Loss	Total
ARC	57.8	−$1663	$2625	−3600	−$2638
BEL	67.2	− 1120	1000	−1120	− 1240
IP	72.4	− 1690	1100	−1040	− 1630
UPJ	89.2	− 1403	1650	−1740	− 1493
FDX	59.7	− 1900	2063	−2650	− 2487
				Total	−$9488

*ARC did not rise above the put striking price of 65. Therefore, the puts would be exercised, resulting in a "loss" of $0.50 × 5 × 100 = $250 that partially offsets the $2625 income received.

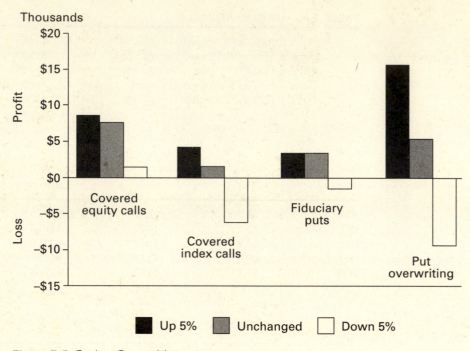

Figure 7-5 Option Overwriting

The five percent rise in the market causes the DEC 385 calls to be substantially in-the-money, and this results in a loss that exceeds the income received from writing the options.

Writing Fiduciary Puts In this strategy, no shares of stock are owned. Instead, funds are placed in an interest-bearing account and the options manager writes index put options in anticipation of the underlying stocks moving up in price.[8] This arrangement is called writing a **fiduciary put** (also called a **cash-secured put**). Table 7-8 (p. 164) shows the hypothetical results of this strategy.

The greatest gain occurs if the market advances or remains unchanged. Because the chosen puts are out-of-the-money, they expire worthless if the market is flat or moves up. Declining market prices cause the puts to go in-the-money, resulting in a loss to the put writer.

Put Overwriting The final strategy, put overwriting, is the most aggressive. Put overwriting can result in significant losses if security prices decline, as we see in the example in Table 7-9 (p. 165).

---

[8]Individual equity put options could be used instead of index puts.

The greatest gain occurs when the market advances. In this situation the stock appreciates and the put premiums decline (to the benefit of the put writer). Declining security prices result in losses from both the long stock positions and from the rising put premiums.

Risk/Return Comparisons   Figure 7-5 shows the relative profits and losses resulting from these four strategies under the three scenarios used. Put overwriting has the most potential losses and gains, while the other strategies are more conservative. (Although this example ignores commission costs, covered equity call writing and put overwriting would be affected by them the most.

It is *not* the case that the writing of covered equity calls is always superior to the writing of "covered" index calls. Any example is sensitive to the market conditions used in its illustration. As it happens here, the use of equity calls dominates the use of index calls in each scenario, but this result should not be generalized.

SUMMARY

Index options are extremely popular. The principal difference between them and ordinary equity options is that index options are cash-settled; there is no delivery mechanism.

The most widely used index option is on the S&P 100 stock index, ticker symbol OEX. Based on the value of 100 stocks, this index has little unsystematic risk so is consequently a useful portfolio hedging tool.

The OEX contract is also popular in option overwriting strategies, which involve writing options (usually calls) to increase portfolio income. Margin rules govern how many options can be written and still be covered. A principal advantage of index options in overwriting accounts is the fact that option exercise will not result in any individual security being called away. This is due to their cash settlement feature.

QUESTIONS

1. Do you think that the margin requirements for the writing of index options should be different from those for equity options? Why or why not?
2. Would you expect the delta of an OEX call option to increase or decrease as the striking price rises?
3. Suppose the holder of a diversified portfolio decided to hedge against a market downturn by writing OEX calls instead of buying OEX puts. Explain the steps the person would take to do this.

4. Would it make sense for someone to construct an index option spread by buying an OEX call and simultaneously writing an XMI call with the same expiration?

5. What should a portfolio manager consider before embarking on a put overwriting program during a bear market?

6. Why is writing an in-the-money put more risky than writing an out-of-the-money put?

7. Someone's primary portfolio objective is capital appreciation. Would it ever make sense for this person to write covered calls?

8. How do index options simplify operational problems with option overwriting?

9. A fund manager wants to hedge against a market downturn. Would it make sense to write index calls, and use the proceeds to buy index puts?

10. How can writing calls potentially "jeopardize" a tax exempt fund's ability to carry out its charitable purpose?

11. Write a 150-word paragraph explaining the term "margin." Assume the paragraph is for the business column of your local newspaper.

12. Suppose someone recommends a change in the rules such that a short put is considered covered if the put writer is simultaneously *short* shares of the underlying stock. Does this make sense to you?

13. How is the risk of a fiduciary put different from the risk of a non-fiduciary short put?

14. Comment on the following statement: "Writing covered index calls is always preferable to writing covered equity calls."

15. Write a 150-word article explaining the relative merits (and the potential risk) of "improving on the market" by writing deep-in-the-money covered calls.

16. The text indicates that option buyers seldom acquire options with the intent of exercising them. Why, then, would stock ever be called away?

17. List four things an option overwriting program should be expected to do.

18. Why does option overwriting lower the risk of investing in the stock market?

PROBLEMS

1. Suppose an investor constructs a bull spread using the OEX DEC 390/395 call options. What is the maximum gain and loss?

2. Refer to Figure 7-3. A friend announces that he is going to set up a

"riskless" bull spread using OEX options by buying 10 November 400 calls and writing 10 November 405 calls at the indicated prices of ¹⁄₁₆ each. Is the strategy riskless? Will it work?

3. You buy 1000 shares of XYZ at $27 on February 1. On April 2, you write 10 JUL 30 calls for $3 each. The options are exercised on April 20, and you sell your shares at the exercise price.
   (a) What is your holding period return?
   (b) What is the *true* rate of return, i.e. the internal rate of return?

4. You manage a $10 million endowment fund, and would like to write index calls to generate some income. The July 320 OEX call sells for $1⅛, and the current level of the index is 315.66. How much income can you generate:
   (a) in a cash account?
   (b) in a margin account using cash equivalents?
   (c) in a margin account using common stock?

5. Suppose you write 50 July 320 calls in problem four. What are the dollars and cents implications to you if, at option expiration, the level of the OEX index is 334.96?

6. You manage a $5 million stock portfolio, which is held in a margin account. How much income can you generate by writing DEC 385 OEX puts from Figure 7-3?

7. Refer to Figure 7-3. You hold $2 million in stock, with a portfolio beta of 1.15. You write 10 DEC 390 OEX calls and write 10 DEC 380 puts. What is your estimate of the total portfolio gain if, at option expiration, the S&P 100 index is 385.00?

8. Suppose you manage a $2 million stock portfolio with a beta of 0.95. Using the data in Table 7-2, how many DEC 385 puts must you purchase to remove *half* the portfolio's market risk?

9. Refer to Problem 8. How many JAN 380 puts must you purchase to remove *all* the market risk?

◉ 10. Suppose the OEX index stands at 400.00, T-bills yield 3.3%, MAR options expire in 65 days, and the MAR 410 call sells for $3½. If you write 10 of these contracts while holding a $5 million stock portfolio with a beta of 1.10, what percentage of market risk has been removed?

◉ 11. In Problem 10, suppose you *also* buy 15 MAR 390 puts.
   (a) What do you estimate the puts would cost?
   (b) What percentage of market risk would be removed by writing the calls *and* buying the puts?

◙ **12.** In Problem 10, suppose 25 days pass and the OEX index moves to 404.00. What do you estimate the aggregate gain or loss on the entire portfolio (stock and option positions) to be?

PART

THE FUTURES MARKET

8 Fundamentals of the Futures Market

As near as I can learn, and from the best information I have been able to obtain on the Chicago Board of Trade, at least 95% of the sales of that Board are of this fictitious character, where no property is actually owned, no property sold or delivered, or expected to be delivered but simply wagers or bets as to what that property may be worth at a designated time in the future. . . . Wheat and cotton have become as much gambling tools as chips on the farobank table. The property of the wheat grower and the cotton grower is treated as though it were a "stake" put on the gambling table at Monte Carlo. The producer of wheat is compelled to see the stocks in his barn dealt with like the peas of a thimblerigger, or the cards of a three-card-monte man. Between the grain-producer and loaf eater, there has stepped in a "parasite" between them robbing them both.

Senator William D. Washburn (D-Minn),
before Congress, July 11, 1892

KEY TERMS

Acapulco trade
arbitrage
basis
broker
cash price
Clearing Corporation
contango market
crack
crush
daily price limit
day trader
deck
delivery month
expectations hypothesis
full carrying charge
  market

futures commission
  merchant
good faith deposit
hedger
intermarket spread
intercommodity spread
intracommodity spread
inverted market
limit order
mark to the market
market order
market variation call
normal backwardation
open interest
open outcry
outtrade

pit
position trader
price discovery
price risk
processor
scalper
speculator
spot price
stop order
stop price
Tapioca City
Unmatched Trade
  Notice

The futures market is a very useful, and very misunderstood, part of our economic system. It enables farmers, businesses, financial institutions, and the managers of investment portfolios to lessen **price risk,** the risk of loss because of uncertainty over the future price of a commodity or financial asset. As with options, the two major market participants are the **hedger** and the **speculator,** with the former transferring some price risk they bear to the latter.

Futures contracts trade on a variety of assets, including grains, petroleum products, precious metals, and cattle, among others. Financial futures, like those traded on Treasury bonds, stock indexes, and foreign currencies are an extremely popular and fast-growing segment of the futures market. While this chapter introduces them, the primary discussion of financial futures is in Chapters 9 through 12.

First we look at the role of futures markets in the financial system. Then we will see how the trading system functions, followed by a review of basic principles of futures contract pricing.

THE CONCEPT OF FUTURES CONTRACTS

What Futures Are

Futures contracts are promises; the person who initially sells the contract promises to deliver a quantity of a standardized commodity to a designated delivery point during a certain month called the **delivery month.** The other party to the trade promises to pay a predetermined price for the goods upon delivery. 'buyer of contract'

> A futures contract is a promise to buy or to deliver a certain quantity of a standardized good by a specific date.

See p. 18

There are some analogies between futures contracts and options contracts. Both involve a predetermined price and contract duration. But an option is precisely that: an *option.* The person holding the option has the *right*, but not the obligation, to exercise the put or the call. If an option has no value at its expiration, the option holder will normally allow it to expire unexercised. With futures contracts, a trade *must* occur if the contract is held until its delivery deadline. Futures contracts do not "expire" unexercised. One party has promised to deliver a commodity that another party has promised to buy.[1]

For instance, a trader may purchase a July soybean contract at the Chicago Board of Trade. The purchase price might be $6.22 per bushel. This contract calls for the delivery of 5000 bushels of No. 2 yellow soybeans to a specially designated regular warehouse at an approved delivery point by the last business day in July. Upon delivery, the purchaser of the contract must pay $6.22 for each of the 5000 bushels, or a total of $31,100. If the current price (called either the **spot price,** or the **cash price**) for soybeans is greater than $6.22, the purchaser of the contract will profit. A spot price of $6.33, for instance, results in a profit of 11 cents on each of 5000 bushels, or $550. On the other hand, if the spot price were only $6.15, the buyer would lose $0.07 per bushel, or $350.

Alternatively, a speculator may anticipate that long-term interest rates are going to rise. This means that the price of treasury bonds will fall. One contract of treasury bonds calls for the delivery of $100,000 face value of bonds that have at least 15 years until their maturity. Because the speculator thinks the price of the bonds will fall, he or she might sell a futures contract at a price of 93, thereby promising to deliver $100,000 face value of these bonds at a price of 93% of par, or $93,000. If the value of the bonds subsequently drops to 92.5% of par, the speculator gains 0.5% of $100,000, or $500.

An important idea to keep in mind with futures is that the purpose of the contracts is not to provide a means for the transfer of goods. Stated another way, property rights to real or financial assets cannot be transferred with futures contracts. Futures contracts do, however, enable people to reduce some risks they assume in their business.

▌ Property rights cannot be transferred with futures contracts.

Most futures contracts are eliminated before the delivery month. This is analogous to the exercise of stock options. People who buy puts or calls do not usually intend to exercise them; valuable options are sold before expiration day. A speculator who is long a corn futures contract does not want to take delivery of 5000 bushels of the commodity. It also may be that a farmer who has hedged by selling a contract prefers to sell the wheat locally rather than deliver it to an approved delivery point. In either case the contract obligation can be satisfied by making an offsetting trade, or "trading out" of the contract. The speculator with a long position would sell a contract, which

---

[1]As we will see, it is also possible for one or both parties to the trade to transfer their half of the promise to someone else via an offsetting trade.

would cancel the long position. The farmer with a short position would buy. Both individuals would be out of the market after these trades.

Why We Have Futures Contracts

Perhaps no other part of the financial marketplace has received as much scrutiny as the futures market. Unlike other markets where tangible items change hands (stock certificates, diamonds, real estate), the participants in the futures market deal in promises. A trader can buy or sell thousands of bushels of wheat or tons of soybean meal and have absolutely no intention of ever growing the commodity or taking delivery of it. In fact, fewer than 2 percent of the commodities underlying all futures contracts are ever actually delivered! The quantity of a commodity as represented by the total number of futures contracts sometimes exceeds the available supply world-wide. These facts give a clue why the commodity markets are frequently attacked by would-be market reformers.

Let's look at an example of how the futures market benefits a specific group of people: college students. Many graduating seniors buy themselves a class ring, often made of gold. Rings are typically ordered months before graduation. When ordering, buyers want a firm price quotation from the manufacturer; they do not want to hear "it depends on the price of gold when we make your ring". A company like Jostens or Balfour can lock in the price they have to pay for gold by appropriate trades in the futures market. Because the firm wants the gold, they *buy* contracts, promising to pay a set price for the gold when it is delivered. A gold mining company, on the other hand, would *sell* contracts, promising to deliver the gold.

I'm not a gambler. I'm not in a crapshoot . . . I'm a speculator. Here's the difference. In gambling, you create the risk. In speculating, you assume the risk.

Lee Stern
Owner of the Chicago Sting Soccer Team and member of the CBOT

Assume a futures trade occurs at a price of $475.50 per ounce, with delivery set for December. There are 100 troy ounces[2] of gold in one contract. This means that the mining company will deliver 100 ounces and receive $47,550 for them, regardless of the price of gold at delivery time. The suppliers of gold know their ultimate selling price, and the manufacturers of the rings knows their major material cost. If these two companies were not able to lock in the future price of gold, the price to the consumer would be

---

[2]A troy ounce weighs 9.7 percent more than a standard (avoirdupois) ounce.

significantly higher to account for the added price risk faced by both the miner and the manufacturer.

Unfortunately, there are still influential people who share the views Senator Washburn expressed in the quotation at the beginning of this chapter. They are in the minority. The commodity exchanges are continually adding new products, and the number of people and organizations who find useful opportunities with futures is increasing. The basic function of the commodity futures market is to transfer risk from some businessperson (the hedger) to someone who is willing to bear it (the speculator). The speculator assumes this risk because of the opportunity for profit. We will discuss these people in greater detail later.

Ensuring the Promise is Kept

A reasonable question is "What happens if someone decides not to pay for the commodity as promised or if a particular farmer is unable to deliver the wheat?" If it were possible to back out of the trade without fulfilling your part of the promise, the futures exchanges would die a quick death. People would lose confidence in the system, and it would not be attractive to either hedgers or speculators. Eliminating this uncertainty is the role of the **Clearing Corporation.**

Each exchange has a clearing corporation that performs a critical duty: ensuring the integrity of the futures contract. Although trades in the pit occur between two specific individuals, the trades actually become sales to or by the Clearing Corporation. By interposing itself between buyer and seller, the Clearing Corporation becomes a party to every trade.[3]

The clearing corporation ensures the integrity of each futures contract by interposing itself between each buyer and seller.

Futures contracts are promises, and promises must be kept. A trader's account may fluctuate in value by more than a million dollars daily. Misfortune or incompetence sometimes forces a member into bankruptcy, yet that member's positions still are promises with other exchange members.

The Clearing Corporation assumes the responsibility for those positions when a member is in financial distress. If this were not so, the integrity of the trading system would break down, and members would tend to trade only with other members who were financially strong. In such a situation it is likely that prices at the exchange would become less competitive.

You cannot overstate the value of a sound clearing system at a commodities exchange. The Chicago Mercantile Exchange publishes a short document

---

[3]This is the same function performed by the Options Clearing Corporation.

entitled "The Financial Safeguard System of the Chicago Mercantile Exchange." One section of this paper deals with financial integrity of the marketplace and reads in part as follows.

> The accounts of individual members and non-member customers doing business through the facilities of the CME must be carried and guaranteed by a clearing member. *In every matched transaction executed through the Exchange's facilities, the Clearing House is substituted as the buyer for the seller and the seller for the buyer.* The Clearing House is an operating division of the Exchange and all rights, obligations and/or liabilities of the Clearing House are rights, obligations, and/or liabilities of the CME. Clearing members assume full financial and performance responsibility for all transactions executed through them and positions they carry. The Clearing House, dealing exclusively with clearing members, holds each clearing member accountable for every position it carries regardless of whether the position is being carried for the account of an individual member, for the account of a non-member customer or for the clearing member's own account. Conversely, as the contraside to every position, the Clearing House is held accountable to the clearing members for performance on all open positions.

Because of the possibility that the collective members of the Clearing Corporation might have to absorb large losses due to the default of one or more members, stringent financial conditions are a condition of membership. These requirements are strictly enforced. **Good faith deposits** (or performance bonds)[4] are required from every member on every contract to help ensure that members have the financial capacity to meet their obligations should things not go their way.

▌The clearing corporation guarantees the integrity of the contracts trading within the jurisdiction and bylaws of the exchange.

Let us turn now to a discussion of how a futures contract is established on the exchanges.

MARKET MECHANICS

Types of Orders

See p. 27-28

A broker in commodity futures is called a **futures commission merchant (FCM).** It is important that there be no misunderstanding between the FCM

---

[4]In practice, the good faith deposit is usually called a margin deposit, or margin requirement. As with the margin requirement on certain stock option spreads, this use of the term *margin* does not imply that money is borrowed or that interest is paid.

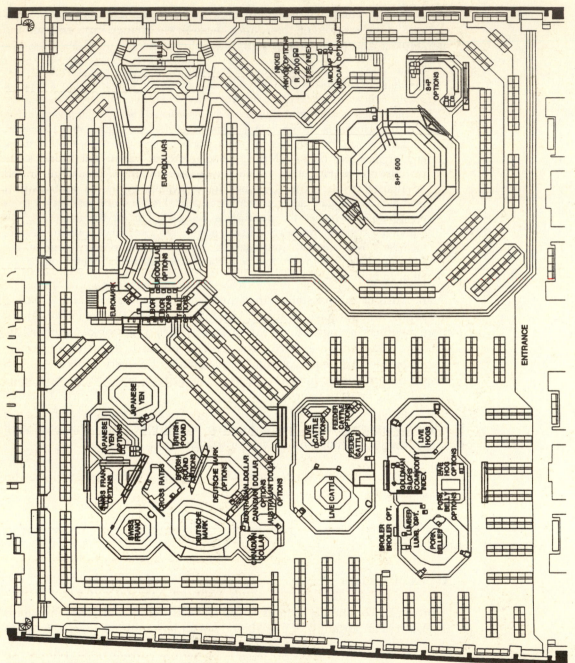

Figure 8-1 Trading Floor at the Chicago Mercantile Exchange
SOURCE: Chicago Mercantile Exchange.

and the individual who places an order. When placing an order, the client should specify the type of order, because each type involves different responsibilities and instructions. The simplest order is a **market order.** This instructs the broker to execute a client's order at the best possible price at the earliest opportunity. For instance, the price board may show the last price for soybeans at 530 ($5.30 per bushel), and the broker may observe that this commodity is trading at "9½ to ¾." This means that there are bids to purchase soybeans at 529½ and that there are sellers of soybeans at 529¾. A client placing a market order to buy is instructing the broker to buy at the best available price, so the broker would likely buy at 529¾. The broker could offer to pay 531 and be certain of attracting attention in the pit and getting the order filled, but this would not be in the client's best interest and would be inappropriate broker behavior.

Ex   With a **limit order,** the client specifies a time and a price. For instance, the order might be to sell five December soybeans at 540, good until canceled. Here the client will accept a selling price of $5.40 per bushel or more, but no less. "Good until canceled" indicates that this is an open order, and that the broker is to execute the order whenever a price of 540 or better can be obtained, even if that price does not occur until weeks from now. Instead of a good-until-canceled instruction, the client might have specified "for the day." This means that if the order cannot be filled during trading hours today, the order is canceled, and the client would have to enter a new order to sell the commodity at a later date.

A third, very useful type of order is a **stop order.** A stop order becomes a market order when the **stop price** is touched during trading action in the pit. Stop orders, when executed, close out an existing commodity position. A stop order to buy would be placed by someone with an existing short position; a stop order to sell would be placed by persons with a long position.

Ex   A person using a stop order to buy might be a short seller who wants protection against large losses due to rising commodity prices. A stop order to buy three September soybeans at 533 means that if the price of soybeans advances to $5.33 per bushel, the broker is to buy three contracts at the best available price (which may be higher than 533).

Ex   Another speculator might place a stop order to sell at 528. This would mean that if the price of September soybeans falls to $5.28, then "sell my soybeans and get me out of the market." This person could be minimizing losses or protecting an existing profit. Note that a person with a long position always places the stop price below the current price, while a person with a short position does the opposite.

With a "buy stop," the stop price is below the current price. With a "sell stop," the stop price is above.

Protecting profits is a very important use of a stop order, although few individuals make use of stop orders for this purpose. Suppose someone bought five September soybean contracts at 520 and they now trade at 530. Each contract is 5000 bushels; when beans advance 10 cents per bushel, the owner of five contracts has a profit of $2500 in their account. To protect most of this profit, the speculator might place a stop order at 528. If prices fall to this level, the speculator will be traded out of the market and most of the profit preserved. If, instead, soybeans rise to 533, the stop price can be moved, perhaps to 531, thus helping to ensure another $750 in profits. Moving a stop price up behind a rising commodity leaves your profit potential untouched but reduces your downside risk.

It is important to remember that stop orders become *market* orders when the commodity (or financial instrument) trades at the stop price. Unlike a limit order, where the person placing the order knows that a trade, if it occurs, will be at a certain price or better, the person using a stop order *is not certain* of trading at the stop price. When the stop is touched, this gives your broker instructions to trade out of the contract immediately at the going price, which may be more or less than the stop price. In a fast market, prices can change very quickly, so the price realized via the stop order may be substantially different than the stop price.

▌The three primary types of orders are market orders, limit orders, and stop orders.

Ambience of the Marketplace

The visitor to a commodity exchange is often struck by the apparent confusion in the exchange. Trades occur by **open outcry** of the floor traders, meaning that offers to buy and sell are called out by the traders. There is no standing in line or computerized order entry; traders stand in a sunken area called the **pit** and bark their offers to buy or sell at certain prices to others within the trading circle.

Besides spoken offers, traders use a series of hand signals to signal their wishes concerning quantity, price, and whether they wish to buy or to sell. Figure 8-2 shows some of these signals for Treasury bond futures.

Only members of the exchange are allowed in the trading pit itself. There are 1402 full members of the Chicago Board of Trade; a full membership gives the right to trade in any of the commodities at the exchange. There are also 725 associate members, with more limited trading privileges, and 200 holders of trading permits, which allow trading in a single commodity. The price of a full membership varies and can fluctuate widely. As an example, a full membership at the Chicago Board of Trade sold for $530,000 on October 6, 1987. The first sale of a seat after the market crashed on October 19th was on October 29th at a price of $321,000. On July 15, 1993, a seat sold for $400,000.

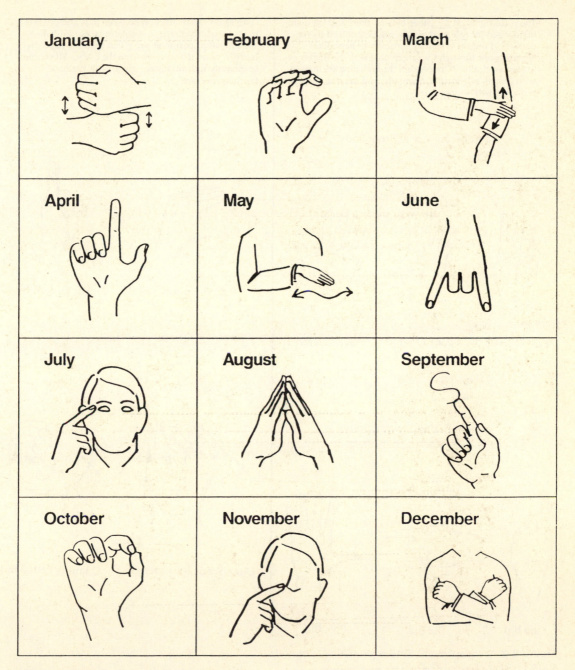

Figure 8-2 Treasury Bond Trading Signals
SOURCE: Chicago Board of Trade.

The price signalled for either bids or offers and the quantity desired for sale or purchase are determined by the number of fingers extended vertically or horizontally. Numbers one through five are quoted with the fingers extended vertically. Numbers six through nine are quoted with fingers extended horizontally, and the number zero is quoted with a closed fist.

Once again, the distinction between bids and offers is made by which direction the palm faces. IMPORTANT: All price quotes are given with the hand directly in front of and away from the body. All volume or quantity indications are given with the hand touching the face.

Palm Facing Away From Body

Two Offered   Four Offered   Five Offered

Call Option   Put Option

Palm Facing Toward Body

One Bid   Six Bid   Five Bid

Quantity of 100 Offered   Quantity of 100 Bid

Figure 8-2 Treasury Bond Trading Signals *(Continued)*
SOURCE: Chicago Board of Trade.

Many newcomers to the exchange choose to lease a membership from someone while trying to develop the expertise and capital to warrant getting their own membership. At the Chicago Mercantile Exchange, it cost about $800 per month in late 1987 to lease a seat.[5]

Next to each trading pit is a raised structure called a *pulpit*, where representatives of the exchange's Market Report Department enter all price changes into the price reporting system. The walls surrounding the trading area are covered with a massive electronic wallboard, which reflects price information about the commodities being traded. Current prices, as well as the two previous prices, are shown, with the high and low prices at which a particular contract has traded during its life. This wallboard also powers a network of price information to which investors and brokerage firms subscribe around the world.

Hundreds of order desks, where telephone/teletype personnel from member firms receive orders from clients and relay order confirmations, line the perimeter of the exchange. Most telephone clerks tape their conversations to protect themselves against alleged order errors. There are approximately 1200 work stations at the Chicago Mercantile Exchange, and 153,600 telephone lines.

The Chicago Board of Trade building houses more computer screens than any other building in the world except NASA headquarters. There is so much activity within the building that in the history of the exchange it has seldom been necessary to turn on the heat!

Visitors to any of the exchanges will note the colorful display of trading jackets worn by people on the trading floor. Exchange policy requires every employee to wear either a business suit or a trading jacket. The Chicago Mercantile Exchange provides red jackets to any member who desires one, and for a nominal fee will provide a freshly laundered one every Wednesday. At all exchanges, brokers from a particular firm have the option of wearing some distinctive jacket color to make it easier for their messenger and clerical people to locate them. At the Chicago Board of Trade, yellow jackets are worn by all messenger people, royal blue signifies a telephone/teletype person, price reporting supervisors wear tan, and dark brown jackets are worn by price reporters.

For certain commodities, there are designated areas within the pit for the trading of a particular delivery month. The pit itself is either octagonal or polygonal, with steps descending into the center. The edge of the pit is approximately waist high to an observer outside. Each trader in the pit wears a large badge containing a two- or three-letter (up to four at the Merc) personal identification code and an indication of which firm he or she works for (or clears trades through—more on this later).

---

[5]Exchanges sometimes impose restrictions on seat leasing. The Chicago Board of Trade, for instance, stopped this practice during 1991 and 1992.

Box 8-1   STARRING IN THE ARTICHOKE PIT

Starring in the artichoke pit

A woman visiting an exchange is studying the action when a floor trader shouts, "Hey guys! Check out that hot commodity!" Trading stops as the pit looks.

Traders have been known to ogle, but they rarely stop trading to do it — except in the cartoon world of Brenda Starr, the famous and beautiful redheaded reporter.

Brenda started trading artichoke futures early this year on an exchange that exists only in the imagination of Mary Schmich, Brenda's alter ego.

Schmich, a feature writer for the *Chicago Tribune*, writes Brenda Starr as a free lancer for Tribune Media Services, which syndicates the comic strip. Schmich decided to put Brenda "in the midst of rough and tumble insanity" by making her a commodities trader after Brenda lost her job as a reporter.

"I'm always looking to put Brenda in certain unexpected settings," she says. "I particularly like to put her in settings that are male dominated."

Male dominated they are, especially in the comic strip. At one point Brenda visits the "Belly Up Bar," where she is reading up on commodities when a man asks her if she's reading a beauty book.

No shrinking violet, Brenda responds, "It's a book on commodities. You know, things like cattle, pork bellies, sexist pigs."

Schmich, who has written Brenda Starr for two years, works with New York-based artist Ramona Fradon, who draws the cartoon from Schmich's scripts.

To prepare for this story, Schmich read books on trading and received a CME tour from a friend, *Wall Street Journal* reporter Jeff Zaslow, who is the model for the strip's Zazley Jeffrow, reporter for the *Easy Street Journal*. The bow-tied Jeffrow is investigating two traders, who have befriended Brenda, for rumor-mongering. The traders are purely fictional, Schmich adds.

Brenda's adventures have appeared in the CME's weekly clip sheet. However, Schmich suggests traders not read the strip too closely because "her grasp of the market is quite shaky." Perhaps, but she's often on the mark. For example, after her first week of trading, Brenda was $50,000 richer but hurt her arm in the pit.

Brenda Starr writer **Mary Schmich** *likes to put Brenda in male areas.*

"I told you trading was risky business," a trader says.

"No more dangerous than war or aerobics," she says.

Schmich says Brenda will return to journalism because — once again proving her accuracy — "Money's not (Brenda's) thing."

Ginger Szala

BRENDA STARR®
By Ramona Fradon and Mary Schmich

Source: Tribune Media Services

Reprinted from *Futures,* 219 Parkade, Cedar Falls, Iowa 50613, June 1987.

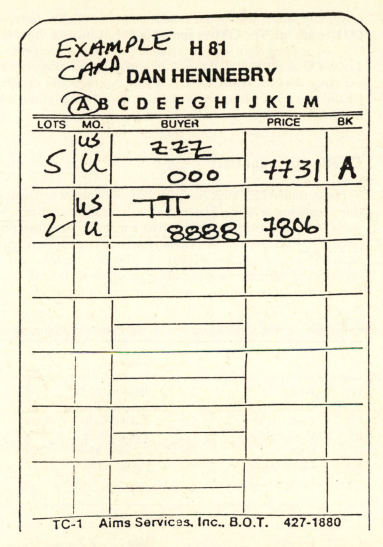

Figure 8-3 A Trader's Card

As in most professions, there is a parochial lingo with which people on the trading floor quickly become familiar. On days when there is little trading activity, people say you can "see through the pit." An unusually large trade by someone who normally trades just a few contracts at a time is called an **Acapulco trade**, presumably because if you are successful with the trade it will finance your trip to exotic places. When traders incorrectly assess the market and lose all their trading capital, they have "busted out," or gone to **"Tapioca City."** A sudden rush of pit activity for no apparent reason is called a "fire drill." A big price move is a "lights out" move. Traders who are riding a winning streak joke about establishing an "O'Hare Spread," referring to O'Hare airport. The O'Hare spread is "Sell Chicago, Buy Mexico."

The trading floor will occasionally observe a moment of silence from 11:00 a.m. until 11:01. This will happen when a long-time member of the exchange dies, or when there is a national or world disaster (such as the Challenger space shuttle explosion or the Chernobyl nuclear power plant accident).

Creation of a Contract

Suppose trader ZZZ buys five contracts of September Treasury Bonds from Dan Hennebry at $77^{31}/_{32}$. The trading unit for Treasury bonds is $100,000 par value of U.S. Treasury bonds that have a maturity of at least fifteen years. The price of $77^{31}/_{32}$ means $77^{31}/_{32}$ *percent of par*, or $77,968.75. A price change of $^{1}/_{32}$ would be the equivalent of $31.25. The two traders confirm their trade verbally and with the hand signals appropriate to the U.S. Treasury bond pit. Each of them then fills out a card recording this information. (See Figure 8-3,

TABLE 8-1   COMMODITY SYMBOLS AT THE CHICAGO BOARD OF TRADE

			Commodity			
W	Wheat	TY	Treasury Notes	AG	Silver
C	Corn	US	Treasury Bonds	AC	Silver Calls
CY	Corn Calls	CG	T Bond Calls	AP	Silver Puts
PY	Corn Puts	PG	T Bond Puts	S	Soybeans
O	Oats	SM	Soybean Meal	CZ	Soybean Calls
MX	Major Mkt Index	BO	Soybean Oil	PZ	Soybean Puts

	Delivery Month				
	Current Year:				
F	January	K	May	U	September
G	February	M	June	V	October
H	March	N	July	X	November
J	April	Q	August	Z	December
	Following Year:				
A	January	E	May	P	September
B	February	I	June	R	October
C	March	L	July	S	November
D	April	O	August	T	December

Source: Chicago Board of Trade *Commodity Trading Manual*

p. 185, for an example.) One side of the card is blue, where one records purchases. The other side is red and is for sales. Each commodity has a symbol, and each delivery month has a letter code. These symbols for commodities traded at the Chicago Board of Trade are listed in Table 8-1. On Dan Hennebry's card, we see his notation that he sold five contracts of September U.S. Treasury bonds at a price of 77$\frac{31}{32}$ to trader ZZZ at firm OOO. The letter A is circled and written in at the far right of the card. This is the time block at which the trade occurred. The first thirty minutes of trading is block A, the second thirty minutes block B, and so on until the close of trading. Normally a trader will either circle the letter or write it in, but not both. The time block helps to ensure that orders are correctly matched during the clearing process. This card also shows a second, independent trade to TTT for two contracts of September T-Bonds at a price of 78$\frac{6}{32}$.

At the conclusion of trading, each trader submits their cards (called their **deck**) to their clearinghouse, where all the cards are matched up and errors identified. The role of the clearing operation is crucial to a well-functioning exchange, and is discussed shortly. First, let's look at the principal players in the futures market.

MARKET PARTICIPANTS

There need to be two types of participants in order for a futures market to be successful: hedgers and speculators. Without hedgers the market would not exist, and there would be no economic function performed by speculators.

Hedgers

In the context of the futures market, a hedger is someone engaged in some type of business activity where there is an unacceptable level of price risk. For instance, a farmer must decide each winter what crops to put in the ground in the spring. The farmer knows about such things as crop rotation but still may face a decision between soybeans and wheat, for instance. To a large extent, the welfare of the farmer's family or business depends on the price of the chosen commodity. If the prices are consequently high, the farmer will earn a fair profit on the crop. Should prices be low because of overabundance or reduced demand, prices may fall to such a level that operating costs cannot be recovered. To reduce this risk, the farmer may choose to hedge in the futures market. Farmers transfer the risk they are unwilling to bear to the speculators who are willing to bear it.

Hedgers transfer price risk to speculators who are willing to bear it.

In March, for instance, September soybeans might be selling for $5.80. Assume the farmer finds this price attractive, because it provides for a reasonable profit level and eliminates the price risk associated with growing the commodity. The farmer can hedge the price risk by promising to sell all or part of the crop through the futures market to someone who is willing to pay $5.80 per bushel for it. As long as the farmer grows the crop and delivers it, he or she will receive the agreed-upon $5.80 per bushel.

It is important to recognize that the farmer cannot eliminate the risk of a poor crop through the futures market; only price risk can be eliminated. Crop insurance may perhaps protect against such an eventuality, but the futures market cannot.

The futures market provides no protection against crop failure.

With agricultural futures the hedger normally goes short in the futures market, because the farmer wants to deliver something. The farmer promises to deliver, with the speculator going long (promising to pay). It is also possible for a hedger to go long to protect some economic interest. Consider the manufacturer of college class rings who must quote prices to upcoming graduates all across the country in early fall for spring delivery of the rings. Should the price of gold rise dramatically after the price quotation on the rings, the manufacturer could see the entire profit eroded. This risk could be hedged by the manufacturer going long sufficient gold contracts to guarantee a supply of gold at reasonable prices. This is a *long hedge* or a *buying hedge*.

Processors

Another market participant is closely allied with the hedger, but is important enough to consider separately. Some people earn their living by transforming certain commodities into another form. A good example is the soybean **processor** who buys soybeans and crushes them into soybean meal and soybean oil. By themselves, soybeans are not particularly useful. Before they can be fed to animals or used as flour they must be ground into meal. The oil from crushing beans is used in salad dressings and in industrial applications.

A common activity of the soybean processor is putting on a **crush.** When the processor discovers a profit margin that is acceptable, this profit can be locked in by appropriate activities in the futures market. Consider the following example.

The processor knows or observes this information:

1. 1 bushel of soybeans weighs 60 pounds; the processor knows that each bushel produces

---

47 lb meal
11 lb oil
2 lb water

---

2. 1 futures contract of <u>soybeans</u> is 5000 bushels, priced in <u>cents/bu.</u>
   1 futures contract of <u>soy meal</u> is 100 tons, priced in $/ton.
   1 futures contract of <u>soy oil</u> is 60,000 pounds, priced in <u>cents/lb.</u>
3. The morning's *Wall Street Journal* lists these prices for the three commodities:

1 ton = 2,000 lbs.

cents/bu.	May beans	654¾ ÷ 100 cents = $6.5475 /bu.
cents/lb.	July soy oil	19.96
$/ton	July soy meal	196

The primary statistic the processor wants to learn is the profit margin implied in these prices. Because the processor uses beans as a raw material and sells oil and meal as finished products, "<u>putting on a crush</u>" involves <u>buying beans, selling oil, and selling meal in the futures market.</u>

One bushel of beans costs $6.5475 (from prices above).

$$\text{meal} = \frac{\$196 \text{ } cents}{one \text{ ton}} \times \frac{1 \text{ ton}}{2000 \text{ lb}} = \$0.098/\text{lb}$$

$$\frac{\$0.098}{one \text{ lb}} \times \frac{47 \text{ lb}}{one \text{ bu}} = \$4.606/\text{bu} \text{ } meal$$

$$\text{oil} = \frac{\$0.1996}{one \text{ lb}} \times \frac{11 \text{ lb}}{one \text{ bu}} = \$2.1956/\text{bu}$$

Cost of raw products purchased:
    soybeans   −$6.5475
Revenue from goods sold:
    from meal $4.6060
    from oil   2.1956
        Total   + 6.8016
    Gross Profit   0.2541

The processor must decide if $0.2541 per bushel is enough profit to cover <u>the other costs</u> of processing, such as electricity, labor, etc. If so, then the processor can lock in this profit by this crush. The last step is to figure out <u>how many</u> contracts of each type of commodity need to be bought or sold. Suppose the processor's crushing capacity is 100,000 bushels of beans.

$$\text{beans: } \frac{100,000 \text{ bushels}}{5000 \text{ bushels/contract}} = 20 \text{ contracts}$$

Decision: BUY 20 contracts soybeans

$$\text{oil: } 100,000 \text{ bu} \times \frac{11 \text{ lb}}{\text{bu}} \times \frac{1 \text{ contract}}{60,000 \text{ lb}} = 18.33 \text{ contracts}$$

Decision: SELL 18 contracts soy oil

$$\text{meal: } 100,000 \text{ bu} \times \frac{47 \text{ lb}}{\text{bu}} \times \frac{1 \text{ contract}}{100 \text{ tons}} \times \frac{1 \text{ ton}}{2000 \text{ lb}} = 23.5 \text{ contracts}$$

Decision: SELL 23 contracts soy meal

Because fractional contracts of futures are not allowed, it is not possible for the processor to hedge perfectly. In general, the processor does not want to promise to deliver more than will be produced, so the number of contracts sold is rounded down. This means that after the processing is complete, there will be a small amount of soy meal and soy oil to be sold in the cash market.

Oil refiners engage in a similar activity called a **crack.** This strategy involves the purchase of crude oil, and the sale of futures contracts in gasoline and #2 heating oil. Precisely the same principles apply in determining a profit margin and locking it in.

Speculators

In order for the hedgers to eliminate an unacceptable price risk, they must find someone who is willing to bear that risk in their place. This person is the *speculator.* The speculator has no economic activity requiring use of futures contracts, but rather finds attractive investment opportunities in the futures market and takes positions in futures in hopes of making a profit rather than protecting one. In certain respects, the speculator performs the same role that insurance companies perform when they prepare policies. The person who buys insurance is unwilling to bear the full risk of economic loss should an accident occur and so chooses to transfer that risk to the insurance company. The insurance company is willing to bear the risk because it feels there is a profit to be made by providing this coverage in exchange for the insurance premium. One pricing theory holds that the hedger does, in fact, pay a premium for such "insurance"; this theory will be examined later, in the section on pricing fundamentals.

In some respects, speculators perform the same role as insurance companies.

As stated above, the speculator normally goes long. As with other types of securities, it is conceptually easier for most investors to envision price rises

Figure 8-4 Good Advice

PRICE

rather than declines, but speculators may also go short if they feel that current prices are too high. Speculators might promise to deliver 5000 bushels of wheat at $4.00 for September delivery if they feel wheat will not sell for that much at delivery time. Most speculators cannot conveniently deliver wheat because they do not grow it; this does not matter, though, since any speculator can quickly exit the market by buying a September wheat contract to cancel the position. The difference in price on the two trades will be the speculator's profit or loss.

Speculators are sometimes classified as either **position traders** or **day traders.** A position trader is someone who routinely maintains futures positions overnight, and sometimes keeps a contract open for weeks. Day traders close out all their positions before trading closes for the day, taking whatever profits or losses they have incurred.

Scalpers

Scalpers are individuals who trade for their own account, making a living by buying and selling contracts in the pit. Studies have shown that the most successful trades made by a scalper are those where the time between the purchase and sale of the contract is less than 30 seconds! Scalpers may buy and sell the same contract often during a single trading day. The value of their account can change drastically on days with wide price swings.

In Figure 8-3 (p. 185) we saw that Hennebry sold 5 contracts of September Treasury bonds to ZZZ. Hennebry is a scalper, and what he wants to do after this trade is buy 5 contracts at a lower price as quickly as he can. Perhaps a customer phones his broker and places a market order to sell 5 September Treasury bond contracts. When this order reaches the pit, the scalpers will all attempt to provide the other side of the trade at a favorable price. Suppose Hennebry gets this trade, and that he buys the 5 contracts at $77^{29}/_{32}$. Having sold five contracts earlier at $77^{31}/_{32}$, this is a gain of $^2/_{32}$ on each of five contracts, so the total dollar profit he just made is

$$ ^2/_{32}\% \times \frac{\$100,000}{\text{contract}} \times 5 \text{ contracts} = \$312.50 $$

Three hundred bucks for a minute's work isn't bad!

Scalpers are also called *locals*, meaning that they are "part of the neighborhood" and someone with whom it is desirable to maintain good relations. Although the business of commodity trading for a living is treacherous, locals place a high emphasis on integrity and accuracy, and these traders will sometimes help each other out of a jam in the pit. Doing so usually involves one or more other locals incurring small opportunity losses through lost trades or channeling business to a trader who has had a bad day. The trader in trouble gets a tick here and a tick there, and hopefully recovers from an otherwise catastrophic loss. (A *tick* is the smallest permissable price change in a particular contract.)

It is important to recognize that the scalpers play a crucial role in the economic functioning of the futures markets. By their active trading with each other, they help keep prices continuous and accurate, which is the hallmark of the U.S. financial system. The futures market would be much less liquid without the scalpers.

THE CLEARING PROCESS

Integrity, honesty, and accuracy are crucial features of a viable trading system. At the Chicago Board of Trade, more than one hundred thousand futures contracts change hands each day, with a total dollar value in the billions. Large sums of money are made and lost each minute in the trading pits; it is imperative that a mechanism be in place to ensure that the promises made are in fact kept, even when large wealth transfers occur. Making sure promises are kept is the role of the clearing process.

Each trader in the pit prepares trading cards on their transactions. The clearing process begins with attempts to match up the cards describing a particular trade. In Figure 8-3, we saw Hennebry's trade of five September U.S. Treasury bond contracts at $77^{31}/_{32}$ to buyer ZZZ of firm OOO. Somewhere in the system there should also be a card from ZZZ showing a purchase from Hennebry with similar terms. When these two cards are matched, a futures contract exists. Besides matching trades, the clearing process performs other functions: guaranteeing trades, supervising the accounting for performance bonds, handling intramarket settlements, establishing settlement prices, and providing for delivery. We now examine each of these functions in greater detail.

Matching Trades

It is the responsibility of each trader on the floor to ensure that his or her deck promptly enters the clearing process. Every trade must be cleared by or through a member firm of the Board of Trade Clearing Corporation. Scalpers make arrangements with a member firm to process their decks each day. Scalpers normally use only one clearing house, and the name of this organization will be displayed on their trading jackets. This name will be the "firm name" entered on trading cards by parties to the scalper's trades.

Brokers are people in the pits who are members of the exchange trading for their own account and for whatever public accounts they choose to accept. They also can be hired by brokerage houses such as Merrill Lynch to handle the firm's transactions on the exchange floor. Brokers also fill out trading cards, but it is common practice for them to submit their cards periodically while trading rather than turning in a deck at the end of the day. A visitor to the exchange is usually amazed with the accuracy with which a person in the pit can sail the heavy cardboard trading cards across the room to their firm's trading desk. This is a distance of ten yards or more, and the desk reporters can usually catch them without leaving their post. This practice is against exchange rules, but it happens on busy days.

While the Clearing Corporation is associated with the Board of Trade, it is an independent organization with its own officers and rules. Some members of the Board of Trade are also members of the Clearing Corporation. These people can clear their own trades, and, for a fee, will sometimes clear trades for non-members. Scalpers might pay $1.50 per trade to a member firm for clearing their trades. All trades must go through the clearing process.

After trading cards are received by a Clearing Corporation member, the information on them is edited and checked by computer. Cards with missing information are returned to the clearing member for correction. The information on valid cards is stored in computer memory. Once all cards have been edited and fed to the computer, the computer attempts to match cards for all trades that occurred on the exchange that day.

Sometimes it is not possible to match all trades exactly. These mismatches, called **outtrades,** result in an **Unmatched Trade Notice** being sent to each clearing member. It is the responsibility of the traders themselves to sort out their outtrades and arrive at a solution to the mismatch. A "price out," where the two traders wrote down different prices for a given trade, sometimes occurs when one person writes down a price that is away from the market, or far away from the current trading range. For instance, soybeans might trade between $5.97 and $6.01 during time block C on a given day. Writing a price of $5.01 rather than $6.01 would result in an outtrade that is easily reconciled by the two participants to the trade. Where the error is not obvious, such as a price of $5.97¼ and a potential match with a price of $5.97½, the two traders often compromise by splitting the difference.

Another mismatch is the "house out," where an incorrect member firm is listed on the trading card. This is normally easy to rectify because there will likely be two trades that do match except for the firm. A "quantity out" occurs when the number of contracts in a particular trade is in dispute. A trader may think he bought eight contracts, while the seller sold eighteen. "Strike out" and "time out" occur primarily with futures options, when errors occur with either the striking price or the delivery month. The worst outtrade is the "sides out," when both cards show the same side of the market, i.e., both indicate buy or both indicate sell. These are difficult to reconcile but do not happen very often.

Despite the reason for the Unmatched Trade Notice, it is the trader's individual responsibility to resolve the error. On the rare occasions when this cannot be done, the dispute may be taken to arbitration with the Clearing Corporation.

At the Chicago Board of Trade, outtrades account for 1 or 2 percent of daily volume. It is estimated that floor brokers lose between 10 percent and 17 percent of gross billings to outtrades. A preliminary run is completed at the Chicago Board of Trade by 5 p.m. each trading day. A listing of unmatched trades is distributed by the clearinghouse to each firm with apparent outtrades from this preliminary run. Many entries on the listing are

Box 8-2   **GOING TO 'COURT'**

Although most out-trades are cleared up between brokers and traders before the market opens, some disputes do go to arbitration.

This isn't a popular step. In fact, only about 30 arbitration hearings took place at the Chicago Board of Trade (CBT) from January to October this year. Only a fraction of those dealt with out-trade disputes.

The general perception from exchange floors seems to be that arbitration committees normally just split the difference between the two sides. Therefore, most traders save time and energy and negotiate their own splits before the markets open. However, exchange officials contend that perception is wrong. They say it's not unusual for arbitration panels to award one member the total amount in question.

For those disputes that can't be settled, complaints must be filed with the exchange arbitration committee. At the CBT, that committee is made up of 20 members appointed by the chairman and approved by the board of directors. It is divided into four groups representing floor locals, floor brokers, members affiliated with brokerage firms and members affiliated with commercial firms. A panel includes one representative from each group and a chairman.

The Chicago Mercantile Exchange (CME) arbitration committee is made up of 70 members divided into financial and agricultural groups. Seven members are asked to the arbitration hearing, although only five sit on the hearing panel. Both the complainant and defendant have the option to disqualify a member of the initial panel.

At the CBT, the member against whom a complaint is lodged has 10 days to make a reply. CBT rules make it mandatory for the member to appear at a hearing.

The CME gives the defendant 21 days to respond to the complaint. No response constitutes that the complainant is right.

At the hearings, panels hear evidence from both sides. Anything, including documentation (time cards, orders, etc.), tape recordings or witnesses can be presented. These hearings can take anywhere from two hours to two days. The panel is not bound by formal rules of evidence during deliberation.

At the CBT, the decision and award made by the committee is final; there are no appeals. If the member who loses the decision fails to make a payment within 30 days, the CBT can suspend his membership and sell his seat to make the payment. Appeals are allowed at the CME but must go through a hearing process first.

There are fees to file a complaint at both exchanges. At the CBT, if the loss is $2,500 or more, the fee is $100; if it is less, the fee is $50. At the CME, the fee to file is $150.

Reprinted from *Futures*, 219 Parkade, Cedar Falls, Iowa 50613. December 1986.

TABLE 8-2 SAMPLE FUTURES TRANSACTIONS

[handwritten: Price is cents/bu. 5000 bu. per contract]

	Trading Account Balances						
	Speculators				Hedgers		
Transaction	A	B	C	D	A	B	C
Day 1: Hedger A decides to sell 1 contract at 530. This is an opening transaction, and a hedger's margin of $1,000 is required.					$1,000		
Speculator A buys this contract, also as an opening transaction, and deposits speculative margin of $2,000.	$2,000						
Settlement price at the end of the day is 527. *[handwritten: $5.27]*					*[+150]*		
Accounts are marked to market. *[handwritten: ($5.30 − 5.27) = .03 × 5000 bu = $150]*	⟨150⟩ $1,850				$1,150		
Day 2: Speculator A takes his loss and gets out of the market by an offsetting transaction. He sells his contract at 527. *[handwritten: CLOSING TRANSACTION]*	takes $1,850 home						
Speculator B buys the contract from Speculator A and deposits margin of $2,000. *[handwritten: OPENING TRANS.]*		$2,000					
Hedger B sells two contracts (opening transaction) at 528 and deposits $2,000.						$2,000	
Speculator C sells one contract (opening transaction) at 528 and deposits $2,000.			$2,000				
Speculator D buys three contracts (opening transaction) from Hedger B and Speculator C, depositing $6,000.				$6,000			
Settlement price at the end of the day is 531.							
Accounts are marked to market. *[handwritten: (#5.31 − 5.27) = .04 × 5000 bu = $200]*		+200 $2,200	⟨150⟩ $1,850	+450 $6,450	⟨200⟩ $950	⟨300⟩ $1,700	
Day 3: Speculator B decides to take his profit and sells his contract at 533 (closing transaction).		takes $2,300 home					
Speculator C elects to get out of the market and buys the contract from Speculator B (closing transaction).			takes $1,750 home				
Settlement price at the end of the day = 532. Accounts are marked to market.				$6,600	$900	$1,600	

[handwritten at bottom: 5.31 − 5.28 = .03 × 5000 = 150]

TABLE 8-2   SAMPLE FUTURES TRANSACTIONS

| | Trading Account Balances | | | | | | |
| | Speculators | | | | Hedgers | | |
	A	B	C	D	A	B	C
Day 4: Hedger C buys 3 contracts at 534 (opening transaction) and deposits $3,000.							$3,000
Speculator D sells 3 contracts (closing transaction) to Hedger C.				takes $6,900 home			
Settlement price at the end of the day = 535. Accounts are marked to market.					$750	$1,300	$3,150
Day 5: Hedger B delivers 2 contracts, receiving $5.28 per bushel and also getting his $2,000 margin back.						takes $54,800 home	
Hedger C receives 2 contracts from Hedger B and pays $5.34 per bushel for them. Hedger C also gets $2,000 of his margin back.							pays $51,400 net
Hedger A delivers 1 contract, receiving $5.30 per bushel and getting his $1,000 margin back.					takes $27,500 home		
Hedger C receives his remaining contract from Hedger A, paying $5.34 per bushel and recovering the other $1,000 of his good faith deposit.							pays $25,700 net

simply clerical errors. Firms have until 8 p.m. to make corrections. Large firms, which clear for many scalpers, sometimes have preliminary run listings several inches thick. Trade checkers attempt to resolve mismatches by checking order cards and calling clearing clerks in other firms. Any mistakes discovered are submitted to the clearinghouse, and another computer run then occurs. According to the market report department at the Chicago Board of Trade, about 90 percent of outtrades are cleared by the second computer run. The remainder must be cleared the following morning by an individual trader involved before the trader begins trading for the day. The exchanges employ outtrade clerks to help in the process of reconciling trades. This job is a stressful one, since outtrades are no fun, and the parties involved are not always in the best of moods. Price disputes are frequently settled by simply splitting the difference.

After resolving all outtrades, the computer prints a daily Trade Register showing a complete record of each clearing member's trades for the day. Within this Register are subsidiary accounts for each customer clearing through the firm. These accounts show all positions in each commodity and delivery month, much like other types of brokerage statements.

Accounting Supervision

The performance bonds deposited by the member firms remain with the Clearing Corporation until each firm closes out its positions by either making an offsetting trade or by delivery of the commodity. When successful delivery occurs, good faith deposits are returned to both parties, payment for the commodity is received from the buyer and remitted to the seller, and the warehouse receipt for the goods is delivered to the buyer.

On a daily basis, the accounting problem is formidable, even when no deliveries occur. Unlike most other types of investment accounts, futures contracts are **marked to the market** every day, meaning that funds are transferred from one account to another based on unrealized (or paper) gains and losses. For instance, if the initial deposit in a member's account is $2000 on a purchase of a soybean contract at $6.00 per bushel, a decline in the price of the soybeans to $5.99 would result in a $50 paper loss, and the member's account would show only $1950 remaining from the $2000 deposit. After each trading day the Clearing Corporation makes these transfers and prepares a summary of positions and cash in the account for each member.

Tables 8-2 and 8-3 present a series of transactions in the soybean commodity futures market and show how the various transactions are handled. The example begins with soybeans selling at $5.30 per bushel. When someone initially establishes a futures position, the trade that does so is called an opening transaction, just as in the options market. Each opening transaction creates half a futures contract. Each closing transaction eliminates half a futures contract. Closing transactions can occur by either delivery

TABLE 8-3   CASH WITH THE CLEARING HOUSE

		Open Interest	Cash Received	Cash Paid	On Hand
Day 1:	Hedger A	+ ½	$ 1,000		$ 1,000
	Speculator A	+ ½	$ 2,000		$ 3,000
		1			
Day 2:	Speculator A	− ½		$ 1,850	$ 1,150
	Speculator B	+ ½	$ 2,000		$ 3,150
	Hedger B	+1	$ 2,000		$ 5,150
	Speculator C	+ ½	$ 2,000		$ 7,150
	Speculator D	+1½	$ 6,000		$13,150
		4			
Day 3:	Speculator B	− ½		$ 2,300	$10,850
	Speculator C	− ½		$ 1,750	$ 9,100
		3			
Day 4:	Hedger C	+1½	$ 3,000		$12,100
	Speculator D	−1½		$ 6,900	$ 5,200
		3			
Day 5:	Hedger B	−1		$54,800	−$49,600
	Hedger C	−1	$51,400		$ 1,800
	Hedger A	− ½		$27,500	−$25,700
	Hedger C	− ½	$25,700		0
		0			

At the end of Day 5, all positions have been eliminated (open interest is zero) and all cash has been disbursed from the clearing house.

---

of the commodity or by an offsetting trade. A short seller, for instance, can get out of the market by buying an identical contract or by delivering the promised commodity.

Open interest is a measure of how many futures contracts in a given commodity exist at a particular time. This is the same idea as exists with stock options. There is no set number of option or futures contracts. When someone writes an option, they create a new contract. Similarly, when someone decides to go short a futures contract, they have created a new contract. The number of futures "promises" can increase or decrease every day, depending on the relative proportion of opening and closing transactions.

Open interest increases by one every time two opening transactions are matched and decreases by one every time two closing transactions are matched. If a trade involves a closing transaction by one participant and an opening transaction by the other, then open interest will not change: the number of "promises" remains unchanged, although the players may change. This is a consequence of the fungibility of futures contracts. If Delta Dick owes $10 to Gabby Gamma, and Gabby Gamma owes $10 to Thaddeus Theta, then Gabby Gamma does not need to be in the picture: the Clearing Corporation can close her out and instruct Delta Dick to pay Thaddeus Theta. The clearing house maintains information about open interest and publishes these figures in the financial pages daily. Large open interest figures are desirable to ensure a competitive market.

Open interest is different from trading volume. A single futures contract might be traded often during its life. A bank that hedges interest rate risk by buying T bond futures might keep this position for several months. But the speculators who take the other side of this trade might exchange their half of the promise 100 times before the delivery date.

Figure 8-5 is an extract from the Monday, March 29, 1993, *Wall Street Journal.* Look at the listing for soybeans at the Chicago Board of Trade (CBT). At the end of the listing we see that open interest is 137,403, which is up 423 from the previous day. Trading volume for the previous Friday is estimated[6] at 27,000; the volume Thursday was 51,729.

When people leave the market by an offsetting trade, their profit or loss comes from the gains or losses that have been posted to their account each day after trading. In Day 1 of Table 8-2 (pp. 196–97), we see Speculator A buy a contract at $5.30 per bushel. Instead of advancing, the price of soybeans went down the following day. This speculator chose to "take his lumps" and get out of the market. The broker was able to sell his contract at $5.27. This $0.03 per bushel loss is incurred on each of the 5000 bushels represented by a single soybean contract, so the speculator loses $150. Although the initial good faith deposit was $2000, only $1850 goes back home.

Another important point is illustrated by the activities on Day 5. Hedger C receives 10,000 bushels of beans from Hedger B. When Hedger B entered the market, he sold beans for 528. Hedger C, however, agreed to pay 534. Because Hedger C pays more than Hedger B receives does not mean there is something wrong with the market or that there is a "parasite," to use Senator Washburn's words. All market participants perform exactly as promised, and by the end of Day 5 we see that everything nets out exactly to zero. Open interest is also zero after the last closing transaction occurs.

Intramarket Settlement

On rare occasions, commodity prices move so much in a single day that good faith deposits for many members are seriously eroded even before the day

---

[6]It usually takes a day to accurately determine volume because of the need to resolve outtrades.

FUTURES PRICES

Friday, March 26, 1993

Open Interest Reflects Previous Trading Day.

GRAINS AND OILSEEDS

CORN (CBT) 5,000 bu.; cents per bu.

	Open	High	Low	Settle	Change	Lifetime High	Lifetime Low	Open Interest
May	229	229¼	228	228¾	....	284¾	218¼	80,653
July	235¾	235¾	234½	235¼	....	286	225	111,924
Sept	239½	239¾	238¾	239¼	....	271½	230½	20,420
Dec	245¼	245½	244¼	245	- ½	268½	233¾	41,842
Mr94	251¾	252	250½	252	....	254¾	240½	3,282
May	254½	255	254½	255	- ½	257½	248¼	721
July	257¾	259	257½	259	....	327	252	1,057
Dec	247½	248½	247¼	248½	....	253½	246	300

Est vol 32,000; vol Thur 57,693; open int 260,199, +5,850.

OATS (CBT) 5,000 bu.; cents per bu.

	Open	High	Low	Settle	Change	Lifetime High	Lifetime Low	Open Interest
May	138½	139	137¼	138¾	+ ¾	177¼	126	4,614
July	138	138½	136¾	138¼	+ ¾	163½	129½	2,214
Sept	138	138	137¼	138¼	+ ¾	156	133¾	267
Dec	139	139	138½	139¾	+ ¼	159	134¾	1,004

Est vol 750; vol Thur 1,263; open int 8,124, -28.

SOYBEANS (CBT) 5,000 bu.; cents per bu.

	Open	High	Low	Settle	Change	Lifetime High	Lifetime Low	Open Interest
May	588	589	585¼	587½	+ ¾	668½	546	48,163
July	594	595	590¼	592¾	+ ¾	671	551	52,098
Aug	596¼	596¾	592¾	595½	+ 1	655	551	5,857
Sept	598	598	594	596½	+ ¼	630	554	4,695
Nov	602½	603	598½	601¼	....	620	555½	22,758
Ja94	611	611	606½	608¾	+ ¼	616¼	576½	2,634
Mar	617	617	613	615¼	- ¼	623	585	413
May	620½	620½	616	619½	- ½	626	612	146
July	620	620	620	621	- ½	629½	600	192
Nov	606	606	603	604	- 1	610½	588	403

Est vol 27,000; vol Thur 51,729; open int 137,403, +423.

SOYBEAN MEAL (CBT) 100 tons; $ per ton.

	Open	High	Low	Settle	Change	Lifetime High	Lifetime Low	Open Interest
May	185.20	185.90	184.90	185.80	+ .60	210.00	177.00	25,497
July	186.60	187.00	186.00	186.90	+ .50	208.00	179.00	23,167
Aug	187.80	188.00	186.90	187.80	+ .60	193.50	180.10	4,887
Sept	188.60	189.00	188.00	188.80	+ .80	193.50	181.00	2,981
Oct	189.90	189.90	188.80	189.50	+ .50	194.50	181.70	2,495
Dec	191.80	191.80	191.00	191.70	+ .30	194.00	183.40	3,930
Ja94	191.70	191.70	191.50	191.70	....	193.50	184.80	361
Mar	192.00	192.20	192.00	192.10	- .40	194.00	186.50	164

Est vol 15,000; vol Thur 28,797; open int 63,492, +2,685.

SOYBEAN OIL (CBT) 60,000 lbs.; cents per lb.

	Open	High	Low	Settle	Change	Lifetime High	Lifetime Low	Open Interest
May	20.96	20.98	20.73	20.86	- .11	23.50	18.85	30,521
July	21.25	21.25	21.00	21.16	- .09	23.20	19.15	19,526
Aug	21.35	21.35	21.14	21.21	- .12	23.25	19.29	5,192
Sept	21.35	21.40	21.25	21.28	- .12	23.25	19.40	2,921
Oct	21.60	21.60	21.39	21.47	- .03	22.35	19.55	1,502
Dec	21.67	21.70	21.45	21.64	- .03	23.45	19.76	6,497
Ja94		....	....	21.70	- .03	22.25	21.10	311
Mar		....	....	21.90	- .10	....	....	114

Est vol 15,000; vol Thur 16,675; open int 66,771, +821.

WHEAT (CBT) 5,000 bu.; cents per bu.

	Open	High	Low	Settle	Change	Lifetime High	Lifetime Low	Open Interest
May	349	349¾	341½	342½	- 6¾	375	318	14,693
July	306	306¼	302¾	304¼	- ¾	373	301	22,773
Sept	307½	308	304¾	306¾	- 1¼	353	304¾	3,600
Dec	316½	317	314	315¾	- ¼	360	314	2,702
Mr94	319	319	319	320	+ 1	353	319	113
July	314	314	312½	313	....	325	303½	162

Est vol 11,000; vol Thur 15,650; open int 44,221, +252.

WHEAT (KC) 5,000 bu.; cents per bu.

	Open	High	Low	Settle	Change	Lifetime High	Lifetime Low	Open Interest
May	329¾	331½	328¼	329¼	- ½	350	310¾	10,875
July	300	301	298½	299	- 1	359	298½	9,797
Sept	303	303	301¼	301¾	- ¾	339	301¼	2,812
Dec	311½	311½	310	310½	- 1	342½	310	555

Est vol 4,188; vol Thur 5,927; open int 24,071, -219.

WHEAT (MPLS) 5,000 bu.; cents per bu.

	Open	High	Low	Settle	Change	Lifetime High	Lifetime Low	Open Interest
May	332	333	328½	329½	- 2	372½	310	10,045
July	309½	310½	308	308½	- ½	350½	306½	2,773
Sept	300½	301	299	300¼	....	336	299	823

Est vol 2,912; vol Thur 2,924; open int 13,710, +335.

BARLEY (WPG) 20 metric tons; Can. $ per ton

	Open	High	Low	Settle	Change	Lifetime High	Lifetime Low	Open Interest
May	84.00	84.10	83.70	83.80	- .20	100.50	82.50	1,942
July		....	....	87.10	....	100.70	86.30	919
Oct	91.30	91.50	91.30	91.40	- .10	102.40	90.40	1,420
Dec		....	....	93.50	- .20	96.20	92.50	1,516

Est vol 165; vol Thur 308; open int 5,797, -34.

FLAXSEED (WPG) 20 metric tons; Can. $ per ton

	Open	High	Low	Settle	Change	Lifetime High	Lifetime Low	Open Interest
May	254.00	254.00	252.00	252.00	- 1.50	299.00	251.10	2,490
July	259.00	259.20	257.50	257.50	- 1.50	298.90	255.00	1,072
Oct	264.80	265.20	264.80	265.00	- 1.00	301.80	260.00	1,359
Dec	269.80	269.80	269.60	269.60	- 1.70	300.50	265.40	835

Est vol 240; vol Thur 137; open int 5,756, +16.

CANOLA (WPG) 20 metric tons; Can. $ per ton

	Open	High	Low	Settle	Change	Lifetime High	Lifetime Low	Open Interest
June	334.80	335.00	333.10	333.90	- .90	352.20	278.50	13,327

	Open	High	Low	Settle	Change	Lifetime High	Lifetime Low	Open Interest
Nov	21.91	21.93	21.90	21.93	+ .02	21.95	21.25	1,797
Ja94	21.78	21.79	21.75	21.75	- .05	21.92	21.35	280
Mar	21.80	21.80	21.77	21.77	- .03	21.80	21.35	1,555
May	21.78	21.78	21.78	21.78	- .06	21.90	21.35	353

Est vol 802; vol Thur 1,195; open int 10,871, -446.

COTTON (CTN)-50,000 lbs.; cents per lb.

	Open	High	Low	Settle	Change	Lifetime High	Lifetime Low	Open Interest
May	60.83	61.35	60.65	61.05	+ .23	66.25	52.15	14,358
July	61.75	62.30	61.60	62.05	+ .28	65.80	53.00	11,338
Oct	61.80	62.20	61.60	62.00	+ .23	64.40	54.40	1,915
Dec	60.75	61.20	60.75	60.90	+ .07	64.25	54.60	8,086
Mr94	61.90	62.25	61.80	61.90	- .10	64.00	55.62	929
May		....	....	62.45	- .12	64.50	59.88	131

Est vol 4,000; vol Thur 6,053; open int 36,808, -405.

ORANGE JUICE (CTN)-15,000 lbs.; cents per lb.

	Open	High	Low	Settle	Change	Lifetime High	Lifetime Low	Open Interest
May	87.00	87.90	84.00	84.15	- .75	122.75	69.25	10,573
July	89.25	90.00	87.00	87.35	- .60	130.00	72.50	5,180
Sept	91.60	92.25	90.30	90.35	+ .10	117.25	75.10	1,360
Nov	93.00	94.00	92.00	92.00	- .50	116.75	78.50	898
Ja94	96.00	97.00	95.70	94.80	+ .30	117.00	82.15	811
Mar	97.50	99.50	97.50	97.80	+ 1.80	109.00	84.50	307

Est vol 2,500; vol Thur 1,172; open int 19,172, -191.

METALS AND PETROLEUM

COPPER-HIGH (CMX)-25,000 lbs.; cents per lb.

	Open	High	Low	Settle	Change	Lifetime High	Lifetime Low	Open Interest
Mar	96.20	96.20	95.50	95.50	- 1.65	114.80	92.80	409
Apr	95.85	95.85	95.85	95.65	- 1.60	111.80	94.00	982
May	96.40	96.60	95.85	96.05	- 1.60	112.10	93.70	22,187
June		....	....	96.40	- 1.55	109.60	95.20	1,347
July	97.00	97.25	96.65	96.80	- 1.45	110.70	95.00	8,431
Aug		....	....	97.15	- 1.40	106.70	96.10	233
Sept	97.75	97.90	97.30	97.50	- 1.35	110.10	95.80	4,296
Oct		....	....	97.65	- 1.30	104.30	96.75	240
Nov		....	....	97.90	- 1.30	104.35	97.10	131
Dec	98.70	98.80	98.45	98.25	- 1.30	109.20	97.00	4,583
Ja94		....	....	98.40	- 1.30	104.40	98.00	157
Feb		....	....	98.65	- 1.30	99.20	97.90	101
Mar		....	....	98.90	- 1.30	107.50	98.25	1,291
May	99.50	99.50	99.50	99.45	- 1.25	102.20	99.00	644
July		....	....	100.00	- 1.20	102.95	99.55	396
Sept		....	....	100.55	- 1.15	105.30	99.90	151

Est vol 4,700; vol Thur 4,394; open int 45,586, -394.

GOLD (CMX)-100 troy oz.; $ per troy oz.

	Open	High	Low	Settle	Change	Lifetime High	Lifetime Low	Open Interest
Mar	332.40	332.40	332.40	332.40	- .30	334.50	326.00	0
Apr	332.80	333.40	332.30	332.50	- .30	410.00	325.80	21,711
June	334.40	335.00	334.00	334.20	- .20	418.50	327.10	37,979
Aug	336.00	336.00	335.50	335.50	- .20	395.50	328.50	13,942
Oct		....	....	337.00	- .20	395.00	330.80	2,001
Dec	338.80	339.30	338.70	338.50	- .20	402.80	331.70	14,961
Fb94	340.50	340.50	340.50	340.10	- .10	376.80	333.80	5,910
Apr		....	....	341.70	....	360.00	335.20	3,897
June		....	....	343.20	....	383.50	339.40	2,676
Aug	345.00	345.00	345.00	344.90	....	351.80	341.50	3,085
Oct		....	....	346.70	....	346.00	344.00	1,211
Dec		....	....	348.70	+ .10	383.00	343.00	2,645
Ju95		....	....	355.20	+ .30	352.00	351.00	1,024
Dec		....	....	362.80	+ .30	403.00	358.00	752
Ju96		....	....	371.30	+ .30	370.90	370.90	487
Dec		....	....	380.50	+ .30	382.00	379.60	389

Est vol 28,000; vol Thur 36,304; open int 112,670, +408.

PLATINUM (NYM)-50 troy oz.; $ per troy oz.

	Open	High	Low	Settle	Change	Lifetime High	Lifetime Low	Open Interest
Apr	357.10	357.50	355.50	356.80	- .20	393.00	335.50	2,574
July	356.10	357.00	353.00	355.30	- .70	389.50	334.50	7,342
Oct	355.00	355.00	354.30	354.30	- .70	371.00	336.00	1,791
Ja94		....	....	353.30	- .70	366.00	335.50	352
Apr		....	....	352.80	- .70	348.00	335.00	289

Est vol 1,334; vol Thur 4,378; open int 12,348, +605.

PALLADIUM (NYM) 100 troy oz.; $ per troy oz.

	Open	High	Low	Settle	Change	Lifetime High	Lifetime Low	Open Interest
Mar	110.00	110.00	109.75	109.75	+ .30	120.00	83.00	11
June	108.00	108.45	107.00	108.25	+ .30	117.50	83.00	2,714
Sept	106.00	106.50	106.00	106.00	+ .30	116.00	93.70	358
Dec	105.00	105.00	103.75	103.75	+ .30	114.50	91.85	1,114

Est vol 208; vol Thur 705; open int 4,198, +149.

SILVER (CMX)-5,000 troy oz.; cents per troy oz.

	Open	High	Low	Settle	Change	Lifetime High	Lifetime Low	Open Interest
Mar	372.0	372.0	372.0	371.9	+ 1.3	513.0	351.0	26
Apr		....	....	372.3	+ 1.3	367.0	358.0	1
May	372.0	374.5	371.5	373.2	+ 1.2	473.0	353.5	40,387
July	374.5	376.5	374.0	375.7	+ 1.3	470.5	356.0	22,595
Sept	379.0	379.0	376.5	378.1	+ 1.3	469.0	358.0	4,923
Dec	381.5	382.5	380.0	381.7	+ 1.3	462.0	362.0	10,736
Mr94	384.0	385.5	384.0	385.5	+ 1.3	450.5	366.0	7,210
May	384.0	384.0	384.0	388.0	+ 1.3	435.0	371.0	860
July		....	....	390.7	+ 1.3	406.0	372.5	369
Sept	393.5	393.5	393.0	393.5	+ 1.3	400.5	376.5	332
Dec		....	....	398.3	+ 1.4	414.0	380.0	460

Est vol 13,000; vol Thur 19,307; open int 87,936, +2,293.

SILVER (CBT)-1,000 troy oz.; cents per troy oz.

	Open	High	Low	Settle	Change	Lifetime High	Lifetime Low	Open Interest
Mar		....	....	370.0	+ 2.0	375.0	349.0	0

	Open	High	Low	Settle	Change
Oct	1.985	1.985	1.970	1.980	- .00
Nov	2.130	2.135	2.120	2.130	- .00
Dec	2.290	2.295	2.275	2.280	- .00
Ja94	2.270	2.273	2.260	2.265	- .00
Feb	1.965	1.990	1.960	1.985	+ .00
Mar	1.855	1.860	1.825	1.855	+ .00
Apr	1.820	1.830	1.805	1.830	....
May	1.825	1.850	1.810	1.840	....
June	1.820	1.850	1.820	1.850	....
July	1.830	1.865	1.830	1.865	- .00
Aug	1.850	1.890	1.850	1.890	...
Sept	1.885	1.920	1.885	1.920	+ .00
Oct	1.990	2.010	1.990	2.010	+ .01

Est vol 10,610; vol Thur 14,172; open ir

BRENT CRUDE (IPE) 1,000 net bbls.

	Open	High	Low	Settle	Change
May	18.75	18.80	18.60	18.75	- .0
June	18.81	18.89	18.68	18.83	+ .0
July	18.80	18.87	18.68	18.81	....
Aug	18.72	18.86	18.71	18.82	- .0
Sept	18.83	18.84	18.83	18.82	- .0
Oct	18.80	18.92	18.80	18.84	....
Nov	18.86	18.88	18.86	18.87	+ .0
Dec	18.88	18.88	18.88	18.88	....

Est vol 22,644; vol Thur 21,876; open ir

GAS OIL (IPE) 100 metric tons; $ per

	Open	High	Low	Settle	Change
Apr	174.50	175.25	173.50	173.50	- .5
May	173.25	173.25	171.50	171.50	+ .2
June	171.75	172.00	170.75	170.75	+ .2
July	172.50	172.75	171.75	172.25	+ .7
Aug	174.00	174.75	174.00	174.00	+ .7
Sept	176.50	176.50	175.75	176.00	+ .5
Oct		....	....	178.50	+ .2
Nov		....	....	180.50	+ .2
Dec	182.50	182.50	182.25	182.25	+ .5
Ja94	182.25	182.25	182.00	182.00	+ .5
Feb	179.50	179.50	179.50	180.00	+ .5
Mar	176.00	176.00	176.00	176.50	+ .5
Sep		....	....	175.50	+ .5

Est vol 11,201; vol Thur 6,940; open int 7

INTEREST RATI

TREASURY BONDS (CBT)-$100,00

	Open	High	Low	Settle	Chg
June	110-06	110-06	109-02	109-04	- 41
Sept	108-25	108-25	107-27	107-28	- 41
Dec	107-07	107-14	106-23	106-23	- 40
Mr94	105-30	105-30	105-21	105-21	- 39
June	104-28	104-28	104-20	104-20	- 38
Sept	....	....	....	103-21	- 37
Dec	....	....	....	102-25	- 36

Est vol 350,000; vol Thur 208,146; op in

TREASURY BONDS (MCE)-$50,000;

	Open	High	Low	Settle	Chg
June	109-22	109-30	108-30	108-30	- 34

Est vol 4,700; vol Thur 3,683; open int

TREASURY NOTES (CBT)-$100,000

	Open	High	Low	Settle	Chg
June	111-09	111-09	110-19	110-21	- 24
Sept	109-27	109-27	109-14	109-14	- 25
Dec	108-21	108-21	108-09	108-09	- 25

Est vol 72,000; vol Thur 45,592; open in

5 YR TREAS NOTES (CBT)-$100,00

	Open	High	Low	Settle	Chg
June	110-18	110-19	110-05	10-055	- 17.0
Sept	109-12	109-12	109-04	109-04	- 16.5

Est vol 33,800; vol Thur 19,572; open in

2 YR TREAS NOTES (CBT)-$200,00

	Open	High	Low	Settle	Chg
June	106-19	06-207	06-167	106-17	- 6¼

Est vol 1,000; vol Thur 579; open int 20,

30-DAY FEDERAL FUNDS (CBT)-$5

	Open	High	Low	Settle	Chg
Mar	96.94	96.94	96.93	96.93	- .01
Apr	96.97	96.98	96.97	96.97	- .01
May	96.97	96.97	96.96	96.97	- .02
June	96.95	96.95	96.94	96.94	- .03
July	96.92	96.92	96.91	96.91	- .04
Aug	96.88	96.88	96.88	96.88	- .04
Sept	96.81	96.81	96.80	96.80	- .05

Est vol 555; vol Thur 155; open int 11,2

TREASURY BILLS (CME)-$1 mil.;

	Open	High	Low	Settle	Chg
June	97.00	97.00	96.97	96.99	- .02
Sept	96.84	96.85	96.82	96.83	- .06
Dec	96.47	96.49	96.47	96.49	- .09

Est vol 3,158; vol Thur 1,788; open int 3

LIBOR-1 MO. (CME)-$3,000,000; poin

	Open	High	Low	Settle	Chg
Apr	96.81	96.81	96.80	96.80	- .01
May	96.78	96.78	96.77	96.78	- .01
Jun	96.76	96.76	96.74	96.75	- .03
Jul	96.70	96.70	96.69	96.70	- .02

Figure 8-5 Futures Listing, *WSJ* 3/29/93

*"I can't help thinking how much nicer
it would have been if you'd made your bundle
in gold instead of pork bellies."*

Reprinted by permission of Brenda Burbank, *The Rotarian.*

Figure 8-6 Bringing Home the Bacon

ends. When deemed necessary, the President of the Clearing Corporation may call on members to deposit more funds into their account during the day. This is a **market variation call,** and these funds must be deposited within one hour from the time the call is issued. This procedure also helps to ensure the integrity of commodity futures contracts.

Settlement Prices

In the commodity pits it is difficult to tell precisely what the last trade was when the bell rings to signal the end of the trading day. This is understandable with the traders calling their bids and offers and where other traders in the pit do not always see every trade that occurs. Because all commodity accounts are marked to market at the close of each day, it is essential that a price be established so that funds can be transferred among accounts. The settlement price is analogous to the closing price on the stock exchanges, and it is this figure that will appear in the morning's financial pages. While procedures vary slightly from commodity to commodity, the settlement price is normally an average of the high and low prices during the last minute or so of trading. Establishment of the official settlement price is another of the Clearing Corporation's functions.

Unlike the prices established on most exchanges, many commodity futures prices are constrained by a **daily price limit.** This means that the price of a contract is not allowed to move by more than a predetermined amount each trading day. For instance, if the daily price limit for soybeans is 30 cents, this means that today's settlement price cannot be more than 30 cents higher or 30 cents lower than yesterday's settlement price. Commodities are said to be "up or down the limit" when a big move like this occurs. Trading will simply stop for the day once a limit move has occurred. Sometimes it may take several days for prices to work their way to a new equilibrium price.

The prices of some futures contracts are constrained by daily price limit restrictions.

Delivery

Although the Clearing Corporation interposes itself between every buyer and seller, it never takes or makes delivery of any commodity. It does provide the framework that ensures accurate delivery. Let's look at the delivery procedure for a grain contract at the Chicago Board of Trade.

When a seller decides to deliver, a *Notice of Intention to Deliver* is filed with the Clearing Corporation. This shows the seller's intention to deliver the commodity on the next business day. Delivery can occur anytime during the delivery month, and the first business day before the first day of the delivery month is called *First Notice Day.*

On the day prior to first notice day, each member with long positions in his or her account must submit a Long Position Report to the Clearing Corporation. This document shows all the members' long positions and their date of purchase. This document also must be updated each day during the delivery month. The date when this report is required is known as *Position Day.* On the next day, *intention day,* the Clearing Corporation may assign delivery to the member with the oldest long position in the particular commodity. The price of the delivered commodity is adjusted for quality differentials and any other associated costs such as temporary storage or transportation.

As a rule, speculators and their brokers do not like to handle deliveries. Given that delivery can occur anytime in the delivery month, speculators tend to move out of the market in the few days prior to first notice day.

Delivery procedures vary somewhat among the exchanges, and are quite different when financial futures are involved. At the Chicago Mercantile Exchange, for instance, both buyers *and* sellers of its Treasury Bill contract may initiate delivery, and delivery must occur on a single, predetermined day of the delivery month.

PRINCIPLES OF FUTURES CONTRACT PRICING

In considering what makes a futures contract valuable and what makes the price of the contract fluctuate from day to day, it is important to remember that a futures contract is a promise to exchange certain goods at a future date. You must keep your part of the promise unless you get someone to take the promise off your hands (i.e., you make a closing transaction). The promised goods are valuable now, and their value in the future may be more or less than their current worth. Prices of commodities change for many reasons, such as new weather forecasts, the availability of substitute commodities, psychological factors, and changes in storage or insurance costs. These factors all involve shifts in demand for a commodity, changes in the supply of the commodity, or both.

General principles of futures pricing are included in this chapter. Specific examples of pricing with financial futures are included in Chapters 9, through 11.

There are three main theories of futures pricing:

1. the expectations hypothesis,
2. normal backwardation, and
3. a full carrying charge market.

The Expectations Hypothesis

Remember Senator Washburn's comments about these "fictitious contracts." Of course, the contracts are very real, with brokerage houses and the Clearing Corporation to enforce compliance with the terms of the contract. Because the contract calls for delivery of a specified good in the future, it seems likely that one of the major determinants of the futures contract value is the current value of the commodity in the cash market. This is exactly what we find.

The most simple generalization about this relationship is the **expectations hypothesis.** This states that the futures price for a commodity is what the marketplace expects the cash price to be when the delivery month arrives. If September soybeans are selling in the futures market for $5.00 per bushel, then this means that $5.00 is what the marketplace expects soybeans to sell for in September. There is considerable evidence that the expectations hypothesis is a pretty accurate description of the way things happen. This is a very important fact for the user of the futures market, because it provides an important source of information about what the future is likely to bring. If I want to know what people expect the price of heating oil to be this fall, I can look in the *Wall Street Journal* for the price of a heating oil futures contract and know that this figure is a reliable estimate based on current information.

(Remember that the price for the retail customer would be somewhat higher than the price that a wholesale distributor would pay.)

The information provided through futures prices are so important that one of the major functions of the futures market is normally listed as **price discovery.** Nowhere in finance do people like uncertainty; wherever possible, we seek to resolve the unknown. The futures market serves a useful role when we ponder the price of important commodities at a future date.

For instance, an investor may be interested in knowing what "the market" thinks the price of gold or German Deutschmarks will be a year from now. According to the expectations hypothesis, the best place to look for an estimate is in the financial pages. You simply need to see what a futures contract with a delivery month one year hence settled at yesterday.

We have previously seen that there needs to be a relationship between the price of a commodity in the cash market and the price of that commodity in the futures market. There is a definite relationship among the cash price of a commodity, the various storage costs associated with the commodity, and the futures price.

We know that in a well-functioning marketplace, arbitrage opportunities will not appear often, and that if they do they will quickly be eliminated as people exploit them. Consider the situation where in June, cash corn sells for $2.00 per bushel, the local grain elevator charges 5 cents per bushel per month to store the grain, and an August futures contract sells for $2.15. If these prices were accurate, an arbitrage opportunity would be there for the taking. Simply buy corn in the cash market, sell a futures contract promising to deliver the corn in two months for $2.15 per bushel, store the corn in the elevator for two months, and then arrange for delivery. You would have $2.10 invested in the corn ($2.00 cost plus 10 cents storage costs) and you would receive $2.15 from the Clearing Corporation when you deliver. You have made 5 cents per bushel profit, without taking any risk.

Normal Backwardation

Remember that investors do not like risk and that they will only take a risk if they think they will be properly rewarded for bearing the risk. If the futures price is what people think the cash price will be at delivery time, then why would anyone be interested in speculating? It seems that the hedger can get rid of their price risk without any cost and that the speculator agrees to take the risk off the hedger's back for nothing. This seems improbable in real life.

The idea of **normal backwardation** is attributed to the famous economist John Maynard Keynes. Like much of good economics, the idea is simple and very logical. A hedger who uses the futures market is essentially buying insurance. Price risk is eliminated by locking in a future price that is acceptable. When we obtain insurance we pay for it, because the insurance company could not remain in business if it offered this protection for nothing. Keynes argues that this means that the futures price must be a downward biased estimate of the future cash price. In other words, come delivery time the cash price will actually be somewhat higher than the price predicted by the futures market. This is because the speculator must be rewarded for taking the risk that the hedger was unwilling to bear. The hedger might really believe that the cash price of soybeans in September will be about $5.04, but might also be perfectly willing to take $5.00 per bushel for certain. Though this is less than the anticipated price, the risk that the soybean market might collapse to $4.75 or less is unacceptable. The peace of mind that $5.00 per bushel brings is valuable.

The speculator, on the other hand, has access to the same information as the hedger, and might agree that $5.04 is a good bet for the cash price of beans in September. Remember that one contract of soybeans is 5000 bushels, so if the speculator can promise to pay $5.00 per bushel and turn around and sell them for $5.04, this is a $200 gain. The high leverage associated with futures contracts can make this an impressive rate of return when annualized. On the other hand, prices could take a dive and result in big losses for the speculator (but not for the hedged farmer).

The concept of normal backwardation does not really mean that the expectations hypothesis is wrong. Keynes agrees that the futures market provides useful information about the future. With the logic of normal backwardation, though, we may be able to fine-tune our estimate of future cash market prices.

A Full Carrying Charge Market

Commodities can be bought in the cash market and stored for later consumption. As we have seen, the person who performs the storage function gets a fee for this service. It is necessary to keep grains dry, to protect against fire, to keep the rat population to a minimum, and to provide insurance on the stored commodities. Insurance is necessary to protect against loss of the goods due to tornadoes, floods, fire, and even explosion. Every few years we read of spectacular blow-ups of a grain elevator. The dust and fine seed particles that can get suspended in the air during filling and storage will, under certain circumstances, ignite with a vengeance. A **full carrying charge market** occurs when futures prices reflect the cost of storing the commodity until the delivery month.

In a world of certainty, the futures price P_f is equal to the current cash price P_c, plus the carrying charges C until the delivery month:

$$P_f = P_c + C$$

All participants in the futures market are very concerned with the idea of

basis. Basis is the difference between the futures price of a commodity and the current cash price. Normally, the futures price exceeds the cash price; this is a **contango** market. If the futures price is less than the cash price, the market is called an **inverted market.** As the gap between the futures price and the cash price narrows, we say that the basis has strengthened; basis weakens if the gap gets wider.

To calculate *basis*, subtract the cash price from the futures price.

BASIS = FUTURES PRICE − CASH PRICE

Although we do not live in a world of certainty, the difference in price between a futures price and the cash price is often quite close to the carrying costs between the two points in time. In such a market, this has important implications for the speculator. Suppose in early September we see prices as follows:

Cash price for soybeans = $4.85
Futures prices: Nov. = $4.90
                     Jan. = $4.95
                     Mar. = $5.00

The speculator might be trying to decide between the January and March delivery months. If the speculator wants to go long (thinking that soybean prices will increase), it is wise to buy the near delivery month (January). To go short (anticipating a downturn in prices), it is best to sell the far delivery month (March). Let's see why.

Arbitrage exists if someone can buy a commodity, store it at a known cost, and get someone to promise to buy it later at a price that exceeds the cost of storage. In a full carrying charge market like in this example, the basis must either stay the same or strengthen; it cannot weaken because that would produce an arbitrage situation. In other words, the difference between an August and a September contract could become less than 5 cents, but it should never be more.[7] If it were more, then you could buy August, sell September, pay a nickel storage for one month, and still be a penny per bushel ahead without having taken any risk.

Although there is never certainty in any investment situation, in a full carrying charge market the bullish speculator who buys the near contract can be very confident of one of two things. If the price of soybeans does go up, then August soybeans should rise by more than September beans. If soybean prices fall, then August soybeans should fall less than September beans. In either case, the speculator is better off buying the near delivery month.

---

[7] This assumes that monthly storage costs remain constant. The example also assumes that the arbitrageur can deliver the corn in the right grade as required.

The logic holds true in reverse for the speculator who is bearish: go short the far contract, because it will either fall in value more or rise in value less than the near delivery month.[8]

Reconciling the Three Theories

The three theories of futures pricing are actually quite compatible. The differences in them are somewhat like the chicken and the egg question, in that it may not be easy to decide which comes first. The expectations hypothesis says that a futures price is simply the expected cash price at the delivery date of the futures contract. People know about storage costs and other costs of carry (insurance, interest, etc.), and we would not expect these costs to surprise the market when they are incurred. It therefore seems logical that people would "expect" the futures price to be partially determined by these costs.

The essence of normal backwardation is that the hedger is willing to take a bit less than the actual expected future cash price for the peace of mind that comes with insurance. Because the hedger is really obtaining price insurance with futures, it is logical that there be some cost to the insurance. The hedger might expect a higher price, but be willing to accept a lower price to reduce risk. The full carrying charge market, the futures price reflects the actual cost of storing a commodity until delivery time. This is consistent with the expectations theory.

SPREADING WITH COMMODITY FUTURES

We have previously seen how the risk and return relationship of a stock option position can be altered by the inclusion of one or more other option positions in the portfolio. The same general result is true with futures contracts. Spreading is a type of speculation and involves taking "offsetting" positions in two related commodities or in the same commodity. As with options, spreads have less risk than an outright long or short position in a particular commodity.[9] Also, there may be special margin requirements with commodity spreads, which means that the speculator has to put up a smaller good faith deposit than would be true on two trades made individually.

---

[8] This relationship is less obvious with financial futures. The interest rate yield curve is seldom flat, and this means that the cost of carry varies according to the time span covered. The shape of the yield curve can change in such a fashion that the strategy described above was, in fact, not the best when viewed after the fact.

[9] This is not always true with spreads in the futures market, particularly with old year/new year or intercommodity spreads.

Intercommodity Spreads   *Different commodities*

An **intercommodity spread** involves a long and short position in two related commodities, perhaps corn and live cattle. A speculator might feel that the price of corn is too low relative to the price of live cattle, and that this differential should correct itself in the near future. So, the speculator might sell live cattle (anticipating a price decline) and buy corn (anticipating a price rise). This type of spread is risky, because there is no assurance that your hunch will be correct. It is entirely possible that corn could decline while live cattle prices increased further, in which case you would lose on both investments. For this reason, there is not always a special margin treatment for an intercommodity spread.

Intermarket Spreads

With an **intermarket spread** a speculator takes opposite positions in two different markets. Wheat trades on both the Chicago Board of Trade and on the Kansas City Board of Trade. Any difference in price between these two locations should be based primarily on transportation expenses or other administrative costs.

Some international investment houses routinely spread gold in the cash market between major financial centers. It may be possible to buy gold in Zurich at $350 an ounce and simultaneously sell it in London at $355. If this $5 difference is sufficient to overcome shipping costs, then a person who bought Zurich gold and sold London gold would realize a profit.

Intracommodity Spreads   *Same commodity*

An **intracommodity spread** is also called an *intermonth spread;* it involves taking different positions in different delivery months, but in the same commodity. For instance, a speculator who was bullish on wheat might buy September and sell December. (Remember from the earlier discussion that a bullish speculator would usually buy the near month in a situation like this). These spreads are rather common since they involve a low margin requirement and reduce risk substantially.

An important consideration with these spreads is the difference between a "same crop" spread and a "new crop/old crop" spread. A spread using November and January soybeans would be a same crop spread, because these beans were harvested during the same crop year. Buying July 1994 beans and selling November 1994 beans would be a new crop/old crop spread, and much more risky because the conditions affecting the price of soybeans may be very different next year.

One final thought on commodity spreads involves the extent to which your losses are known or limited. Suppose that in March a speculator reads that September meal sells for $174.60 and that December meal sells for $179.60. The speculator, being bullish, buys a September contract and sells a December contract.

Suppose that in August we see that soy meal has risen (as the speculator had hoped), and that current futures prices are $184.60 for the September contract and $194.60 for the December contract. If the speculator were to close out these two contracts at this point in August, the combined positions would show a loss, even though commodity prices moved in the anticipated direction. On the long side, the contract price rose by $10 per ton, while on the short side the price rose by $15 per ton. Since the speculator was short the December contract, this $15 price rise really translates into a $15/ton loss. Combining this with the $10 per ton gain on the long side yields a net loss of $5 per ton. With 100 tons in a soy meal contract, this means that the combined positions lost $500 even though prices advanced. The reason for this is that the basis on the short position changed adversely relative to the basis on the long position.[10]

Why Spread in the First Place?

It should be obvious that there can be huge gains and losses in the futures market. Some people, including professional commodity traders, are uncomfortable with the magnitude of loss that could occur from a "lights out" move. Acapulco is very nice, but we need to remember that Tapioca City is out there somewhere.

Many people choose to trade the basis rather than simply go long or short a particular futures contract and hope that prices move your way. I may expect the basis to strengthen or to weaken, but in either event my maximum loss is likely to be much less than with a single futures position. Playing the basis involves more than one contract, and this is by definition a spread. Most intracommodity spreads are basis plays.

Intercommodity spreads are not necessarily risk-reducing strategies. In the example earlier, where a speculator sold live cattle and bought corn, it is certainly possible that both contracts could move adversely. Such a spread is closer to two separate speculative positions than to a spread in the stock options sense.

Intermarket spreads are really arbitrage plays based on discrepancies in transportation costs or other administrative costs. When arbitrage is spotted, a spread is the way to take advantage of it: buy in the cheap location and sell where it is dear.

---

[10] This is not something we have to worry about with bull spreads using stock options.

SUMMARY

Futures contracts are promises to buy or to deliver a certain quantity of a carefully defined commodity by a certain date. Futures contracts enable farmers, bankers, or anyone else with economic interests in a particular commodity to hedge price risk. The futures market cannot provide protection against crop failure or against making bad investments.

To ensure the integrity of the contract, all trades are actually sales to or purchases from the Clearing Corporation. Both hedgers and speculators post a good faith deposit to show their capacity to sustain any losses that might accrue to them.

There are three main theories of futures pricing: the expectations hypothesis, the concept of normal backwardation, and the concept of a full carrying charge market. Rather than competing philosophies, these three theories are different perspectives on the fundamental result that futures prices are primarily determined by today's cash price, by the cost of storing and transporting commodities, and by expectations about how the cash price is likely to change in the future.

QUESTIONS

1. How is it possible for the trading volume in a particular futures contract to exceed the open interest in that commodity?

2. Why is a delivery mechanism essential to a well-functioning futures market?

3. Do you think that daily price limits make sense?

4. Under current rules, hedgers must post a smaller good faith deposit than speculators. Do you feel this is a reasonable rule?

5. Explain how it is possible for a hedger to *benefit* from a narrowing basis in a particular commodity.

6. Why is it that your maximum losses and gains are *not* predetermined with a commodity spread (like they are with most option spreads)?

7. "Closing all futures exchanges would probably be inflationary because of the added risk the producers would have to bear." Do you agree?

8. Suppose you were on a commission that was evaluating several proposals for new futures contracts. What would you want to know before you could make a decision on whether the proposals should be approved?

9. Do you think it would be possible for futures contracts to trade via the *specialist* system? Why or why not?

10. Commodities whose prices are particularly volatile lend themselves to futures trading. Lettuce is usually considered to be the grocery store commodity whose price is most uncertain. One day it is 47 cents a head, the next day it is 99 cents. Some people argue that futures contracts will never work for *perishable* commodities like lettuce. Do you agree?

11. A farmer anticipates having 50,000 bushels of wheat ready for harvest in September. What would be the implications of hedging by **(a)** selling 8 contracts, **(b)** selling 10 contracts, and **(c)** selling 12 contracts of September wheat?

12. Give examples of someone who might profitably use a *long hedge* in **(a)** corn, **(b)** gold, and **(c)** soybeans.

13. Briefly explain why prices for futures contracts on grains are generally higher for more distant delivery months.

14. "Individual speculators tend to lose money on their purchase of futures contracts." Do you agree?

PROBLEMS

Note: To solve these problems, refer to the *Wall Street Journal* clipping in Figure 8-5 as needed. Assume that today is March 29, 1993

1. Suppose two weeks ago a speculator purchased 4 contracts of September soybeans at 630½. What is the person's gain or loss as of the date of this newspaper?

2. Suppose a farmer anticipates harvesting 50,000 bushels of wheat in September. How much money would the farmer receive **(a)** today and **(b)** at delivery from hedging by selling 8 contracts of September wheat at the Chicago Board of Trade (using the settlement price shown in today's paper)?

3. Assume a soybean processor has a 100,000 bushel capacity. Calculate the processor's profit margin according to the *WSJ* prices and put on a crush for October delivery. Assume it takes one month to complete the processing operation.

4. Refer to the CBT wheat prices in the clipping. Explain how yesterday's volume could be 11,000 contracts, yet open interest rose by only 84 contracts.

5. According to the expectations hypothesis, what is the best estimate for the price of orange juice in March 1994?

6. An American importer anticipates a need for 8 million Deutschmarks in several months. How many futures contracts would this person need to *buy* or *sell* to hedge this requirement completely?

7. Look at the prices for copper futures at the Commodities Exchange (CMX). What do you think accounts for the rising price pattern for more distant delivery months?

 **Stock Index Futures**

*B*uy and you'll be sorry
Sell and you'll regret
Hold and you will worry
Do nothing and you'll fret.

The Trader's Lament

KEY TERMS

basis convergence	market risk
beta	stock index
cash settlement	synthetic index portfolio
fair premium	systematic factors
hedge ratio	unsystematic factors

The number of underlying assets on which futures contracts are available is constantly growing. There have been proposals for new commodity contracts before the exchanges and other regulatory bodies almost continuously since 1985. The fastest growing segment of the futures market is in financial futures. In 1972, physical commodities such as agricultural products, lumber, and metals comprised over 95 percent of all futures volume. Today, these combined contracts amount to only about one-third of total futures volume. This chapter and the next two review a representative from each of the three subgroups of the financial futures: stock index futures, foreign exchange futures, and interest rate futures.

STOCK INDEXES AND THEIR FUTURES CONTRACTS

The first thing to understand about an index futures contract is the nature of the underlying asset. What is the **stock index** that people promise to deliver or to buy? Someone can hold a handful of soybeans or corn, but what about the Standard & Poor's 500 index? How can someone "buy" or "sell" a stock index? These are reasonable questions that are asked somewhere in the United States every day by banks, retirement funds, and individual investors who are learning the potential role these contracts have in their portfolios.

Stock Indexes

While the Dow Jones Industrial Average may be the best known stock index, there is no futures contract on the DJIA. The exchanges and Dow Jones were never able to resolve certain trademark concerns. The Major Market Index, known in the trade by its ticker symbol XMI, is a proxy for the DJIA. Over a lengthy period, the correlation of returns on the XMI with the DJIA is over 98 percent.

Futures contracts also trade on the S&P 500 (Chicago Mercantile Exchange, colloquially known as the Merc), S&P MIDCAP 400 (Merc), Nikkei 225 (Merc), and the New York Stock Exchange Composite (New York Futures Exchange). Figure 9-1 (p. 216) summarizes these and other major stock indexes. The examples to follow focus on the best-known, most general, and most popular contract: the S&P 500 stock index futures contract.

The Standard and Poor's Corporation has prepared the S&P 500 index since 1917; it was originally intended as a standard against which portfolio managers and investment advisors might be judged. Initially there were only 200 stocks in the index, with expansion to 500 in 1957. Of the five hundred companies, 400 are industrial firms, 40 are public utilities, 40 are financial

STOCK MARKET DATA BANK   3/25/93

MAJOR INDEXES

HIGH	LOW (†365 DAY)		CLOSE	NET CHG		% CHG	†365 DAY CHG		% CHG	FROM 12/31		% CHG
DOW JONES AVERAGES												
3478.34	3136.58	30 Industrials	x3461.32	+	15.94	+ 0.46	+	193.65	+ 5.93	+	160.21	+ 4.85
1589.61	1204.40	20 Transportation	1553.55	+	7.05	+ 0.46	+	161.55	+ 11.61	+	104.34	+ 7.20
241.99	200.74	15 Utilities	x241.74	+	1.32	+ 0.55	+	37.81	+ 18.54	+	20.72	+ 9.37
1286.34	1107.47	65 Composite	x1280.25	+	6.04	+ 0.47	+	111.01	+ 9.49	+	75.70	+ 6.28
432.78	371.37	Equity Mkt. Index	427.72	+	2.78	+ 0.65	+	42.81	+ 11.12	+	14.43	+ 3.49
NEW YORK STOCK EXCHANGE												
251.36	217.92	Composite	248.33	+	1.42	+ 0.58	+	22.84	+ 10.13	+	8.12	+ 3.38
303.16	273.18	Industrials	298.55	+	1.90	+ 0.64	+	15.69	+ 5.55	+	4.16	+ 1.41
113.31	91.57	Utilities	113.31	+	0.45	+ 0.40	+	19.32	+ 20.56	+	8.48	+ 8.09
234.89	182.66	Transportation	230.94	+	0.48	+ 0.21	+	28.64	+ 14.16	+	16.22	+ 7.55
220.56	165.40	Finance	217.41	+	1.09	+ 0.50	+	43.43	+ 24.96	+	16.58	+ 8.26
STANDARD & POOR'S INDEXES												
456.33	394.50	500 Index	450.88	+	2.81	+ 0.63	+	43.02	+ 10.55	+	15.17	+ 3.48
524.99	470.91	Industrials	517.27	+	3.46	+ 0.67	+	31.72	+ 6.53	+	9.81	+ 1.93
394.95	307.94	Transportation	378.19	−	0.07	− 0.02	+	34.41	+ 10.01	+	14.44	+ 3.97
172.07	135.59	Utilities	171.83	+	0.74	+ 0.43	+	32.87	+ 23.65	+	13.37	+ 8.44
45.43	32.40	Financials	44.73	+	0.29	+ 0.65	+	10.20	+ 29.54	+	3.84	+ 9.39
166.77	136.02	400 MidCap	162.32	+	1.59	+ 0.99	+	15.04	+ 10.21	+	1.76	+ 1.10
NASDAQ												
708.85	547.84	Composite	681.01	+	6.65	+ 0.99	+	65.61	+ 10.66	+	4.06	+ 0.60
757.05	581.60	Industrials	702.61	+	9.69	+ 1.40	+	7.94	+ 1.14	−	22.33	− 3.08
868.27	589.03	Insurance	846.47	+	1.95	+ 0.23	+	230.98	+ 37.53	+	42.56	+ 5.29
626.03	385.46	Banks	621.34	+	1.63	+ 0.26	+	228.10	+ 58.01	+	88.41	+ 16.59
314.39	242.25	Nat. Mkt. Comp.	301.68	+	2.99	+ 1.00	+	30.03	+ 11.05	+	1.12	+ 0.37
303.87	232.48	Nat. Mkt. Indus.	281.56	+	3.95	+ 1.42	+	4.46	+ 1.61	−	9.84	− 3.38
OTHERS												
423.08	364.85	Amex	419.12	+	0.84	+ 0.20	+	20.26	+ 5.08	+	19.89	+ 4.98
281.38	238.81	Value-Line(geom.)	278.05	+	1.67	+ 0.60	+	18.02	+ 6.93	+	11.37	+ 4.26
232.36	185.81	Russell 2000	226.45	+	1.52	+ 0.68	+	20.21	+ 9.80	+	5.44	+ 2.46
4475.25	3849.10	Wilshire 5000	4416.32	+	25.92	+ 0.59	+	407.70	+ 10.17	+	126.58	+ 2.95

†-Based on comparable trading day in preceding year.

Figure 9-1 Summary of Major Index Stocks

Reprinted by permission of *Wall Street Journal*, © 1993 Dow Jones & Co., Inc. All Rights Reserved Worldwide.

companies, and 20 are transportation firms. The stock of these 500 companies adds up to about 80 percent of the total value of securities traded on the New York Stock Exchange. The S&P 500 Index is currently one of the Commerce Department's leading indicators.

This index is weighted to give greater importance to larger companies. In calculating the index, each of the 500 share prices is multiplied by the number of outstanding shares in that particular firm. These figures are then added together and compared with an arbitrary starting value of 100 established during a 1941–43 base period.

Stock Index Futures Contracts

Chapter 8, "Fundamentals of the Futures Market," discussed basic principles: the role of the hedger, the importance of the speculator, standardization of the underlying commodity, and the delivery procedure. Stock index futures contracts are similar in every respect to a traditional agricultural contract *except* for the matter of delivery, which will be discussed shortly. As with other futures contracts, a stock index future is a promise to buy or sell the standardized units of a specific index at a fixed price at a predetermined future date.

The S&P 500 Stock Index Futures Contract   Table 9-1 lists the characteristics of the S&P 500 stock index futures contract. Unlike most other commodity contracts, there is no actual delivery mechanism at expiration of the contract. All contracts are completed with a **cash settlement.** It is not practical to have speculators or hedgers deliver 500 different stock certificates in the appropriate quantities to satisfy the requirements of the contract. The value of the index is known at "delivery time," and it is much more convenient to credit or debit accounts with gains or losses that have accrued to them.

There is no delivery mechanism with stock index futures; all closing contracts are settled in cash.

Pricing of Stock Index Futures   The traditional factors that influence the stock market also determine the level of the SPX index: political events,

---

TABLE 9-1   CHARACTERISTICS OF S&P 500 STOCK INDEX FUTURES

Contract size = $500 × index value.
Minimum price change is 0.05 ($25).
Initial good faith deposit for a speculator is $15,000 (subject to change).
Contracts are marked to market daily.
Delivery of stocks does not occur; contracts are settled in cash.
The contract does not earn dividends.
Trading hours: 9:30 AM—4:15 PM EST
Settlement months and ticker symbols:
          Futures: SP   Cash Index: SPX
    MAR (H) JUN (M) SEP (U) DEC (Z)
Final trading day: Thursday before the 3rd Friday of the contract month
These contracts are nicknamed SPOOZ in the trading pit.

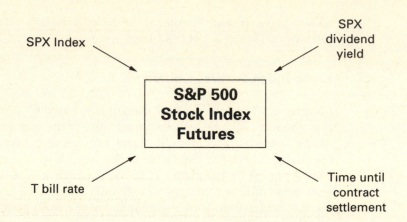

Figure 9-2 Determinants of Stock Index Futures Value

money supply, inflation worries, and investor optimism. The *futures* value depends on four elements:

- the level of the index itself
- the dividend yield on the 500 stocks in the index
- the current level of interest rates
- the time until final contract cash settlement

These determining factors are similar to the determinants of a call option premium.

In finance most pricing relationships center on arbitrage arguments; equivalent securities should sell for the same price. An institution could have a long position in all 500 securities comprising the SPX index. A more convenient alternative might be to have a long position in the futures contracts. While these positions are similar, they are not equivalent. A major difference lies in the fact that stocks pay dividends while the futures contracts do not. We know from elementary investment principles that on ex-dividend dates stock prices tend to fall by about the amount of the dividend earned. An investor is not indifferent to receiving the dividend or not receiving it (everything else being equal), so the fact that dividends are not received should be reflected in the futures price.

Also, no return is earned on a stock purchase unless the stock appreciates or pays dividends. Purchase of a futures contract requires the posting of the good faith deposit, which can be satisfied with interest-earning U.S. treasury bills. Satisfying the margin requirement this way, the speculator will earn interest while speculating on the general level of the stock market. No interest accrues from holding stock, and the futures price reflects this difference. The gist of this comparison is that the futures price should equal

(handwritten margin note: LONG STOCK POSITION vs LONG FUTURES POSITION)

TABLE 9-2 STOCK INDEX FUTURES INFORMATION

current level of the cash index	329.83
T bill yield	6.02%
S&P 500 dividend yield[1]	2.65%
futures price	334.30
days until delivery	121

the dollar value of the index, plus the short-term interest cost and less the dividend yield received.

Suppose we have the information shown in Table 9-2:

The T bill rate exceeds the dividend yield on the S&P 500, so there is a relative advantage to buying the futures contract over the cash index. We can find whether the actual futures price is too high or too low by calculating the **fair premium** for the time remaining in the futures contract. The steps shown in Table 9-3 do this.

If, as Table 9-3 (p. 220) shows, the fair value of the futures contract is 333.51, the current market price of 334.20 (as shown in Table 9-2) is too high. The actions of market participants should cause the price of the futures contract to return to their no-arbitrage level.

An alternative, but essentially equivalent, way of determining the fair value of a futures contract is by assuming that the dividend stream occurs continuously (rather than discretely). Equation 9-1 is used for this calculation:

$$F = S\,e^{(r - d)t} \tag{9-1}$$

where F = fair futures price

$\quad S$ = current level of the index

$\quad r$ = T bill rate

$\quad d$ = S&P 500 dividend yield

$\quad e$ = base of natural logarithms

$\quad t$ = years until delivery date (decimal: $\dfrac{days\ until\ delivery}{365}$)

In this example,

$$S = 329.83$$
$$r = .0602$$
$$d = .0265$$

and $t = \dfrac{121}{365} = 0.3315$

---

[1] The S&P 500 dividend yield is conveniently obtained from the Standard and Poor's *Outlook*, which is available at most public library reference desks.

TABLE 9-3 DETERMINATION OF FAIR PREMIUM FOR S&P 500 FUTURES

T Bill rate	6.02%	
S&P 500 dividend yield	−2.65%	
Fair Annual Premium	3.37%	
In percentage points, the adjusted fair premium:		
121/365 × 3.37%	=	1.12%
In index points, the adjusted fair premium:		
1.12% × 329.83	=	3.68 points
The fair value of futures		
329.83 + 3.68	=	333.51

Using equation 9-1, the fair value of the futures is

$$F = 329.83 \ e^{(.0602 - .0265)(.3315)} = 333.54$$

↳ natural antilogarithm = EXP in math mode of HP 17B II

This figure is only slightly different from the value shown in Table 9-3 and is easier to calculate.

Table 9-4 shows the essence of the pricing relationship. The concept of a **synthetic index portfolio** is an important result. It means that large institutional investors such as life insurance companies and pension funds can replicate a well-diversified portfolio of common stock by simply holding a long position in the stock index futures contract and *margining*[2] the position with T bills. Added benefits of the futures approach are (1) commissions will be much lower on the futures contracts than on 500 separate stock issues, and (2) the portfolio will be much easier to follow and manage. There are still many fiduciary restrictions (many clearly outdated) that preclude widespread use of futures as a substitute for stock ownership, but the number of futures users grows daily.

Uses of Stock Index Futures

There are three broad uses of stock index futures contracts: speculation, arbitrage, and hedging.

Speculation   A person who anticipated that the stock market was about to advance could obtain substantial leverage by buying S&P contracts. Each one-point movement in the index translates into $500. Significant profits (and losses) can occur via speculation in these futures contracts.

---

[2]Providing collateral for an investment position is sometimes called margining.

PRICING RELATIONSHIP BETWEEN FUTURES AND STOCK

TABLE 9-4   CREATION OF A SYNTHETIC INDEX PORTFOLIO

Long stock index futures	+	Long treasury bills	=	Long index portfolio
(subtract 3.37% premium)		(add 6.02% yield)		(equals 2.65% dividend yield)

Arbitrage   Arbitrageurs are important players in the financial marketplace. Their activities help keep the market efficient and functioning well. The previous example showed a situation where the actual market price of the futures contract differed from the price expected by pricing theory. Expecting that the futures contract and the value of the cash index will soon return to their "normal" relationship, an arbitrageur might short the futures contracts and buy stock. As the gap between the two prices narrows, the arbitrageur earns a profit.[3]

Hedging   As with any futures contract, the primary purpose of S&P futures is to facilitate risk transfer from someone who bears undesired risk to someone else who is willing to bear the risk because of the anticipated profits that might be made. Stock index futures contracts are widely and successfully used for this purpose by most large commercial banks and by many pension funds and foundations. Hedging applications are the subject of the following section.

HEDGING WITH STOCK INDEX FUTURES

A hedger seeks to eliminate price risk; using the S&P 500 futures contract, a portfolio manager can largely eliminate the risk of paper losses on the portfolio from declining security prices.

Systematic and Unsystematic Risk

Stock prices fluctuate because of two sets of factors. **Systematic factors** are those that influence the stock market as a whole, and include such things as market interest rates, economic indicators, the political climate, regulatory policy, and fiscal or monetary policy. Systematic risk is also called **market risk** and is also called beta. **Unsystematic factors** are unique to a specific

---

[3]This is the motivation behind program trading, which is discussed later in the book.

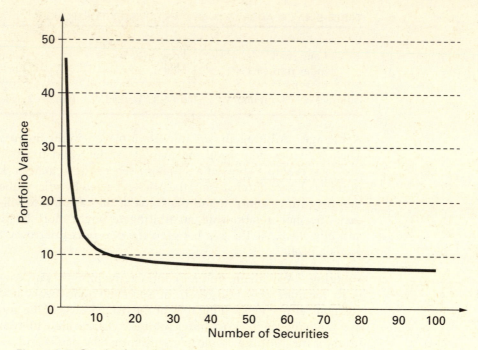

Figure 9-3 Graph of Portfolio Variance

company or industry and include earnings reports, technological developments, labor negotiations, cost of materials, and merger or acquisition
activity.

Properly diversifying a portfolio can eliminate unsystematic risk. In fact,
a principal result of capital market theory is the fact that investors are not
rewarded for bearing unsystematic risk: the "market" assumes that you have
been smart enough to reduce risk through diversification as much as possible
for a given level of anticipated return.

A well-known study by Evans and Archer[4] shows how portfolio variability declines as the number of securities in the portfolio increases. Figure 9-3
shows these famous results. A portfolio containing 15 or 20 unrelated stocks
provides a very high degree of diversification; adding more securities results
in very little additional risk reduction.

Beta is also a measure of the relative riskiness of a portfolio compared to
a benchmark portfolio like the S&P 500 index. By definition, the benchmark
has a beta of 1.0. Portfolios that are riskier than the benchmark have a beta
greater than one, while more conservative portfolios have a beta less than

---

[4]Evans, John L. and Stephen H. Archer. "Diversification and the Reduction of Dispersion,"
Journal of Finance, December 1968, 761–767.

one. Suppose a portfolio has a beta of 0.92. This means that for every 1 percent change in the value of the S&P 500 index, the portfolio should change in value by 0.92 percent.

In order for a hedge to be effective, the hedging device one chooses is normally as similar as possible to the commodity being hedged: farmers do not hedge their wheat crop by using corn futures, nor should an equity manager hedge stock holdings with a bond index. The wheat farmer will hedge with wheat futures, and the stock portfolio manager will hedge with a stock index. The S&P 500 index is a well-diversified portfolio and is effective in hedging the investment portfolios of endowment funds, mutual funds, and other broad-based portfolios.

The Need to Hedge

Suppose you are the portfolio manager for a $75 million stock fund. You anticipate a downturn in the market soon, but remain bullish for the long term. However, you also know that a declining portfolio value would look bad in the end-of-year report your fund will provide to its interested parties. What can you do?

One obvious alternative is to sell everything before prices fall. This solution would protect your gains, but would be expensive in terms of commissions. Also, you do not want to suffer the embarrassment of reporting that your "equity" fund contains only cash equivalents.

Another approach is to hedge the stock portfolio. Futures hedging involves taking a position in the futures market that offsets a position you hold in the "cash" market. If you are long stock, logically you should be short futures. Just as the farmer needs to figure out how many contracts to sell, the portfolio manager must calculate the number of contracts necessary to counteract likely changes in the portfolio value.

The Hedge Ratio

Portfolios are of different sizes and different risk levels. It is necessary to recognize these differences in order to build a proper hedge. Though there is a high degree of leverage with futures, a single contract will not have much effect on the total risk of a $1 billion stock portfolio. Large portfolios require more contracts than do small ones. Similarly, risky portfolios fluctuate more than the market average; thus they require a larger hedge.

The **hedge ratio** incorporates the relative value of the stocks and futures and accounts for the relative riskiness of the two "portfolios." One portfolio (the S&P 500 index) has a beta of 1.0 by definition, and the second portfolio (the stocks) may be more or less risky than this. If the stock portfolio is less

INDEX

S&P 500 INDEX (CME) $500 times index

```
                                              Open
        Open   High   Low  Settle  Chg   High   Low  Interest
June  449.00 452.90 448.50 452.00 + 2.80 458.10 391.00 164,053
Sept  449.70 453.35 449.30 452.70 + 2.90 458.55 391.00   2,978
Dec   450.95 454.30 450.20 453.40 + 3.00 459.30 429.70     434
   Est vol 43,284; vol Wed 52,939; open int 167,466, +3,007.
   Indx prelim High 451.75; Low 447.93; Close 450.88 +2.81
```
S&P MIDCAP 400 (CME) $500 times index
```
June  161.00 162.80 161.00 162.60 + 1.60 167.50 138.60   7,697
   Est vol 180; vol Wed 273; open int 7,711, +73.
   The index: High 162.33; Low 160.74; Close 162.32 +1.59
```
NIKKEI 225 Stock Average (CME)—$5 times Index
```
June 18930. 18990. 18930. 18950. + 300.0 19350. 14550. 15,460
   Est vol 945; vol Wed 1,311; open int 15,518, +223.
```

Figure 9-4 S&P 500 Stock Index Futures Contract (CME)

risky, it will be necessary to use fewer futures contracts. If the stock portfolio has a beta greater than one, then more futures contracts are necessary. To hedge a long position, the manager needs to go short the futures contracts. Because these are not available in fractional amounts, the portfolio manager must round to a whole number.

There are three pieces of information needed to determine the hedge ratio:

1. the value of the chosen futures contract
2. the dollar value of the portfolio to be hedged
3. the beta of the portfolio

The first of these is easy to determine. The size of an S&P 500 futures contract is established as $500 times the value of the S&P 500 index. Figure 9-4 shows the S&P 500 stock index futures prices from March 25, 1993.

Suppose the manager of a $75 million stock portfolio (beta equal to 0.92) studies a possible hedge using the September S&P 500 futures. Figure 9-3 shows that the prior day's closing value for the S&P 500 index was 450.88, and that the SEP S&P 500 futures contract closed at 452.70. The value of the futures contract is therefore $500 × 452.70, or $226,350.

The hedge ratio for this example is calculated below:

$$HR = \frac{\text{Dollar value of portfolio}}{\text{Dollar value of S\&P contract}} \times \text{beta}$$

(9-2)

$$= \frac{\$75 \text{ million}}{\$500 \times 452.70} \times 0.92 = 305 \text{ contracts} \quad (\text{SHORT})$$

Consider the consequences of several different market scenarios at the final delivery day for the contract.[5]

---

[5]Dividends are ignored in these examples; they would be the same in each scenario.

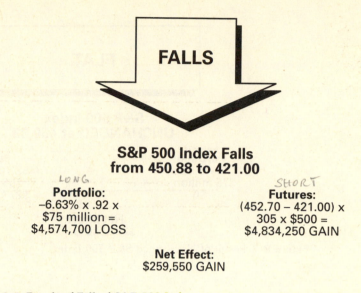

**S&P 500 Index Falls
from 450.88 to 421.00**

LONG

Portfolio:
–6.63% x .92 x
$75 million =
$4,574,700 LOSS

SHORT

Futures:
(452.70 – 421.00) x
305 x $500 =
$4,834,250 GAIN

Net Effect:
$259,550 GAIN

Figure 9-5 Result of Fall of S&P 500 Index

1. *The Market Falls.* This is what the portfolio manager expected to happen. There will be a loss in the stock portfolio and a gain in the futures market. Suppose the S&P 500 index falls from 450.88 to 421.00.

   This is a decline of 6.63 percent. This means the portfolio should have fallen by 6.63% × 0.92 = 6.10%, or $4,574,700. This is a *loss* to you.

Figure 9-6 Result of Rise of S&P 500 Index

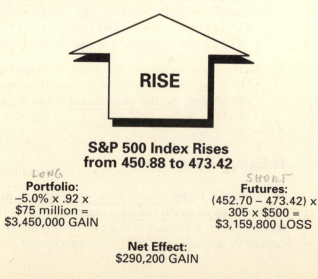

**S&P 500 Index Rises
from 450.88 to 473.42**

LONG

Portfolio:
–5.0% x .92 x
$75 million =
$3,450,000 GAIN

SHORT

Futures:
(452.70 – 473.42) x
305 x $500 =
$3,159,800 LOSS

Net Effect:
$290,200 GAIN

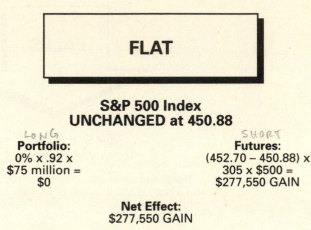

Figure 9-7 Result of Unchanged S&P 500 Index

In the futures market, you have a *gain*. You sold 305 contracts short at 452.70. At the expiration of the futures contract, you can close out the 305 short contracts by buying 305 contracts at 421.00. (At expiration, the price of the futures contract should exactly equal the index itself.) This gives you a gain of 31.70 points × $500 × 305 contracts = $4,834,250. The combined positions (cash and futures market) result in a gain of $259,550.

2. *The Market Rises.* Suppose the index rises from 450.88 to 473.42. This market rise of 5 percent means the portfolio, with its beta of 0.92, should rise by 4.60%, or $3,450,000. You will lose money on the futures position, because you sold them short and they rose in price to 473.42 at expiration. The loss is (473.42 − 452.70) × $500 × 305 = $3,159,800. The combined positions result in a gain of $290,200.

3. *The Market is Unchanged.* There is no gain on the stock portfolio. There is, however, a gain in the futures. The basis will deteriorate to zero at expiration, so the short hedger has a gain of (452.70 − 450.88) × $500 × 305 = $277,550.

Hedging in Retrospect

In practice, a hedge of this type will never be perfect: there is usually some relatively small profit or loss when the hedge is lifted. There are two reasons for this. First, it is usually not possible to hedge exactly because the futures contracts are only available in integer quantities. This means the portfolio manager must round to the nearest whole number. Second, stock portfolios seldom behave exactly as their beta says they should. In the example above, the portfolio *should* change by 92 percent as much as the general market. Betas are estimated, and the portfolio may change by more or less than this amount.

If you examine the results in each of these scenarios carefully, you will note that the basis works to the advantage of the short hedger. Even if the market remains unchanged, the value of the futures contracts will decline as the delivery month approaches. On the last day of a futures contract's life, its market price should equal the spot price. This means the basis becomes zero. This phenomenon is called **basis convergence** and is true for all futures contracts, whether they be agricultural, financial, or another category.

Analogous to convergence phenomenon for stock options on p. 69.

Convergence of the futures contract with the cash index works to the advantage of the short hedger.

m: Why?

The gains earned from the deteriorating basis are modest in percentage terms. In the "market unchanged" scenario, there was a combined gain of $277,550. On a $75 million portfolio, this is a percentage return of 0.37 percent over six months, or less than one percent per year. This represents the differential between the T bill rate and the dividend yield on the stock index. Note also that hedging is not a free lunch; in the case where the market advances, the portfolio would have fared better had the hedge not been used.

It is by no means necessary for a portfolio manager to hedge the entire portfolio. Instead of using 305 contracts as in the examples above, the manager might decide to hedge only 80 percent of the portfolio, using 244 contracts. This allows greater upside appreciation if the portfolio manager is wrong about a forthcoming downturn, but would still provide substantial protection against a declining market.

SUMMARY

Financial futures are the fastest growing segment of the investment field. These contracts are popular with both speculators and hedgers. Stock index futures can be used to reduce systematic risk associated with a well-diversified stock portfolio. The price of a stock index futures contract is determined by adjusting the current value of the index for the differential between the dividend yield on the index portfolio and the prevailing treasury bill rate.

Accurate hedge ratios are essential to proper hedging. With stock index futures, the hedge ratio depends on the size of the portfolio, its beta, and the value of the chosen futures contract.

QUESTIONS

1. Suppose you manage a $25 million insurance company stock portfolio. Do you see any advantage in the S&P 500 future contract as a hedging device over the Major Market Index?

2. Comment on the following statement: "Because the basis works to the benefit of the short hedger with stock index futures, a calendar spread where you are long the near month and short the far month (where the basis is higher) is usually a winner."

3. Suppose that, instead of holding a diversified portfolio of common stock, a mutual fund announces its intent to hold stock index futures and T bills. Give arguments for and against this practice as a substitute for more conventional equity investing.

4. Comment on the following statement: "Over the long term, people who are long stock index futures contracts are going to be net losers."

5. Why does convergence of a stock index futures contract with the cash index work to the advantage of a short seller?

6. Under what circumstances do you think stock index futures could trade in an inverted market?

7. Could the S&P 500 stock index futures contract be used to hedge a portfolio of only five stocks?

8. What role does beta play in the construction of a hedge ratio for a stock portfolio?

9. In hedging a portfolio, is there anything philosophically wrong with only hedging part of it?

10. Suppose a number of companies in the S&P 500 index simultaneously increase their dividends. What influence would this likely have on the value of an S&P 500 futures contract?

PROBLEMS

1. Suppose that the current level of the S&P 500 index is 340.00, the dividend yield on the index is 2.55%, and Treasury bills yield 5.88%. What is the theoretical price of an S&P 500 futures contract with delivery in 63 days?

2. In problem 1, suppose the T bill rate falls to 4.25%. What is the theoretical price of an S&P 500 futures contract with 120 days until final delivery?

3. As the manager of a $200 million stock portfolio with a beta of 0.88, you have decided to hedge 80 percent of the value of your portfolio using the S&P 500 futures. Refer to the prices for September delivery in Figure 9-4. What is the appropriate hedge ratio, and how many contracts will you buy or sell?

4. Refer to the data in problem 3. Suppose you want to hedge the portfolio using the DEC S&P 500 stock index futures contracts shown in Figure 9-4. How many of these contracts do you need to buy or sell?

5. As the manager of a $750 million stock portfolio with a beta of 1.12, you have decided to hedge 40 percent of the value of your portfolio using the S&P 500 futures. Refer to the prices for September delivery in Table 9-4. What is the appropriate hedge ratio, and how many contracts will you buy or sell?

6. Solve problem 1 assuming continuous compounding of the dividends, i.e., use equation 9-1.

7. The SPX index stands at 450.00. An S&P 500 futures contract with delivery in 85 days sells for 455.50. If the dividend yield on the SPX is 2.2%, what T bill rate is implied in these prices?

Foreign Exchange Futures

*T*he inventory of this market is uncertainty.

E. B. Harris
Former Chairman
Chicago Mercantile Exchange

KEY TERMS

accounting exposure
covering the risk
deflation
economic exposure
exposure
foreign exchange risk
forward exchange rate
inflation premium

interest rate parity
nominal interest rate
purchasing power parity
real rate
risk premium
spot exchange rate
transaction exposure
translation exposure

In the world of finance, the capital markets across the globe have become one giant playing field. Consider the following:

- The financial press carries prices on popular foreign securities in the daily newspaper.
- Financial information services such as Quotron allow you to access the price of gold in London, Zurich, Paris, or New York simply by appending the letter L, Z, P, or N to the GLD symbol for gold.
- Many morning radio programs begin the day by reporting on the action on foreign stock exchanges and on the overnight strength of the dollar.
- Major brokerage firms have ready access to foreign capital markets and can confirm an overseas trade made on your behalf in a matter of minutes.

Public pension funds are increasingly finding attractive investment opportunities abroad. Their overseas investment totals over $20 billion. Michael Howell, European equity strategist for Salomon Brothers in London, expects that U.S. pension fund managers will have between 20 percent and 25 percent of their assets invested overseas by the year 2000. (The current figure is about 4 percent.)

Overseas investments or international business dealings often generate foreign exchange risk. Understanding how foreign currency futures contracts can be used to reduce this risk is the primary objective of this chapter. A recent survey[1] of corporate treasurers indicates that the primary corporate use of derivative assets is hedging foreign exchange exposure (see Table 10-1). In the next section we look at the sources and different dimensions of the foreign exchange risk that corporate treasurers seek to reduce.

TABLE 10-1 ANSWER TO THE QUESTION, *"FOR WHAT PURPOSE DO YOU USE DERIVATIVE INSTRUMENTS?"*

77%	To hedge foreign exchange risk exposure
56%	To hedge floating rate debt
54%	To create synthetic floating rate debt at a lower cost
43%	To hedge income/profits
41%	To create synthetic fixed rate debt at a lower cost
40%	To achieve strategic liability management
24%	To hedge overseas investment
19%	To hedge commercial paper issuance
10%	To access global capital markets
10%	Other uses
3%	To access foreign equity markets

[1]Reported in "The Way It Is," *Treasury* (Spring 1993): 19–20.

FOREIGN EXCHANGE RISK

We have seen that with the appropriate hedging strategy, farmers can reduce price risk, and portfolio managers can minimize market risk. In the world of international business, another significant risk is **foreign exchange risk,** which is the chance of loss due to changes in the relative value of world currencies.

When a U.S. investor buys a foreign security, there are really two relevant purchases. The actual purchase of the security is one of them, but before you can do this you must exchange U.S. dollars for the necessary foreign currency. In essence, you are buying the foreign currency, and its price can change daily. To an investor, the changing relationships among currencies of interest constitute *foreign exchange risk.* Modest changes in exchange rates can result in significant dollar differences. On a holding of 1 million units of foreign exchange, for instance, a price change of 1 cent per unit amounts to $10,000.

A Business Example

Suppose an American importer agrees to purchase forty New Zealand leather vests at a price of NZ$110 apiece, for a total of NZ$4400. The vests will take approximately two months to produce, and the importer has agreed to pay for them before they are shipped.

The *Wall Street Journal* might show that today's spot exchange rate for New Zealand dollars is $0.5855/NZ$. To the U.S. importer, this means that each vest costs NZ$110 × $0.5855/NZ$, or $64.41. The importer has arranged with a local specialty shop to sell these vests wholesale at $100 apiece; the shop owner is confident they can be sold at retail for $150.

The importer's concern is obvious. If the U.S. dollar weakens between now and vest shipping time, the "cost of goods sold" will go up. Suppose, however, the dollar has been strengthening for months, and the importer remembers the investment saying "The trend is your friend." If the dollar continues to strengthen, the importer's profit will increase. The trader's proverb advises letting the dollar strengthen further before locking in a purchase price that you expect to decline.

To show the effect of modest exchange rate changes, we can calculate the impact of two different scenarios. If the dollar strengthens and the value of the New Zealand dollar falls to $0.5500, the cost of the vests becomes $2420. On the other hand, if the dollar falls to $0.6200/NZ$, the cost of the vests translates into NZ$4400 × $0.62/NZ$, or $2728. This is $151.80 more than the original price. The important thing to note here is that the vest manufacturer's published prices do not change with international exchange rates. A vest still costs NZ$110. What does change price in this example is the New Zealand dollar.

The change in the exchange rate for foreign currencies is the principal issue with foreign exchange risk. Before someone can buy a foreign good, they must first buy the appropriate foreign currency. If an American sells goods abroad and receives payment in the local currency, the proceeds cannot be spent at home until the foreign currency is converted into the American "currency of account," the U.S. dollar.

Also, note that the vests can become more expensive or they can become cheaper. This is price volatility, and price volatility constitutes risk. The fact that the volatility might work in your favor does not reduce the risk.

An Investment Example

Through your broker you might place a market order to buy 1000 shares of Foster's (the Australian beer company), trading on the Sydney Stock Exchange. Assume you get the shares at A$1.45. Your brokerage statement will show the value of this purchase in U.S. dollars. The exchange rate might be $0.7735/A$ at the time you buy the stock. This means the shares cost you 1000 × A$1.45 × $0.7735/A$ = $1121.58.

If the shares appreciate to A$1.95, the result is a holding period return of

$$\frac{(A\$1.95 - A\$1.45)}{A\$1.45} = 34.5\%$$

Over this period, however, the value of the Australian dollar might fall from $0.7735 to $0.7000. If you were to sell the shares, you would receive 1,000 × A$1.95 × $0.7000/A$, or $1365.00. From your perspective, the holding period return was not 34.5 percent. Rather, it was ($1,365 − $1,121.58)/ $1121.58 = 21.7 percent. This is still a good return, but you were obviously hurt by the foreign exchange risk.

From Whence Cometh the Risk?

It is said that when the United States sneezes, the world catches a cold. While this may be a little parochial, the point is that events in one industrial country affect the rest of the world. When a big player, like the United States government, changes its economic policy, suffers a recession, or experiences high unemployment, these events have significant economic consequences elsewhere in the world. Interest rates are often a good barometer of these events. They are particularly relevant to an understanding of foreign exchange risk.

The Role of Interest Rates   Students of finance learn that the **nominal interest rate** (the stated rate) can be expressed as the sum of three components: the *real rate,* an *inflation premium,* and a *risk premium.*

| The nominal rate of interest is the aggregate of the real rate, an inflation premium, and a risk premium.

The Real Rate of Interest   The **real rate** is an economic abstraction that we cannot directly observe. Theoretically, it reflects the rate of return investors demand for giving up the current use of funds. In a world of no risk and no inflation, the real rate indicates people's willingness to postpone spending their money.

The Inflation Premium   The **inflation premium** reflects how the general price level is changing. Inflation is normally positive (negative inflation is called **deflation**), and it therefore measures how rapidly the money standard is losing its purchasing power. If inflation is 5% per year, an average $100 purchase today will cost $105 in one year.

The Risk Premium   The **risk premium** is the component of interest rates that is toughest to measure; security analysts earn their pay by their efforts to decipher it. Risk-averse investors will not take unnecessary risks, and they expect to be compensated over the long term for any risks they choose to take. This is why the average return on common stocks (which are risky) is higher than the average return on U.S. treasury bills (which are assumed to have no risk). Investors will not purchase risky securities offering the same return as a riskless security. The price of a risky security must reflect a risk premium to entice someone to buy it; the magnitude of the risk premium depends on how much risk the security carries. The more risk, the higher the risk premium, and therefore the lower the price. (Anything can become an attractive investment if its price falls low enough.)

Forward Rates   Before discussing interest rates further, it is useful to look at the difference between *spot* and *forward* exchange rates.

If the New Zealand importer cashes a U.S. dollar traveler's check while abroad, the exchange occurs at the **spot exchange rate.** This is the current exchange rate for two currencies, and it is the rate that is posted on signs at international airports and in banking centers. The spot rate changes daily and can increase or decrease.

| The spot rate is the current price of a foreign currency.

The **forward exchange rate** is a contractual rate between a commercial bank and a client for the future delivery of a specified quantity of foreign currency. Forward rates are normally quoted on the basis of one, two, three, six, and twelve months, but other terms can be arranged. Widely-traded currencies can have a forward market as long as five years ahead.

We also know from academic research[2] that the forward foreign exchange rate is an unbiased estimate of the future spot rate for foreign exchange. The foreign exchange section of the financial pages can provide information on the direction "the market" feels relative currency values will travel in the months ahead. If forward rates show that the dollar is expected to strengthen, it would make sense to delay paying New Zealand dollars as long as possible. If the dollar is expected to weaken, then you should lock in a rate now before your cost goes up.

The forward rate is a contractual rate between a commercial bank and a client for future delivery of foreign exchange.

There is no active forward market for the New Zealand dollar, so let's look at an example using another currency: the German mark. On a particular day, the *Wall Street Journal* might list the spot exchange rate as $0.5122/DM and a 90-day forward rate as $0.5147/DM. Suppose a portfolio contains DM120,000 par value in 8.33% German corporate bonds that mature in 90 days. To avoid the foreign exchange risk, the portfolio manager could "lock in" the maturity value of these bonds by entering into a forward contract to deliver 120,000 Deutschmarks. (You want to deliver DM because you will receive them when the bonds mature.) This could be done at a local commercial bank.[3]

Note that under the forward contract the future dollar price of the Deutschmark is more than the prevailing spot rate. This means that the marketplace expects the value of the U.S. dollar to decline relative to the German mark in the next 90 days. The difference between the two rates can be quoted as an annual premium or discount using the formula in Table 10-2.

For the German mark, we find a forward discount of 1.94%:

$$\frac{\$0.5122 - \$0.5147}{\$0.5147} \times \frac{12}{3} \times 100 = -1.94\%$$

Having discussed this, let's now examine the notion of interest rate parity and see why we get this result.

Interest Rate Parity   The **interest rate parity** theorem states that differences in national interest rates will be reflected in the currency forward market. If

---

[2]See, for instance, Bradford Cornell's article, "Spot Rates, Forward Rates, and Exchange Market Efficiency," *Journal of Financial Economics* (August 1977): 55–65.

[3]A small community bank will probably arrange this contract through a larger bank with which the small bank has a correspondent/respondent relationship.

TABLE 10-2 FORWARD CONTRACT PREMIUM OR DISCOUNT

$$\text{Forward premium or discount} = \frac{\text{spot rate} - \text{fwd rate}}{\text{forward rate}} \times \frac{12}{n} \times 100$$

where n = the contract length in months

there are no transaction cost differentials, two securities of similar risk and maturity will show a difference in their interest rates equal to the forward premium or discount, but with the opposite sign.

Using the example above, if 90-day U.S. Treasury bills yield 8.05%, the interest rate parity theorem requires that German T bills yield 1.94% more, or 9.99%. (This assumes that the world considers the two securities equally risky. If this is not so, there will be a risk premium reflected in the riskier security's interest rate.)

Forward rates reflect differences in national interest rates.

A Treasury bill rate for any country is a nominal rate. Recall that the nominal rate is the aggregation of the real rate, the inflation premium, and a risk premium. If some economic event happens that causes interest rates in the United States or in Germany to change, the relative value of the two currencies will change. This, by definition, is foreign exchange risk.

Purchasing Power Parity   The concept of **purchasing power parity** is an extension of the interest rate parity theorem, stating that, for two currencies that are initially in equilibrium, a relative change in the prevailing inflation rate in one country will be reflected as an equal but opposite change in the value of its currency.

As an example, consider two hypothetical countries, A and B, whose currencies are in equilibrium: 1 unit of currency A equals 2 of B. Countries A and B are contiguous, and people freely cross the border to purchase goods from their foreign neighbors. If inflation in country A suddenly rises by 2 percent more than in country B, country A's currency will depreciate by 2 percent relative to country B's currency. This means the new equilibrium exchange rate will become 1.02A = 2B, or A = 1.9608B.

The reason for this change stems from the behavior of the international trading partners. People naturally want to buy a particular good for the least cost. In country A, the higher level of domestic inflation causes the prices of goods to increase, making them less desirable to people in both country A and country B. Fewer people are now going to buy goods in country A; it is cheaper to get them in B. The end result is that country A will export fewer goods, while country B will sell more. This can cause country A to develop a trade deficit with country B. Less international trade means people in country B will have less demand for country A's currency because they are not buying as much in country A. This reduced demand will cause the price of the currency to fall to a new equilibrium level, where residents of country B are again motivated to cross the border to buy goods in country A.

▌Unexpected inflation causes the value of the home currency to fall.

Table 10-3 provides a tongue-in-cheek example of this phenomenon. If you neglect transaction costs such as airline tickets, apparently you can appease your Big Mac attack at the least cost if you buy them in Hong Kong.

There are other relevant economic issues that complicate this simple example substantially. The important point is the fact that differentials in international inflation rates can be a source of foreign exchange risk.

Dealing with the Risk

Having seen some primary sources of foreign exchange risk, we now look at its practical meaning to the international investor.

The Concept of Exposure   **Exposure** is the extent to which you face foreign exchange risk. Unfortunately, there is not always a quick and convenient way

TABLE 10-3 BIG MAC PARITY

Country	Local Price of Big Mac	*Implied* Local Price of the U.S. Dollar (and Big Mac)	*Actual* Exchange Rate; Units of Foreign Currency per U.S. Dollar*
Australia	A$2.25	1.19 ($1.70)	1.32
Britain	£1.14	0.60 ($1.84)	0.62
Canada	C$1.86	0.98 ($1.58)	1.18
France	FF14.92	7.89 ($2.62)	5.70
Hong Kong	HK$8.00	4.23 ($1.02)	7.81
Japan	¥370	195.76 ($2.42)	152.90
S. Korea	Won2,181	1,153.97 ($3.14)	694.95
U.S.—Chicago	$1.89	— ($1.89)	—
W. Germany	DM3.89	2.06 ($2.30)	1.69
Yugoslavia	Dinar16.94	8.96 ($1.45)	11.68

*As of March 20, 1990

Source: Relationship cited in *The Economist* (April 15, 1989); reported in *Futures* (May 1990): 27.

to measure this. Accountants have fussed over this problem for years, have rewritten the rules several times, and still it remains a thorny issue. In general, there are two types of exposure: *accounting* and *economic*. An investment manager is primarily concerned with the latter type, but should know something about the former, too.

Accounting Exposure   **Accounting exposure** is of greatest concern to multinational corporations that have subsidiaries abroad in several foreign countries. It is also of concern to the person who holds foreign securities and must prepare dollar-based financial reports on the portfolio's composition and performance.

The parent company is normally required to prepare consolidated financial statements "reflecting fairly" the current state of affairs of the company. The financial statements, however, must be prepared in a single currency (the U.S. dollar for an American firm). Turning foreign currencies into dollar equivalents involves two other accounting concepts: **transaction exposure** and **translation exposure.**

The Financial Accounting Standards Board provides good intuition into the concept of *transaction exposure* in its statement number 8:[4]

> A transaction involving purchase or sale of goods or services with the price stated in foreign currency is incomplete until the amount in dollars necessary to liquidate the related payable or receivable is determined.

This means that if I promise to pay 4400 New Zealand dollars for the forty vests, I have a transaction exposure until I exchange U.S. dollars for enough New Zealand dollars to pay the bill.

Translation exposure stems from the holding of foreign assets and liabilities that are denominated in currencies other than U.S. dollars. The values of foreign real estate holdings and foreign mortgages, for instance, must be "translated" into U.S. dollars before they are incorporated into a U.S. balance sheet. There is a precise set of rules for how this translation is done, but they are for the accountants to worry about and are not a routine investment management activity.

Economic Exposure   **Economic exposure** measures the risk that the value of a security will decline due to an unexpected change in relative foreign exchange rates. This is the type of exposure with which security investors are most concerned.

---

[4]Financial Accounting Standards Board, *Statement of Financial Accounting Standards No. 8.*, October 1975, para. 113. FASB 8 has been superseded by FASB 52, but the concept of exposure remains the same.

■ The portfolio manager is most concerned with foreign exchange economic exposure.

In determining the value of a financial asset, the security analyst seeks to measure the present value of all the cash flows that will accrue to the security holder. The present value of these future cash flows is determined by discounting them, using a well-conceived discount factor. Expected changes in exchange rates should be included in this discount rate. Determination of the discount rate is largely a subjective matter, as is the business of forecasting future exchange rates.

For the security investor, the importance of economic exposure is clear. When it comes time to sell a foreign security, an adverse foreign exchange movement since the security was purchased will attenuate a gain, or even turn it into a loss.

Dealing with the Exposure   Having identified foreign exchange exposure, a decision needs to be made about what to do about it. In general, the portfolio manager faces three choices: ignore the exposure, reduce it, or hedge it.

Ignore the Exposure   People often select this choice by default. An investor might be aware of the foreign exchange risk associated with a non-U.S. security but consider that risk to be a fact of life of global investing. This strategy is also appropriate if foreign exchange movements are expected to be modest or if the dollar amount of the exposure is small relative to the cost of doing something about it.

Doing nothing also would be an appropriate action if the U.S. dollar was expected to depreciate relative to the country of the foreign security. This is because the depreciation of the dollar would result in a gain to the U.S. holder of a security denominated in a foreign currency.

Reduce or Eliminate the Exposure   This alternative amounts to getting rid of the foreign security, or at least reducing the size of your position in it. Certainly this is a way to deal with the problem, but a rather extreme one. Still, if the dollar is expected to appreciate dramatically, this is an approach that should be considered.

Hedge the Exposure   Hedging involves taking a position in the market that offsets another position. (Hedging foreign exchange risk is also called **covering the risk**.) There are various ways in which foreign exchange exposure can be hedged. The most common methods are via the forward market or the futures market.[5]

As we saw earlier, a forward contract is a private, non-negotiable transaction between a client and a commercial bank. I know that the

DM100,000 par value German bonds in the earlier example will mature on a particular date, and if I so choose I can arrange with my bank to exchange DM for dollars at an exchange rate to be determined now. No money changes hands until the DM are delivered, but I eliminate the foreign exchange risk. The rate the bank promises to pay me for the DM reflects relative interest rates and associated risks, as we saw above.[6]

Foreign Currency Futures

If you understand basic principles of hedging and speculating, you will have no trouble applying those ideas to futures contracts on foreign currencies. Foreign exchange futures contracts trade at the Chicago Mercantile Exchange. They all call for delivery of the foreign currency in the *country of issuance* to a bank of the clearinghouse's choosing.

Hedging with Foreign Exchange Futures

The major players in this market are people representing commercial interests, such as major retailing firms, international banks, and multinational businesses. Scalpers have a smaller role in the foreign currency markets.

A Business Example   When business transactions occur between two countries, the goods or services traded must be valued in some currency. An American importing firm, for instance, might agree to buy a large shipment of woodcarvings, clocks, and candles from a German manufacturer. Suppose the total cost of the items is DM20 million, handshakes occur on the first of April, and the German firm promises to deliver the goods in early December. Payment is to be made upon delivery.

Before the U.S. importers accepted the DM20 million price, they checked the relative value of the U.S. dollar and the German Deutschmark to make sure that the DM price translated into an acceptable U.S. dollar price. Presumably it did, or the transaction would not have occurred.

While the cost of the goods is fixed in Deutschmarks, the price that counts is the U.S. dollar price, and this will almost certainly change before payment occurs. The world political situation, changes in international interest rates, and inflationary fears all contribute to daily fluctuation in relative exchange rates worldwide. From the U.S. importer's perspective, two

---

[5]People also hedge via the foreign currency options market, discussed in Chapter 13.
[6]A principal economic distinction between futures contracts and forward contracts is that futures contracts provide for daily marking-to-the-market, while forward contracts do not.

transactions must occur to complete this sale. First, it is necessary to buy the Deutschmarks, and second, it is necessary to pay for the imported goods. The price of the second transaction is fixed in the sales agreement; the price of the DM will change over time.

Fortunately, this foreign exchange risk can be hedged away in the futures market. Table 10-4 shows DM futures prices from 5 April 1993. The U.S. importer needs to get marks, so it is necessary to buy futures contracts. Because payment will be made in December, the December futures contract is the one to use. The paper shows that yesterday's settlement price for December DM futures was 61.1 cents per DM.

There are 125,000 DM in one contract. To hedge DM20 million, we need 160 contracts exactly. The importer would go long 160 contracts.

Once December arrives, the hedger can do one of two things. Because the DM are needed, one approach would be to simply sit back and wait for delivery to occur. When the DM were received, they could then be transferred to the German manufacturer. Alternately, the importer could trade out of the contracts by selling them before receiving a delivery notice.

If the DM appreciated from April to December (that is, the cost of the DM increased), the hedger would find that there would be a gain in the futures market that offset the higher cost of the DM in the cash market. On the other hand, if the DM depreciated, the lower cost in the cash market would be offset by a loss in the futures market. As in any hedging application, the hedge serves as insurance against some specific type of risk. The fact that you did not need the insurance (the case where the DM fell in value) should not be interpreted to mean that hedging was a bad investment.

An Investment Example Suppose a portfolio contains DM120,000 par value in 8.33% German corporate bonds. These bonds come due next March, when the issuing German firm will mail the bondholders their final check. In our case, this will be a check for DM125,000: this is the DM120,000 principal amount plus the final interest check of DM5,000. These funds will most likely have to be converted into dollars before they can be reinvested, unless the proceeds will be used to buy new German securities.

TABLE 10-4 GERMAN MARK FUTURES PRICES
           5 April 1993; 125,000 marks; $ per mark

	High	Low	Settle	Chg	Lifetime High	Lifetime Low	Open Interest
JUN	.6218	.6180	.6213	+.0023	.6920	.5890	104,020
SEP	.6156	.6132	.6153	+.0023	.6720	.5863	5,789
DEC	.6102	.6102	.6110	+.0023	.6650	.5830	194

$$\frac{20,000,000}{125,000} = 160 \text{ contracts}$$

The spot rate for the German mark might be $0.5400. This means that DM125,000 are currently worth $67,500. Between now and next March, this value can go up or down as the dollar depreciates or strengthens. I do not know for certain what the dollar value of the DM check I receive next March will be.

If I am uncomfortable with this uncertainty and want to hedge the foreign exchange exposure, I can do so using the DM futures contract. Because I will be receiving DM, I want to promise to deliver them to a buyer, so I go short (sell) in the futures market. By doing so I am promising to sell the Deutschmarks for $0.5530 apiece, for a total value of $69,125.

In March, there will be a gain or a loss in the futures market that will largely offset the gain or loss experienced when I convert the DM to dollars. Suppose the spot exchange rate in March is $0.5600. The check I receive from the bonds would be worth DM125,000 × $0.56/DM, or $70,000. This is $875 more than the value locked in with the hedge. I will now close out my futures position at the spot price of $0.5600 by buying one contract. I bought at $0.5600 and sold at $0.5530, losing $0.0070 on each of DM125,000 for a loss of $875. The loss in the futures market exactly cancels the gain in the spot market.

If the dollar had depreciated by March, and the spot exchange rate became $0.5000, then the DM check would be worth $62,500. The price locked in was $69,125; the check is worth $6,625 less than that. In the futures market, I sold at $0.5530 and bought at $0.5000; this is a gain of $6,625, which exactly cancels the reduced value of the check I receive.

Pricing of Foreign Exchange Futures Contracts

Futures prices are simply a function of the cash price plus the cost of carrying the particular asset or financial instrument. With foreign currency, the "cost" of holding one currency rather than another is really an opportunity cost measured by differences in the interest rates prevailing in the two countries. Table 10-5 presents a basic pricing model for foreign currency futures contracts.

TABLE 10-5   FOREIGN EXCHANGE FUTURES PRICING MODEL

$$P_f = \text{spot rate} \times \left[1 + (I_{ed} - I_{lc}) \times \frac{\text{days to delivery}}{365} \right]$$

where P_f = futures price
I_{ed} = Eurodollar rate
I_{lc} = local currency rate

Note: 360-day years are used to calculate Deutschemark, French franc, Japanese Yen, and Swiss franc rates.

The local currency rate is the "risk-free" interest rate prevailing in the country of concern. Suppose that in the Land of Leptonia interest rates are 10.00% and that the current dollar price of a Lepton is $0.4817. Also suppose that the current Eurodollar deposit rate is 7.50%. For how much should a 90 day futures contract sell? Using the formula, we find that the equilibrium price is

$$0.4817 \times \left[1 + (0.075 - 0.100) \times \frac{90}{365} \right] = 0.4787$$

This means that the futures price for Leptons should be *less* than their cost in the spot market.

Foreign exchange futures are priced this way because of the theory of interest rate parity. This states that securities with similar risk and maturity should differ in price by an amount equal to (but opposite in sign) from the difference between national interest rates in the two countries. In this example, Leptonia's interest rates are 2.5% (on an annual basis) higher than the U.S. rate. For 90 days, or one fourth of a year, Leptonia's rates are 0.625% higher. Therefore, Leptons for delivery in 90 days should sell at a 0.625% discount from their spot value, and this is exactly what we find.

Any futures price is a function of the cash price and the carrying cost associated with holding the commodity or financial instrument.

Consider one more example. Suppose I sell a Country X foreign currency futures contract to someone residing in Country X. By selling a contract as an opening transaction, I promise to deliver a certain quantity of foreign currency. Assume the contract calls for delivery in six months, and that the interest rates in my country are higher than the interest rates in Country X. I can invest the currency until I must deliver it. Similarly, the buyer of the futures contract can invest the funds that will be used to pay for the foreign exchange. Because my interest rates are somewhat higher than those of the Country X resident, I have an advantage: I will earn more interest. This differential is reflected in "compensation" to the Country X futures contract buyer via a discounted futures contract price.

Key Issues in Foreign Exchange Risk Management

For many portfolio managers, foreign exchange risk is a very modest component of total risk, and often one that is for all practical purposes immaterial. Still, if foreign exchange risk is ignored, it should be ignored on purpose rather than through ignorance. The steps in good foreign exchange risk management are these:

1. define and measure foreign exchange exposure;

2. organize a system that monitors this exposure and exchange rate changes;
3. assign responsibility for hedging;
4. formulate a strategy for hedging.

SUMMARY

Foreign exchange futures are used to reduce foreign exchange risk, or the risk of loss due to shifting relative values in national currencies. These contracts are priced according to the theory of interest rate parity, which is really just another version of the cost-of-carry pricing model.

Foreign exchange risk can be hedged via the forward markets, the foreign currency options markets, or the foreign exchange futures markets.

QUESTIONS

1. Comment on the following statement: "If you have a lot of foreign holdings scattered around the world, foreign exchange risk is not much of a problem, because the various translation gains and losses all average out to zero long term."

2. If a person anticipated receiving a quantity of a foreign currency in 90 days, why not hedge this transaction by using a 30-day forward contract and replacing it twice? Wouldn't this give you greater flexibility over locking in the 90 day rate?

3. At present, one unit of currency X equals three of currency Y. Interest rates are 6% in X and 8% in Y. Inflation in both countries suddenly rises by 3%. What effect would you expect this to have **(a)** on the respective interest rates, and **(b)** on the relative exchange rates?

4. Why is economic exposure more important to a portfolio manager than either type of accounting exposure?

5. Comment on the following statement: "I've never made any money in the currency forward market."

6. How might someone use foreign exchange futures in a *short hedge*?

7. Suppose you are a speculator in Deutschmark futures, and you are currently long three contracts. You hear a rumor about interest rates rising in Germany. Is this good news for you?

8. Why might overhedging be considered speculation?

PROBLEMS

1. The current exchange rate is one U.S. dollar equal to 1.4456 units of currency G. In the United States, the T-bill rate is 8.68%. The 60-day forward rate for currency G is $0.7100/G. What country G interest rate is implied in these prices?

2. Check the *Wall Street Journal* for 90 day forward prices on the German mark. What is the forward premium or discount?

3. Using your answer to Problem 2, and assuming 90-day T bills yield 9%, what should a 90 day German T bill yield if both governments are considered equally risky?

4. Suppose a Canadian dollar costs seventy-five cents in United States money. If the market begins in equilibrium, what should the new exchange rate be if U.S. inflation is one percent greater than the Canadian rate?

5. Using data from a recent edition of the *Wall Street Journal,* find the U.S. and Canadian prime interest rates. Based on these values, what change does the market expect in the value of the Canadian dollar relative to the U.S. dollar during the next year?

6. You have SF1,000,000 in bonds that will mature in 90 days. Using current data from the *Wall Street Journal*, show how you can hedge the foreign exchange risk by **(a)** using the forward market, and **(b)** using the futures market.

7. Suppose the U.S. prime interest rate is 9.75%, and the Japanese prime rate is 8%. The spot exchange rate for the Japanese yen is ¥136.15/$. If the 180-day forward rate is 135.90¥/$, is the market in equilibrium?

8. Refer to Table 10-5. You hold securities in Germany valued at DM58 million. How many DEC DM futures should be bought or sold to hedge the foreign exchange risk?

9. Based on your answer to Problem 8, suppose the value of the German securities rises to DM60 million, but the Table 10-5 information remains unchanged. How should you adjust the hedge from problem 8?

 **Interest Rate Futures**

Better be wise by the misfortunes of others than by your own.

Aesop

We saw in the previous chapters that an investor can remove much of the worry about adverse stock market fluctuations or foreign exchange movements by hedging that risk away by using stock index futures or foreign exchange futures, respectively.

Many portfolios, especially those with income as a primary objective, contain securities that are **interest rate sensitive.** That is, their value can be adversely affected if market interest rates rise. Equity securities are subject to market risk, while debt securities face interest rate risk.

Corporate and government bonds, for instance, are interest rate sensitive. Bond prices move inversely with interest rates. This means that the value of a bond portfolio will decline if market interest rates increase.

A passbook savings account, on the other hand, is not interest rate sensitive. There is no way that the principal value of such an account can decline, regardless of what happens to interest rates. The rate of interest paid on the account can change, but the value of the account will never decline unless the owner withdraws money from it.

In this chapter and the next, we look at several methods of reducing the level of interest rate risk associated with interest rate sensitive assets. The most efficient way of doing this requires the use of interest rate futures, so we begin with a discussion of the characteristics of these financial future contracts.

INTEREST RATE FUTURES

Interest rate futures contracts have enjoyed the same success as stock index futures. These contracts[1] have traded for over a decade now. The T bond contract is the most successful futures contract in the world, if you measure success by trading volume. Daily volume is usually well over 300,000 contracts, of which between 4 and 5 percent will ultimately be settled by delivery. Many financial institutions routinely use these contracts to hedge interest rate risk or lock in yields.

Categories of Interest Rate Futures

These futures contracts on debt are customarily grouped into short-term, intermediate-term, and long-term categories.

Short-term Contracts The two principal short-term contracts are **Eurodollars (EDs)** and U.S. Treasury bills. Eurodollars are simply American

---

[1]Avoid referring to futures contracts as "securities." They are *contracts* and are regulated by the Commodity Futures Trading Commission rather than the Securities and Exchange Commission.

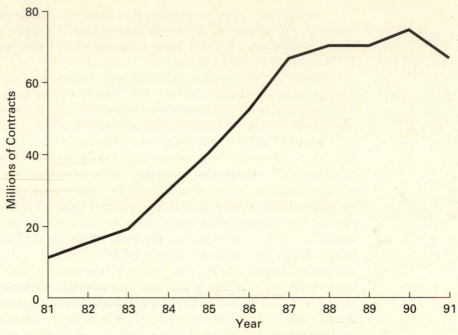

Figure 11-1 Treasury Bond Futures Contract Trading Volume
Source: Chicago Board of Trade

dollars on deposit in a bank outside the United States; there are at least $3.5 trillion of them. Eurodollars came about in the 1950s during the Cold War between the United States and the Soviet Union, Eastern Europe, and Red China. These countries feared the evolution of circumstances that might cause the U.S. government to freeze or confiscate their deposits in New York's money center banks. (This did happen to Iranian bank accounts following the hostage crisis in 1979.) To avoid this possibility, Communist countries transferred their dollar balances to banks in Europe.

The term "Eurodollar" refers to any dollar-denominated account outside the U.S.

Today, the term Eurodollars applies to any U.S. dollar deposit outside the jurisdiction of the U.S. Federal Reserve Board. Banks often prefer Eurodollar deposits to domestic deposits because EDs are not subject to reserve requirement restrictions. This means that every ED received by a bank can be reinvested somewhere else. This bank preference for EDs translates into a slightly higher interest rate on ED deposits.

Although EDs have this important advantage, they also carry more risk than a domestic deposit. They could be confiscated or frozen by the government of the country in which they are located, and there is not necessarily any deposit insurance outside the United States.

The Chicago Mercantile Exchange Eurodollar contract began trading in December, 1981, and is extremely popular with corporate treasurers and other hedgers. On November 1, 1991, open interest in ED futures topped the 1 million mark for the first time, representing more than $1 trillion Eurodollars.

Intermediate and Long Term   The contract on U.S. Treasury notes is the only member of the intermediate-term category, and Treasury bonds are the principal player in the long-term category. There are also contracts available on municipal bonds and on a U.S. dollar index, but these are special purpose contracts and have a limited following. The mechanics of using the long- and intermediate-term contracts for hedging or speculating are similar.

Treasury Bills and Their Futures Contracts

Characteristics of U.S. Treasury Bills   Unlike most other fixed income instruments, U.S. Treasury bills sell at a discount from their par, or face, value. The government sells 91-day (13-week) and 182-day (26-week) T bills at a weekly auction. The minimum denomination of a T bill is $10,000; much higher amounts are available. The more you pay for them, the lower the yield to you, and the less interest the government must pay. An investor might pay $9852 for a T bill that matures in 91 days. At maturity, the investor receives $10,000, earning $148 in interest. Treasury bills do not carry a stated interest rate. The interest rate their owner earns depends on the time until maturity and the price you paid for the bill.

Although these are simple discount securities, years of tradition have resulted in several ways of measuring their yield or calculating their price. Using traditional present value and future value notation, the pricing relationship for these simple discount securities seems straightforward:

$$\text{price} = \frac{\text{par value}}{(1 + r)} \tag{11-1}$$

where r = yield to maturity

For the Treasury bill described above, we can quickly solve for the yield to maturity:

$$\$9{,}852 = \frac{\$10{,}000}{(1 + r)}$$

Rearranging terms,

$$r = (\$10{,}000/\$9{,}852) - 1$$
$$= 0.01502 = 1.502\%$$

This rate is for one-fourth of a year. To annualize the rate and make it easier to interpret, it is necessary to multiply by 4, giving a yield to maturity of about 6.01%.

The industry practice is to do this slightly differently. A common format is:

T bill price = face value − discount amount
discount amount = face value × (days to maturity/360)   (11-2)
× ask discount

The **ask discount** is the discount associated with the current asking price for the Treasury bill. As with all publicly traded securities, there is always a bid price (the current highest buying price) and an ask price (the current lowest selling price). With an ask discount of 6.10%, we find a discount amount of

$10,000 × (91/360) × 6.10% = $154

The T bill price is then

$10,000 − $154 = $9,846

This differs slightly from the previous value, because in the first example we multiplied by 4 rather than by 360/91.

T bill yields can also be calculated as a **bond equivalent yield,** as follows:

$$\frac{\text{discount amount}}{\text{discount price}} \times \frac{365}{\text{days to maturity}} = \text{bond equivalent yield} \qquad (11\text{-}3)$$

If the T bill sells for $9,852, the bond equivalent yield is

$$\frac{(\$10,000 - 9,852)}{\$9,852} \times \frac{365}{91} = 6.025\%$$

The bond equivalent yield adjusts for two things: (1) the fact that there are 365 days (not 360) in a year, and (2) the actual investment required is the discounted price, not the face value. The value of this measure is that it enables you to compare more directly the yield on T bills with competing investment alternatives.

Alternatively, we could use $(1 + r)^{.25}$ in the denominator of equation 11-1. This changes the answer to 6.15%. This method assumes that your interest can be compounded into subsequent T bills, thereby earning a higher effective rate.

The Treasury Bill Futures Contract   Treasury bill futures contracts call for the delivery of $1 million par value of 90-day T bills on the delivery date of the futures contract. This means that on the day the Treasury bills are delivered, they mature in 90 days.

Table 11-1 is an extract of prices from the financial pages. Note that prices for the contract are presented both as a percentage of par and as a

TABLE 11-1 DEC T BILL FUTURES INFORMATION

PERCENTAGE OF PAR					ANNUAL Discount		
Open	High	Low	Settle	Chg	Settle	Chg	Open Interest
93.69	93.69	93.64	93.64	−0.09	6.36	+0.09	221

discount from par. The settlement price of 93.64 represents 93.64% of 100, or a discount of 100.00% − 93.64% = 6.36% *from* par. This figure of 6.36% is the market's best estimate of what 90-day T bills will yield near the end of December.

Remember that 6.36% for 90 days is different than 6.36% for one year. The rate published in the *Wall Street Journal* is an annual rate; we need to make a calculation to convert the price in the paper to our actual cost.

Suppose someone buys a DEC T Bill futures contract at a price of 93.64. What specifically does this mean in dollars and cents? To find out, the annual yield must be converted back into the true yield for the time the T bill is held (here, 90 days). By custom, 360 day years are used in computations like this. So 6.36% per year becomes 90/360 × 6.36% = 1.5900% for 90 days. When you buy a T bill futures contract, you are promising to buy $1 million in T bills, and the price you are promising to pay is

$$\frac{\$1 \text{ million}}{(1 + .00159)} = \$984,348.85$$

PER TEACHER'S METHOD
100−1.59 = 98.41 × 10,000 = $984,100

.0159

Suppose that in the middle of December interest rates have risen to 7.00%. Here, the *WSJ* price will be 93.00. We calculate the new price of the futures contract as follows:

$$90/360 \times 0.0700 = 0.0175$$

$$\frac{\$1 \text{ million}}{1.0175} = \$982,800.98$$

This means that a speculator who bought a T bill at 93.64 has lost money:

	$982,800.98	received
−	984,348.85	paid
$	1,547.87	LOSS[2]

It is an obvious point, but worth stressing: The price of a fixed income security moves inversely with market interest rates. In this example, our

---

[2]The futures contract holder will in all likelihood not pay or receive anywhere near this much. Instead, they will trade out of the contract before the delivery month. Their account will then be credited or debited with their gain or loss on the futures market transaction.

speculator was long a T bill contract and interest rates rose. Consequently, he lost money.[3]

Small movements in the relative level of interest rates translate into significant amounts of money. A change of one basis point (0.01%) in the price of a T Bill futures contract results in a $25 change in the value of the contract.

Let's look at another example, this time as a hedger. Suppose you learn that an educational foundation whose assets you manage will receive $10 million from an estate in three months. As the portfolio manager, you would like to invest the money now because you believe that interest rates are going to fall soon. When you are talking about sums of money this large, even a few basis points translate into many dollars.

> Speculators buy T bill contracts when they expect short-term rates to fall and sell contracts when rates are expected to rise.

Using the futures market, you can lock in the current interest rate. To do this, it is necessary to buy T bill futures, because you want the T bills. If you had the money, you would buy them now; but you will not receive the money for another three months. We saw in the example above that you are promising to pay $984,348.85 for $1 million in T bills if you buy a futures contract at 93.64. You will receive $10 million from the estate, so perhaps you decide to buy 10 DEC T bill futures contracts. (Ten of these contracts have a market value of slightly less than $10 million.)

> To lock in a current interest rate, buy T bill futures.

Three months later you receive your money as expected. Now you can remove your hedge by selling the futures contracts. Suppose that interest rates did fall, and that 90-day T bills now yield 5.5%. $1 million in T bills would then cost

$$\frac{\$1 \text{ million}}{1. + (90/360 \times 0.055)} = \$986,436.50$$

This is $2087.65 more than the price at the time you established the hedge. You are buying $10 million face value in T bills, so the total added cost to your fund is $20,876.50.

In the futures market, however, you have a gain that will offset the increased purchase price. A yield of 5.5% means the futures contracts will be

---

[3]The question is not necessarily whether rates will fall, but whether the T bill rate at contract expiration will be higher or lower than that implied by the futures contract price. For instance, the speculator may buy contracts if he or she expects a smaller drop in rates than the market seems to expect.

quoted in the paper as 94.50. When you close out these futures positions, you will sell your contracts for more than you paid for them. In fact, your gain in the futures market will be $20,876.50, exactly equal to your "opportunity cost" from the decline in interest rates.

Treasury Bonds and Their Future Contracts

Characteristics of U.S. Treasury Bonds Treasury bonds are similar to corporate bonds in almost every respect. They pay semiannual interest, have a maturity date of up to 30 years from time of issuance, and are readily traded in the capital markets. The two differences between a Treasury *bond* and a Treasury *note* is that notes, by definition, have a life of less than ten years at the time they are initially offered, and that T bonds are callable fifteen years after issuance. (Treasury notes are not callable.)   *may be*

> Treasury bonds may be callable after 15 years.

EX The Treasury seldom calls bonds, but it does happen. On October 9, 1991, the Treasury called the 7.5% bonds of August, 1993. Treasury rules require a 4-month notice, and so the bond was retired with the final coupon payment on February 15, 1992. The last call of a Treasury bond prior to this was in December, 1962. The subsequent refinancing of these particular bonds of 1993 saved the U.S. government about $18 million. Immediately prior to its call, the bond sold for 101$\frac{13}{32}$. It was retired at par. The loss in market value due to the call illustrates why investors should be aware of call provisions.

All new Treasury bonds and notes are issued in book entry form only and are registered in someone's name. Actual bond certificates are no longer issued. There are still coupon (bearer) bonds around, but no new ones are being issued. Despite the fact that registered bonds do not require the bondholder to clip a coupon, we still refer to a bond's *coupon rate*. This is the stated interest rate that determines the dollar amount of interest the bond pays. If a $1000 par bond has a coupon rate of 8½%, this means the bond will pay 8½% of par value per year, or $85. (In actual practice, this would be paid in two $42.50 installments, six months apart.)

Bonds are identified by the issuer, the coupon, and the year of maturity. We might refer, for instance, to the U.S. government "nines of 1997." This means the Treasury bonds with a 9% coupon rate that come due in 1997.

Pricing of Treasury Bonds Pricing of Treasury bonds is a straightforward process. We know the price of the bond, its maturity date and par value, and the timing and magnitude of the interest payments. With this information,

m: Price is set in mkt place, must know the price in order to solve for YTM.

m: US GOVT BONDS USE ACTUAL DAYS METHOD OF COUNTING DAYS -- i.e., 1 YEAR = 365 DAYS.

[handwritten: includes face pmt of value at maturity]

TABLE 11-2 BOND PRICING RELATIONSHIP

$$P_0 = \sum_{t=1}^{n} \frac{C_t}{(1 + r)^t}$$

where P_0 = current price of bond
n = number of periods until maturity
r = yield to maturity
t = time period
C_t = cash flow at time t *[handwritten: (coupi int + face value)]*

[handwritten: (discount rate]

we can <u>solve for the interest rate that equates the present and future values.</u>[4] This interest rate is the bond's <u>internal rate of return, or yield to maturity</u>. Table 11-2 outlines the pricing relationships.

[handwritten: Also see P. 259   Ex]

Suppose the U.S. government 9's of 2000 mature in six years and currently sell for 98% of par, or $980. We can <u>solve for the yield to maturity by finding the discount rate</u> (r) that makes the pricing equation hold.

To do this, we can either look at a "<u>bond book</u>," use a spreadsheet package like <u>Lotus 1-2-3</u>, or use a <u>trial and error</u> approach in which we estimate r and search for the value that makes the equation hold. Because the <u>bond sells at a discount from its par value of $1000</u>, we know that the <u>yield to maturity will be slightly</u> greater than its coupon rate of 9%. We might use 9.1% as a first estimate. Here is the equation:

[handwritten: face value + last coup pmt]

$$\$980 = \frac{42.50}{(1 + r)^{0.5}} + \frac{42.50}{(1 + r)^{1.0}} + \frac{42.50}{(1 + r)^{1.5}} + \frac{42.50}{(1 + r)^{2.0}} + \ldots + \frac{42.50}{(1 + r)^{5.5}} + \frac{1042.50}{(1 + r)^{6}}$$

For this bond, the yield to maturity (r) is 9.44%.

A <u>callable bond</u> is really a package of two securities: a <u>long position in a non-callable bond</u> and a <u>short call option</u> on the bond. The value of a callable bond, then, equals the value of a comparable non-callable bond minus the value of the "written" call.

The Treasury Bond Futures Contract This contract calls for the delivery of $100,000 face value of U.S. Treasury bonds that have a <u>minimum of 15 years</u> until maturity (and, if callable, have a <u>minimum of 15 years of call</u> protection). Bonds that meet these criteria are **deliverable bonds.**

[handwritten right margin: p. 174]

[handwritten left margin: Per p. 272, find institutions are among the largest users of T. bond futures to hedge interest rate risk.]

Defining the underlying commodity for the T bond futures contract, however, is <u>more involved than</u> with other commodities. An important feature of all commodity contracts is <u>fungibility</u>. Hedgers and speculators

---

[4]Technically, the <u>bond's yield to maturity assumes that coupon proceeds are reinvested at the</u> yield to maturity as they are received.

both want to be able to trade out of their contracts without having to go through the delivery process.

Some commodity traders consider the T bond pit to be the most sophisticated arena at the exchange. It is one of the largest and most difficult for an observer to follow; there are sometimes over 700 people in the pit at the opening bell.

As with the T bill contract, speculators buy T bond contracts when they expect interest rates to fall,[5] and go short when they expect them to rise. While an exchange-inspected bushel of wheat is the same as any other such bushel, a Treasury bond with a 9% coupon and twelve years until maturity is not the same as another bond with an 11% coupon and 23 years to maturity. Unlike stock index futures, delivery does actually occur with Treasury bill, bond, and note futures, although most contracts are closed via an offsetting trade. Only about 4% of Treasury bond contracts, for instance, are settled by delivery.

To "standardize" the $100,000 face value T bond contract traded on the Chicago Board of Trade, a **conversion factor** is used to convert all deliverable bonds to bonds yielding 8%.

Conversion factors are used to "standardize" bonds for futures delivery.

These conversion factors (or adjustment factors, as they are also called) are published by the Chicago Board of Trade. They are a function of the remaining life of a particular bond and its coupon rate. Bonds that have coupons higher than 8% are more valuable than bonds with lower yields, so these bonds "count extra" if delivered. Similarly, bonds with yields less than

TABLE 11-3 SAMPLE CHICAGO BOARD OF TRADE CONVERSION FACTORS FOR T BONDS

Remaining Life (Years & Months)	Coupon Rate			
	7%	8%	9.5%	10¼%
16–0	0.9106	1.0000	1.1297	1.1945
18–6	0.9043	1.0000	1.1436	1.2154
20–9	0.8994	0.9998	1.1504	1.2258

[5]They also buy when they expect a smaller drop than the rates implied in the futures contract, and vice versa.

8% have adjustment factors less than one. Table 11-3 (p. 255) shows some example correction factors.[6]

The Matter of Accrued Interest

Bondholders earn interest each calendar day they hold a bond. This is unlike the situation with common stock, where the dividend is an "all-or-nothing" item.[7] Despite this, firms only mail interest payment checks twice a year. Someone might buy a bond today and receive a check for six months' interest two weeks later. This would be a substantial return in two weeks' time. Things do not work this way, however, for the story is incomplete.

When someone buys a bond, they pay the **accrued interest** to the seller of the bond. Similarly, the bond seller receives accrued interest from the new bond owner. One day's interest accrues for each day the bond is held. At the end of the interest payment period, the bond issuer sends one check for the entire six months' interest to the current bond holder.

Figure 11-2 shows how bond interest accrues over the calendar year. This example is for a bond with a 9% coupon that pays interest on the first day of February and of August. A 9% coupon bond pays $90 in interest each year. This amounts to $0.2466 per day. A person who buys one of these bonds on May 5th, for instance, gets the bond 94 days into the interest cycle. The buyer must pay $0.2466/day × 94 days = $23.18 in accrued interest to the seller of the bond. If this bond were purchased at a price of 95, the buyer would pay $950 (the principal) plus $23.18 (the accrued interest) for a total of $973.18. On top of this would be any brokerage commission paid.

After the calendar year, bond investors must report the interest they have earned to the Internal Revenue Service. Your interest income is equal to the interest checks you received from the company plus accrued interest received from bonds you sold *minus* accrued interest you paid during the year to buy bonds.

---

[6]You can calculate these factors yourself if you need to. For instance, if the bond has an even number of quarters remaining in its life (that is, the bond is not in the middle of an interest payment period), the conversion factors are determined as follows:

$$CF = \sum_{t=1}^{n} [C_t/(1.04)^t]/100,000$$

where CF = correction factor
n = number of semi-annual periods until maturity (rounded down)
t = time period
C_t = cash flow at time t

[7]If you buy stock before an ex-dividend date, you get the entire forthcoming dividend. If you buy it on the ex-dividend date or later, you are not entitled to the next dividend.

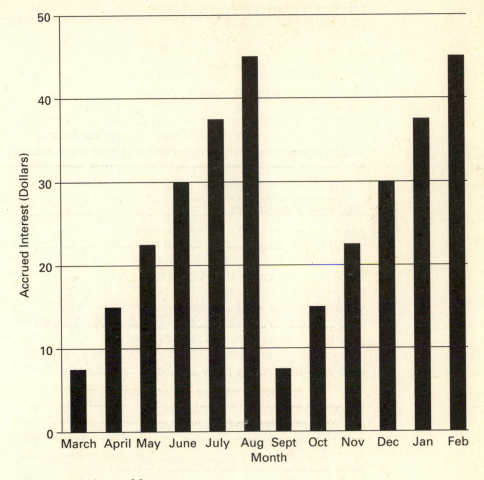

Figure 11-2 Accrued Interest
9 percent interest payable February 1 and August 1.

The Invoice Price

Deliverable bonds are standardized by multiplying the settlement price by the conversion factor, and then adding any accrued interest. The **invoice price** is the amount that the deliverer of the bond receives when a particular bond is delivered against a futures contract. It is calculated via equation 11-4:

$$
\begin{array}{c}
\text{invoice} \\
\text{price}
\end{array}
=
\left|
\begin{array}{c}
\text{settlement price} \\
\text{on position day}
\end{array}
\times
\begin{array}{c}
\text{conversion} \\
\text{factor}
\end{array}
\right|
+
\begin{array}{c}
\text{accrued} \\
\text{interest}
\end{array}
\qquad (11\text{-}4)
$$

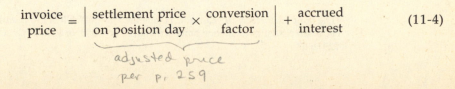

adjusted price
per p. 259

TABLE 11-4   CALCULATING DURATION : TRADITIONAL DURATION CALCULATION

$$D = \frac{\displaystyle\sum_{t=1}^{N} \frac{C_t \times t}{(1+Y)^t}}{P_0}$$

where D =   duration
C_t =   cash flow at time t
Y =   yield to maturity
P_0 =   current price of bond
N =   number of years until maturity

Delivery Procedures

Position day is when you notify the clearinghouse of your intent to deliver bonds against your futures contracts. This is two business days before the day you deliver the bonds (**delivery day**). Delivery is actually accomplished via wire transfer between accounts, and funds are transferred the same way.

Ex   Suppose, for instance, someone wants to deliver a 7% bond with 20 years, 11 months remaining in its life, and that the settlement price for the T bond futures contract on position day is 91-00. Chicago Board of Trade policy requires that remaining maturity be rounded down to the nearest quarter, giving twenty years and three quarters. The invoice price is then

0.9100	futures settlement price
× $100,000	contract size
× 0.8994	correction factor (conversion or adjustment factor on P. 255, Table 11-3)
$81,845.40	
+ 2,916.67	accrued interest[8] for 5 mos.
$84,762.07	invoice price

At any given time, there are usually several dozen bonds that are eligible for delivery on the T bond futures contract. Normally, only one of these bonds will be **cheapest to deliver.**

As we have seen, the yield on a bond depends on the bond price, the coupon, and the time until maturity. Bonds with coupons of 8%, for instance, may yield more or less than 8%, depending on their price. Only if they sell for exactly par will they yield 8% exactly. Other bonds, perhaps with a coupon of 7%, may also yield 8%, but this means they sell for less than their par value.

---

[8] The bond matures in 20 years and *11 months*. This means it is five months into the interest rate cycle. Accrued interest on one bond is therefore 5/6 × $35, or $29.17. On $100,000 par, the total is $2916.67.

The conversion factors make all bonds equally attractive for delivery only when the bonds under consideration yield 8%. If they yield more or less than this, one bond is going to have the (lowest) adjusted price, and hence be cheapest to deliver.

Fortunately, the bond cheapest to deliver is usually quickly determined: It is normally the bond with the highest **duration.**[9] This is the case when long-term interest rates are above 8%, as they normally are.

*NOTES
p. 285*

Duration

When applied to bonds, the duration statistic is the weighted average number of years necessary to recover the initial cost of the bond, where the weights reflect the time value of money. Duration's principal value to the financial manager or industrial engineer is that it is a direct measure of interest rate risk; the higher the duration, the higher the interest rate risk.

see p. 272

▌ Duration is the weighted average number of years necessary to recover the initial cost of the bond.

Calculating Duration   Table 11-4 presents the traditional duration calculation.

✓ P. 254

In the example above using the U.S. government 9's of 94, we found a yield to maturity of 9.44%. We calculate this bond's duration as follows.

r = YTM = 9.44%

$$D = \frac{\begin{array}{c} \dfrac{45 \times 0.5}{(1.0472)^{0.5}} + \dfrac{45 + 1.0}{(1.0472)^{1}} + \dfrac{45 \times 1.5}{(1.0472)^{1.5}} + \dfrac{45 \times 2.0}{(1.0472)^{2}} \\[2ex] + \dfrac{45 \times 2.5}{(1.0472)^{2.5}} + \dfrac{45 \times 3.0}{(1.0472)^{3}} + \dfrac{45 \times 3.5}{(1.0472)^{3.5}} + \dfrac{45 \times 4.0}{(1.0472)^{4}} \\[2ex] + \dfrac{45 \times 4.5}{(1.0472)^{4.5}} + \dfrac{45 \times 5.0}{(1.0472)^{5}} + \dfrac{45 \times 5.5}{(1.0472)^{5.5}} + \dfrac{1045 \times 6.0}{(1.0472)^{6}} \end{array}}{980} = 4.80 \text{ yrs.}$$

$\left(\dfrac{1+r}{2}\right)^{t}$
$\left(1 + \dfrac{.0944}{2}\right)^{t}$
$(1 + .0472)^{t}$

$1000 \times 98\% = $980

Duration is measured in years. This bond has small cash flows received every six months for five and one-half years, and one large cash flow at year six when the principal is returned with the last interest payment. The weighted average time to receive these cash flows is 4.80 years.

Equation 11-4 provides some intuition into the duration statistic in that it shows time weighted by the present value of the cash flows received in each period, but the calculation is unwieldy. Fortunately there is a simpler method: the closed form formula for duration.

---

[9]Another reasonably quick way to find the cheapest to deliver bond is to divide the deliverable bonds' market prices by their respective conversion factors. Whichever bond has the lowest ratio is the cheapest to deliver.

Closed Form Duration   The traditional calculation of duration can be tedious, because of the need to work through the summation. Fortunately, there is an easier way: The closed form duration equation is in equation 11-5.

$$D = \frac{C\left[\dfrac{(1 + Y)^{N+1} - (1 + Y) - YN}{Y^2\,(1 + Y)^N}\right] + \dfrac{F \times N}{(1 + Y)^N}}{P} \tag{11-5}$$

where D = duration
 C = coupon payment per period
 F = face (par) value of the bond
 N = number of periods until maturity
 Y = yield to maturity of the bond *per period*
 P = current market price of the bond

| The bond cheapest to deliver is normally the eligible bond with the longest duration. When Y/T mkt interest rates are above 8%, per p. 262 See notes, p. 285

Let's look at an example to help show the meaning of cheapest to deliver. Consider the information in Table 11-5.

If I have to buy bonds to deliver against a futures contract, I want to get these bonds as cheaply as possible. Table 11-5 shows that if I use the 7.25's of 2016, they would cost me $97,494.14. The other bond would cost more:

TABLE 11-5   CALCULATION OF CHEAPEST TO DELIVER
(Date of Calculation is January 15, 1990)

Bond	Price	Duration	Conversion Factor
7.25% of May 2016	89¹⁶/₃₂	11.14	0.9180
8.125% of Aug 2019	99¹¹/₃₂	10.92	1.0137

7.25% of May 2016

Time until maturity = 26 years 4 mo → 26 years, 1 quarter
Conversion factor = 0.9180
Cost of buying 100 bonds to deliver:
100 bonds/0.9180 = 108.932 bonds
108.932 bonds × $895.00/bond = $97,494.14

8.125% of Aug 2016

Time until maturity = 26 years 7 mo → 26 years, 2 quarters
Conversion factor = 1.0137
Cost of buying 100 bonds to deliver:
100 bonds/1.0137 = 98.649 bonds
98.649 bonds × $993.4375/bond = $98,001.62

per contract
$100,000 ÷ $1000 = 100

1 bond futures contract = $100,000

10 contracts
× $100,000
1,000,000

$98,001.62. The 7.25's are cheapest to deliver, and we note that they also have the longest duration, as expected.

The way the delivery system actually works is slightly different from this example. If I am short 10 T bond futures contracts, I promise to deliver $1,000,000 million face value of bonds. I will deliver 100 bonds; I cannot deliver fractional bonds. Consequently, the "correction factor" adjustment influences the *amount I receive* from the person who receives the bonds I deliver. The lower the coupon on the bond I deliver, the less I receive for it. The buyer pays an "invoice price," calculated as we saw in equation 11-4.

In practice, theoretical calculations regarding T bond futures and their hedge ratios are all based on the characteristics of the cheapest to deliver bond.

Delivery Options[10]

Some of the most sophisticated research in finance deals with the Treasury bond futures contract. This research identifies and seeks to value three distinct options held by someone with a short futures position.

1. *The Quality Option* A person with a short futures position has the prerogative to deliver any T bond that satisfies the delivery requirements. This is called the **quality option.**
2. *The Timing Option* The holder of a short position can initiate the delivery process anytime during the delivery month. This is the **timing option.**
3. *The Wild Card Option* Treasury bonds cease trading at 3 pm eastern standard time. A person may choose to initiate delivery anytime between the 3 p.m. settlement and 9 p.m. (EST) that evening. Changes in market conditions may change the desirability of delivery. In essence, the short hedger may make a transaction and receive cash based on a price determined up to six hours earlier.

   This important, and valuable, option is called a **wild card option.** If T bond prices were to decline late in the day, one could buy at the new, lower price and deliver at the previous, higher price.

SUMMARY

Financial futures are the fastest growing segment of the investment field. These contracts are popular with both speculators and hedgers.

Interest rate futures are divided into short-term, intermediate-term, and

[10]See Hugh Cohen, "Evaluating Embedded Options," *Economic Review* (Nov/Dec 91): 9–16, for a good discussion of embedded options.

long-term. Eurodollars are the most popular short-term futures contract. Treasury notes and Treasury bonds are the most popular in the latter two categories. These contracts can be used to hedge interest rate risk such as that faced by financial institutions.

Conversion factors are used to turn eligible T bonds into "equivalents" for futures delivery. Bonds with coupons above 8% count extra, while bonds with lower coupons do not count as much.

Treasury bonds are priced based on a bond that is the cheapest to deliver. When long-term market interest rates are above 8%, the bond with the highest duration will normally be the cheapest to deliver.

T bond futures contain a number of embedded options available to the short hedger. The quality option allows choice of which bond to deliver; the timing option permits selection of which day to deliver; the wild card option permits the delivery decision to be made up to six hours after the settlement price.

See notes, P. 285

QUESTIONS

1. Briefly explain why it is necessary to translate all bonds into "8 percent equivalents" in the delivery process for Treasury bond futures.

2. What is the purpose of calculating the "bond equivalent yield" with Treasury bills?

3. Suppose you are the manager of a money-market mutual fund. Would it matter if you hedged interest rate risk using Treasury bond futures instead of T bill futures?

4. Why is it necessary to include the provision about call protection in the definition of bonds eligible for delivery against the T bond futures contract?

5. Who might logically use T bills or Eurodollars in a hedge designed to reduce interest rate risk?

6. Do you feel that the need to hedge short-term interest rates is as important as the need to hedge long-term rates?

7. Explain why the cheapest to deliver bond has the lowest ratio of market price to conversion factor.

8. Look at a current *Wall Street Journal.* Compare the settlement prices of the different Treasury bill futures contracts. Why do you think they are different?

9. In hedging a portfolio, is there anything philosophically wrong with only hedging part of it?

10. Why might overhedging be considered speculation?

11. How can there be a "quality option" if all U.S. Treasury bonds are of equal default risk?

12. What is the difference between the "timing option" and the "wild card option?"

13. What is the relationship between the price of a callable bond and the price of an otherwise similar non-callable bond?

PROBLEMS

1. The newspaper price for a T bill futures contract is 93.33. What is the value of the T bills promised at delivery based on this price?

2. A speculator goes long 4 T bill contracts at 93.34 and closes them out three weeks later at 93.40. Calculate this person's gain or loss in dollar terms.

3. A T bill comes due in 88 days and sells for $9800. Calculate
   (a) the ask discount
   (b) the bond equivalent yield

4. Using a current *Wall Street Journal*, find the five deliverable T bond with the highest durations. Determine which of these is cheapest to deliver. (See Footnote 9 in this chapter.)

5. Zero coupon bonds are securities that pay no periodic interest. They have one cash flow: the return of principal at maturity. What is the duration of a zero coupon bond?

6. You deliver 16-year T bonds with a 7% coupon on an interest payment date against a futures contract position. If the T bond settlement price on position day is 92, what is the invoice price?

7. Refer to a current issue of the *Wall Street Journal*. Without doing any calculations, which Treasury bond do you think is cheapest to deliver?

8. A Treasury bond matures in 21 years and has a coupon of 7⅝%. What is its conversion factor?

9. A Treasury bond matures in 21 years and has a coupon of 9%. What is its conversion factor?

10. A T bond futures contract was purchased at 92. The hedger chooses to deliver bonds with a 6½% coupon that mature in 24 years, 5 months. If delivery occurs exactly halfway through an interest payment cycle, what is the invoice price?

11. You expect to receive $4.5 million to invest in Treasury bills in one month. Using current price information from the *Wall Street Journal*, show specifically how to lock in a current interest rate using Treasury bill futures.

12. A 10% bond sells for 110% of par, and matures in exactly 16 years. Calculate its conversion factor.

◉ **13.** Refer to problem 10. Suppose, instead, the bond chosen for delivery is a 9%, 20-year bond. Other conditions remain the same. What is the invoice price?

14. Repeat problem 11, except lock in a long-term rate using Treasury *bond* futures.

◉ **15.** You deliver 16-year T bonds with a 7% coupon on an interest payment date against a futures contract position. If the T bond settlement price on position day is 92, what is the invoice price?

◉ **16.** A 10% bond sells for 110% of par, and matures in exactly 16 years. Calculate its conversion factor.

17. You expect to receive $4.5 million to invest in Treasury bills in one month. Using current price information from the *Wall Street Journal*, show specifically how to lock in a current interest rate using Treasury bill futures.

18. Repeat problem 17, except lock in a long-term rate using Treasury *bond* futures.

 **Immunization and Spreading Strategies**

The most expensive real estate in Chicago is the top step of the bond pit.

Dale Lorenzo
Vice Chairman, CBT

bank immunization
basis point value (BVP)
bullet immunization
duration shifting
funds gap
immunization

LED spread
LIBOR
MOB spread
NOB spread
rate sensitivity
TED spread

One of the most important classes of strategies using interest rate futures is that involving portfolio immunization. The classic economic function of the futures market is hedging unwanted risk, and immunization epitomizes this practice in the financial markets.

Spreads are another popular futures market endeavor. These are enormously popular among arbitrageurs, marketmakers, and individual speculators. By attracting participants in the marketplace, spreading activities contribute to enhanced liquidity in the trading pits, and therefore better pricing for everyone.

THE CONCEPT OF IMMUNIZATION

Immunization means precisely what the name implies. An immunized bond portfolio is largely protected from "catching a disease" from fluctuations in market interest rates. Nonetheless, it is seldom possible to eliminate interest rate risk completely. Just as with childhood vaccinations, there is always a possibility that someone will develop a disease against which they were immunized.[1]

It is seldom possible to completely eliminate interest rate risk.

Continually immunizing a fixed-income portfolio is a time-consuming and technical chore. If it is necessary to be absolutely precise in the process, there are some fine points that must be considered, all of which complicate the process considerably. The references section of this book contains a sampling of published work regarding theoretical immunization issues. People involved in fixed income security management should continue their education by learning about the assumptions, shortcomings, and popularity of the various immunization techniques. Two broad groups of immunization-type tactics are duration matching and duration shifting. The next section covers them.

Duration Matching

There are two main applications of duration matching: *bullet immunization* and *bank immunization.*

Bullet immunization   **Bullet immunization** seeks to ensure that a predetermined sum of money is available at a specific time in the future. The objective

---

[1]Sometimes the marketplace does not behave like it is "supposed to," as evidenced by the widespread apparant arbitrage during the Crash of 1987.

is to offset the effects of interest rate risk and reinvestment rate risk. If market interest rates rise, coupon proceeds can be reinvested at a higher rate, but the increase in interest rates will reduce the value of bonds. Proper immunization will make sure that the "dollars and cents" effects of these two sources of risk net to zero.

| Bullet immunization is concerned with getting the effects of interest rate risk and reinvestment rate risk to cancel.

Ex

Suppose we have a requirement to invest $936 in bonds and ensure that the money will grow at a 10% compound rate over the next six years, at which time the funds will be withdrawn. This means in six years the fund needs to be worth $1,658.18.[2]

Over the six-year period, interest rates will most likely change. If they go up, the reinvested coupons will earn more interest, but the market value of the bonds held will go down. The account will be liquidated after six years, so there is a possibility of a capital loss on the bonds, causing the account to end with a value below the target.

This risk can be reduced by properly selecting the bonds in which to invest. The task is to invest $936 in some asset or portfolio of assets such that its yield to maturity is 10% and its duration is 6.00 years (the investment horizon). This is the essence of bullet immunization: *investing the present value of the payout(s) and matching the durations of the deposits and the withdrawals.*

Suppose there is a bond selling for exactly $936 with a coupon of 8.8%, a maturity in eight years, and a yield to maturity of 10.00%; its duration is calculated to be 6.00 years. For the sake of simplicity, assume the bond pays its interest annually, and that market interest rates change only once, after the third year. Table 12-1 (p. 268) shows three scenarios: rates remaining unchanged, rates falling from 10% to 9%, and rates rising from 10% to 11%.

If interest rates remain constant, after year six the value of the accumulated (and reinvested) interest proceeds plus the value of the bond[3] equals the amount targeted (rounding errors ignored).

If rates fall to 9% the interest accumulated is $14.54 less than in the "constant rate" scenario, but the bond price is $17.30 higher. Rising rates increase the interest received by $13.50, but the bond price falls by $16.90.[4]

---

[2]$936 × (1.10)^6 = $1658.18   *at end of 6 yrs*

[3]We must solve for the hypothetical bond value. For example, given an 8.8% coupon, a 10% yield to maturity, and 2 years of remaining life, the bond value is $979.20.

[4]Note in scenarios 2 and 3 that the resulting portfolio value does not exactly equal the target figure of $1658.18. Duration is a first-derivative statistic, and it works well for small changes in interest rates. Larger changes result in a divergence between actual price changes and those predicted by duration.

TABLE 12-1 THE EFFECTS OF IMMUNIZATION

Requirement: Invest $936 at a guaranteed rate of 10% per year for six years. No cash withdrawals until year six, when the entire amount is withdrawn.
Solution: Invest $936 in a security (or portfolio of securities) with a yield to maturity of 10.00% and a duration of 6.00 years.

One possibility is an investment in the single bond below:

bond price	=	$936
bond annual coupon	=	8.8%
bond maturity	=	8 years
bond yield to maturity	=	10.00%

Scenario 1: Interest rates remain constant at 10%

	(Reinvestment Rate at End of Year)					
	10%	10%	10%	10%	10%	—
	Value of Cash Flows					
Year	1	2	3	4	5	6
1	88.00	96.80	106.48	117.13	128.84	141.72
2		88.00	96.80	106.48	117.13	128.84
3			88.00	96.80	106.48	117.13
4				88.00	96.80	106.48
5					88.00	96.80
6						88.00
Total	88.00	184.80	291.28	408.41	537.25	678.97
	+ Bond Value at end of year six					979.20
	Total Portfolio Value					**$1658.17**

Scenario 2: Interest rates fall to 9% after 3 years

	(Reinvestment Rate at End of Year)					
	10%	10%	9%	9%	9%	—
	Value of Cash Flows					
Year	1	2	3	4	5	6
1	88.00	96.80	105.51	115.01	125.36	136.64
2		88.00	96.80	105.51	115.01	125.36
3			88.00	95.92	104.55	113.96
4				88.00	95.92	104.55
5					88.00	95.92
6						88.00
Total	88.00	184.80	290.31	404.44	528.84	664.43
	+ Bond Value at end of year six					996.50
	Total Portfolio Value					**$1660.93**

TABLE 12-1   THE EFFECTS OF IMMUNIZATION

Scenario 3: Interest rates rise to 11% after 3 years

	(Reinvestment Rate at End of Year)					
	10%	10%	11%	11%	11%	—
	Value of Cash Flows					
Year	1	2	3	4	5	6
1	88.00	96.80	106.48	118.19	131.19	145.63
2		88.00	96.80	107.45	119.27	132.39
3			88.00	97.68	108.42	120.35
4				88.00	97.68	108.42
5					88.00	97.68
6						88.00
Total	88.00	184.80	291.28	411.32	544.56	692.47
		+ Bond Value at end of year six				962.30
		Total Portfolio Value				**$1654.77**

"Total" shows end-of-year value of reinvested coupon proceeds. Coupons are received at the end of the year.

Bank Immunization   The example above showed how an independent bond portfolio can have its interest rate risk reduced by lowering the average duration of the portfolio. The problem is slightly different if interest-sensitive liabilities are simultaneously held. This kind of problem is often called the **bank immunization** case.

Banks have an investment officer. Besides managing portfolios like anyone else, the bank investment officer often is also concerned with certain balance sheet effects associated with changes in the value of the banks assets *and* liabilities. Books on the management of financial institutions go into this topic in much greater detail than we will here.

Assume that the bank holds the bonds in Table 12-2 and that these are part of the balance sheet shown in Table 12-3 (p. 270).

TABLE 12-2   BOND PORTFOLIO

Par	Company	Coupon	Maturity	Price	Yield	Duration
$ 50,000	XYZ	10⅛	2001	$ 50,860	9.78%	5.20
75,000	DEF	8	2006	63,728	10.20%	7.55
40,000	ALQ	9½	2002	40,376	9.33%	5.79
60,000	LLG	7⅞	2009	48,810	10.35%	8.38
70,000	FFQ	8½	1996	69,972	8.52%	1.88
$295,000				$273,746		5.55

ON BALANCE SHEET

Average duration

TABLE 12-3 SIMPLE NATIONAL BANK BALANCE SHEET (1 JANUARY 1994)

interest-sensitive assets	$273,746	non-interest-sensitive liabilities	26,000
non-interest-sensitive assets	500,000	interest-sensitive liabilities	400,000
		Net Worth	347,746
Total Assets	$773,746	Total L&NW	$773,746

A bank's **funds gap** is its interest rate sensitive assets (RSA) minus its interest rate sensitive liabilities (RSL). An asset that has **rate sensitivity** is one whose value changes as market interest rates change. If the bank wants to immunize itself from the effect of interest rate fluctuations, it must reorder its balance sheet such that the following condition holds:

$$\$_A \times D_A = \$_L \times D_L \tag{12-1}$$

where $\$_{A,L}$ = dollar value of interest rate sensitive assets
or liabilities

and $D_{A,L}$ = dollar-weighted average duration of assets or
liabilities

Assume that the bank's interest sensitive assets are limited to the bonds in Table 12-2 (p. 269); the duration of this bond portfolio is 5.55 years. Assume also that the rate sensitive liabilities have a duration of 1.00 year.[5] At the moment the bank is not immunized from interest rate risk:

Assets: $273,746 × 5.55 years = 1,519,290.30 $-years
Liabilities: $400,000 × 1.00 years = 400,000 $-years
1,519,290.30 ≠ 400,000

It is important to understand the implications of this. The $-duration value of the asset side of the portfolio exceeds that of the liability side. If market interest rates rise, the value of the rate sensitive assets and rate sensitive liabilities will both fall. However, the decline in RSA will exceed the decline of the RSL. The balance sheet must balance, and this means that net worth must decline. Net worth is what determines the value of shares of stock, and management clearly wants to take action to keep share price from falling. From a pure banking point of view, declining net worth also will cause problems with capital adequacy ratios of the type that bank examiners watch.

To immunize the portfolio, the bank needs to do one or more of the following:

1. get rid of some RSA;
2. reduce the duration of the RSA;

---

[5]These might be the bank's own bonds, which the bank was previously issued in the capital market.

3. issue more RSL;

4. raise the duration of the RSL.

Practical considerations make certain of these alternatives more attractive than others. Issuing more debt, for instance, cannot be done quickly, nor can new bonds be sold without flotation costs. A new security offering, especially of debt, may also cause concern in the capital markets; alternative 3 is not normally a feasible means of adjusting the funds gap. Similarly, it is generally not possible to alter the duration of the existing liabilities. This eliminates alternative 4.

This reduces the choices to the left-hand side of the balance sheet. The bank could sell some investment bonds it holds and put the proceeds into non-RSA. The remaining alternative is to put the proceeds from the sale of high-duration bonds into lower duration bonds.

Banks usually make duration adjustments by altering the *left* side of the balance sheet. (ASSET SIDE)

With one equation and two unknowns (the dollar amount of RSA and their duration), there are theoretically an infinite number of solutions to the problem. In practice, the fact that bonds are sold in increments of $1000 par value will limit the number of possibilities.

Looking carefully at the existing bond portfolio, it is apparent that the ultimate solution will require a reduction in RSA. The lowest duration bond is the FFQ 8½s96, with a duration of 1.88 years. If all the other bonds are sold and the proceeds are invested in more FFQ bonds, the '$-years' value would be $273,746 × 1.88 years = 514,642 $-years, which is still more than the target value of 400,000 $-years. This means the RSA must be reduced.

Note that reducing the RSA does not imply that anything is being thrown away. The bank has plenty of other assets (like cash, overnight federal funds, and non-negotiable certificates of deposit) that are not RSA. RSA money can be shifted into these as needed.

A good computer programmer can prepare an algorithm that will search the possible ways of rearranging the portfolio and produce a list of the most desirable options. Without such a program, the problem can still be solved reasonably quickly.

One feasible solution to the problem is to sell all the bonds except XYZ and FFQ. These are the bonds with the lowest duration. This changes the portfolio as Table 12-4 (p. 272) shows. This portfolio has $120,832 of RSA with an average duration of 3.28 for a total of $120,832 × 3.28 years = 396,328 $-years. This is close to the target figure of 400,000 $-years.

TABLE 12-4 MODIFIED BOND PORTFOLIO

Par	Company	Coupon	Maturity	Price	Yield	Duration
$50,000	XYZ	10⅛	1998	$50,860	9.78%	5.20
70,000	FFQ	8½	1996	69,972	8.52%	1.88
			Total RSA	120,832		
		Cash Equivalents (non-RSA)		152,914		
				$273,746		3.28

Duration Shifting

Changing Components Duration is a measure of interest rate risk. The higher the duration, the higher the level of interest rate risk. Faced with the prospect of rising interest rates, the bond portfolio manager should reduce the duration of the portfolio. This is called **duration shifting.**

See p. 259

Duration is lowered by reducing maturities and raising coupons. This means the portfolio manager wants to sell long-term bonds and replace them with short-term bonds, and sell bonds with low coupons, replacing them with bonds carrying higher coupons.

If interest rates are expected to rise, bond portfolio managers can reduce the anticipated damage by lowering the duration of the portfolio.

If the bonds' durations are known, the task can be accomplished in one step: Sell bonds with high durations and replace them with bonds of lower duration.

Suppose we have a portfolio like the one in Table 12-2 (p. 269). This portfolio has a market value of $273,746, and, based on this market value, its average duration is 5.55 years. What can be done if interest rates are expected to rise? Reduce duration is the obvious answer. An extreme approach would be to sell all these bonds and replace them with the shortest duration securities we can find. Thirty-day Treasury bills would be one solution, as would bank repurchase agreements or short-term certificates of deposit.

Hedging with Interest Rate Futures Some of the largest users of the T bond futures contract are financial institutions, which use them to hedge interest rate risk. A commercial bank usually maintains a substantial portion of its assets in government securities like Treasury bonds. If interest rates were to rise, the market value of these bonds would fall, and this would result in a reduction in equity on the right-hand side of the balance sheet. If such a rate rise were anticipated, the institution could go short T bond contracts to hedge the risk.

p. 254

To properly prepare such a hedge requires the calculation of a hedge ratio similar to that used with stock index futures. Instead of using beta, it is necessary to know the duration of the bond or mortgage portfolio being hedged.[6]

E×

Suppose a bank portfolio manager holds $10 million face value in government bonds, with a market value of $9.7 million and an average yield to maturity of 7.8%. Assume also that the weighted average duration of the portfolio is 9.0 years, and that the cheapest to deliver bonds have a duration of 11.14 years and a yield to maturity of 8.1%. Perhaps the manager is afraid that interest rates are going to rise, which will cause the value of the bond portfolio to decline. The portfolio can be immunized via interest rate futures by calculating a hedge ratio as follows:[7]

$$HR = CF_{ctd} \times \frac{P_b \times D_b \times (1 + YTM_{ctd})}{P_f \times D_f \times (1 + YTM_b)}$$

where P_b = price of bond portfolio as a percentage of par
D_b = duration of bond portfolio
P_f = price of futures contract as a percentage of 100%   (12-2)
D_f = duration of cheapest to deliver bond eligible for delivery against the futures contract
CF_{ctd} = correction factor for the cheapest to deliver bond.
YTM_{ctd} = yield to maturity of the cheapest to deliver bond
YTM_b = yield to maturity of the bond portfolio[8]

The hedger wants to select a quantity of futures contracts with characteristics such that

$$P_{c2} - P_{c1} + HR (P_{f2} - P_{f1}) = 0$$
where P_{ct} = price of cash portfolio at time t
P_{ft} = price of futures contracts at time t (12-3)
HR = hedge ratio

This is the goal of immunization: getting the change in value of one set of securities to offset the change in value of another set.

As stated, the cheapest to deliver bonds have a duration of 11.14. Suppose the portfolio manager chooses to hedge using a futures contract

---

[6]There are many different strategies for hedging interest rate risk. This duration-based example is just one of them. It assumes that if interest rates change, the shift in the yield curve will be parallel. That is, all maturities will change yields by the same amount.
[7]A good overview of some of the theoretical issues regarding interest rate hedge ratios is in Kolb and Chiang, "Improving Hedging Performance Using Interest Rate Futures," *Financial Management* (Autumn 1981): 72–79.
[8]In many cases the yields to maturity of the cheapest to deliver bond and the hedged portfolio are approximately the same. Consequently, the YTM factors are often dropped from the hedge ratio equation, since they do not materially change the answer.

(where does this come from? [Just arbitrarily given?)

with a market price of $90^{22}/_{32}\%$ of par, or 0.906875. The hedge ratio is then

$$HR = 0.9180 \times \frac{0.97 \times 9.0 \times (1.081)}{0.906875 \times 11.14 \times (1.078)} = 0.7954$$

CONVERSION FACTOR

To reduce the portfolio duration, it is necessary to go short futures contracts. The number sold depends on portfolio size and the hedge ratio. (Recall that a T bond futures contract calls for the delivery of $100,000 par value of T bonds.)

$$\# \text{ contracts} = \frac{\text{portfolio par value}}{\$100,000} \times HR \qquad (12\text{-}4)$$

$$= \frac{\$10 \text{ million}}{\$100,000} \times 0.7954$$

$$= 79.54 \text{ contracts} \rightarrow 80 \text{ contracts}$$

This procedure is very similar to the computations used with stock index futures.

A word of caution is in order. Financial futures are sophisticated financial instruments. There are many nuances in their pricing, including assumptions about such things as yield curve behavior and delivery procedures which have not been covered here. There are, for instance, at least five other ways of calculating the appropriate hedge ratio with financial futures. To learn more about strategy and the technical application of these contracts, the references for this chapter are helpful.

Increasing Duration with Futures While immunization activities are customarily oriented toward reducing the duration of a portfolio, it is sometimes appropriate to increase the duration. Adding long futures positions to a bond portfolio will increase the duration, and it is useful to know how to do this to achieve the desired duration.

A common way of determining the best way to achieve a target duration is via the **basis point value (BPV)** method. The basis point value is the change in the price of a bond for a one basis point change in the yield to maturity of the bond. Changing the duration of a portfolio by this method requires the calculation of three basis point values: one for the current portfolio, one for the target portfolio, and one for the cheapest to deliver bond. The number of futures contracts to buy is then determined by equation 12-5:

$$\# \text{ contracts} = \frac{(BPV_{\text{target}} - BPV_{\text{current}})}{BPV_{\text{futures}}} \qquad (12\text{-}5)$$

For the current and target portfolios, basis point value depends on duration, yield to maturity, and portfolio size, as equation 12-6 shows:

$$BPV = \frac{\text{duration} \times \text{portfolio size} \times 0.0001}{(1 + r/2)} \tag{12-6}$$

where r = portfolio yield to maturity[9]

The *BPV* of the cheapest to deliver bond is also a function of the relevant Chicago Board of Trade conversion factor and is calculated by equation 12-7:

$$BPV = \frac{\text{duration} \times \text{portfolio size} \times 0.0001}{(1 + r/2) \times \text{conversion factor}} \tag{12-7}$$

EX

Suppose a portfolio has a market value of $10 million, a yield to maturity of 8.5%, and a duration of 4.85. A forecast of declining interest rates causes a bond manager to decide to double the portfolio's interest rate risk exposure by doubling the portfolio duration to 9.70. Assume also that the cheapest to deliver Treasury bond sells for 98% of par, has a yield to maturity of 9.22%, duration of 9.7, and a conversion factor of 0.9100. The relevant BPVs can then be calculated as shown in Table 12-5.

Applying equation 5, the number of futures contract to buy to double the portfolio duration is then

$$\frac{\$9304.56 - \$4652.28}{\$101.90} = 45.66 \text{ contracts}$$

TABLE 12-5 DETERMINING BASIS POINT VALUES

Current Portfolio	
$\dfrac{4.85 \times \$10 \text{ million} \times 0.0001}{(1 + 0.085/2)}$ =	$4652.28
Target Portfolio	
$\dfrac{9.70 \times \$10 \text{ million} \times 0.0001}{(1 + 0.085/2)}$ =	$9304.56
Futures Contract	
$\dfrac{9.70 \times \$100000 \times 0.0001}{(1 = 0.0922/2) \times .9100}$ =	$101.90

4.85 × 2 = 9.70 →

[9]The portfolio yield to maturity is a conceptual number. Seldom do all portfolio components mature at the same time, so there are actually numerous relevant maturity dates. The portfolio yield to maturity can be calculated as a weighted average of the component yields to maturity, but it is important to remember the implicit assumption that all intervening cash flows are reinvested at the average portfolio YTM.

By buying 46 contracts, the bond manager will effectively double the portfolio duration, resulting in capital gains should the market interest rates fall as expected. Of course, by increasing the risk, the consequences of an interest rate rise also increase.

Disadvantages of Immunizing

If immunization is a good idea, why doesn't everyone do it?[10] For one thing, there are potential disadvantages. It is probably not a good idea to immunize continuously for the reasons discussed below.

▌Continuous immunization is probably not an optimum strategy.

Opportunity Cost of Being Wrong   Immunization strategies may be based on certain assumptions about the future direction of interest rates, or they may simply be based on the assumption that future rates will be volatile. If the market is efficient, it is very difficult to forecast changes in interest rates. With an incorrect forecast, immunized portfolios can suffer an opportunity loss.

Consider the sample bank balance sheet in Table 12-3 (p. 270). This bank has more $-years in RSA than in RSL. We went through an exercise to get these two figures approximately equal, because if interest rates rise the bank will suffer a decline in its net worth.

Suppose, however, that contrary to expectations interest rates *declined*. Then, if the balance sheet had been left alone, the value of the RSA would have *risen* by more than the rise in value of the RSL. This would have resulted in an increase in the bank's net worth.

Lower Yield   Another consideration is that immunization usually results in a lower level of income generated by the funds under management. The typical yield curve is upward sloping. This means that everything else being equal, the longer the term of a fixed income security, the higher its yield.

By reducing the portfolio duration, the portfolio return will shift to the left on the yield curve, resulting in a lower level of income for the fund beneficiary. It is a fundamental of finance that lower risk means a lower expected return. This principle holds for immunization strategies, just as with other investment activities.

▌Immunization usually reduces the portfolio yield.

---

[10]Ignorance is a prime reason.

Transaction Costs   Immunization is also not a costless activity. Selling one set of bonds and buying another requires the payment of brokerage commissions. For some investors, these sales may also result in tax liabilities.

There are also commissions associated with the futures market, but these will be much lower than those resulting from wholesale replacement of bonds. This, in fact, is a primary reason why the futures market is the method of choice for immunization strategies among many portfolio managers.

Immunization: Instantaneous Only   A final consideration is the fact that a portfolio may be only temporarily immunized. With each day that passes, durations change, yields to maturity change, and market interest rates change. Unless the portfolio is adjusted periodically, minor changes in duration will result in an increasing divergence between what was expected to happen and what actually occurred. Minor changes will also occur in the hedge ratio (for futures) or the $-years value (for asset shifting).

It is not practical for any but the largest portfolios to make daily adjustments to account for changing immunization needs. Smaller portfolios may be initially immunized, and revised only after weeks have passed or when conditions have changed enough to make revision cost-effective.

Immunization is neither a costless nor a permanent portfolio adjustment.

SPREADING WITH FINANCIAL FUTURES

Many traders actively employ sophisticated strategies simultaneously using more than one of the financial futures traded on the financial futures trading floor. This brief section focuses on two especially popular strategies of this kind: the *TED spread* and the *NOB spread*. Others of lesser importance are also mentioned.

TED Spread

At the International Monetary Market of the Chicago Mercantile Exchange, a popular strategy is "TED spreading," which involves the T bill futures contract and the Eurodollar futures contract. Traders who use this spread are anticipating changes in the relative riskiness of Eurodollar deposits.

The futures contracts on these short-term assets are very popular, even more so than that of the T bill contract. The daily trading volume for Eurodollar futures is often 20 times that of T bill futures. Open interest is over 1.5 million contracts, with a dollar value more than $1 trillion. Eurodollar rates tend to change more rapidly than U.S. T bill rates, although the two rates usually move up or down together. This is one reason the TED spread is popular.

In a nutshell, the **TED spread** is the difference between the price of the U.S. T bill futures contract and the Eurodollar futures contract, where both futures contracts have the same delivery month.

> The TED spread is the price difference between a three-month T bill futures contract and a three-month Eurodollar futures contract, where the two contracts have the same delivery month.

The trading pits for the T bills (ticker symbol TB) and the Eurodollars (ticker symbol ED) are only a few feet apart, thus facilitating spreading. Traders who employ this spread anticipate some change in the TB/ED price relationship. This differential frequently changes in response to developments in the world economy.

Suppose you feel that the gap between the TB and ED yields will widen because of increasing tension in Europe. The T bill yield has always been less than the ED yield, and conversely the T bill price is always more than the ED price. By convention, a person who buys the TED spread buys the T bill and sells the ED. When you sell the TED spread, you sell the T bill and buy the

Figure 12-1 The TED Spread

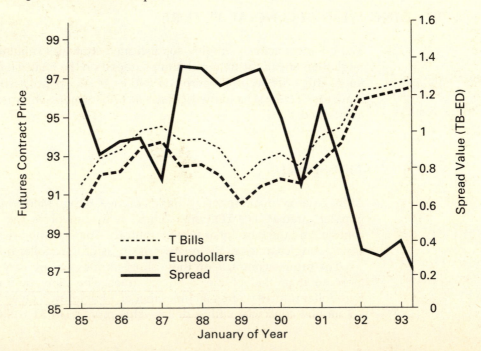

TABLE 12-6 BUYING THE TED SPREAD

Day 1:	buy	10 TB @	93.41	sell	10 ED @	92.00
Day 15:	sell	10 TB @	93.45	buy	10 ED @	91.88
	gain		0.04	gain		0.12

= 10 × $25/tick × 4 ticks   = 10 × $25/tick × 12 ticks
= $1000 *Gain*   = $3000 *Gain*

Net Gain = $4000

ED. If you think the spread will widen, you want to buy the spread. You really do not care if interest rates rise or fall; all that matters is that the spread widens. If this happens, you will make a profit.

Suppose the settlement price for a March 96 ED is 92.00, while the March 96 TB is 93.41. These prices translate into yields of 8.00% for the ED and 6.59% for the TB. This is a difference of 141 basis points. Suppose a speculator can buy a ten-contract TED spread at these prices. Two weeks later, as anticipated, the spread has widened. Current prices become 93.45 for the TB, and 91.88 for the ED; the spread is therefore 157 basis points. If the speculator is able to close out the positions at these prices, there is a profit as calculated in Table 12-6. Each tick (0.01%) is worth $25 per contract.[11]

The NOB Spread

Another popular strategy is "notes over bonds," or the **NOB spread.** A spreader might buy T bond futures and simultaneously sell T note futures. Traders who use these spreads are speculating on shifts in the yield curve. Treasury notes are intermediate-term securities, while Treasury bonds are long term. Normally, long-term interest rates are higher than shorter term rates, but the magnitude of the difference frequently changes. A speculator who anticipates such a change can construct a spread using T note futures and T bond futures in precisely the same fashion as with the TED spread.

The T note futures contract calls for the delivery of $100,000 face value of Treasury notes, just like the T bond contract. Securities deliverable against T note futures have a maturity of no less than 6½ years and no more than 10 years from the date of delivery; deliverable T bonds must have a remaining life of at least fifteen years.

Suppose I feel that the gap between long-term rates and short-term rates is going to narrow. Stated another way, I think that the price of T notes is

---

[11]0.01% of $1 million is $100. The T bill futures contract calls for the delivery of T bills with 90 days until maturity, or one-fourth of a year. T bill yields are quoted on an annual basis, but if they are three-month bills, their actual yield is one-fourth the annual rate. Hence, a tick is $100/4, or $25.

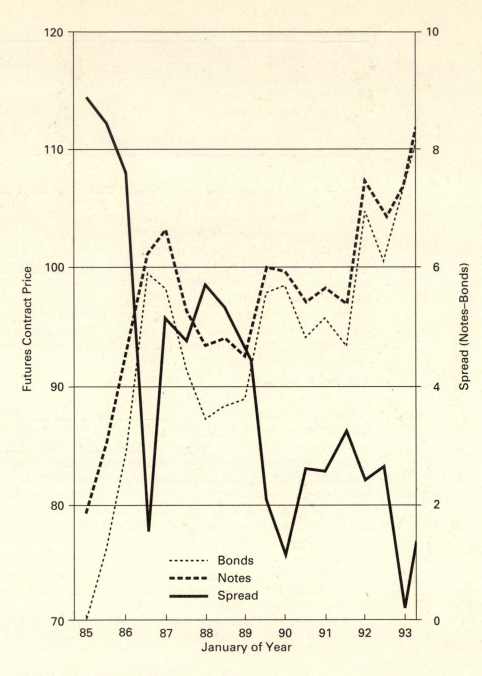

Figure 12-2 The NOB Spread

going to rise relative to the price of T bonds. To take advantage of this belief, I would buy T note futures contracts and sell T bond futures. Conversely, if I felt the spread was going to widen, I would sell T note futures contracts and buy T bonds. My aggregate profit/loss would be determined in the same manner as in Table 12-6 (p. 283).[12]

Other Spreads with Financial Futures

LED Spread   **LED spread** is trader talk for the LIBOR-Eurodollar spread. **LIBOR** is the London Inter-Bank Offered Rate; this rate is the deposit rate associated with inter-bank loans in London. It is much like the federal funds rate in the United States.

The futures contract on the LIBOR implies a one-month Eurodollar time deposit rate. The Eurodollar futures contract is similar to the U.S. Treasury bill futures contract and implies a three-month rate. Normally, the three-month rate is higher than the one-month rate, as the yield curve is usually upward sloping. LED spreaders usually adopt this strategy because of a belief about a change in the slope of the yield curve or because of apparent arbitrage in the forward rates associated with the implied yields.

MOB Spread   The **MOB spread** is "municipals over bonds." In essence, it is a play on the taxable bond market (Treasury bonds) versus the tax-exempt bond market (municipal bonds). Tax-exempt yields are much less than taxable yields on securities of comparable risk, but the gap between them can vary significantly. Regardless, interest rates tend to move together, so there is high correlation between the yields (and therefore the prices) of Treasury bonds and municipal bonds. As with all spreads, the MOB spreader buys the futures contract that is expected to outperform the other and sells (promises to deliver against) the weaker contract. The size of the MOB spread depends on many economic and psychological factors, including tax laws, the general quality and availability of credit in the marketplace, and the shape of the yield curve.

SUMMARY

Immunization is a technique designed to eliminate much of the interest rate risk inherent in a bond portfolio or the net interest rate risk on a balance

[12]Note that both T note and T bond futures trade in 32nds of a point rather than in decimals; do not forget to convert to decimal prices.

sheet. The essence of immunization is turning long-term securities into short-term securities or security equivalents.

Immunization is not a costless activity. It usually lowers the expected return of a portfolio, results in an opportunity loss if you incorrectly forecast the direction of interest rates, and results in higher transaction costs. It also is an instantaneous strategy that requires frequent revision.

Certain spreading strategies with interest rate futures are quite popular. The TED spread (Treasuries over Eurodollars) is a way to speculate on relative changes in the level of international uncertainty. The NOB spread (notes over bonds) facilitates speculation on shifts in the slope of the yield curve. Other less-familiar spreads include the LED spread (LIBOR over Eurodollars) and the MOB (municipals over bonds).

QUESTIONS

1. What does "immunization" mean?
2. Explain the difference between bullet immunization and bank immunization.
3. Explain the relationship between interest rate risk and reinvestment rate risk in a bullet immunization strategy.
4. Explain the concept of "funds gap."
5. Which side of the balance sheet do banks generally alter as part of their immunization strategies? Why?
6. Give examples of assets that are "rate sensitive" and others that are not.
7. List several ways the duration of a portfolio can be changed.
8. Why are some bonds cheaper to deliver than others?
9. Explain the idea of "basis point value."
10. What are the disadvantages of immunizing?
11. Why is immunization "instantaneous only"?
12. What is the TED spread?
13. Give an example of a situation in which someone might consider using the TED spread.
14. What is the NOB spread?
15. Suppose the slope of the yield curve is expected to flatten. How would a NOB spreader take advantage of this?
16. Why might someone consider using the LED spread?
17. What is the motive of the MOB spreader?
18. Briefly explain why it is necessary to translate all bonds into "8% equivalents" in the delivery process for Treasury bond futures.

PROBLEMS

1. Refer to Table 12-1 (p. 268–69) in this chapter. Suppose that interest rates changed instantaneously to 8% after two years. Show the resulting portfolio value, as with the rest of the table.

2. Refer to Table 12-2 (p. 269). Suppose the portfolio manager sold all the XYZ bonds and put the money into 90-day T bills. What is the new portfolio duration? (Ignore commissions and accrued interest.)

3. Make up a bullet immunization example, using *two* of the bonds in Table 12-2. Show the cash flow, etc., as in Table 12-1. Assume the bonds pay interest annually.

4. Suppose a bank has rate sensitive assets of $45 million, rate sensitive liabilities of $23 million, total assets of $100 million, and equity of $50 million. The duration of the RSA is 3.3, while the duration of the RSL is 13.5. What is the bank's funds gap?

5. If the cheapest to deliver bond has a duration of 7.5, a price of 100, and a conversion factor of 0.9150, how many futures contracts (selling for 98) must be used to hedge a $10 million portfolio with a duration of 14.6?

6. If the cheapest to deliver bond has a duration of 9.5, a price of 90, and a conversion factor of 0.8450, how many futures contracts (selling for 99) must be used to hedge a $130 million portfolio with a duration of 8.6?

7. What is the conversion factor for a 7⅝% coupon bond that matures in 21 years, 4 months?

8. What is the conversion factor for a 9% coupon bond that matures in 16 years, 11 months?

9. A bond portfolio has a market value of $56 million, a yield to maturity of 8.7%, and a duration of 6.44. What is its basis point value?

10. Assume the cheapest to deliver T bond sells for 97, has a yield to maturity of 6.6%, a duration of 5.5, and a conversion factor of .8124. What is the basis point value of the associated futures contract?

11. Refer to a current *Wall Street Journal*. How many basis points is the September "next year" TED spread?

3

PART

SPECIAL TOPICS

13 Futures Options and Other Derivative Assets

You may not get rich by using all the available information, but you surely will get poor if you don't.

Jack Treynor

foreign currency option
futures option
warrant

warrant hedge
when-issued stock

This chapter covers futures options and other well-established derivative securities: warrants, when-issued stock, and foreign currency options. In recent years, the rocket scientists of finance have spawned derivative products faster than theoretical physicists have proposed new subatomic particles. While these newer securities (such as CAPS, PERCS, and LEAPS) are also derivative assets, Chapter 15 (Financial Engineering) covers them.

FUTURES OPTIONS

I once heard these securities described as "uniquely worthless." This is wrong. They are versatile financial instruments, clearly worth exploring.

Characteristics

When the idea of listed options on futures contracts was first proposed, some observers felt that these securities served no economic purpose and were simply gambling instruments. Few informed people continue to share this view, however. **Futures options** give users of the futures market an enhanced ability to tailor their risk/return exposure to individual needs. They also provide an opportunity for the speculator to avoid the unlimited losses that are theoretically possible with futures contracts.

> Futures options give users of the futures market an enhanced ability to tailor their risk/return exposure to specific needs.

Only since 1982 have options been permissible on non-agricultural futures, and only since 1984 on traditional agricultural commodities like wheat and soybeans. The Commodity Futures Trading Commission Act of 1974 provides that futures contract markets must be "not contrary to the public interest," and such products as might be traded on the exchanges must serve legitimate hedging purposes.

In principle, these options are no different from listed options on stocks or stock indexes. Calls give you the right to buy, and puts give you the right to sell. As you would expect, the futures option gives you the right to buy or sell a commodity futures contract. It is important to recognize that *the underlying security is the futures contract, not the physical commodity represented by the futures contract*. In other words, the owner of a call option on soybean futures has the right to assume a long position in a soybean futures contract. The owner of a soybean futures put has the right to go short a soybean futures contract. Exercise of a futures call does not result in delivery of the underlying commodity. Instead, the exerciser's account will be credited with a long position in the futures contract, and he or she must pay for it.

■ Futures calls give their owner the right to go long a futures contract; a put gives its owner the right to go short.

Writing an equity call and buying an equity put (or vice versa) are not equivalent strategies. They are not equivalent with futures options either, and it is useful to note precisely how they are different. Someone who buys a futures put has the right to go short a futures contract. Someone who writes a futures call has the obligation to go short if the call holder chooses to exercise. Similarly, if I buy a futures option call, I have the right to go long, while a put writer has the obligation to go long if exercise occurs.

Table 13-1 shows selected futures options prices. The format of the listing is similar to that of traditional option quotations. Expiration dates are from left to right, striking prices are listed vertically, and the prices (premiums) for puts and calls are side by side. The price listed for a JAN 575 call option on

TABLE 13-1   FUTURES OPTIONS PRICES
November 20, 1992

SOYBEANS
5000 bu; cents/bu

Strike Price	Calls			Puts		
	JAN	MAR	MAY	JAN	MAR	MAY
500	59½	...	...	⅛	⅝	1⅛
525	34¾	42½	49¾	⅝	1⅞	3½
550	13¾	22	30½	4¼	7	9¼
575	3½	10	17¾	19	19½	21¼
600	¾	4¾	10¼	41¼	39	38
625	¼	2¼	6	...	...	58¾

S&P 500 Stock Index
$500 × premium

Strike Price	Calls			Puts		
	NOV	DEC	JAN	NOV	DEC	JAN
415	11.60	13.55	16.60	0	2.00	4.20
420	6.60	9.55	12.90	0	2.95	5.45
425	1.60	6.20	9.55	0	4.60	7.10
430	0	3.70	6.75	3.40	7.05	9.30
435	0	1.85	4.50	...	10.25	12.00
440	0	0.90	2.85	13.40	14.25	15.35

soybeans is 3½ cents per bushel. A futures option corresponds to a single commodity futures contract, which for soybeans is 5000 bushels.

The person who buys this call pays the premium of 3.50 cents on each of 5000 bushels, for a total of $175.00. The option writer receives this sum and keeps it, regardless of what happens to soybean prices between now and the expiration date of the option.

Like other options, futures options have both *intrinsic value* and *time value*. On the date the Table 13-1 prices were determined the settlement price for January soybeans was $5.59 per bushel. A call option with a striking price of 575 ($5.75 per bushel) is out-of-the-money if the underlying commodity sells for less than this. Therefore, there is no intrinsic value with this option. If we looked at a JAN 575 put, however, it would have intrinsic value of $5.75 − $5.59 = $0.16. Table 13-1 shows that the premium for a JAN 575 put on soybean futures is 19 cents. Because the intrinsic value is 16 cents, its time value must be $0.19 − $0.16 = $0.03.

There is one major way in which futures options differ from equity or index options, and that has to do with their expiration. Generally, the option month refers to the futures contract delivery month. The option expires on a specific date in the *preceding* month. The actual expiration date varies with each contract. For soybeans, expiration is set as "the first Friday preceding the first notice day for the corresponding soybean futures contract by at least 10 business days." So the JAN 550 soybean call actually expires in December. Expiration is not the third Friday of the stated month, as with equity or index options. A calendar is usually necessary to figure out the precise expiration.

Most futures options expire in the month prior to the futures delivery month.

With S&P 500 stock index options, serial expiration of options has been available since July, 1987. For instance, it is possible to trade an October option on the December futures contract. These October options expire in traditional fashion on the third Friday of October. The reason for this distinction is that stock indexes are not deliverable; they are cash-settled. Because there is no delivery mechanism, it is more useful to extend the life of the option into the "delivery" month.

Speculating with Futures Options

The principles of speculation with futures options are very similar to those we have previously discussed. Suppose a speculator anticipates a bumper crop of soybeans and is confident that the price of soybeans is going to drop. He could write naked calls, but might be uneasy about the unlimited risk and predetermined maximum gain characteristic of this strategy. Instead, he decides to buy a put option on the soybean futures, facing the same decisions regarding expiration and striking price as any other options user. The longer the time until option expiration, the greater the likelihood of a favorable price movement, but the more the option costs. The more favorable the striking price, the higher the option premium as well.

After considering these factors and checking his account balance, the speculator decides to buy 3 JAN 550 puts, and does so at the listed price of 4¼ cents. His money at risk is

$$3 \text{ contracts} \times \frac{5{,}000 \text{ bu}}{\text{contract}} \times \frac{\$0.0425}{\text{bu}} = \$1912.50$$

This is the most that the option buyer can lose.

> *PUT ?*
> Buying futures options involves a predetermined, known, and limited maximum loss, just as with options on other assets.

Suppose that by mid-December the price of soybeans falls, as predicted. If the settlement price of the futures contract is $5.3500, the 550 put has intrinsic value of fifteen cents. There is still time value, and the option premium might be twenty cents. Selling the three puts results in a profit of $0.20 (sale price) − $0.0425 (purchase price) on each of 15,000 bushels, for a total gain of $2362.50. On the other hand, if soybean prices remained above $5.50, the value of the puts would approach zero as the expiration date approached.

Spreading with Futures Options

It is also common for speculators in futures options to reduce their money at risk by setting up various types of spreads. An investor who was bullish on the future price of soybeans, for instance, might construct a bullspread by buying calls with one striking price and writing other calls with a higher striking price. Consider the MAR 600 and 625 calls on soybeans from Table 13-1. These show settlement prices of 4¾ cents and 2¼ cents per bushel, respectively. Suppose someone selects these options for a bullspread. Table 13-2 is a profit and loss summary for the strategy.

TABLE 13-2   SOYBEAN CALL OPTION BULLSPREAD

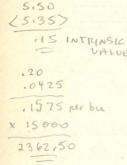

		Futures Settlement Price (cents/bu)					
		600	605	610	615	620	625
buy 600 call	@ 4.75	−4.75	+0.25	+5.25	+10.25	+15.25	+20.25
write 625 call	@ 2.25	+2.25	+2.25	+2.25	+ 2.25	+ 2.25	+ 2.25
		−2.50	+2.50	+7.50	+12.50	+17.50	+22.50

Handwritten margin notes:
5.50
⟨5.35⟩
.15 INTRINSIC VALUE

.20
.0425
.1575 per bu
× 15000
2362.50

HIGHER STRIKE PRICE

(handwritten: WRITE MAR 550 CALL)

(handwritten: BUY MAY 550 CALL)

TABLE 13-3 EFFECT OF CHANGING BASIS ON FUTURES OPTION SPREAD

	Cash Price	March Delivery			May Delivery		
		Futures Price	Basis	Option Value	Futures Price	Basis	Option Value
Nov 20	545	565	+20	22	571	+26	30½
Feb 15	580	595	+15	47	599	+19	53½
change		+30	− 5	+25	+29	− 7	+23

loss on short MAR call:
$0.25 × 5000 = $1250

gain on long MAY call:
$0.23 × 5000 = $1150

net loss = $1250 − $1150 = $100

The maximum loss is 2½ cents per bushel, or $125 for the 5000 bushels covered by one option. The maximum gain is much more substantial, $1125. This is an attractive risk/reward ratio.

Remember the Chapter 8 discussion on the implications of changing basis with agricultural commodities. Someone who buys a January soybean contract and sells a November contract, for instance, runs a substantial basis risk, because these two contracts have a *different* basis, and it is possible that both contracts could move against you.[1]

The same warning is appropriate with futures options. If I construct a calendar spread with soybean calls, perhaps by buying the MAY 550 and writing the MAR 550, I run a basis risk. The MAY 550 call gives me the right to go long a May futures contract. The short position in the March call gives someone else the right to go long a March futures contract, and because I am the one who created the option, it is I who must go short a March futures contract. The pricing of the March and May contracts can be quite different.

Suppose that on November 20th, when we are looking at the *WSJ* with the prices shown in Table 13-1 (p. 288), we also find that the futures prices for soybeans are 565 for March delivery, and 571 for May delivery. Also suppose that on this day the cash price for soybeans is 545.

On November 20 we buy the MAY 550 call for 30½ cents, and write the MAR 550 call, receiving 22 cents. The net cost of the spread is 8½ cents per bushel. There are 5000 bushels covered by one contract, so the spread requires a cash outlay of 5000 bu × $0.085/bu = $425.

Over the next three months, there is a major increase in the price of soybeans because of concern about a newly discovered crop disease with unknown implications. The cash price increases to 580, and the futures

---

[1]Under most circumstances each delivery month of an agricultural commodity futures contract will move together. Unusual storage circumstances or demand patterns could cause some deviation from this, however.

contracts rise to 595 for the March contracts and 599 for the May contracts. The value of the options changed to 47 cents for the March calls, and 53½ cents for the May calls. Table 13-3 (p. 291) shows the net effect. Because the May contract basis change is more than the March contract basis change, this results in a loss for the spreader.

check this

Hedging with Futures Options

There are as many ways to hedge with futures options as there are with equity or index options. Any hedge serves to limit risk with some tradeoff in potential return. In the commodities market, there are sometimes several levels of hedging going on when futures options are involved.

Suppose a Midwest family operates a 1500 acre farm and knows from experience that they can expect to harvest between 30 and 40 bushels of soybeans per acre. The family plans on an expected harvest of 50,000 bushels. The futures market can be used to hedge the price risk faced by the family. Because there are 5000 bushels of soybeans in one contract, they might decide to go short 10 soybean contracts.[2]

Unexpected problems with the crop (weather, bugs, tornadoes, etc.) sometimes make it impractical (or impossible) to deliver the full 50,000 bushels called for by the futures contracts. So they indirectly hedge again by going short 9 contracts only. The purpose of this partial hedge is to reduce the inconvenience and cost of having to either close out some contracts at a financial loss or acquire soybeans in the cash market to deliver against the short contracts.

Finally, the family might feel that there is a substantial chance that this year's soybean prices will be higher than in the past. Hedging in the futures market locks in a price, and this price might well be less than the one that prevails at harvest time. So they can hedge again by buying a few soybean calls. This way, if prices advance sharply, they will recover some of what would have otherwise been an "opportunity loss." The cost of the call options is analogous to insurance against missing out on a good market price at harvest time.

Futures options are particularly useful to the individual investor who speculates with interest rate or stock index futures. If someone buys an S&P 500 index futures contract, for instance, a market decline results in their account balance dwindling as it is marked to market each day. As protection against these potentially disastrous losses, puts on the S&P futures could be purchased. (You also could write call options, but this would provide less protection.) Similarly, the person who is short S&P 500 futures might buy calls or write puts as a hedge.

---

[2]In practice, most farms only hedge between 25% and 50% of their overall potential crop.

Early Exercise of Futures Options

Listed call options will not normally be exercised early, because doing so results in an abandonment of the remaining time value of the option. With futures options, there are circumstances in which it is optimal to exercise a call early. Fortunately, this can be explained by intuition without complicated equations.

Someone who buys a call option has a net cash outlay. This money is the option writer's to keep no matter what happens. When I buy (go long) a futures contract, I put up a good faith deposit that is still my money; in fact, I can satisfy most of the good faith deposit with Treasury bills on which I earn interest.

Suppose that the value of a futures contract rises dramatically, leaving certain call options deep-in-the-money. The deeper in-the-money any option goes, the more it behaves like the underlying security itself (and the closer the absolute value of *delta* gets to one). A deep-in-the-money futures call is a valuable asset, and it could be sold to generate cash; it earns no interest, however. Because this option will behave very much like the futures contract itself, there is little reason to prefer the call to the futures contract.

In fact, there is a good reason to prefer the futures contract over the call. The investment characteristics of the two securities are similar. If I exercise the call, though, I get to go long the futures contract, and my cash investment begins to earn interest, whereas if I keep the call I earn no interest. Of course, you also could sell the call, but this would get you out of the market entirely. This position is not equivalent to either the "long call" or "long futures" position, so it is not part of the early exercise question.

Early exercise of futures options is sometimes optimal when they become deep-in-the-money.

Pricing Futures Options

Fisher Black (of Black-Scholes fame) extended the principles of the BSOPM to futures pricing. Although this model is limited to European options (which can only be exercised at maturity), it is a useful starting point for determining a theoretical futures option premium. Table 13-4 (p. 294) shows the model.

Suppose (1) a two-month (0.1667 year) call option is available on the S&P 500 stock index futures, (2) T bills yield 6%, (3) the S&P 500 futures contract currently sells for 270.00, (4) the option has a striking price of 275.00, and (5) that volatility is 35 percent. What is the theoretical value of the call?

TABLE 13-4 BLACK FUTURES CALL OPTION PRICING MODEL

$$C = e^{-rt}[FN(a) - KN(b)]$$

$$\text{where } a = \frac{ln(F/K) + \sigma^2 t/2}{\sigma\sqrt{t}}$$

$$b = a - \sigma\sqrt{t}$$

and
C	=	futures call option premium
e	=	base of natural logarithms
r	=	risk-free interest rate
t	=	time in years until option expiration
K	=	option striking price
F	=	futures price
σ	=	annual volatility of the futures price
$N(\cdot)$	=	cumulative normal density function

First, solve for the arguments a and b:

$$a = \frac{ln\,(270/275) + [0.35^2(0.1667)]/2}{0.35\,\sqrt{0.1667}}$$

$$= \frac{-0.01835 + 0.1225(0.1667)/2}{0.14289}$$

$$= -0.05698$$
$$b = -0.05698 - 0.14289$$
$$= -0.19987$$

Next, find the $N(\cdot)$ values:[3]

$$N(a) = N(-0.05698) = 0.4773$$
$$N(b) = N(-0.19987) = 0.4208$$

Now substitute values:

$$C = e^{-.06(2/12)}[270(0.4773) - 275(0.4208)]$$
$$= \$13.02$$

These calls should sell for about $13.

The futures call option pricing model can be readily adapted to a futures *put* option pricing model. See Table 13-5.

It is also possible to use the principles of put/call parity to value a put option once we know the value of an associated call. Table 13-6 shows how.

---

[3]As with Black-Scholes values, accuracy is important in calculating $N(\cdot)$ values. In this example, for instance, if you round $N(a)$ and $N(b)$ to two decimals, it will make a difference of about $1 in the predicted call value!

TABLE 13-5   BLACK FUTURES PUT OPTION PRICING MODEL

$$P = e^{-rt} [KN(-b) - FN(-a)]$$
$$\text{where } P = \text{put premium}$$

and all other variables are as defined in Table 13-4.

TABLE 13-6   PUT PRICING MODEL BASED ON PUT/CALL PARITY

$$P = C - e^{-rt} (F - K)$$

with all variables as defined in Table 13-4.

Let's solve for the equilibrium value of a put on the S&P 500 index futures using the put/call parity version of the model. We have already solved for the value of the call: $13.02. Therefore,

$$P = \$13.02 - e^{-.06(0.1667)} [275 - 270] = \$17.97$$

These puts should sell for $18.

As with other options, the holder of a futures option has three alternatives: (1) keep the option, (2) exercise it, or (3) sell it. A review of the pros and cons of each choice follows.

The risk of holding onto the option is that prices may move adversely, resulting in a decline in the value of the option. Conversely, of course, prices may move in your favor and the value of the option could increase.

The early exercise of options is normally not smart. The exerciser abandons any remaining time value when he or she does this. Options that are deep-in-the-money have little time value; they sell for very close to their intrinsic value. It *is* often advantageous to exercise these early as discussed above.

It is often advantageous to exercise deep-in-the-money futures options early.

Selling the option has the merit of capturing the remaining time value (and the intrinsic value). This alternative also gets you out of the market. (When you exercise a futures option, you are still in the market. If you exercise a call, you acquire a long futures position; if you exercise a put, you acquire a short futures position.)

This means that when the holder of a valuable futures option decides to leave the market, the option will normally be sold rather than exercised.

Futures Option Deltas   Using calculus, you can see from Tables 13-4 and 13-5 that the delta for futures options is slightly different from delta for equity or index options. The derivative of the option price with respect to the futures price is $e^{-rt}N(a)$ for calls and $e^{-rt}N(-b)$ for puts.

NOT same as p. 296

Futures call delta: $\Delta_c = e^{-rt} N(a)$
Futures put delta: $\Delta_p = -e^{-rt} N(-a)$

Implied Volatility Implied volatility is an important idea with futures option pricing, just as with the pricing of other options. Implied volatility is the standard deviation of returns that will cause the pricing model to predict the actual option premium.

Calculating implied volatility must be done via a trial and error process as with other options, because it is not possible to isolate sigma in the valuation equation.

FOREIGN CURRENCY OPTIONS

Foreign currency options began trading at the Philadelphia Stock Exchange in 1982. Today options trade on the Australian dollar, the British pound, the Canadian dollar, the German mark, the French franc, the Japanese yen, and the Swiss franc. These options are successful and their use is growing steadily.

Characteristics

Like equity and index options, these contracts are guaranteed by the Options Clearing Corporation. Striking prices are standardized, as are expirations and margin requirements. Foreign currency options expire on the Saturday *preceding the third Wednesday* of the expiration month.

Foreign currency *options* are different from options on foreign currency *futures*. It is important to be precise with your terminology here. A foreign currency call option gives you the right to buy a certain quantity of the foreign currency; a foreign currency futures option gives you the right to go long the futures contract.

Foreign currency options are not the same as foreign currency futures options.

One interesting perspective on foreign currency options is noteworthy. If an American buys a Swiss Franc call denominated in dollars, this gives him or her the right to exchange U.S. dollars for Swiss Francs. This is no different from a U.S. dollar put denominated in Swiss Francs. Such a security would give its owner the right to deliver U.S. dollars and receive Swiss Francs.

A foreign currency call is the same as a dollar put.

The contract size for foreign currency options is currently set at one half the size of the futures contract for the same currency. The primary purpose for this is to keep the option premium at a relatively modest level. Unlike futures, where only a good faith deposit is required, options must be paid for in full (if purchased) or a significant margin posted (if the option is written). The futures contract for the German Deutschmark, for instance, covers 125,000 marks; the DM option covers 62,500 marks.

Speculating with Foreign Currency Options

Table 13-7 shows a listing of foreign currency options from the financial pages.

Looking at the German mark, you see that yesterday's closing exchange rate for the US $ and DM was 62.60 cents per Deutschmark. A speculator who anticipated that the dollar was going to strengthen relative to the mark expects that the price of marks is going to decline. If this is true, then buying DM puts would be an appropriate strategy. Suppose a speculator buys a contract of January 61 Deutschmark puts for the premium listed, 1.10 cents per DM. This costs $687.50, as there are 62,500 DM covered by the option. This is also the speculator's maximum loss.

Suppose the DM does fall, and that near expiration the new $/DM exchange rate is 0.5925. The 61 put is then intrinsically worth (0.6100 − 0.5925) × 62,500, or $1093.75. The speculator made $406.25 before commis-

TABLE 13-7 FOREIGN CURRENCY OPTIONS
November 24, 1992

DMARK		Calls			Puts		
		DEC	JAN	MAR	DEC	JAN	MAR
62.60	60	r	r	3.04	0.21	0.79	1.41
62.60	60½	r	r	s	0.31	0.86	s
62.60	61	1.77	r	r	0.44	1.10	1.86
62.60	61½	r	r	s	0.62	1.23	s
62.60	62	1.00	1.58	r	0.81	1.57	2.35
62.60	62½	0.80	r	s	1.08	1.80	s
62.60	63	0.60	1.12	r	1.40	2.08	2.82
62.60	63½	0.44	r	s	r	r	s
62.60	64	0.32	r	r	2.10	r	3.64

r = not traded

s = no option offered

62,500 German marks; cents per Deutschmark

sions. As with other options, it is unlikely that many speculators would ever find it advantageous to exercise the option; they will sell it instead. Exercise involves the inconvenience of actually having to pay for the foreign currency, and then converting it into dollars. This latter step is probably costly. Fungibility makes life much simpler.

Hedging with Foreign Currency Options

Chapter 10 showed how a U.S. importer could hedge foreign exchange risk on a purchase from a German supplier by using foreign exchange futures. The same type of protection is available in the options market. In this example, the American store owner needed to get Deutschmarks to pay for woodcarvings and other gift shop items. Because the store owner needs the DM, the appropriate hedge is a long one, with the store owner promising to buy the DM at a predetermined price.

In the options market, a call gives you the right to buy, but not the obligation. This could be attractive to the store owner, who could not afford the risk of adverse price movements in the value of the dollar, but who felt there was a significant chance the value of the dollar would increase between now and the payment time. Rather than locking in a price, the store owner might "hedge his or her bets" by buying calls. This way, if the DM appreciates, the call will become more valuable and partially offset the higher purchase price of the woodcarvings. If the DM depreciates, then the call will be allowed to expire worthless, but the actual cost of the gifts will be less than it would have been if the futures market were used.

It is not possible to say that one method is clearly superior to the other. Options require payment in full, while the futures contracts require only a good faith deposit. Hedging with futures locks in a price; options perhaps reduce the likelihood that you will have an opportunity loss from locking in a "bad" price.

A Note on the Pricing of Foreign Currency Options

You might expect that the Black-Scholes Option Pricing Model would work with these options just like it does with equity options. Unfortunately, there is a problem with the behavior of currency exchange rates and the assumptions of the option pricing model. Specifically, the variance of exchange rate changes is not constant and the distribution of these changes is not normally distributed. This introduces substantial error into the Black-Scholes forecasts.

The Black-Scholes model does not work well with foreign currency options.

WARRANTS

Characteristics

Warrants are curious securities. They are also rare; it is unusual for more than two dozen to be listed at any given time on the New York Stock Exchange, with a smaller number on the American Stock Exchange.

Warrants are really long-term call options issued by a corporation. They give the owner the right to purchase a set number of shares of stock directly from the company issuing the warrant. There is a predetermined exercise price and expiration date, which can be as far as twenty years in the future.

> Warrants are long-term call options issued by the underlying company.

Corporations often issue warrants in conjunction with a new bond issue; the potential benefits of such securities usually allow the company to sell the bonds at a slightly lower interest rate than would otherwise be necessary. Warrants pay no dividends, and their owners have no voting rights, but investors like them because of the leverage they provide. Like a call option, warrants let you assume a bullish position on a stock but with a lower investment than would be necessary if you bought the stock outright. Warrant holders can make enormous profits during bull markets or merger waves, but their downside risk is limited.

You have to do a little homework to get details about the trading terms of a warrant. One convenient source of information is the Standard and Poors' *Stock Guide.* Other sources are the Standard and Poors' *Stock Report* or the *Value Line Investment Survey.*

As an example, Sport Supply Group (GYM, AMEX) has warrants outstanding, each of which gives its owner the right to buy 1 share of GYM stock at a price of $12.50 anytime until February 28, 1997. If the value of GYM stock rises above $12.50, the warrants will become in-the-money and will have intrinsic value, just like a call option.

Unlike call options, which are based on some logical round number of units of the underlying security, warrants do not always cover a logical number of shares. For instance, Hasbro (the toy manufacturer) has a warrant issue in which 4 warrants are required to buy 1 common share at $18.92.

Warrant prices are determined by the same factors determining option prices. Assuming that arbitrage situations will not last for long, we can use logic to determine the theoretical maximum and minimum prices at which warrants should sell.

We can think of a warrant as in- or out-of-the-money. If it is out-of-the-money, then the warrant value will approach zero as the expiration date

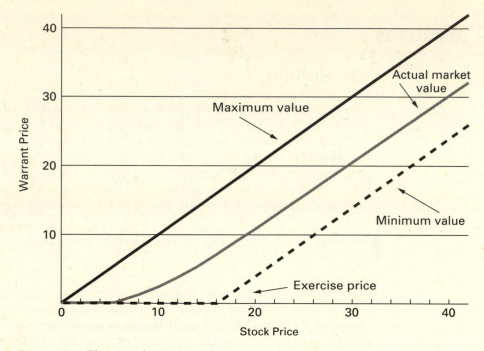

Figure 13-1 Theoretical Warrant Values

nears. An in-the-money warrant, on the other hand, should never sell for less than the current stock price minus the exercise price of the warrant. The theoretical maximum price for a warrant is the stock price itself. These relationships all assume each warrant covers exactly one share of stock. This relationship is diagramed in Figure 13-1. Because a warrant is very much like a long-term call option, this relationship is similar to that predicted by the Black-Scholes option pricing model.

Hedging with Stock Warrants[4]

The strategy of using a **warrant hedge** is similar to a covered call writing strategy. The outcome to the hedger is the same, but warrant hedging involves an extra player—the warrant lender. Under this strategy, an investor buys shares of stock and simultaneously sells short warrants on the

---

[4]Much of the material in this section is from Robert A. Strong and Steven V. Fischetti, "Hedging with Stock Warrants: A Free Lunch?" *American Association of Individual Investors Journal* (November 1984): 9–13.

same company. To sell short, the investor borrows the warrants, and then sells them.

If, at warrant expiration, the stock price is below the exercise price of the warrants, the warrants will not be exercised; they are worthless. This effectively means that the person who sold the warrants short owes the lender nothing and can pocket the full proceeds from the short sale. The loss in value of the underlying stock is cushioned by the proceeds from the warrant sale.

If, however, the stock price rises, the warrants will be exercised by the holder, who will then purchase the shares *from the company* at the exercise price. Because the warrants are valuable, the investor must repay *the lender* that which was borrowed, although he still pockets the proceeds from the short sale. The obligation is to return the warrants—or the equivalent—and, in general, this is fulfilled by the investor selling the shares at the exercise price to the warrant lender. The investor's profit on the deal is limited to the exercise price at which it was necessary to sell the shares, plus the proceeds from the short sale. The outcome is the same as in a covered call writing strategy, except that the investor now owes stock to the warrant lender, whereas in call-writing he would owe stock to the call holder.

Let's look at a hypothetical example of a warrant hedge. Suppose the common stock of company XYZ is selling for $21, and that there are warrants trading for $5 that entitle their owner to buy one share of XYZ common stock at $24.25 anytime between the time of purchase and January 1, 1996. An investor buys 1,000 shares of XYZ, and simultaneously sells short 1,000 warrants. No further action is taken until the expiration of the warrants.

If, at expiration, the stock price is $24.25 or less, the warrants will expire worthless and the investor makes $5,000 on the short position: 1,000 warrants were sold at $5 and were "reacquired" at $0. In addition, the investor is still long 1,000 shares of stock.

If the stock rises above $24.25, the warrants will be valuable. Warrant holders will exercise them, and the short seller will have to cover their short position by buying warrants on the open market, or by delivering shares of stock at $24.25 despite the higher market price. In this example, the investor's maximum gain is $8.25 per share plus any dividends paid over the period. This maximum profit occurs at any stock price of $24.25 or more. At this price, the investor will make $3.25 on the stock ($24.25 − $21.00) and $5.00 on the warrant. Profit is limited even if stock prices move higher, because the shares must be delivered at $24.25.

If the stock price declines, losses are offset by the $5000 proceeds from the short sale and any dividends received. Share prices could actually fall to $16 before the investor began to lose money (even lower if dividends were received).

If the stock price is unchanged at expiration of the warrant, there is no capital gain on the stock, but there is still a $5000 gain from the short sale of the warrants.

In a study of the profitability of this strategy, Strong and Fischetti found that over the period 1968–81 warrant hedges showed above-average risk-adjusted performance. This means that after considering the volatility of the warrant hedge relative to the overall market, the returns from warrant hedges were higher than predicted by financial theory. More research is necessary to understand precisely how the marketplace determines a price for these securities.

OTHER DERIVATIVE ASSETS

When-Issued Stock

A good case could be made for the claim that **when-issued stock** is the least understood financial asset. Few stockbrokers, finance professors, or investors are familiar with these curious securities, yet their prices appear in the financial pages every day.

In the stock listings you can routinely find an entry like the one in Table 13-8.

The code *wi* following the second entry for SaraLee in the listing indicates these are when-issued shares. Don't confuse the *wi* with the *wt* abbreviation for warrants. The two securities are quite different.

Common Stock Trading on a When-Issued Basis[5]   When a firm splits its stock, the post-split price of shares will reflect the change in the number of outstanding shares. In a two for one split, for instance, an investor who owns 300 shares will receive a new stock certificate for another 300 shares, making a total of 600. But the investor's wealth does not double, because the price of the post-split shares will be approximately one half the pre-split price.

The New York Stock Exchange permits investors to trade shares of stock issued in conjunction with a stock split even before these new shares are distributed to existing shareholders. The motivation for this policy is unclear, but the NYSE *Company Manual* indicates that it is considered desirable, from the standpoint of public interest, to provide when-issued trading to investors.

The specialist on the floor of the exchange begins to make a market in the lower-priced split shares shortly after the recapitalization has been approved by the shareholders, and *both the new shares and the old shares trade simultaneously*. The period of simultaneous trading is short, generally ranging from 4 days to 35 days.

As with a cash dividend, the old shares will go ex-distribution on the fourth business day before the date of record established for the stock split.

---

[5]Much of the material in this section comes from Dosoung Choi and Robert A. Strong, "The Pricing of When-Issued Common Stock: A Note," *Journal of Finance* (September 1983): 1293–98.

TABLE 13-8 WHEN-ISSUED STOCK LISTING

Stock	Sym	Div	Yld %	PE	Vol 100s	Hi	Lo	Close	Net Chg
SaraLee	SLE	1.00	1.7	24	2688	61	60⅛	60½	+⅜
SaraLee wi		...	...	...	29	30½	30¼	30½	...

Anyone purchasing the old shares after this date will purchase them *with a due bill* for the additional shares. This due bill will be noted on the investor's purchase confirmation. Holders of the due bill are entitled to the new shares when they are issued.

Although both the old shares and the new shares are proportional claims on the same cash income stream, their adjusted prices may logically differ due to the manner in which trades in when-issued shares are settled. Investors who buy or sell the old shares have their accounts debited or credited for the net amount of the transaction on the fifth business day following the trade. Trades in the when-issued securities, on the other hand, do not settle until six business days after the date of distribution. Thus, the purchase of when-issued shares is analogous to buying the stock on 100 percent margin with no interest charged on the debit balance.

When-Issued Shares and Reality To test whether this could actually be true, I once opened a special brokerage account and purchased some when-issued shares. No money was required to do this; these were the only securities in the account. Before the delivery of the new shares, I sold these same when-issued shares. Never did I deposit any money into the account, and the entire transaction netted me a small profit after commissions.

We would expect the price of the when-issued shares to exceed that of the old shares by the value of this interest concession. In a study by Choi and Strong, they found that even after adjusting prices for the time value of money, the when-issued shares consistently sell for a slight premium over their theoretical value. This seems to show that if you are interested in selling shares of a stock that recently declared a stock split, and you are in no hurry for your money, it may make sense to sell them on a when-issued basis.

In any event, further research is necessary to discover how the market assigns value to these curious securities.

Hybrid Securities

There is a growing number of hybrid derivative securities, most of which are designed for some special purpose. The most important of these are discussed in the Financial Engineering chapter of this book.

SUMMARY

Futures options are options on futures contracts; futures calls give the call holder the right to *go long* a futures contract at a predetermined price, while futures puts give the put holder the right to *go short*. Futures options can be theoretically priced using a cousin of the Black-Scholes Option Pricing Model.

Foreign currency options are not futures contracts. They are options that give you the right to buy or sell a given quantity of foreign exchange. These options cannot be accurately priced with the BSOPM or its futures counterpart because the behavior of foreign currencies violates an important assumption of the OPM.

Warrants are like long-term call options issued *by the company* rather than another investor. Certain hedging strategies using warrants appear to be unusually profitable.

When-issued stock usually comes about because of a stock split. These new shares and the old shares trade simultaneously for a brief period, and at some brokerage firms when-issued shares can be purchased without any cash outlay.

QUESTIONS

1. Remembering that the purchase of a futures contract requires only a good faith deposit (which can be satisfied by the deposit of interest-bearing Treasury bills), and the formula for put-call parity from Chapter 5, what relationship would you expect between the prices of *at-the-money* futures puts and calls on the same underlying commodity?

2. Refer to Figure 13-1 (p. 300). At what stock price do warrants sell for their greatest premium over intrinsic value? Is this what you would expect from the Black-Scholes OPM?

3. What do you consider to be the advantages and disadvantages of buying *when-issued* stock rather than "regular way" shares?

4. The issuing firm sometimes extends the life of a warrant that is about to expire. **(a)** Why do you think the firm might do this? **(b)** What effect, if any, would this have on the warrant hedging strategy described in the chapter?

5. Suppose someone is interested in speculating on an increase in the value of the U.S. dollar relative to the German Deutschmark. What are the relative advantages of using foreign currency options rather than foreign currency futures options?

6. Warrants are like long-term call options issued by a company. Would it make sense for a firm to create a new type of security that was essentially a long term *put* option? Such a security could conceivably provide a floor value to shares of common stock, because the shareholder could exercise the "put" and sell them back to the company at this price.
7. Explain how a farmer who normally used a short hedge on his crop could logically use futures options on his crop, too.
8. Explain how a farmer can eliminate price risk using futures puts.
9. How is buying a futures call different than writing a futures put?
10. Explain the following statement: "From the perspective of a U.S. investor, a Deutschmark call option is the same as a U.S. dollar put option."
11. Explain why "serial expiration" works for stock index futures options, but would be impractical for an agricultural commodity futures contract.
12. Why do most futures options expire in the month prior to the futures delivery month?
13. Explain why basis is especially important to a futures option spreader.
14. Why is early exercise of futures options sometimes appropriate?
15. Would you expect an at-the-money futures option ever to be exercised early?

PROBLEMS

1. Using the S&P 500 futures option prices from Table 13-1 (p. 288)
   (a) calculate the breakeven price for a person who buys a DEC 430 call;
   (b) determine this person's gain or loss in dollars if, at option expiration, the S&P 500 index is 447.45.
2. Draw a profit and loss diagram for an S&P 500 DEC 425/435 call option bullspread.
3. Do problem 2 by using put options.
4. Refer to Table 13-1. Suppose there are 58 days until expiration of the December options, and the December S&P 500 futures settled at 430.00. Using the 430 calls and a T bill rate of 3%, what is the implied volatility of the option?
5. Using the answer to Problem 4, what is the theoretical value of an S&P 500 DEC 445 call?
6. A futures option has a striking price of 55. The underlying asset sells for 53, has a volatility of 0.25, and the option has 110 days of life remaining. If interest rates are 3.3%, what is the delta of this option?

7. A speculator is long 5 contracts of DEC S&P 500 futures, with initial conditions as listed in Problem 4. If the speculator writes 3 DEC 440 calls,

   (a) how much per month will be received?

   (b) what will the position delta become?

8. A warrant has an exercise price of $20, a market value of $7, and the underlying stock price is $18. You decide to set up a warrant hedge by buying 100 shares of the stock and selling 100 warrants short; assume each trade occurs at the prices listed above. Each warrant covers 1.12 shares of stock.

   At warrant expiration, you have received a total of $48 in dividends on the stock. What is your gain or loss in dollars if, at expiration, the stock price is   (a) $15,   (b) $18,   (c) $35?

9. Refer to Table 13-1. Suppose a speculator buys three MAR 600 soybean puts.

   (a) Calculate the gain or loss in dollars if, at option expiration, the futures contract sells for 602.

   (b) Prepare a profit/loss worksheet for the purchase of one of these put options.

14 Risk Management

*L*ife wasn't designed to be risk-free. The key is not to eliminate risk, but to estimate it accurately and manage it wisely.

William Schreyer,
former Chairman and CEO
Merrill Lynch & Company

KEY TERMS

delta management	option beta
Itô's lemma	option elasticity

It is difficult to write about the futures and options markets without incorporating risk management into almost every example. Risk management is the primary reason these markets exist. Each previous chapter discussed at least a small aspect of the topic. Any strategy using derivative assets, such as covered calls, protective puts, or futures hedges, alters the risk/expected return characteristics of a portfolio.

A clairvoyant equity manager will be either 100 percent in the market or 100 percent out of it at any point in time. For the rest of us, changing market conditions cause our stock market optimism to periodically refashion itself. Consequently, the proportion of our portfolios held in stock is subject to frequent change.

This chapter provides additional perspective on the power of derivative assets as tools to the financial risk manager. Futures and options are neutral products; how someone uses them determines how they impact portfolio risk.

> Futures and options are neutral products; how they are used determines how they impact portfolio risk.

MANAGING COMPANY RISK

Delta Management Revisited

Option pricing theory and its offspring have turned modern portfolio management on its nose during the last decade. Few option traders can talk shop for more than a minute without paying homage to the delta god. People actively practice **delta management.** This term refers to any investment practice that monitors the position delta and seeks to maintain it within a certain range. Delta is an extremely useful idea for many reasons, one of which is particularly material here: It is a direct measure of the "degree of bullishness" represented in a particular security position or portfolio.

As previously discussed, delta is the first derivative of the option pricing model with respect to the price of the underlying asset, and ranges from -1.0 to 1.0. A call option might have a delta of 0.70; this means for every $1 change in the value of the underlying asset, the value of the option will increase by 70 cents.

A long futures contract has a delta of $+1.0$; a position that is short 100 futures has a delta of -100.00. Call options have deltas near 1.0 if they are deep-in-the-money and near zero if they are far out-of-the-money. Puts have deltas near -1.0 when deep-in-the-money and near zero if far out-of-the-money. When the option striking price is near the price of the underlying asset, the option delta will be near 0.5 (for calls) or -0.5 (for puts).

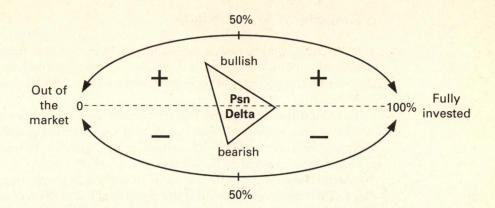

Figure 14-1 Risk Exposure

If someone owns 10,000 shares of Toys R Us (TOY, NYSE), that person's position delta in TOY is 10,000 × 1.0, or 10,000: each share of stock counts "one delta point." The TOY position delta is simply the sum of the deltas contained therein from TOY stock and the related option position.

Suppose recent events cause the portfolio manager to be slightly less optimistic regarding the TOY position. Establishing the initial 10,000 share block as a 100 percent bullish position, there are several ways market risk can be reduced.

An obvious way is to sell shares and hold cash. Selling 5000 shares, for instance, would reduce the position delta to 5000 (50 percent of the original value). Relative to the starting point, the portfolio manager is now "50 percent bullish." A problem with this method of adjusting the portfolio is the potential for cries of churning[1] if the shares are bought back after the economic smoke clears.

Another alternative is to go short against the box,[2] if you are willing to pay the commissions. You also could buy TOY puts (which add *negative* deltas to the portfolio total), but, because you have to pay for long options, this would involve a cash outflow. You also could write TOY calls (adding negative deltas), or you could do some combination of the above.

In any event, the immediate investment objective is temporarily altering the risk level of the portfolio. The method the manager uses depends on circumstances and what has previously occurred. The following short case study shows one typical scenario.

---

[1]"Churning" is generating commissions through unwarranted trades.

[2]Selling short against the box is when someone owns shares of stock, borrows similar shares from their broker, sells the borrowed shares, and eventually replaces the borrowed shares with the owned shares. The most common motivation for selling short against the box is to shift tax liabilities from one year into the next.

A Case Study: Avon Products

This example shows how a portfolio manager can use options to alter temporarily the risk exposure in a position, generate income in the process, and restore the portfolio to its original state with little disruption.

Initial Conditions Suppose that on January 26 a portfolio manager holds 10,000 shares of Avon Products (AVP, NYSE), currently selling for $33. Changing market conditions cause him or her to decide to reduce the AVP exposure to 90 percent of the initial level.

At first, the AVP position delta is 10,000; each share counts one delta point. The objective is to reduce the position delta to 90 percent of this, or 9000. There are three choices:

1. sell 1,000 shares of AVP and hold cash;
2. buy put options;
3. write call options.

Selling stock is a possibility, but the transaction does involve costly commissions and may violate portfolio policy, especially if the manager were to reacquire the shares shortly after that. Buying puts has the disadvantage of requiring a cash outlay. Considering all this, suppose the decision is to write calls.

Perhaps the AVP MAR 35 call sells for $2 and has a delta of 0.441. The manager determines that writing 23 of these contracts will reduce the position delta appropriately:

$$10,000 - (N \times 0.441 \times 100) = 9000$$
$$1,000 = 44.1N$$
$$N = 22.68, \text{ rounded to } 23$$

This brings $4600 in premium income into the portfolio. The position delta is now 8986:

$$(10,000 \text{ shares} \times 1.0) - (2300 \text{ calls} \times 0.441) = 8986$$

TABLE 14-1 AVON PRODUCTS POSITION DELTA

Stock: 10,000 shares × 1.0	=	10,000
Calls: 10,000 short calls × −0.404	=	− 4,040
Puts: 3,100 long puts × −0.310	=	− 961
		4,999

Result: 49.99 percent bullish relative to starting position

Relative to the starting position delta of 10,000, the portfolio is now 89.86 percent bullish.

One Week Passes   After one week, AVP stock sells for $32½. The MAR 35 calls now have a delta of 0.404. The position delta changes to 9071:

(10,000 shares × 1.0) − (2300 calls × 0.404) = 9071

The manager decides to reduce the AVP exposure further, to 50 percent of the original level. Again, there are three methods for doing this:

1. sell 4071 shares of AVP and hold cash;
2. buy put options;
3. write more call options.

The manager selects the latter.

The MAR 35 calls should now sell for $1⅝. Writing 77 more of these generates $12,513 in premium income. The position delta is now 5960:

(10,000 shares × 1.0) − (10,000 calls × 0.404) = 5960
Result: 59.60% bullish relative to starting position

The AVP holding is still too bullish; any additional short calls will be uncovered, and the manager does not want to do this. Unless stock is sold, the manager must buy puts.

Buying Puts   The APR 30 puts would sell for $1.95 and have a delta of −0.310. The manager figures out that the purchase of 31 contracts will adjust the position delta to the desired level as Table 14-1 shows.

At March Expiration   At option expiration in March, AVP stock is at $33. The manager's fears about the company never materialized, and he or she decides to return to the original 100 percent bullish position, with a position delta of 10,000.

The MAR 35 calls expire worthless. The APR 30 puts can be readily sold, and, according to the BSOPM, should be worth $0.96. Table 14-2 summarizes the total option income associated with this risk management case study.

TABLE 14-2   TOTAL OPTION INCOME

23 calls sold on Jan 26:	+ $ 4,600
77 calls sold a week later:	+ 12,513
31 puts bought @ $1.95:	− 6,045
31 puts sold @ $0.96:	+ 2,976
Net income from options:	$14,044

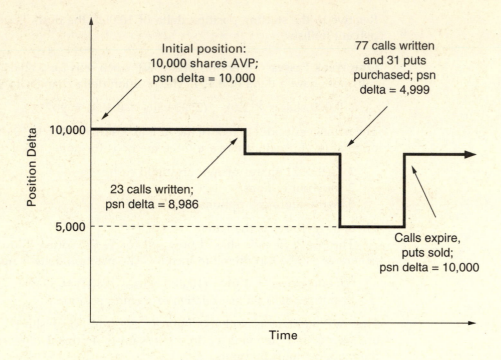

Figure 14-2 Adjusting Company Position Delta

The portfolio manager used options periodically to alter the risk exposure of an individual security position. He or she did so without disturbing the equity portfolio; the risk adjustments came from the inclusion of option positions in the correct "delta quantity."

MANAGING MARKET RISK

The example above showed how options can be used to adjust company-specific risk. Perhaps the more important risk management use of derivative assets is altering total market risk, as discussed in Chapter 7. This section introduces some new twists to the process.

Traditional Derivative Asset Methods

Using Futures Contracts   Stock index futures contracts, like those on the S&P 500 (SPX), are widely used to reduce market risk. As discussed in Chapter 9, by shorting SPX futures, the manager of an equity portfolio can reduce the risk of adverse market swings.

The hedge ratio determines the number of futures contracts necessary to eliminate market risk. In practice, most institutional use of SPX futures is to reduce risk rather than eliminate it. Notice the quotation from William Schreyer, former CEO of Merrill Lynch, at the beginning of this chapter. A principle of finance is that risk and expected return are directly related. If you eliminate risk, returns will be very modest in a well-functioning marketplace.

Most institutional use of SPX futures is to reduce risk rather than eliminate it.

This means that a portfolio manager who employs a practice of continually hedging the entire portfolio will not be very successful. Futures contracts, like options, are risk management tools that should be used judiciously.

The elimination of risk can reduce expected return. Risk management tools should, therefore, be used judiciously.

Using Index Options   The most common use of stock index options is in overwriting programs designed to increase the income from a portfolio. Writing calls is a bearish activity, however, because short calls have negative deltas. Introducing negative deltas into a portfolio will reduce its market risk.[3]

Still, index options can specifically be used to alter market risk. Writing calls may be appropriate for slight reductions in risk, while buying puts may be best for large reductions. The crafty manager may write calls in sufficient quantity to generate the funds necessary to buy puts, and in so doing achieve a desired position delta with little cash outlay.[4]

Using Futures Options

As stated above, stock index futures (like the S&P 500) and index options (like the OEX) are very useful for reducing market risk without disrupting the underlying portfolio, and are widely used for this purpose. *Futures options* can do the same thing, and sometimes may be the preferred alternative.

A major advantage of futures and options is that these derivative assets allow you to alter market exposure (position delta) without making wholesale changes in the underlying asset portfolio. By combining futures or their

---

[3] If the portfolio position delta goes below zero, though, writing more calls will increase the market risk.

[4] There is an example of this in Chapter 6.

Box 14-1 **WRITING FUTURES OPTIONS**

Just as with options on equity securities or indexes, there are two types of futures options: calls and puts. A futures call gives its holder the right to go long a predetermined futures contract at a predetermined price. A futures put gives its holder the right to go short.

A person who writes a futures option is obligated to take the other side of the futures contract if the option holder chooses to exercise. The person who owns a call has the right to go long, so the call writer has an obligation to go short if the call is exercised. A put writer has an obligation to go long if the put holder chooses to exercise and go short.

As with other options, the option writer gets to keep the option premium no matter what happens, and all players can trade out of their option positions anytime before the exercise date.

---

options in the correct proportion, the manager can dial in the desired market exposure.

Fiduciary Concerns   Few fiduciaries have total freedom to use options and futures in any fashion they wish. Writing truly naked options may violate investment covenants because of the potential risk. Similar restrictions may apply to the purchase of futures positions that are not part of a hedge.

If a manager writes puts, there is an obligation to go long if the puts are exercised. As long as you do not write more puts than the number of futures contracts you are short, the puts are "covered," in the sense that exercise of the puts simply requires you to remove the futures hedge.

Writing calls carries an obligation to go short if the calls are exercised, so it may not be feasible to write more calls than the equivalent "futures contract value" of the stock portfolio. Stated another way, if the calls are exercised, the call writer must, in effect, put on a hedge by going short futures contracts, and a fiduciary may not want to go short by so many that the position delta moves into negative territory.

As an example, suppose you manage a $115 million stock portfolio with a beta of 0.98 and that a particular S&P 500 futures contract trades for 365.00. One futures contract has a value of 365.00 × $500 = $182,500, so the $115 million portfolio is "worth" 630 futures contracts: $115,000,000/ $182,500 = 630. Because the beta is slightly less than one, the number of futures needed to hedge the portfolio completely is less than this: 98% of 630 is about 620 contracts.

The portfolio manager may not ever want to be short more than 620 futures calls, because if they were exercised the combined position delta of the stock and the resulting short futures would be less than zero.

Box 14-2   "COVERED" FUTURES OPTIONS FROM A FIDUCIARY VIEWPOINT

To be "covered," a fiduciary may not want to write more futures puts than the number of futures contracts that are currently short. Otherwise, there is a risk that the excess options may leave you with a long futures position if the options are exercised. Similarly, a fiduciary may not want to write more futures calls than the number of futures equivalents represented in the stock portfolio.

Finding the Optimum Mix   Many option contracts could be chosen for hedging purposes. In this example, two out-of-the-money S&P 500 futures options (100 days until expiration) are chosen: a 355 put and a 375 call. Writing both these options produces a position commonly called a short strangle. Assuming a volatility of 15 percent and a current futures price of 365.00, the Black futures option pricing model predicts a delta of 0.372 and a premium of $7.11 for the call. For the put, the delta is −0.340 and the premium is $6.83.

The accompanying figure shows the optimum mix of S&P 500 futures and their puts and calls to hedge varying amounts of the $115 million portfolio's market risk, where optimum is defined as the alternative that achieves the correct position delta and generates the most cash.

The optimum mixes for various position deltas are determined using a simple linear program designed to maximize the income generated by the hedge. If it is necessary to hedge 100 percent and completely remove market risk, you would sell 620 futures. This situation corresponds to the far left portion of the figure. A position delta of 50 percent, on the other hand, is best achieved using futures *and* short strangles. Specifically, maximum income is generated if you go short 276 futures, write 344 puts, and write 276 calls. In this example, reductions in position delta down to 63 percent are best accomplished using futures calls only. Writing covered strangles is not the answer to every portfolio problem. It is simply one alternative in a long list.

Gamma Risk

Gamma is the second derivative of the option pricing model and is a measure of how sensitive delta is to changes in the price of the underlying asset. There are several aspects of gamma that should be understood when using derivative assets in risk management.

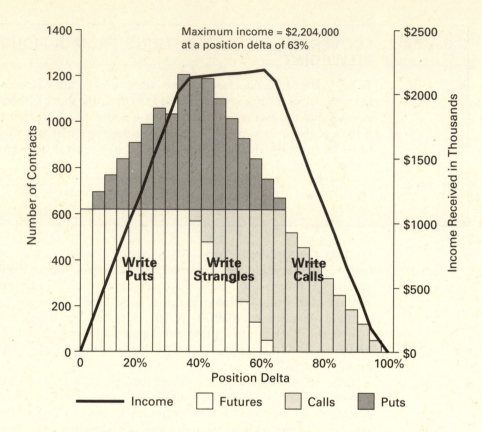

Figure 14-3 Delta Management via Covered Strangles

Itô's Lemma The manager using options in delta management should be aware of the fact that, by itself, delta works fine for modest changes in the value of the underlying asset, but major price movements will introduce error into the estimated position delta. Figure 14-4 illustrates theoretical Black-Scholes option prices. If new option prices are predicted using delta alone, the forecast error increases with the size of the underlying asset price change.

Itô's lemma is a useful result from stochastic calculus that can improve new option premium forecast accuracy. While the derivation and proof of this result is beyond the scope of this book, the implications are not. The simplest form of the lemma is shown in equation 14-1:

$$dC = \Delta\, dP + (1/2)\, \gamma\, (dP)^2 \tag{14-1}$$

In words, this equation says that the change in call premium is equal to delta multiplied by the change in the underlying stock price, plus one half gamma multiplied by the square of the underlying stock price change. The value of Itô's lemma is best seen with an example.

Call Premium

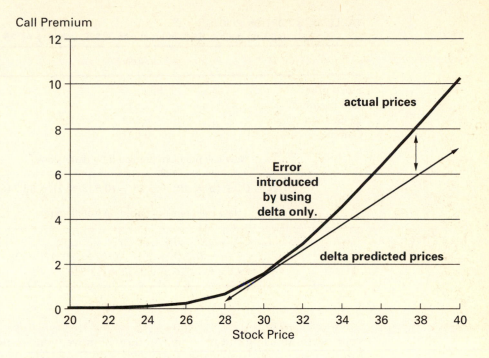

Figure 14-4 Theoretical Option Values

Suppose we have the initial and subsequent conditions as Table 14-3 shows. If the stock price changes instantaneously from \$50 to \$52, the Black-Scholes call premium will rise from \$2.65 to \$3.87. Using delta alone, the predicted call premium is about \$3.75, for a forecast error of 3.1 percent (based on the actual premium). Using Itô's lemma, the predicted call premium is \$3.81, for a forecast error of 1.56 percent. This reduces the forecast error by half.

The above example assumed that the underlying stock price changed instantaneously, with no passage of time. This simplifies the example, but need not be the case. Other versions of Itô's lemma provide for additional variables, such as time. Equation 14-2 shows this form, where dT represents the change in time remaining until option expiration and Θ is the option theta:

$$dC = \Delta\, dP + \Theta\, dT + (1/2)\, \gamma\, (dP)^2 \tag{14-2}$$

Gamma Risk   Suppose you compare two methods of reducing your position delta by 50 percent: (1) using futures only, and (2) using futures *and* covered strangles. Returning to the earlier example, because your portfolio is "worth" 620 futures contracts, you would go short 310 futures to hedge half

TABLE 14-3 OPTION PRICES
(striking price = $50, interest rate = 3%, volatility = .25, time = 90 days)

	Initially	Moments later
Stock price	$50	$52
Call premium	2.65	3.87
Delta	0.548	0.669
Gamma	0.0319	0.0292

New call premium predicted by delta alone:

$$C_1 = C_0 + (\Delta \times dP) = 2.65 + (0.548 \times 2) = \$3.746$$

New call premium based on Itô's Lemma

$$C_1 = C_0 + (\Delta \times dP) + (1/2) \times \gamma \times (dP)^2$$
$$= 2.65 + (0.548 \times 2) + (1/2) \times 0.0319 \times (2)^2$$
$$= 2.65 + 1.096 + 0.0638 = \$3.810$$

your portfolio using futures only. As shown above, you would go short 276 futures, write 344 puts, and write 276 calls using the latter method of hedging.

If the market breaks and the futures contract falls to 350.00, the portfolio hedged with futures only will still have a position delta of approximately 50 percent of its unhedged value. Minor differences will occur because of basis convergence and because stock portfolios do not always behave according to their beta.

The option deltas will change dramatically, however. Assuming the options have 80 days of life remaining, the new deltas would be 0.169 for the call and −0.557 for the put. The revised position delta would then be 620 (stock) − 276 (short futures) + 192 (short puts) − 47 (short calls) = 489. This is considerably higher than the 310 target. Instead of remaining 50 percent bullish, your position has become 79 percent bullish.

Futures contracts have a gamma of zero; options have gammas that are non-zero. The implication of this is that two hedged portfolios, one using futures only and the other using futures or options, can have the same position delta, but the portfolio using options will be imperfectly hedged if the market breaks sharply.

Still, writing futures options is a convenient, income-producing method of hedging. It should be considered as a viable alternative whenever you want to hedge less than 100 percent of your position, and is especially attractive when you want to hedge less than half.

RISK MANAGEMENT AND BETA

Option overwriting, the purchase of puts (equity or index), and shorting stock index futures will reduce portfolio risk. Logically, these activities will also reduce a portfolio's beta, and it is useful to know how much. Written in sufficient quantity, calls can cause the total portfolio position delta to turn negative. If this happens, it is important to be aware of the fact.

Estimating Beta With Index Option Overwriting

Suppose a manager chooses to write 56 OEX call contracts as a means of generating additional income from a $1 million stock portfolio with a beta of 1.08. The options have a delta of 0.324, and the current level of the index is 298.96.

For starters, it is necessary to turn the stock portfolio into "OEX equivalents." This is done the same way as with stock index futures:

$$\text{Hedge ratio} = \frac{\text{portfolio value}}{\text{contract value}} \times \text{beta}$$

$$= \frac{\$1 \text{ million}}{298.96 \times \$100} \times 1.08$$

$$= 36.13 \text{ contracts}$$

The stock portfolio is theoretically equivalent to 36.13 at-the-money contracts of the OEX index. Although no OEX option has a striking price of 298.96, we can still substitute 298.96 for the striking price in the Black-Scholes model and determine a theoretical delta. Suppose this value is 0.578.

The stock portfolio position delta can now be estimated as Table 14-4 (p. 320) shows. The stock portfolio has a beta of 1.08 and is equivalent to 36.13 at-the-money OEX contracts, with a delta contribution of 2,088.31. After writing the calls, the position delta is only 273.91. The resulting portfolio beta, then, can be roughly estimated by a simple proportional relationship, as shown here:

$$\frac{\text{initial portfolio delta}}{\text{initial portfolio beta}} = \frac{\text{final portfolio delta}}{\text{final portfolio beta}}$$

$$\frac{2,088.31}{1.08} = \frac{273.91}{\text{beta}}$$

$$\text{beta} = 0.14$$

TABLE 14-4   CALCULATION OF POSITION DELTA

Stock Portfolio

OEX equivalents		Delta		Contribution
36.13	×	0.578 × 100	=	2,088.31

Short Index Calls

Contracts		Delta		Contribution
56	×	−0.324 × 100	=	−1,814.40
		Position Delta		273.91

Writing 56 of the OEX calls against this stock portfolio removes most of the market risk, as shown by the drastically reduced position delta and the small beta. As time passes or the value of the S&P100 index changes, so will the position delta and the portfolio beta.

This heuristic relies on the following logic. Before any options are written, the portfolio has a beta of 1.08. If calls are written such that the portfolio becomes delta neutral, by definition the portfolio's value will not change with small price movements in the underlying asset. This means a delta neutral portfolio has a beta of zero (0).

Caveats

The method shown above is only approximate. Delta and beta are not normally in a linear relationship. In general, an option beta is equal to **option elasticity** multiplied by the beta of the underlying asset.

Recall that delta measures the change in *dollar* value of an option associated with a dollar change in the value of the underlying asset. An IBM call with a delta of 0.40, for instance, will rise in value by forty cents if IBM stock rises by $1. Beta measures the *percentage* change in an asset price that is expected from a given percentage change in the price of the underlying asset. If IBM stock has a beta of 1.05, a 1 percent rise in the overall stock market means that IBM stock probably would rise by 1.05 percent.

An option's elasticity is its delta multiplied by the ratio of the underlying stock price and the current option premium. Letting C = option premium and S = price of the underlying asset,

$$\text{elasticity} = \text{delta} \times \frac{S}{C} \qquad (14\text{-}3)$$

Elasticity will always be greater than or equal to one for a call option, and less than or equal to one for a put option.

The **option beta** is the elasticity multiplied by the beta of the underlying asset:

$$\beta \text{ option} = \text{delta} \times \frac{S}{C} \times \beta_s \qquad (14\text{-}4)$$

Given that call elasticities can never be less than 1.0 (and are usually much greater), equation 14-4 shows that the call option beta will normally be greater than the stock beta, and that put betas will normally be negative.

Option deltas are a function of a number of variables in the Black-Scholes OPM. As time passes, interest rates change, the underlying stock price moves, or volatility expectations shift, so the option delta also will change. This means that an option beta can change even if the underlying asset beta does not. Consequently, the relationship between option betas and their corresponding stock betas changes continually. The mathematical relationship is well-established, but option betas are very nonstationary. It makes little sense to publish option betas because of their dynamic nature.

▌An option beta can change even if the beta of the underlying asset does not.

SUMMARY

Derivative assets are extremely useful in altering the risk exposure of a portfolio. Their particular advantages are the ability to maintain the original equity portfolio undisturbed and the generation of premium income, a frequent risk adjustment by-product.

Delta is a good predictor of future option prices for small changes in the price of the underlying asset. Large changes, however, result in forecast error. Itô's lemma is an important result of stochastic calculus that uses gamma to improve forecast accuracy.

Usually there are many ways in which a portfolio manager can attain a desired position delta. Mathematical programming techniques help in the search for the optimum way of adjusting delta.

Altering position delta also alters the aggregate portfolio beta. Beta is the principal measure of market risk, and the revised beta value is useful to know whenever options are used with a stock portfolio. This calculation comes from a simple proportional relationship between before and after deltas and betas.

An option's elasticity is equal to its delta multiplied by the ratio of the price of the underlying asset and the option premium. The option beta is the elasticity multiplied by the beta of the underlying asset.

QUESTIONS

1. "The concept of hedging is patently inconsistent with the efficient market hypothesis, as it assumes the hedger can forecast the market." Do you agree with this statement?

2. "A clairvoyant equity manager will be either 100 percent in the market or 100 percent out of it at any point in time." Why is this true?

3. What does it mean to say "futures and options are neutral products"?

4. In the context of portfolio risk management, explain the phrase "100 percent bullish."

5. Suppose a portfolio contains 100,000 shares of General Electric. List three ways in which the GE position delta could be decreased.

6. Compare covered call writing and the purchase of protective puts as a means of lowering position delta.

7. A manager writes covered calls against a stock position. If the underlying stock price does not change, explain how the position delta could go up or down with the passage to time, depending on the options that were written.

8. Why do you think most institutional use of stock index futures is to reduce risk rather than to eliminate it?

9. Explain the idea of a "covered futures call" from a fiduciary standpoint.

10. In words, what is the usefulness of Itô's lemma?

11. Explain the concept of gamma risk.

12. Why does stock index option overwriting alter a portfolio beta?

13. What is the difference between an option's elasticity and its beta?

14. Why will the beta of a call option normally exceed that of the underlying asset? Under what circumstances would this not be true?

15. If a stock beta remains constant, how can an associated option beta change?

PROBLEMS

Note: Use the following information in problems 1–3: XYZ stock price = $44, striking price = $45, time until expiration = 110 days, riskfree interest rate = 3.3%, volatility = 0.30

■ 1. A portfolio contains 50,000 shares of XYZ. If the manager writes 40 of the above calls against it,
   (a) what is the position delta?

(b) what is the "degree of bullishness" relative to the original position?

◎ **2.** Suppose all the initial data remain the same, except that 25 days pass.
  (a) What is the position delta now?
  (b) What is the degree of bullishness relative to the original position?

◎ **3.** Assume that 85 days remain until option expiration. If the manager now buys 15 $45 *puts*, what is the position delta?

Note: Use the following information in problems 4–6: S&P 500 futures price = $400, striking price = $410, time until option expiration = 50 days, riskfree rate = 3.3%, volatility = 0.20

  4. A portfolio with a beta of 0.95 contains securities worth $10 million. How many S&P 500 futures are necessary to hedge 80 percent of the portfolio?

◎ **5.** How many of the above call options are necessary to hedge 50 percent of the portfolio?

  6. How many of the above call options could be written and be considered covered from a fiduciary standpoint?

◎ **7.** An equity call option sells for $2, has 45 days until expiration, the T bill rate is 3.4%, the stock price is $54, and the striking price is $55. Suppose the stock price instantaneously changes to $56. Estimate the revised call premium
  (a) using delta alone.
  (b) using Itô's lemma.

  Compare these answers to the actual result.

◎ **8.** Suppose in problem 7 that all the data remain the same except that three days pass before the stock price changes to $56. Estimate the revised call premium using Itô's lemma, including theta.

  9. Suppose the OEX index is 435.56. A $5 million portfolio (beta = 1.22) has 156 index call contracts written against it, each of which has a delta of 55.6. Estimate the new portfolio beta.

◎ **10.** A stock (beta = 1.20) sells for $45. A 90-day $45 call sells for $3, with market interest rates at 2.9%.
  (a) What is the elasticity of this call?
  (b) What is the beta of this call?

◎ **11.** In Problem 10, suppose 15 days pass and the stock price moves up to $48. What is the new option beta?

◎ **12.** In Problem 10, suppose 15 days pass and the stock price moves down to $42. What is the new option beta?

15 Financial Engineering, Globex, and Program Trading

*T*he most complicated risk management structure can be broken down into components that any high school graduate should be able to understand thoroughly. Ph.D.'s with various specialities—the "rocket scientists" described in the press—play an important role in financial risk management. But a Ph.D. is not necessary to understand any single aspect of financial risk or to evaluate the overall effectiveness of risk control.

Gary L. Gastineau
Swiss Bank Corporation

KEY TERMS

Americus Trust
cap price
CAPS
DOT system
financial engineering
GLOBEX
LEAPS

PERCS
PRIME
program trading
SCORE
termination claim
unit
vega

Although the world has had a century to react to Senator Washburn's comments (see the opening quotation for Chapter 8), futures and options continue to generate controversy, partly because of the rapid pace of market change and the difficulty outsiders have in understanding the products. In this chapter, we look primarily at financial engineering, a rapidly growing derivative asset subfield. Related to this is the proliferation of hybrid securities such as CAPS, PERCS, PRIMES, and SCORES.

GLOBEX is the futures and options market's response to the rapid integration of world economies and exchanges. This computerized trading system will eventually make possible 24-hour trading in many financial futures from a terminal in your study.

The chapter ends with a review of program trading, a poorly understood trading technique, but one that contributes to market efficiency and fair pricing. The appendix to the chapter reviews what we know about the Crash of 1987.

FINANCIAL ENGINEERING

Financial engineering is the popular name for constructing asset portfolios that have precise technical characteristics, particularly when those characteristics are not conveniently available in an existing exchange product.

Engineering an Option

Suppose that the S&P 500 index is at 326.00 and that the level of world uncertainty is such that long-term downside protection is prudent. An equity manager might want insurance against a market collapse over the next two years, but also want to retain the potential for upside appreciation. There is a variety of tactics by which wealth can be protected without disturbing the underlying portfolio.

Normal hedging by shorting S&P 500 futures would provide the downside peace of mind, but at the opportunity cost of future gains in the portfolio. A futures hedge "locks in" a price level, precluding further price appreciation.

Writing a call option provides limited downside protection. Receiving a premium of $1 provides exactly $1 in downside protection and has the further disadvantage of attenuating gains at the striking price. This is not an appropriate tactic when the objective is keeping the road to profits open while defeating most of the downside risk.

Buying a put is probably the most appropriate tactic. For a cost, puts provide reliable protection without prejudice to the upside potential of the portfolio. Table 15-1 (p. 326) reviews these alternatives.

TABLE 15-1 PORTFOLIO PROTECTION ALTERNATIVES

Choice	Advantages	Disadvantages
Short futures	Low trading fees; easy to do	Lose upside potential; possible tracking error
Write calls	Generate income	Lose most upside potential; inconvenient if exercised; limited protection
Buy puts	Reliable protection	Premium must be paid; hedge may require periodic adjustment

Having decided to use puts, the equity manager still faces choices, because the available put arsenal includes options on at least three different types of underlying assets: individual equities, stock market indexes such as the S&P 100 (OEX), and index futures contracts like the S&P 500 futures contract.

Extensive purchase of individual equity puts is inefficient in a large portfolio. Because a portfolio may contain dozens of stocks, buying equity puts would involve expensive trading fees, managerial time, and a significant premium cost. Either index options or futures options are best suited to this mission, and in many applications the two categories are interchangeable.

Figure 15-1 Ways to Provide Downside Protection

Objective

Acquire downside protection for a stock portfolio while leaving profit potential open.

Choices

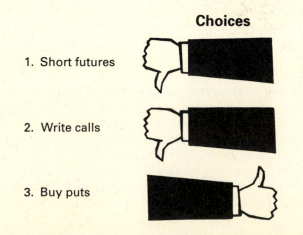

1. Short futures

2. Write calls

3. Buy puts

TABLE 15-2 OPTION PRICING MODEL DERIVATIVES

Delta—measures the sensitivity of the option premium to changes in the value of the underlying asset

Gamma—measures how quickly delta changes as the value of the underlying asset changes

Theta—measures the rapidity with which time value deteriorates

Vega—measures the sensitivity of the option premium to changes in anticipated volatility in the underlying asset. Vega is also called *kappa*

Suppose the decision is to use options on S&P 500 futures. These options have lives of less than a year, so it is not possible to purchase a 2-year put directly. However, you can construct one via a judicious combination of the options that are available. The greater the range of striking prices and expirations from which you may choose, the easier the task.

We know from option pricing theory that an option is reasonably well-defined by its pricing model derivatives. The most important of these are delta, gamma, theta, and **vega**,[1] reviewed in Table 15-2.

Assuming Treasury bills yield 8% and market volatility is 15%, the Black Options Pricing Model predicts the theoretical variables for a 2-year S&P 500 futures put option with a 325.00 striking price shown in Table 15-3.

Now assume that the eight options shown in Table 15-4 (p. 328) are available. They can be purchased or written. (Their pricing model sensitivities are shown.) The chore is assembling these options in the right combination to get position derivatives that match the theoretical values of the desired put.

Linear programming is a mathematical technique simplifying discovery of the least-cost combination of the available options giving the required position derivatives. Figure 15-2 shows one solution generated from a linear program. The synthetic two-year put includes two long call positions (820

TABLE 15-3 THEORETICAL VALUES FOR A 2-YEAR S&P 500 FUTURES PUT
(Striking price = 325.00; Current level of the index = 326.00)

Option Premium	=	$23.15
Delta	=	−0.388
Theta	=	−0.011
Gamma	=	0.016
Vega	=	1.566

---

[1]Vega does not have the everyday applications that delta, theta, and gamma do. Most individual and institutional users of options do not worry about vega; it is the most linear of the option pricing model derivatives. In a financial engineering application, however, vega may be important.

TABLE 15-4 THEORETICAL VALUES

Striking Price		CALLS		PUTS	
		JAN	MAR	JAN	MAR
320	Premium	$9.97	$13.25	$4.02	$7.38
	Delta	.645	.595	−.346	−.384
	Theta	−.069	−.045	−.071	−.046
	Gamma	.071	.047	.071	.047
	Vega	.411	.651	.411	.651
330	Premium	$4.88	$8.36	$8.84	$12.28
	Delta	.413	.445	−.578	−.533
	Theta	−.074	−.047	−.074	−.047
	Gamma	.075	.049	.075	.049
	Vega	.433	.672	.433	.672

March 320s and 1000 March 330s), three long put positions (1000 Mar 320s, 82 January 330s, and 1000 March 330s), two short calls (833 January 330s and 556 January 320s), and one short put (1000 January 320s).

"Smaller" puts can be constructed by scaling down each of the above positions proportionately. Table 15-5 shows the calculations; the slight error in the totals is due to rounding.

The tough part of engineering an option is dealing with the dynamic nature of the product. Any synthetic option portfolio requires frequent adjustment if it is to continue to mimic the desired theoretical option. This

TABLE 15-5 PORTFOLIO SUMMARY

Position	Contribution to Position			
	Delta	Gamma	Theta	Vega
long 820 MAR 320 calls	487.90	38.54	−36.90	533.82
long 1000 MAR 330 calls	445.00	49.00	−47.00	672.00
short 556 JAN 320 calls	−358.62	−39.48	38.36	−228.52
short 833 JAN 330 calls	−344.03	−62.48	61.64	−360.69
short 1000 JAN 320 puts	346.00	−71.00	71.00	−411.00
long 82 JAN 330 puts	− 47.40	6.15	− 6.07	35.51
long 1000 MAR 320 puts	−384.00	47.00	−46.00	651.00
long 1000 MAR 330 puts	−533.00	49.00	−47.00	672.00
Total	−388.15	16.73	−11.97	1564.12
[scaled down by 1000:	−0.388	0.017	−0.012	1.564]
	Net Cost = $25.99			

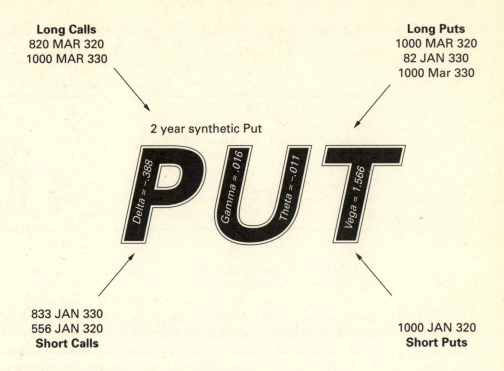

Long Calls
820 MAR 320
1000 MAR 330

Long Puts
1000 MAR 320
82 JAN 330
1000 Mar 330

2 year synthetic Put

Delta = -.388 Gamma = .016 Theta = -.011 Vega = 1.566

833 JAN 330
556 JAN 320
Short Calls

1000 JAN 320
Short Puts

Figure 15-2 Synthetic Two-Year Put

means that adjustments to the long and short positions in the portfolio will be required as time passes and the value of the underlying asset changes.

After two days, for instance, the level of the cash index might have fallen one point, to 325.00. The passage of time and the change in the value of the underlying asset will cause the pricing model derivatives to change also. Table 15-6 shows the new position characteristics compared to those of the theoretical put we seek to replicate.

To keep the engineered put behaving like a "real" one, it is necessary to adjust the option positions that comprise it. Using updated pricing model derivatives and new option premiums, the linear program can be modified

TABLE 15-6 POSITION DERIVATIVES AFTER TWO DAYS

	Target	Actual
Delta	−0.388	−0.394
Theta	−0.011	−0.006
Gamma	0.016	0.013
Vega	1.566	1.555

TABLE 15-7 ORIGINAL AND ADJUSTED OPTION PORTFOLIO TO EXACTLY REPLICATE A TWO-YEAR PUT

	Original Position	New Position	Action
Jan 320 calls	short 556	short 1000	sell 444
Mar 320 calls	long 820	long 793	sell 27
Jan 330 calls	short 833	short 408	buy 425
Mar 330 calls	long 1000	long 1000	—
Jan 320 puts	short 1000	short 248	buy 752
Mar 320 puts	long 1000	long 1000	—
Jan 330 puts	long 82	short 589	sell 671
Mar 330 puts	long 1000	long 1000	—

slightly to find a new basket of options that will have the desired characteristics. Table 15-7 shows this.

These extensive adjustments are necessary if we wish to replicate the two-year put option exactly. We are probably most interested in the position delta as time passes, and the new position delta of -0.394 is not so different from the original target of -0.388. Many managers would not choose to adjust the portfolio merely because of this slight deviation from the target figure. How frequently you should reconstruct the portfolio to fine-tune delta depends on the rest of your market positions and the magnitude of the trading fees you pay, in addition to how rapidly the market has moved since you first built the put.

Hybrid Securities[2]

PRIMES and SCORES These were arguably the first of the engineered hybrid securities. Although they are now out of existence, they provide a good case study. **PRIME** is the acronym for "Prescribed Right to Income and Maximum Equity"; **SCORE** stands for "Special Claim on Residual Equity." Rather than being issued by the underlying company, these were issued by a separate legal entity called the **Americus Trust.** There were 24 separate companies on which an American Trust **unit** was issued in 1986. Each unit contained one PRIME and one SCORE. These securities provided investors a means of separating a stock's income and capital appreciation potential. Both types of securities had a five-year initial life and were marketable.

---

[2]In preparing this section, I received very helpful information from Emmett J. Harty of the Parallax Group, Inc., 315 Post Road West, Westport, CT, 06880, (800-227-2057) and from Joanne M. Hill of PaineWebber Derivative Products Research Group (212-713-3322).

A person who bought a PRIME obtained all the rights of ordinary equity ownership except unlimited upside potential.[3] Above a certain price level, the PRIME owner received no further capital gains. This is analogous to the profit/loss characteristics associated with the writing of a covered call.

▌Owning a PRIME is like a covered call position.

Owning a SCORE is like owning a long-term European call option.[4] The SCORE owner received nothing other than the intrinsic value of the option at its "expiration." Rather than a striking price, the SCORE had a **termination claim.** If the stock price was above the termination claim at the dissolution of the trust, the SCORE was valuable.

▌Owning a SCORE is like owning a long-term call option.

The holder of Americus Trust securities could become an ordinary stockholder by redeeming a PRIME and a SCORE, receiving a share of common stock in exchange. Figure 15-3 (p. 332) shows the relationship. A *unit* contained both a PRIME and a SCORE; a unit could be exchanged for a share of stock, or a PRIME and a SCORE could be exchanged for a unit. A share of stock, however, could not be exchanged for a unit.

PERCS   The fact that the Americus Trusts were scheduled to end after five years was partially responsible for the creation of **PERCS.** This term stands for "Preferred Equity Redemption Cumulative Stock." These securities are like PRIMES, except they are issued directly by the corporation. PERCS have a larger dividend than the common stock, so are more like a cumulative preferred stock with a call written against it. Among the companies that have issued PERCS are General Motors, K-Mart, Texas Instruments, R. J. Reynolds, AON Corporation, and Tenneco.

▌PERCS are like PRIMES except they are issued by the underlying company.

PERCS have a three-year life and are callable over this period. The call price progressively declines to a final call premium of about 30%. After the

---

[3]The PRIME holder receives the same dividends as the underlying shareholder minus a small fee associated with the administration of the trust. This is about a penny per share per quarter.

[4]SCORES resemble long-term call options more than warrants. Warrants are issued directly by the company and can dilute earnings per share. SCORES and listed options are issued by an entity other than the underlying company.

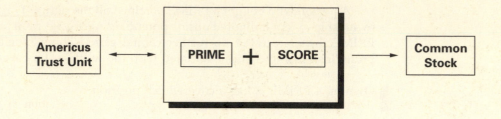

Figure 15-3 Redeeming an Americus Trust Unit

three-year period the PERC holder is required to convert the security to common stock. When the PERC is called, it is exchanged for common stock based on the call price. This means if the stock price exceeds the call price the PERC holder will receive less than one full share for each PERC. The call premium, then, amounts to a cap on appreciation potential. Many equity investors would seek to sell their PERCS if the stock price advances beyond the call price.

A functional difference between a covered call and a PERC is that with the former, the compensation for the short call comes immediately as the option premium. With a PERC, the compensation comes from the enhanced income stream.

LEAPS   A **LEAP** is a "Long-term Equity AnticiPation Security." LEAPS are analogous to SCORES, except that LEAPS are created by the options exchanges rather than a separate trust. The CBOE issued the first LEAP in October, 1990, with the other option exchanges following suit shortly after that.

LEAPS are analogous to SCORES.

LEAPS are issued with durations of 1, 2, and 3 years. Both put and call LEAPS trade, both with American exercise features. Three striking prices are established at issuance: an at-the-money strike, a strike 20 percent below the current stock price, and a strike 25 percent above the current stock price. New strike prices are added as necessary so that the 20 percent and 25 percent bounds are maintained.

These securities are still somewhat new, and attempts are underway to standardize certain of their structural features. The exchanges plan eventually to synchronize their offerings such that all LEAPS expire in a January. This would simplify their trading, because after one year a three-year LEAP would

TABLE 15-8 SYNONYMOUS TERMS

Options	Primes	Percs	Scores	Leaps
strike price	termination claim	final call price	termination claim	strike price
expiration date	termination date	mandatory conversion date	termination date	expiration date

Source: Parallax Group, Inc.

be identical with a newly issued two-year LEAP and would be fungible with it. In early 1993 there were LEAPS trading on over 100 individual securities, as well as on the OEX, SPX, and XMI stock indexes.[5] Both the OEX and SPX LEAPS are based on one-tenth of the underlying index; the OEX is American exercise style, while the SPX is European.

LEAPS are attractive to both hedgers and speculators. LEAP puts can provide long-term protection to a stock portfolio (or an individual security position); LEAP calls can be written to enhance portfolio income. A speculator might buy either type of LEAP in anticipation of rising or falling security or market prices.

As described in the paragraphs above, there are certain similarities in PRIMES, PERCS, SCORES, and LEAPS. Table 15-8 shows these.

CAPS   CAPS trade on the CBOE and AMEX, and are much like an option spread packaged as a single security. Call CAPS have a **cap price** equal to the option striking price plus the CAP interval, while puts have a cap price equal to the option striking price minus the CAP interval. At present, the CAP interval is 30 points at the CBOE and 20 at the AMEX. On both exchanges, the options trade via automatic European exercise style; they are automatically exercised and are cash settled, if in-the-money at expiration.

A speculator who buys an OEX 360 cap has a position that is similar to buying a 360 call and writing a 390 call (390 is 30 points over the 360 striking price). No further profits occur above an index level of 390. This is the situation that prevails with a simple bull spread, and the profit and loss diagram for the purchase of a CAP is identical.

It is important to note that a CAP is not identical to a spread, however. The two parts of a spread can be dissembled and traded separately if the spreader chooses. This is not so with a CAP; it cannot be torn apart.

---

[5]Striking prices on the stock index LEAPS are set at either 2½- or 5-point intervals.

Box 15-1 **BIG-TIME TACTICS FOR SMALL INVESTORS**

The public finally prevails in the market. "LEAPS (Long-term Equity AnticiPation Securities) are the only area where the public is ahead of the institutions," says Harrison Roth, senior options strategist with Cowen & Co. in New York.

Swaps, exotic options, basis trading, synthetic asset allocation—only institutional investors with the capital to trade on huge scales can engage in those tactics.

LEAPS stand out because small investors can reap benefits. At a time when small investors need alternatives to lack-luster certificates of deposit yet still shy away from a scandal-prone market and feel uncomfortable with its volatility, LEAPS allow them to participate in familiar blue-chip stocks and avoid the fray.

Basically, investors can buy in-the-money LEAPS with high enough deltas that the options respond almost one-to-one to the underlying stock.

For example, on Aug. 20, a January 1994 General Motors $25 call cost $12 (with the stock at $35¾ a share). "A tremendous bargain," Roth says. Option holders don't collect dividends, but they can compensate. Having bought the option for $12, they can invest the remaining $23¾ in an appropriate maturity Treasury note. That provides an almost risk-free investment which will at least earn as much as the dividend earnings of the stock.

Better yet, the low cost of LEAPS opens the way to what Roth calls "surrogate" strategies. Consider the possibilities that arise from an initial purchase of an IBM LEAP. With the stock at $86, the January 1994 70 call traded at 16.

Again, investors could buy the call and invest the "savings" in T-notes. Alternatively, they could take advantage of the leverage to buy more than one IBM LEAP, but Roth cautions against going overboard.

Most interestingly, investors can use the low price to diversify. Roth explains. A 100-share block of IBM would cost $8,600. But investors could buy one LEAP call each in IBM, Apple, Digital Equipment and Intel. Doing that they avoid the common pitfall of picking the wrong stock in the right industry. "The nature of the options means they can afford to be right on only one of four," Roth says.

They can also do that more broadly, he notes. Along with an IBM LEAP, they could buy Amgen, Pfizer and Philip Morris, or some such mix. Now, Roth says, "they own a little mutual fund." And all for less than 100 shares of IBM would cost.

LEAPS traders can engage in almost all the strategies available with regular options. And for the small investor, there may even be tax advantages.

Roth says a traditional covered call tactic can temporarily shelter income from tax. For example, with Johnson & Johnson trading at $50 a share, the January 1995 50 call was 10. Traders who owned, or bought, 1,000 shares of the stock could sell 10 calls and collect $10,000 in premium. But, he says, for tax purposes there is no taxable event until the option expires, traders repurchase it, or they assign it. Say nothing happens until January 1995 when they assign the option. The first tax on the $10,000 falls due in April 1996—over three years of tax-free use of the money.

Obviously, each investor must study his own tax situation and the suitability of LEAPS given his needs. But equally obvious: LEAPS open the way to new investment dimensions for the average investor.

Source: Futures (Oct, 1992) p. 50.

Surprisingly, CAPS have not enjoyed the investor enthusiasm the exchanges anticipated. Trading volume is very low, and the future of these securities is unclear.

GLOBEX

In economic discussions it is popular to speak of how the world has become one giant marketplace. Barriers to trade are falling, communication links are increasing, and access to global markets is improving. An excellent example of this lies in **GLOBEX,** the global trading system developed by Reuters Limited for initial use by the Chicago Mercantile Exchange and the Chicago Board of Trade. MATIF (Marché à Terme International de France) products began trading on March 12, 1993. The Commodity Exchange, the New York Cotton Exchange, the New York Futures Exchange, and the Coffee, Sugar, and Cocoa Exchange have all agreed in principle to participate in GLOBEX.

A new era has dawned. GLOBEX represents as revolutionary a change for the futures industry as did the introduction of financial futures two decades ago. No doubt, just as it took many years for that revolution to take hold, so will it take time for GLOBEX to become established. Nevertheless, it is inevitable—GLOBEX exemplifies the world of the 21st century.

Leo Melamed, Chairman
GLOBEX Corporation

Characteristics

GLOBEX is designed to extend the trading hours for products that show demand outside regular open outcry trading hours. GLOBEX is a computer-terminal version of the trading pits that allows trading of futures and options contracts after the close of the exchanges. GLOBEX cost $70 million to develop and five years to become functional. Eventually, GLOBEX will permit worldwide trading around the clock,[6] controlled by the GLOBEX Control Center in Chicago. GLOBEX terminals are available to members and member firms of the CME, CBOT, and MATIF. Individual members can place their terminals in an office or at home. The average order response time is only 3 seconds.

GLOBEX opened on June 25, 1992, with about 225 trading terminals up and running. In the first hour of GLOBEX trading volume reached 300 contracts. Nearly 2000 contracts traded the first night. Between its opening and the end of July, average daily trading volume was 1354 contracts.[7] In early 1993, GLOBEX terminals were in use in Chicago, New York, London, Paris, Tokyo, Hong Kong, and Geneva. Frankfurt, Zurich, and Singapore are likely to be added to the list. Initially, only futures and options on Deutchmarks, yen, and 10-year Treasury notes traded. Currency futures and options and interest rate futures and options began trading on March 4, 1993. Other financial futures are likely to be phased into the system, with the notable exception of the S&P 500 stock index futures. The Chicago Mercantile Exchange does not plan to list this contract.

Trading Terms

GLOBEX is limited to limit orders to buy or sell. Orders are matched based on time priority when the limit price is reached. The system also accommodates fill-or-kill orders, which are essentially market orders that may be only partially filled.[8] The system permits trading of both calendar futures spreads and intercommodity spreads (such as the TED spread). No other spreads are currently available for trading.

---

[6]Current GLOBEX trading hours are from 6:00 p.m. Sunday evening through 6:00 a.m. Friday morning, central standard time.

[7]See *GLOBEX Report,* vol. 1, no. 3 (August 17, 1992).

[8]Fill-or-kill orders produce an immediate trade at the best available bid or ask. If the order cannot be completely filled for some reason, the remainder of the order is canceled.

Future Outlook

Some of the most influential individuals in the futures and options business devoted enormous amounts of time to ensuring that GLOBEX would be successful. New exchanges are developing everywhere in the world it seems, and it is increasingly easier for traders to use a different market if tax or regulatory concerns become too egregious in the home country. GLOBEX is both a defensive measure and an attempt to improve the operational efficiency of the hedging/speculating paradigm. While it is probable that the system has some bugs to be worked out, there is a very high likelihood that computerized trading will be part of derivative asset trading in the future.

> We find GLOBEX to be a very efficient way to trade currency futures. The system is easy to use and executions are fast, fair, and clean. . . . While we do not feel GLOBEX will replace the open outcry system, it is an excellent outlet for the Far Eastern and European time zones.
>
> Raymond McKenzie
> Managing Director,
> Morgan Stanley & Co.

PROGRAM TRADING

One fundamental principle of finance is that arbitrage opportunities will be short-lived. When security prices deviate from their "true" value such that riskless profits can be made, some market observers will find the arbitrage, exploit it, and quickly eliminate it.

Definition

Program trading is not easy to define. One use of the term is "any computer-aided buying or selling activity in the stock market." Other people view program trading as synonymous with "stock index futures arbitrage."

Hans Stoll and Robert Whaley, two well-known market researchers, propose that program trading has three key characteristics:[9]

1. It is *portfolio trading,* meaning that an entire portfolio of stocks is traded via a single order;

---

[9]Stoll, Hans and Robert Whaley. "Program Trading and the Monday Massacre." Unpublished paper; November 4, 1987.

2. It is *computerized trading* done with small individual lots of stock rather than large blocks;

3. It is *computer decision making,* where the decisions are triggered by the existence of mispricing (arbitrage).

Program trading is:
1. portfolio trading,
2. computerized trading, and
3. computer decision making.

Arbitrageurs in the marketplace perform a useful function, helping keep the market efficient and ensuring that prices do not deviate from their proper values for very long. As a group, they are not hurting for pocket change, particularly in markets that are popular with the investing public.

Arbitrageurs help keep the market efficient.

Implementation

Computers have made the life of both the arbitrageur and the institutional investor simpler and more profitable. Using the New York Stock Exchange's *Designated Order Turnaround* system, called **DOT,** market orders for less than 2100 shares of a stock may be placed with the stock specialist electronically rather than going through a floor broker. We have seen previously certain relationships that should prevail among security prices, such as the theory of put/call parity and the "fair value" price of stock index futures contracts. With high-speed, on-line computers, it is much easier to identify those instances when arbitrage is present.

A perception that is not accurate is the notion that these watchful computers "call the shots" on which way stock prices are to move next. The computer identifies situations where arbitrage is present but does not cause the situation.

Groups of arbitrageurs often identify profitable opportunities almost simultaneously, and they take advantage of these computer-identified opportunities on a grand scale by collectively buying or selling hundreds of thousands of shares in a matter of minutes. Contrary to popular belief, however, this extra volume is mostly from many small institutional trades rather than massive 100,000-share transactions.

Because the arbitrage situation will normally work in only a single direction (e.g., everyone buys or everyone sells), this large influx of orders can cause prices to change drastically. *Program trading* is the common term describing any strategy that instantaneously recommends buy or sell orders because of arbitrage.

At present, program traders normally fall into one of two groups: (1) institutions that buy stock index futures and Treasury bills to create the equivalent of an index portfolio (long stock index futures + long T bills = long index portfolio), and (2) institutions that combine a well-diversified stock portfolio with short positions in stock index futures to create synthetic Treasury bills (long index portfolio + short index futures = long T bills). If these traders find that they can synthetically create an index fund that yields more than the actual index portfolio, or create synthetic T bills that yield more than actual T bills, they are going to jump on the chance. In doing so, they may collectively buy or sell thousands of shares in the blink of an eye.

Program trading suffers from a bad name because of the alleged impact these programs have on security prices. If the market takes a real tumble or if it is unusually volatile, someone will certainly put the blame on program trading. The stock specialist needs to match buy and sell orders as they arrive, and if program trading leads to the rapid arrival of many DOT orders at once, the specialist can have difficulty maintaining a "fair and orderly market." This situation can lead to increased volatility, which is not desirable.

On September 11, 1986, for instance, the Dow Jones Industrial Average fell 86.61 points (4.61%); the following day it continued to decline, and the total drop was 120 points in two days. On January 23, 1987, there was an intraday swing of 114 points in the DJIA. Program trading was blamed for this disturbing market behavior on both occasions. There were many fingers pointed at program trading as the culprit behind the crash of 1987 (discussed in the appendix). For all investors, changes in the DJIA of this magnitude are thought-provoking.

It is easy to forget that an 80 point drop in the Dow when it is over 2000 is different from an 80 point drop when it is under 1000. Long-time market participants still subconsciously think of 20 point movements in the DJIA as a "major" change. Gary Gastineau, author of the excellent book, *Stock Options Manual,* reported in a publication of the Chicago Board Options Exchange that when the market fell 41.91 points on April 30, 1986, it was the largest one-day *point* decline on record then.[10] However, that 2.3% decline had been exceeded at least 362 times over the previous five years, or an average of once every two months!

Many professional traders and investment managers believe that program trading benefits the public. W. Gordon Binns, vice-president and chief investment funds officer of General Motors, told a congressional panel that the use of program trading enabled GM to reduce average commission costs for the company pension fund from between 7 and 10 cents per share to between 2 and 3 cents per share. This is clearly to the benefit of the many retirees receiving checks from the fund.

---

[10]Gastineau, Gary. "Arbitrage, Program Trading and the Tail of the Dog." Special publication of the Chicago Board Options Exchange, 1986.

To study the impact that futures and options may have on the cash (stock) markets, a study was commissioned jointly by the Federal Reserve Board, the Commodity Futures Trading Commission, and the Securities Exchange Commission. This study reports "futures and options markets do not destabilize cash market prices, and indeed, may work to stabilize them."[11]

The Open Outcry and Specialist Systems

A discussion of program trading often leads into a discussion of the merits and demerits of the two trading systems used in the United States, the specialist system and the marketmaker system. The *specialist system* is used on the American and Philadelphia Stock Exchanges; *marketmakers* are used on the Pacific Stock Exchange and at the Chicago Board Options Exchange. Trading pits, of course, are used at the commodities exchanges. Each system has its own apologists and critics.

Andrew Schwarz, a specialist at the American Stock Exchange, says, "The specialist acts at all times to maintain a fair and orderly market." As specialists buy and sell against the prevailing trend of the market, they incur substantial risks while helping to promote continuous, fair pricing. In exchange for this role, option specialists receive a modest commission of a half dollar or so for each option contract they handle from the public. Because specialists are in a position to make substantial profits from their "book," it is in their interest to make a good market with heavy trading activity.

A different view is expressed by Gary Lahey, CBOE former vice chairman. He states, "If a multitude of people [i.e., marketmakers] in a trading crowd are all trying to do different things, the interaction provides a better market than one individual."

While representatives of the various exchanges logically want to argue the respective merits of their system, there is one area in which consensus is building. High-volume markets seem to lend themselves to the marketmaker system, while low-volume or recently listed securities are best traded via the specialist system. The successful OEX contract is traded at the CBOE via marketmakers, and Schwartz calls the OEX arena "the most efficient marketplace" he has ever seen.

At the AMEX, the success of the XMI contract has led to more than 200 Options Principal Members (i.e., marketmakers) augmenting the specialist in handling this product. This situation at the AMEX is the first example of the two trading systems coexisting and serving a common purpose.

---

[11]"A Study of the Effects on the Economy of Trading in Futures and Options," Board of Governors of the Federal Reserve System, Commodity Futures Trading Commission, and Securities Exchange Commission (December 1984), pp. 1–18 and 1–19.

SUMMARY

Financial engineering is a rapidly growing subfield of the derivative assets business. It is the popular name for the construction of asset portfolios that have precise technical characteristics, particularly when those characteristics are not available in an existing exchange product.

Financial engineers have spawned a number of hybrid securities with unique characteristics. PRIMES, SCORES, CAPS, LEAPS, and PERCS are examples. Each of these offers a particular risk and return package that is often not otherwise available.

GLOBEX is a worldwide computer trading system that permits the trading of most financial futures contracts and their options almost around the clock. It is a joint venture of the Chicago Mercantile Exchange and the Chicago Board of Trade, with other world exchanges interested in participating.

Program trading refers to any activity that contains three key components: the trading of entire portfolios, the use of computers to make the trades, and the use of a computer to decide when to make the trades. Program trading exists because of the periodic short-lived arbitrage opportunities between the stock market in New York and the futures market in Chicago. Computers act on the arbitrage, quickly eliminating it, and helping to keep prices efficient.

QUESTIONS

1. Someone once said "finance is the study of arbitrage." What does this statement mean?
2. Explain the term "financial engineering."
3. Why is buying a put better portfolio protection than writing a covered call?
4. Why does selling stock index futures eliminate upside profit potential on a diversified portfolio?
5. Briefly explain "vega."
6. Suppose a portfolio is long a number of different options. What can you say about its position theta?
7. How does the options concept of position risk affect financial engineering applications?
8. In engineering a put for downside protection, why is gamma important?
9. Why do engineered options need periodic adjustment?
10. Why is a SCORE more like a long-term call option than a warrant?

11. If new Americus Trusts were introduced, do you think it would make sense to allow common stock holders to exchange their shares for units?
12. Would you expect an Americus Trust unit to sell for more, less than, or the same as a share of the common stock?
13. What is the difference between a LEAP and a SCORE?
14. Why is an OEX CAP not identical to an option spread with the same striking price interval?
15. GLOBEX does not plan to list stock index futures. Why do you think this is?
16. Suppose that conclusive proof became available showing that program trading *does* increase the volatility of the security markets. What changes, if any, do you think would be called for?
17. Describe the two principal groups of program traders.
18. Do you believe that the marketmaker system would work in the stock market, where the specialist system has always been used?

PROBLEMS

Note: Use the following data in solving problems 1–4: stock price = $55, interest rates = 4%, volatility = .25, time until MAY expiration = 45 days, time until JUN expiration = 74 days.

1. You hold 5 JUN 45 calls, 5 JUN 55 calls, and are short 5 JUN 60 calls.
   - **(a)** What is the position delta?
   - **(b)** What is the position theta?
   - **(c)** What is the position gamma?
2. In Problem 1, suppose that 10 days pass and the stock price retreats to $54. What are the new position derivatives?
3. In Problem 1, suppose all the options were *puts* instead of calls. Do you need to recalculate values to determine
   - **(a)** position delta?
   - **(b)** position theta?
   - **(c)** position gamma?

   Confirm the new values using the software.
4. What is the theoretical Black-Scholes value for a 3-year put with a striking price of 55?
5. According to Black-Scholes, the premium for a one-year option is less than the sum of the premiums for two successive six-month options. Show that this is true, and explain why this is.
6. Select a LEAP from the *Wall Street Journal* listing. Calculate its implied volatility. Do the same for an ordinary equity option on the same

company. Why do you think the implied volatility values might be different?

● 7. Select a LEAP from the *Wall Street Journal.* Using the software, determine its delta, gamma, and theta.

● 8. Prepare a plot showing time value decay of a 3-year call option. Use the data at the start of this section and a striking price of $60.

 **Appendix: The Crash of 1987**

*A*nyone can hold the helm when the sea is calm.

Publilius Syrus

KEY TERMS

Black Monday
Brady report
bucket trading
circuit breaker

cross trading
portfolio insurance
Terrible Tuesday

October 19, 1987, will be remembered as **Black Monday,** the day the market fell 508 points. During the last hour of trading, the Dow Jones Industrial Average (DJIA) was falling at the rate of 1 point every 17 seconds. What happened to cause this? While no one really knows, the futures and options markets have had many fingers pointed at them. Let's look at the events surrounding the crash and at these accusations.

On October 19, 1987, the Dow Jones Industrial Average fell 508 points, the largest point drop in history.

THE MARKET BEFORE AND AFTER THE CRASH

Figure 15A-1 shows the Dow Jones Industrial Average in the week before and the two weeks following the October 19 crash. Clearly this was a complicated period with unprecedented volatility. The average daily price change in the DJIA over the period October 12 to October 30 was 4.93%. Volatility of this magnitude attracts attention from all quarters, including investors large and small, the exchanges, the regulators, and Congress.

Option speculators who felt that "if ever there was a time for buying index straddles, this is it" were particularly frustrated because of their

Figure 15A-1 DJIA Around the Crash of 1987
Source: Wall Street Journal.

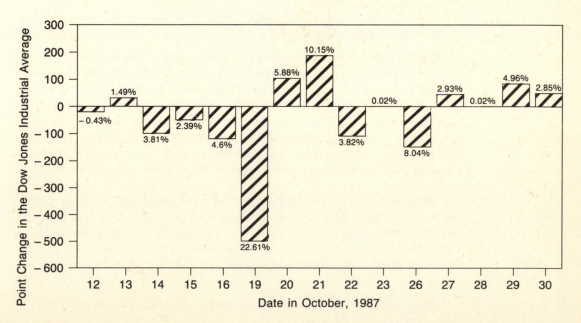

difficulty in trading. On the Friday before the crash, there were 15 striking prices ranging from 280 to 350 listed for the OEX contract. The day after the crash, there were 34 striking prices, ranging from *185* to 350. Some speculators, your author included, called to get price quotes on options with the new striking prices, but prices had moved so much that the Options Price Reporting System was unable to immediately react to the new striking prices. Brokers who punched in the code for a striking price of 220 were still retrieving 320 strike price values.

Similar frustrations were experienced by those who placed market orders during this period of high volatility. Some orders to buy a $5 option were filled at prices in double digits because of the rapid swings in the level of the market.

There is a saying that when Wall Street sneezes, the world catches a cold. The crash of the U.S. markets had repercussions around the world, as exchanges in Tokyo, Sydney, London, and elsewhere also took major dives. What happened to cause this? In the search for someone to blame, many fingers quickly pointed to program trading.

Program Trading and the Crash of 1987

One week after the crash, *Barrons'* reported the following:

> "Monday signaled the end of program trading," Rep. Edward J. Markey, the chairman of the House subcommittee with jurisdiction over the SEC, said Thursday. "This is it. It's over."
> "They have to have a scapegoat," sighed a mutual fund manager. "The last time, it was the shortsellers."[1]

Barrons' goes on to point out the particular irony in this accusation. As we have seen, program trading is intended to eliminate arbitrage situations that develop between the stock market and stock index futures. But the dramatic fall in the market averages made traders reluctant (or unable) to participate in the rollercoaster game. As a consequence, the basis in contracts like the S&P 500 futures diverged substantially from where it "should" have been. This confused and frustrated many portfolio managers. If the program traders had acted on the discrepancies in the market, it might have reduced the volatility of the market.

William Brodsky, President of the Chicago Mercantile Exchange, points out that on "Black Monday" institutions sold over 50,000 contracts of the S&P 500 futures to hedge their massive portfolios. This is equivalent to about 130 million shares of stock. (Total volume on October 19 was 605 million shares.) If these institutions had chosen to sell their shares instead of hedging

---

[1]"Villain or Scapegoat? The Heat's on Program Trading," *Barrons* (October 26, 1987): 9.

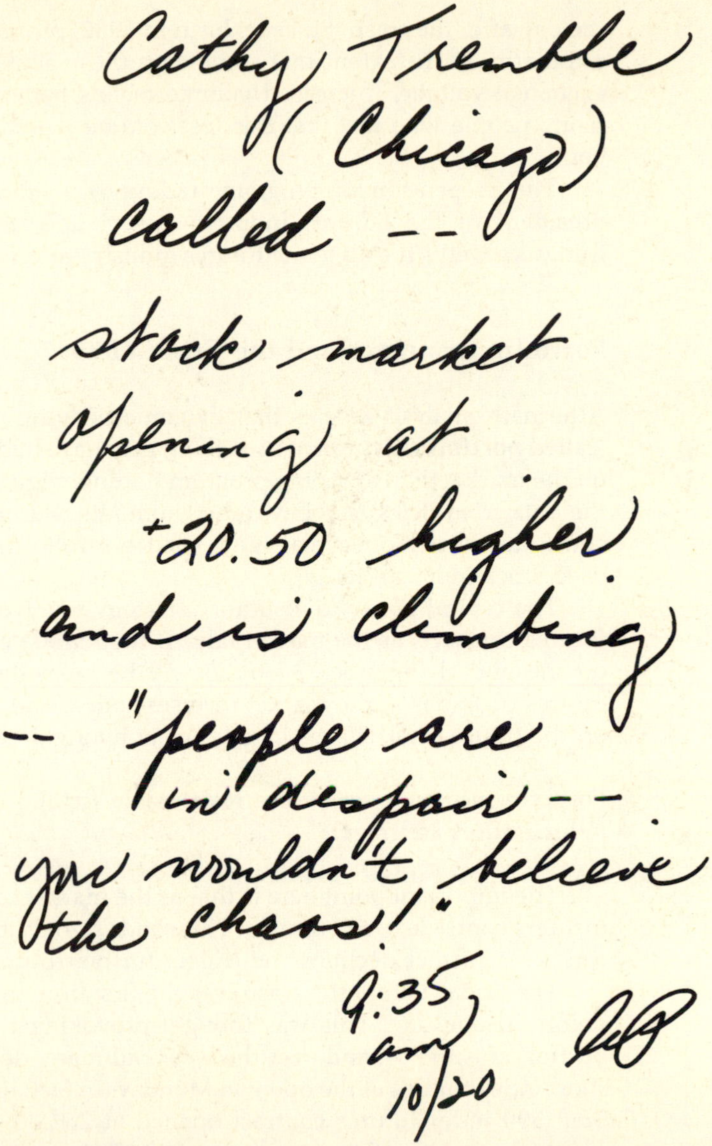

Cathy Tremble
(Chicago)
called --

stock market
opening at
+20.50 higher
and is climbing)
-- "people are
in despair --
you wouldn't believe
the chaos!"
9:35
am
10/20

Figure 15A-2 Copy of a Telephone Message I Received from the Floor of the Chicago Mercantile Exchange on Terrible Tuesday

in the futures market, Brodsky feels that the market would have declined even more than 508 points.

Regardless of whether Brodsky is correct or not, program trading was curtailed by the exchanges on October 20 (now dubbed **Terrible Tuesday**), the day after the crash. Since its birth in 1982, program trading has grown in popularity to the extent that some days these activities account for 10% of exchange volume.[2] Increased volume means better liquidity, and there are many people who feel that this lost volume would do far more harm than good.

The suspension of program trading was lifted on November 9. The president of the Futures Industry Association, John Damgard, summed things up well: "It's up to the futures industry to prove its worth once again."

Portfolio Insurance and the Crash of 1987

Aftermath analysis reveals that dynamic hedging with stock index futures (called **portfolio insurance** back then) may have had a more significant effect on the market than anything program trading might have done. In reviewing the data from Black Monday, the Commodity Futures Trading Commission concluded that money managers used portfolio insurance *more* than they used stock index arbitrage.

The typical portfolio insurance strategy involves selling S&P 500 index futures contracts as the market falls. If the market continues to fall, the loss on the underlying stock portfolio will be partially offset by gains on the futures positions. If the market reverses course and rises, there will be a loss on the futures that will be largely offset by a gain on the stocks.

Portfolio insurance was more responsible for the market crash than stock index futures arbitrage.

The important point here is that as the market continues to fall, portfolio insurers continue to sell futures. This sends signals to the marketplace, which can cause further declines and trigger further futures selling.

The Friday before the crash was the first time the DJIA had ever lost 100 points in one day. This was thought-provoking to many managers using portfolio insurance, and over the weekend many decisions were made to go short index futures at the open on Monday. In fact, on Monday the December S&P 500 index futures contract opened at 264.00, which was down 18.25 points from the settlement price of 282.25 the previous trading day. At the close on Black Monday, the December S&P 500 futures contract stood at 201.50, a remarkable one-day decline of 80.75 points. This means that the value of one contract fell $40,375 in a single day!

---

[2] Over 15 percent of NYSE volume on Black Monday was from program trading.

The important issue with portfolio insurance in the context of the crash is not so much that it *didn't work,* but rather the fact that it *could not be implemented.* We have seen how the basis in S&P 500 index futures is theoretically determined and how it is usually only a few points in magnitude. But at times on October 19 there were gaps of over 20 points between the level of the cash index and the futures contract value. Figure 15A-3 illustrates the S&P 500 futures basis hour by hour on October 19. Normally, the futures contract sells at a premium to the cash index, since interest rates normally exceed the dividend yield of stocks. But the figure shows that during the 500 point plunge futures were occasionally selling at significant *discounts* to cash. Managers who "insured" with futures found that they still lost lots of money.

In the aftermath of the crash, one thing is now clear: There was a severe information shortfall on October 19 and 20. Volume was so heavy and confusion was reigning so supremely that it was very difficult for the people on the exchange floor, much less individual investors trying to call their brokers, to get current price information. A good case could be made for the thesis that "current price" was a nonsequitur on these two days. No one knew an accurate price for anything. This meant that many portfolio insurance signals were false, and that the severity of the information lag caused widespread whipsawing of security and contract prices.

Figure 15A-3 Basis in December S&P 500 Futures

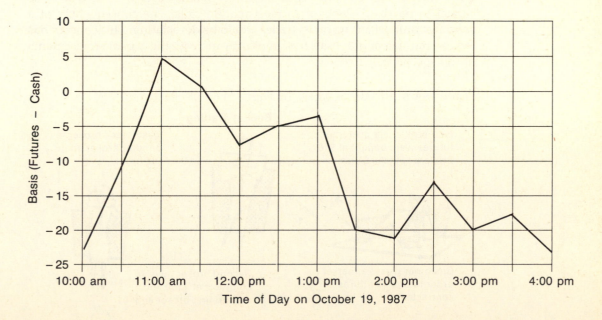

Concerns with the Specialist and Marketmaker Systems

Marketmakers   There is some evidence that a few marketmakers at the Chicago Board Options Exchange may have significantly overcharged customers for options during the hectic days surrounding the crash. In the frenzy of the pit, it is possible to switch customer orders and those for your personal trading account, an illegal practice sometimes called **cross trading.** The temptation to take a better price at the customer's expense becomes stronger as your own financial position deteriorates. Many marketmakers lost millions during this period, and some were completely wiped out. Total marketmaker losses at the CBOE on October 19 are estimated at $150 million, or between 10 percent and 20 percent of their total capital.

Another illegal activity, **bucket trading,** is when a customer is charged more than necessary and two traders split the difference (see Figure 15A-4). Proponents of the specialist system argue that covert overcharging is not possible with a single specialist for the security or option.

Specialists   The specialist's job is traditionally described as "making a fair and orderly market." This involves taking the other side of the market if everyone wants to sell, and vice-versa. During the crash, specialists were forced to buy securities that they did not want. Many of the specialists lost a major percentage of their capital base. Table 15A-1 shows the dramatic decline in seat prices on the various exchanges following the crash. Many of these trades were genuine "distress sales," where seats were sold to raise capital to pay bank debts or to meet margin calls. The consequences of a specialist unit defaulting on its trades would be devastating. This concern has led to a number of proposals to significantly increase the capital requirements of the specialists.

Figure 15A-4 A Model of Bucket Trading

Bucket Trading

First broker tells customer futures were bought at $101. Brokers split the $1 profit.

Customer's broker tells another broker about the order.

Customer places a market order to buy 10 futures contracts.

Second broker buys 10 contracts at $100 and sells to first broker at $101.

TABLE 15A-1   SALES OF EXCHANGE MEMBERSHIPS BEFORE AND
AFTER THE CRASH

	Before Oct. 19		After Oct. 19
CME	$478,000	(Oct. 19)	$325,000 (Oct. 23)
IMM	355,000	(Oct. 19)	275,000 (Oct. 20)
IOM	175,000	(Oct. 14)	95,000 (Oct. 27)
CBT	530,000	(Oct. 6)	321,000 (Oct. 29)
CBOE (full)	440,000	(Oct. 16)	285,000 (Oct. 27)
CBOE (special)	27,200	(Oct. 16)	15,000 (Oct. 26)
NYSE	1,000,000+	(Oct. 15)	625,000 (Oct. 27)
NYFE	600	(Oct. 9)	100 (Oct. 20)
AMEX	345,000	(Oct. 16)	170,000 (Oct. 20)
PHLX	150,000	(Oct. 6)	75,000 (Oct. 20)

Source: Futures Magazine

During the crash, several specialist units also failed to fulfill their obligation to maintain a market in their assigned securities. Trading simply ceased for several major stocks as the specialists' capital disappeared.

WHAT CAUSED THE CRASH?

This question persists around the world. Various commissions and private study groups sought answers. Six factors were clearly important in the market's fall.[3]

1. *Persistent use of portfolio insurance* As stock prices fell, portfolio insurers needed to sell more stock or more futures contracts. This may have accelerated the fall.
2. *Inability to act on stock index arbitrage* The volume of trading swamped the system, and made it impossible to "pick up the five-dollar bills from the sidewalk."
3. *A $1 billion sale of equities by Fidelity Investments*[4] Fidelity is the nation's largest mutual fund management group, and was in an unusually aggressive stance before October 19th.

---

[3] "What Really Ignited the Market's Collapse After Its Long Climb," *Wall Street Journal* (December 16), p. 1.

[4] Although the *WSJ* article does not cite the event, Wells Fargo Investment Advisors (a heavy portfolio insurer at that time) sold nearly $2 billion of stock index futures on Black Monday, and $1 billion in equities.

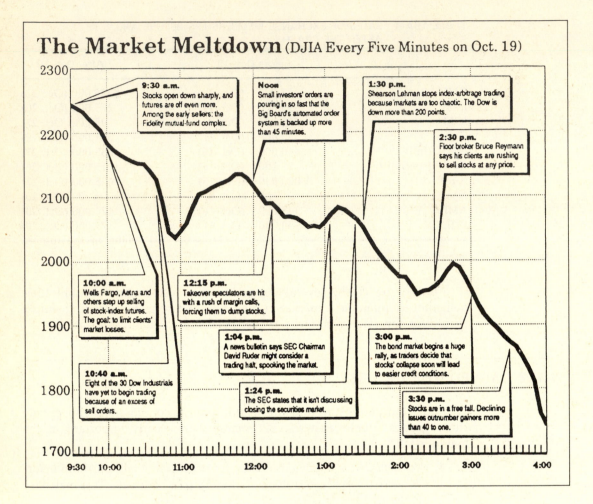

The Market Meltdown (DJIA Every Five Minutes on Oct. 19)

9:30 a.m.
Stocks open down sharply, and futures are off even more. Among the early sellers: the Fidelity mutual-fund complex.

Noon
Small investors' orders are pouring in so fast that the Big Board's automated order system is backed up more than 45 minutes.

1:30 p.m.
Shearson Lehman stops index-arbitrage trading because markets are too chaotic. The Dow is down more than 200 points.

2:30 p.m.
Floor broker Bruce Reymann says his clients are rushing to sell stocks at any price.

10:00 a.m.
Wells Fargo, Aetna and others step up selling of stock-index futures. The goal: to limit clients' market losses.

12:15 p.m.
Takeover speculators are hit with a rush of margin calls, forcing them to dump stocks.

1:04 p.m.
A news bulletin says SEC Chairman David Ruder might consider a trading halt, spooking the market.

3:00 p.m.
The bond market begins a huge rally, as traders decide that stocks' collapse soon will lead to easier credit conditions.

10:40 a.m.
Eight of the 30 Dow Industrials have yet to begin trading because of an excess of sell orders.

1:24 p.m.
The SEC states that it isn't discussing closing the securities market.

3:30 p.m.
Stocks are in a free fall. Declining issues outnumber gainers more than 40 to one.

Figure 15A-5 The Market Meltdown
Reprinted by permission of the *Wall Street Journal* © Dow Jones & Company, Inc., 1987. All Rights Reserved.

4. *Caution by block traders* The nation's largest brokerage firms were selling large blocks from their customers as quickly as they bought them. Block traders were unable to absorb the selling pressure.

5. *Fear of a trading halt* A statement by the Chairman of the SEC regarding a possible trading halt was reported two hours late and may have squelched a brief rally.

6. *Insufficient capital at specialist firms* The magnitude of sell orders made specialists unable or unwilling to fulfill their marketmaking responsibilities.

Figure 15A-5 shows the chronology of events on Black Monday.

In the report[5] of a blue-ribbon panel commissioned by the Chicago Mercantile Exchange, a portion of the conclusion reads:

The debate surrounding October 19 has focused on three major concerns: futures margin policy, index arbitrage, and portfolio insurance.

- We found no evidence that futures either caused the 1987 increase in equity prices, or exacerbated the crash. In contrast, higher futures margins would probably have decreased buying interest in the futures market on October 19 and thus led to further price declines.
- Index arbitrage does not appear to have played a major role in the crash. Arbitrage transmitted selling pressure for the futures market to the stock market on October 19, but did not provide a net source of selling pressure to the equity markets overall.
- Portfolio insurance did contribute significantly to selling in the futures markets. However, this strategy was only one of many sources of selling, and does not by itself explain the magnitude of the crash. Nor can it explain the widespread equity price declines outside the U.S., in markets where portfolio insurance is unknown.

Another much-publicized study is the so-called **Brady Report,** named after its chairman, former Senator Nicholas Brady, R-NJ. This report concludes that the primary reason for the market crash was the failure of the stock and futures markets to act as a single, unified trading place. It also identifies portfolio insurance as a major factor, but only because of the failure of the markets to move together like they "are supposed to."

In a report prepared by the Commodity Futures Trading Commission, no evidence was found to support the "persistent notion" that program trading strategies were at fault for the crash. Rather, the report finds that the crash was the result of a lack of faith in the bull market and that "the bull market in stocks that started several years ago began to trend down in late August and the downward trend was accentuated in early October."

The editorial staff of *Futures* magazine sum things up well. "In the aftermath of the Oct. 19 Black Monday stock market crash, one fact is very clear: Index futures and options did not cause the crash. Fear, then momentary panic, regarding the U.S. and world economy was the root cause. Markets are only a vehicle through which investors express their greed and fear."[6]

Index futures and options did not cause the crash; fear did.

---

[5]"Stock Index Update," *Market Perspectives*, February 1988, p. 3.

[6]"Let the Market Make the Decision on Indexes," *Futures* (December 1987): pp. 40–41.

CURRENT ISSUES REGARDING REGULATION

The crash was not a pleasant event, and we do not want another one. This concern has directed considerable attention to the subject of preventing a reoccurrence.

Recommendations

We will look at three themes regarding regulation of these markets: the recommendations of the Brady Commission, the question of who provides oversight for the markets, and internal policies of the markets.

The Brady Report The bulk of the Brady Report consists of recommendations for better regulatory coordination of the markets, without specifically prescribing a method. The well-known finance professor Merton Miller (who chaired the CME study committee) says, "The Brady Commission says something ought to be done, but it's not clear. It's as if they spent their energy trying to present a narrative of what happened." Another finance professor, Hans Stoll (author of the original put/call parity article) says of the Brady Report, "It's a good starting point." Its principal recommendations follow.

1. Coordination (ideally under a single agency) of the critical issues that crisscross the securities and futures boundary. At present, the Securities and Exchange Commission has authority over the stock and option exchanges, while the Commodity Futures Trading Commission supervises the futures markets. The Brady Report does not say so explicitly, but there are strong inferences that the Federal Reserve Board should be given authority over those issues that cross market boundaries.
2. Unify the clearing systems used on the exchanges and the procedures by which trades are settled. (Recall that the role of the Clearing Corporation is to ensure contract integrity. After the crash, the Options Clearing Corporation took a loss of more than $8.5 million because of the failure of one of its 190 members due to stock index option losses. The other members of the OCC were assessed $6.7 million to replenish the fund, with the other $1.8 million coming from operating income. This was the first time since 1973 that it has been necessary to cover such a loss.)
3. Make margins consistent and comparable to control the use of leverage.
4. Improve the information systems used to monitor both inter- and intramarket activities.
5. Establish a **circuit breaker** system to prevent a market meltdown. Daily stock price limits exist on the Tokyo Stock Exchange, for

instance. The Brady Report does not specifically recommend stock price limits in the United States, perhaps because the suggestion has met with complete opposition both before and after the crash. The report does say that whatever circuit breakers are used must be coordinated across all markets and implemented simultaneously.

The exchanges have installed various circuit breakers since the crash. In July 1990, the NYSE implemented a rule that becomes effective when the DJIA declines 50 points or more from its previous day's close. When this occurs, shares may only be sold via the DOT system on an uptick (when the last change in stock price was up).[7] Between July 31, 1990, and November 7, 1990, there were twenty occasions when this rule took effect. On nine of those days, the market finished the day down less than 50 points.

There remains no clear cause and effect between circuit breakers and market stability. One researcher suggests that an effective circuit breaker mechanism must be coordinated across both the futures and stock markets and satisfy the following criteria:[8]

1. circuit breakers in one market must have counterparts in the other market,
2. counterpart circuit breakers must impose similar restrictions in both markets, and
3. counterpart circuit breakers must trip in both markets at the same time.

Oversight of the Markets   Stock index futures are the principal focus of oversight questions. An article in *Time* says, "The problem is that a stock-index futures contract is neither commodity nor security. Rather, it is an unusual hybrid . . ."[9] At present, the CFTC has jurisdiction over these contracts but only after a rather unfriendly dispute with the SEC in 1982. Later, in early 1988, Nicholas Brady testified before the Senate Agricultural Committee that it would be "counterproductive" for the SEC to pursue its request that Congress award stock index futures jurisdiction to it rather than leaving it with the CFTC.

The securities industry has always been proud of its ability to police itself, although some members of the financial, legal, and trading community question the quality of this self-regulation. One insightful industry analyst sums things up this way: "Right after the market break, there were good guys

---

[7]Another NYSE circuit breaker is tripped when the DJIA falls 250 points from the previous day's close, in which case trading stops for one hour.

[8]Morris, Charles S. "Coordinating Circuit Breakers in Stock and Futures Markets," *Economic Review* (March/April 1990): 35–48.

[9]"Who Will Rule the Futures?" *Time*, February 15, 1988.

Margins soar across the board						
		Futures				
		Speculative margins				**Hedge margins**	
		Before Oct. 19		After Oct. 19		Before Oct. 19	After Oct. 19
		Initial	Maintenance	Initial	Maintenance		
CME	S&P 500 futures	$10,000	$7,500	$20,000	$15,000	$7,500	$15,000
	Eurobonds	750	500	1,500	1,000	500	1,000
	T-bills	750	500	1,500	1,000	500	1,000
	MMI	4,500	3,000	8,000	7,000	3,000	7,000
CBOT	T-bonds	2,500	2,000	5,000	4,000	2,000	4,000
	T-notes	2,000	1,500	4,000	3,000	1,500	3,000
	Municipal bonds	2,000	1,500	4,000	3,000	1,500	3,000
	GNMAs	2,500	2,000	5,000	4,000	2,000	4,000
KCBT	Value Line Index	4,500	3,000	20,000	20,000	3,000	20,000
NYFE	NYSE Composite Index	3,500	1,750	7,000	5,000	1,750 (initial) 1,500 (maintenance)	5,000 (initial & maintenance)

		Options	
		Before Oct. 19	After Oct. 19
CBOE	S&P 100 options	Premium plus 5% of the value of the underlying index, minus any out-of-the-money amount not less than premium plus 2%.	Premium plus 10% of the value of the underlying index, minus any out-of-the-money amount not less than premium plus 5%.
AMEX	XMI		
	XII		

Figure 15A-6 Changing Margin Requirements
Reprinted from *Futures*, 219 Parkade, Cedar Falls, Iowa 50613, December 1987.

and there were bad guys. Now there are shades of gray. And Washington is not good at dealing with shades of gray. There are things shouting for attention, but there's no clean way to get to them. And, for the markets, that's good because the longer Washington doesn't act, the less likely it will act." The exchanges, however, did act. There are now numerous policies and circuit-breaker procedures in place to reduce the likelihood of a market tailspin like the one in 1987.

Margin   One action the futures and options exchanges took immediately after the crash was wholesale revision of margin requirements. Figure 15A-6 shows a doubling of most initial margins and a *quadrupling* of the initial margin on the KC Value Line futures. The thinking was that heftier margins would reduce speculative activity, or at least ensure greater financial integrity of the market participants.

This change is a new chapter in a debate that has raged for over 100 years. The fundamental issue is this: "Why limit speculative activity?" We have seen that speculators are necessary in a well-functioning futures market. To many market observers, it is unclear what economic function is served by reducing their ranks. It may even be counterproductive. In recent testimony before Congress, Alan Greenspan, Chairman of the Federal Reserve Board commented, "Insufficient arbitrage between cash and futures can be a destabilizing force in a declining market . . ."[10]

The term "margin" continues to breed confusion as well. In a *Wall Street Journal* article,[11] George Melloan comments

> The futures exchanges are fighting efforts to "equalize" margin requirements in the various markets. They argue, with some persuasiveness, that margin requirements in the spot securities and index futures markets have two totally different purposes. The one is a downpayment on a security, required by regulators to prevent the excessive borrowing or leverage that occurred before the 1929 Crash. The other is a surety bond on a contract. If the contract value falls the owner is required to put up more money . . .

Program Trading and Stock Index Futures   On February 4, 1988, the New York Stock Exchange moved to curtail program trading via DOT anytime the Dow Jones Industrial Average moved fifty points in one day.[12] This decision has been criticized by Nicholas Brady, since a principal recommendation of his report was the need for coordination of the markets. Here is an important blessing for the futures market: While the New York Stock Exchange feels that stock index arbitrage increases market volatility, Mr. Brady argues that *such a strategy performs the valuable function of keeping the markets linked.*

According to the chairman of the Brady Commission, program trading "performs the valuable function of keeping the markets linked."

Further evidence of the complexity of this issue comes from comparing comments from the current and immediate past Chairman of the Federal Reserve Board. The Chairman of the FED is one of the most influential persons in Washington with respect to matters concerning the exchanges.

Shortly after the crash, Paul Volker, former chairman of the Federal Reserve Board, commented, "It's very hard not to rail at the index futures markets—I don't think these techniques add much to the sum of human endeavor."[13] Contrast this with the remarks of Alan Greenspan, another FED chairman:

---

[10]Testimony by Alan Greenspan before the House Subcommittee on Telecommunications and Finance, May 19, 1988.

[11]Melloan, George. "Congressional Theatrics vs. Real Market Reform," *Wall Street Journal* (May 24, 1988): 29.

[12]This trigger was hit on April 6, 1988, when the Dow Jones Industrial Average rose 64.16 points. Market observers reported that program trading continued in manual form with only a modest loss of efficiency.

[13]Reported in "Volker on the Crash," by Leonard Silk. *New York Times Magazine* (November 8, 1987): 40.

What many critics of equity derivatives fail to recognize is that the markets for these instruments have become so large not because of slick sales campaigns but because they are providing economic value to their users. By enabling pension funds and other institutional users to hedge and adjust positions quickly and inexpensively, these instruments have come to play an important role in portfolio management. The history of futures and options provides numerous examples of contracts that did not provide much economic value and consequently failed . . .[14]

With these opposing views from two distinguished gentlemen, it is no wonder that Congress, and the public, are confused.

FINAL THOUGHTS ON THE CRASH

The Portfolio "Insurance" Lesson and the Infallibility of Market Efficiency

Financial theory spends much of its time showing why arbitrage cannot exist for long and how quickly the five-dollar bills will be recovered from the sidewalk. Similarly, the theory describes the behavior of "rational" people.

The events surrounding October 19 were inconsistent with theory. The negative basis in the S&P 500 futures contract persisted for much of the day and, in large part, was a source of the confusion that prevailed. Portfolio insurance works if the markets "behave as they are supposed to." On October 19 and 20, 1987, they didn't. The Chicago Mercantile Exchange concludes in one of its reports that portfolio insurers "learned that continuous and smooth exit prices are not obtainable when a collective mass move to an exit occurs. Now that this flaw has been widely exposed, we expect excessive use of this strategy will no longer be a problem."

Charles A. Bowsher, Comptroller General of the United States, in testimony on January 26, 1988 before the House Subcommittee on Telecommunications and Finance, provides a good epitaph to this discussion:

The facts of the October crash have been reported so widely that it seems unnecessary to review them here. The cause of those events is less well understood and there may never be complete agreement on that issue. After all, debate continues today on what "caused" the crash of *1929.*

---

[14]Testimony by Alan Greenspan before the House Subcommittee on Telecommunications and Finance, May 19, 1988.

SUMMARY

There is no clear-cut cause of the Crash of 1987 other than fear. The market's 508 point decline was exacerbated by an imbalance in the futures and equity markets, and by traders' inability to act on arbitrage situations. The bulk of the recommendations generated by those who have studied the crash call for steps to promote the integration of the various markets into a single, well-coordinated marketplace.

 **Precious Metals**

*T*he Mind of Man is Devoured by this Supreme Possession

Pindar
Isthmian Ode V, opening lines
circa 400 B.C.

bullion	London fix
corner	numismatic value
gold certificate	platinum group
gold/silver ratio spread	precious metal
good delivery bar	strategic metal
intrinsic value	troy ounce
karat	

This book is entitled "Speculative Markets." Most of the applications discussed so far deal with ways in which derivative assets may be used in hedging applications and with why the speculator may choose to take on the risk the hedger does not want.

Gold is an example of a commodity that, with a few exceptions, is a pure speculative asset. Gold mining companies and jewelry manufacturers have legitimate hedging interests, as may equity portfolio managers who want to reduce their portfolio risk.[1] Most gold players, however, are speculating on a change in the price of the most famous of the precious metals. Gold is sufficiently important in the international monetary community to warrant specific discussion in the study of speculative markets.

The term **precious metal** is applied to gold, to silver, and to the platinum group metals.[2] This chapter covers all three, but focuses on gold, the most popular and best-known precious metal investment. Futures contracts are available on them all.

GOLD

In varying degrees, just about all of us are intrigued by gold. Also called the *heraldic metal*, humans have been influenced throughout history by the distribution of gold in the world. We have envied those who have it, pitied those who don't, moved to where it can be mined, and fought or robbed each other to obtain more of it. Most of us wear some of it every day of our adult lives.[3]

Gold wedding bands are the world's most common piece of gold jewelry.

The Supply of Gold

There is not a lot of gold in the world; what there is, though, has been around a long time. Gold does not tarnish or wear out. A centuries-old gold object looks just as fresh and bright as a newly minted coin. Gold is extremely malleable: it can be melted, reshaped, and melted again without losing its physical characteristics. A single ounce can be stretched into a wire more

[1]Gold returns often show a negative correlation with the stock market, which makes gold a particularly attractive portfolio component.
[2]These elements are also called "noble metals," because they are resistant to oxidations and corrosion.
[3]The National Geographic Society videotape "Gold!" (video number 51084) is an excellent overview of gold's global role. Some of the trivia in the sidebar comes from this presentation.

Box 16-1   **GOLD TRIVIA**

- The lifelines and helmet visors of NASA astronauts are plated with gold to reflect the sun's heat and to protect the wearer's eyes.
- Ft. Knox is the site of the U.S. Government's biggest hoard of gold. The main vault door weighs twenty tons and is only the first of a long series of doors.
- The Bible mentions gold more than 400 times. The first reference is Genesis 2:10–11, where a river leaving the Garden of Eden "compasseth the whole land of Havilah, where there is gold; And the gold of that land is good . . ."
- All the gold ever discovered could be formed into a cube fifty-six feet on a side.
- Of all the gold ever discovered, 40 percent has been mined in the last 100 years.
- It takes 6000 pounds of rock to produce one ounce of gold.
- Gold mines can be more than 2 miles deep and result in about 400 deaths per year.
- Gold (and other precious metals) is measured in troy ounces. A **troy ounce** weighs 9.7 percent more than the standard ounce we use in normal measure. Bulk gold is called **bullion.**
- During the four-day refining process, gold-bearing ore is immersed in a cyanide solution to help remove impurities (such as silver) and then is formed into crude ingots of about 88 percent purity. At the conclusion of the process, most gold is formed into **good delivery bars** of 400 troy ounces (12½ kilograms, or 27.6 pounds), each 99.6 percent pure.
- In Europe and the United States, most good quality gold jewelry is 18 **karat** (75 percent pure). Inexpensive jewelry may be only 9 or 10 karat, but can still legally be described as "gold." In the Third World, gold is usually 21 or 22 karats. Pure gold (24 karat) is too soft for most purposes and is rarely found except in bullion form.
- In India, the wearing of gold is said to bring prosperity and luck, and to promote fertility. At a Hindu wedding, the bride will wear all the gold she owns as "widow's insurance"; by tradition the gold she wears at her wedding is hers alone.
- King Croesus of Lydia struck the first gold coin in 560 B.C.
- The ridged edge on coins today originated with the Romans, who did this to prevent people from cutting off slivers of coins to remelt.
- In 1531 the Spanish conquistador Pizarro killed more than 6000 Inca Indians in a thirty-minute battle, and subsequently melted down approximately thirteen tons of now-priceless artifacts.

than fifty miles long. In the manufacture of gold leaf, a good delivery bar is initially transformed into a thin ribbon more than one-quarter of a mile long. Ultimately, the gold leaf will be 1000 times thinner than a page of this book. Viewed another way, it would take 250,000 sheets of gold leaf to make a stack an inch high. These characteristics of gold make it very possible that the gold we wear today adorned the body of an ancestor thousands of years ago.

World gold supplies come from three sources: gold that has been recently mined, gold that has been ''recycled'' from industrial waste or from old jewelry, and gold from the central banks of governments.

South Africa is the primary source of newly mined gold in the world, accounting for about 50 percent of the annual production. The former Soviet Union is a distant second, with 25 percent. Canada is third with about 5 percent. Gold is mined on every continent except Antarctica. Total annual production approaches 2000 tons.

Most gold in the United States comes from two large mines: Homestake Mining (HM on the New York Stock Exchange) and the Nevada Carlin Mine. About 40 percent of U.S. gold comes as a by-product from the mining of copper.

The world's largest store of gold is held in suspension in the oceans. Scientists estimate they contain about 100,000 times more gold than has ever been mined from the earth's surface. At present, there is no cost-effective technology to recover it.

The Demand for Gold

Jewelry constitutes the principal demand for gold, followed in order by coins, bullion/coinage for investment purposes, and industrial applications. Jewelry accounts for 60 percent of current gold production. About 20 percent is stored by investors; 7 percent, or almost 4 million ounces, goes to electronics; another 7 percent has other industrial uses, and 3 percent goes to dentistry. Cost can limit gold's uses. Gold has a very high degree of conductivity and would be an excellent wire for electrical or electronic purposes. Because gold evenly diffuses heat and does not oxidize, it would make excellent cooking utensils.

The principal demand for gold is jewelry.

The Europeans are particularly fond of owning gold. Many Europeans purchase small amounts of gold on a regular monthly basis via some sort of savings plan offered at a local bank. Throughout Europe, but especially in Germany and Switzerland, children often receive small gold bars as presents for birthdays or other special occasions. The French people have

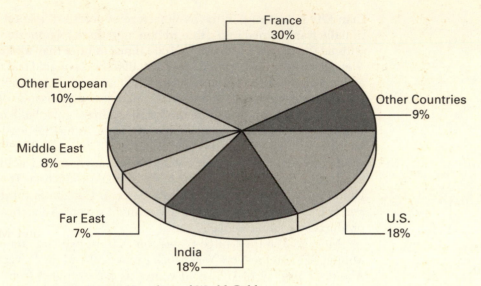

Figure 16-1 Private Hoarding of World Gold

suffered through many wars and other periods of turmoil. Throughout history, gold has been an effective store of value, while national currencies have been devastated by inflation or government bankruptcy.[4] George Bernard Shaw said "If you must choose between placing your trust in government or placing your trust in gold, then gentlemen, I strongly advise you to place your trust in gold." Largely as a consequence of these lessons from history, French citizens own much of the privately held gold in the world, mostly in the form of coins. Figure 16-1 shows estimated distribution of privately held gold worldwide.

During the Great Depression of the 1930s, a kilo of gold (35.36 oz.) would have bought a new Ford, Chevy, or Plymouth. Today, a kilo of gold can still buy a new Ford, Chevy, or Plymouth.

George Gero
Prudential-Bache

Whenever someone fires a gun somewhere, investors look for $800 an ounce gold. This is an unreasonable expectation.

Tom Griffo
Cargill Investors Services

---

[4]Gold does not always weather the storm of global uncertainty. On the first day of the Persian Gulf war in 1991, gold fell $30 an ounce.

Gold also has more exotic uses. Minuscule quantities are used in the labeling of some disposable cosmetic containers. At one ritzy restaurant in France, gold leaf is pompously placed atop elegant desserts. This adds no calories or taste, but looks nice!

There are several factors that can make gold an attractive investment. Gold has often demonstrated returns that are unrelated to the stock market as a whole. This can make gold a powerful diversifying agent in a portfolio.[5] Figure 16-2 (p. 366) illustrates the major participants in the world gold market, and Figure 16-3 (p. 367) shows the annual trading range of the price of gold since 1975.

Factors Influencing the Price of Gold

A Weakening U.S. Dollar   Much of the European and Middle Eastern investment community view investments in gold and the U.S. dollar as mutually exclusive. They sell one when they buy the other. As concerns over such things as the trade balance and protectionism rise, investors dump dollars and buy gold, providing upward pressure on gold prices.

Strong Foreign Currencies   As foreign currencies grow stronger relative to the U.S. dollar, the price of gold as measured in the home currency declines for the foreign investor. This traditionally prompts significant purchases of gold by the Japanese, the Germans, and the Swiss.

Rising Oil Prices   The investment community has never liked inflation. Historically, gold has been a useful inflation hedge, and an increase in the price of oil raises fears of inflation. Figure 16-4 (p. 368) shows the relationship between the price of gold and U.S. inflation rates since 1975.

Uncertainty with International Finance   Third-world loans, mounting debt, and emergence of the U.S. as the world's largest debtor nation worry many investors, who again turn to gold for stability during times of uncertainty.

Japanese Gold Coins   In 1986, Japan imported 565 tons of gold, about half of which was used for the minting of the Hirohito gold coin. This popular gold coin commemorated 60 years of Emperor Hirohito's sovereignty. The previous record for gold imports was set the year before, when Japan imported 197 tons.

---

[5]Like some commodity futures contracts, gold often appears to have a very low or negative beta. The word "appears" is important here; beta is not a stationary statistic. Over the very long term, the price of gold has risen, and so has the general level of stock prices. This implies a positive beta. It is not correct to assume that gold will demonstrate negative beta behavior; it probably is safe to say that gold carries risk reduction potential in most portfolios.

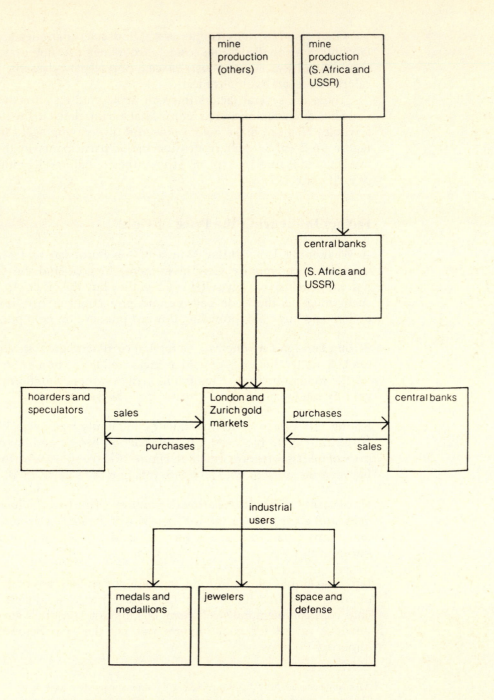

Figure 16-2 Participants in the World Gold Market
Source: *Commodity Trading Manual,* p. 210.

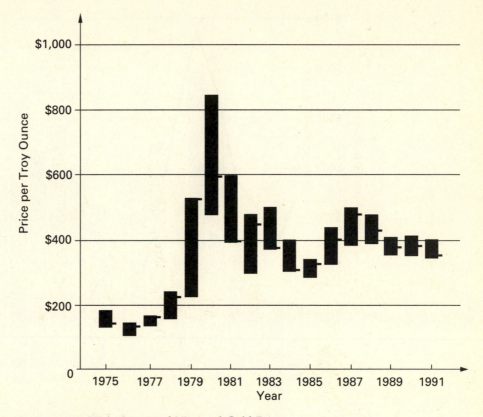

Figure 16-3 High, Low, and Year-end Gold Prices
(London price per troy ounce)

At least 14 million of these coins were minted. Each coin contains 20 grams of gold, and when issued in November of 1986, had a face value equivalent to $650 U.S. dollars. The coins were legal tender, although virtually all were purchased as mementos. Their especially attractive feature is that they can be cashed in at their face value, regardless of what happens to the price of gold in the future.

Supply is generally not the driving force behind gold price movements.

The Gold Institute

Investing in Gold

As indicated above, there is an intrigue about gold that contributes to the popularity of this investment. In addition, there have been many periods

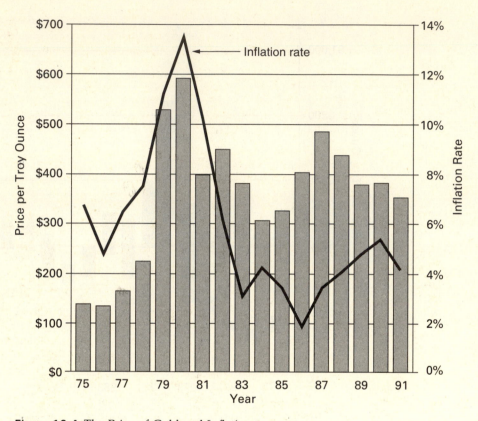

Figure 16-4 The Price of Gold and Inflation
(Year-end Values)
Source: *Metal Statistics* (1992) and Treasury Bulletin

when the percentage price appreciation of precious metals has led the pack of investment alternatives. There are six principal means by which an individual may invest in gold.

Bullion   The rare individual may have the money to buy gold bars and stack them in the basement. Smaller quantities may be stored in one ounce bars, in nuggets, or as gold dust. The one ounce gold bar is a popular investment in the United States. Bullion investments may be exotic, but they have obvious shortcomings. There is a significant risk of theft, and they produce no income until sold. Also, they lack marketability; how quickly could you sell a good delivery bar at a fair price? Finally, unless you have acquired your gold in standardized form (stamped ingots or recognized coins), you may incur an expense in having it assayed when you want to sell.

Despite these factors, at least eight pension funds invest in gold bullion to diversify their other investments. The manager of one fund cites the threat of renewed inflation as a primary motive for holding gold. As a point of interest, the Rhode Island Hospital Trust National Bank is second only to the U.S. Treasury in the amount of gold kept on deposit.

Certificates   It is also possible to purchase documents representing ownership of gold bullion that is kept by someone else on your behalf. A number of banks in the United States and Canada issue these **gold certificates,** which are obligations of the issuer to deliver gold upon demand. You can take delivery at any time if you wish, although it may take a few days to actually receive the gold. Most likely the bullion is kept in a vault at a bank, investment house, or coin dealership. Certificates are registered in your name, adding security to the investment. Certificates may also be readily sold back to the dealer from whom you bought them, although there will be a few percentage points lost in the dealer's bid-ask spread. You generally pay no sales tax when you buy gold this way; state laws vary on whether you have to pay this tax if you buy gold bullion and take it home.

The primary advantage of gold certificates over the bullion itself is convenience. You are freed from worry about storage, delivery, and insurance. Certificates do carry the risk that there is no gold backing them, but if you deal through a major bank or brokerage firm, this risk is minimal (or nonexistent with insurance from the Federal Deposit Insurance Corporation or the Security Investor Protection Corporation). Figure 16-5 (p. 370) is an advertisement from the financial pages for a new offering of gold certificates.

Convenience is the primary advantage of gold certificates over the bullion itself.

Mining Shares   Perhaps the most popular form of gold ownership in the United States is through the purchase of shares in gold mining companies, either directly or through a mutual fund. Homestake Mining is the largest U.S. gold mining company and is a popular investment for those seeking to speculate in gold. An increase in the price of gold directly influences the earnings of a gold mining company.

Several mutual funds specialize in gold or other precious metals; United Services, International Investors, and USAA Gold fund are among the largest. Shares have a major advantages over other forms of ownership in that they are instantly marketable, and they may also generate some income through dividends. It is also possible to invest in shares of South African mining companies, although there is more social risk with these securities. Prices for these companies can be found in the "Foreign Markets" section of the *Wall Street Journal.*

An advantage to investing in gold mining shares is the fact that the firm may provide periodic income via dividends.

Figure 16-5 Gold Certificate Memorandum

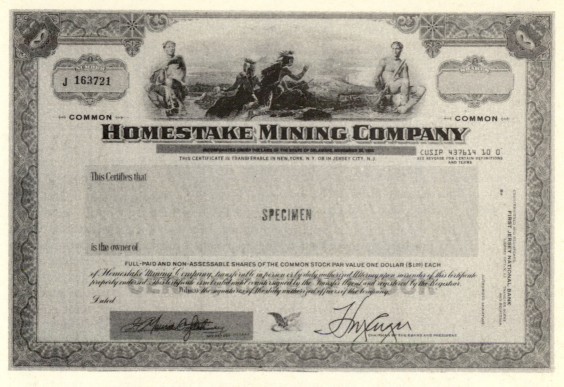

Figure 16-6 Homestake Mining Stock Certificate

Coins   Gold coins are popular with both collectors and with gold speculators. It is important to distinguish between a coin's **intrinsic value** and its **numismatic value.** Collectors may be willing to pay more than the value of gold contained in the coin because the coin is rare or popular. Some people find it difficult to simultaneously be a coin collector and an investor in gold. It is easy to "fall in love" with the coins you bought for their bullion value.

It is important to distinguish between a gold coin's bullion value and its numismatic value.

Table 16-1 (p. 374) lists the most popular coins for investing in gold bullion. The South African Kruggerand, which was once the most popular gold coin, lost much of its investment appeal because of restrictions placed on the importation of these coins in protest of the apartheid policies of the South African government. Although these restrictions have been lifted in the United States, the coin has not regained its original popularity. Some investors avoid the Austrian, Hungarian, and Mexican coins because of their

Box 16-2   **GOLD SHARES VS. GOLD**

All that glitters is not gold, since "you can make a lot more money" by investing in highly leveraged gold-oriented stocks, says Martin McNeill, a senior vice president with Dominick & Dominick Inc.

"Gold shares usually outperform gold on the upside," notes Gil Atzmon, a portfolio manager and mining analyst with the San Antonio-based United Services Funds, which has nearly $340 million invested in three gold-oriented funds.

Stocks tend to bottom before gold, leading some analysts to believe that, after a year of dismal performance, gold stocks and funds may be poised for a breakout.

The stock market crash last October slashed values on volatile gold-based shares by as much as 45%, according to Lucille Palermo, a gold mining analyst with Drexel Burnham Lambert.

Recovery has been slow. From September 1987 to September 1988, funds that invested at least 65% of equity in gold mining companies, bullion, or coins lost 15.5% on average, making them "the worst performing for that time period," reports Lipper Analytical Services Inc.

The 1,445 individual funds that Lipper tracks gained an average of 8.7% for the year. The Dow Jones Industrial Average, excluding dividends, climbed 7.9%, and equity-based funds as a whole rose 9.9%.

While the gold-oriented funds' record over the last year is hardly stellar, Michael Lipper, president of Lipper Analytical says, "the time to be buying gold, historically, is when it acts badly."

The market was acting very badly in September, when spot gold tumbled under $400 per oz. to its lowest level in a year and a half. Charts indicate a cycle low should be reached sometime in mid-October, however. McNeill thinks the market could bottom between $375 and $380. At this point, he predicts, "shares should start to outperform the metal."

Palermo is not so sure, and cautions "if gold flounders here, the shares will flounder," too. "If gold goes up, shares are going to go up a whole lot more," she adds.

Investors who buy shares before a gold rise are likely to get them at bargain basement prices, since the downturn in the cash and futures markets sparked panic selling of gold-oriented issues on the New York, American and Toronto stock exchanges.

Sellers lost sight of the fact that most large gold producers hedge their physical holdings with forward sales and are protected against sliding prices, Atzmon says.

Even if the market remains soft, it costs U.S. producers an average of $200 to produce one ounce of gold, meaning, "gold miners can make strong profits at the $400 price," according to Andrew Economos, an analyst with Scudder, Stevens & Clark Inc.

With bullion trading at an average of $447 in 1987, domestic producers showed an after-tax profit level of $100 to $160 per oz., he notes.

Scudder recently launched its own gold fund and expects to see healthy earnings in 1989 and beyond.

Many funds have decided not to invest in South Africa, the world's largest producer. With the U.S. Congress moving toward tougher economic sanctions against the apartheid state, Europeans are more likely to snap up shares in South African companies, McNeill says.

Gold bugs looking toward Australia may be put off by an income tax on gold producers starting January 1991. The tax will hamper earnings, but has already been "fully discounted in the shares," Palermo says. But other, more favorable, tax changes should help raise Aussie gold dividends, she adds.

Closer to home, McNeill and other stock watchers recommend Canadian and U.S. companies such as Amax Gold Inc., American Barrick, Battle Mountain, Echo Bay, Homestake, Newmont Gold and Placer Dome Inc.

Atzmon advises investors to shy away from high-cost, marginal operators and risky grass roots exploration firms. He favors small start-up companies that have already locked in prices with gold loans, calling them "the shining stars" of the mining industry.

Judith Burns

Futures, November 1988, p. 59

awkward weights. The convenient sizes of the other coins add to their liquidity and popularity.

Gold Futures and Futures Options   Futures contracts for gold are similar in essentially every respect to contracts for other commodities. An individual can buy gold futures if the price of gold is expected to rise, or sell them if prices are expected to decline. A gold hedger might be a manufacturer of university class rings, where it is necessary to quote ring prices months in advance of the actual delivery of the ring.

The futures market for gold is always a *contango market;* there is always an adequate gold supply available from world financial institutions and bullion houses.

Gold futures trade in a contango market.

TABLE 16-1   POPULAR COINS FOR GOLD INVESTMENT

1. American Eagles*
2. Canadian Maple Leaf*
3. Mexican 50 Peso [1.2057 ounces]
4. Austrian 100 Corona [0.9802 ounces]
5. South African Kruggerand*
6. Chinese Panda**
7. Japanese Hirohito
8. Hungarian 100 Korona [0.9802 ounces]
9. California Gold Pieces*

*1 oz, ½ oz, ¼ oz, ¹⁄₁₀ oz sizes

**1 oz, ½ oz, ¼ oz, ¹⁄₁₀ oz, ¹⁄₂₀ oz sizes

The Pricing of Gold

While the actual price of gold is largely determined by basic principles of supply and demand, a ninety-year-old ritual, the **London Fix,** is used to establish the price that is quoted by the news services and the financial press.

Twice each day, at 10:30 a.m. and 3 p.m. London time, representatives of the five member firms of the London Gold Market gather in an office of the London banking firm N. M. Rothschild & Son Ltd. to "fix" the price of gold. At these meetings, the members are in continual telephone communication with their firms as they seek a gold price that will "clear the market," where supply and demand are in balance. This price, stated in U.S. dollars by convention, will reflect the relative balance of buy and sell orders that have been placed with the member firms.

The process begins with a suggested price from a designated representative of one of the member firms. Buyers react to this price, followed by sellers. If the orders do not match, a new price is suggested. Buyers and sellers move in or out as the proposed fix price varies. Usually the process is completed within fifteen minutes of the first suggested price. The record for the longest session was set one afternoon in 1980, when it took 99 minutes to achieve balance. News of the fix is flashed around the world within minutes of its determination.

Although the London fix is an important price, it is not the only one. Gold is traded continuously throughout the world, with trading tracking the sun from London to markets in Singapore, Sydney, Hong Kong, the United States, and elsewhere. Prices are constantly changing in response to economic and political news.

Futures contracts in gold are traded at the Chicago Mercantile Exchange–International Monetary Market, at the Commodities Exchange in New York, at the Chicago Board of Trade, and at the MidAmerica Commodities Exchange. At the CME and the COMEX the contract is for 100 ounces, while the CBT and the MidAmerica Exchange trades a "mini contract" of 33.2 ounces. A futures price for a precious metal will always be greater than the spot price. The general relationship is as follows.

$$FP = SP + BC + SC + TC$$

where FP = futures price
SP = spot price
BC = borrowing cost
SC = storage cost
TC = transportation cost

Basis for a precious metal contract, then, comes from three sources. Borrowing costs reflect the interest I would pay if I were to borrow money to buy gold in the spot market. Storage costs represent the fact that gold must be safeguarded, most likely in a bank vault (for a fee). Transportation costs are incurred when the bullion is shipped to the depository designated by the exchange.

Basis for gold futures is the sum of borrowing costs, storage costs, and shipping costs. These are not the same for every investor.

Figure 16-7 Sources of Gold Futures Price

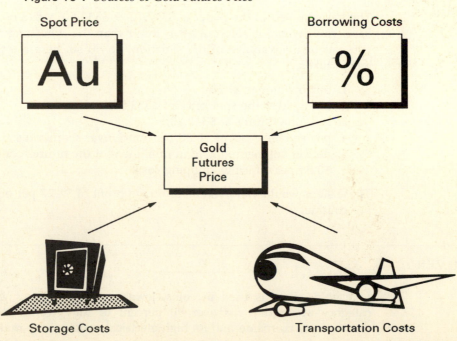

FIGURE 16-8 Gold Futures Prices
Gold (CMX)—100 troy oz/$ per troy oz

	Open	High	Low	Settle	Change
DEC	333.70	334.00	333.40	333.60	−1.80
FEB	337.00	338.00	336.90	337.50	−1.80
APR	341.70	342.00	341.10	341.60	−1.90
JUN	346.90	347.20	346.90	347.10	−1.90

Suppose one morning you read the *Wall Street Journal* quotations reflected in Figure 16-8. On this day, the spot price for gold is $333.50 per ounce. Suppose the CMX June futures call for delivery in about six months. Would it make sense to buy gold at $333.50 per ounce and sell the futures at $347.10, intending to store the gold for six months and then ship it in fulfillment of the contract? The answer depends on the rate at which you can borrow and how much you must pay for storage and transportation. Perhaps your current borrowing rate is 7% per year, storage costs are 5 cents per ounce per month, and shipping costs are 35 cents per ounce. *Your* basis, then, is

$$FP - SP = (0.07/year)(6/12\ year)(\$333.50) + (\$0.05/month)(6\ months) + \$0.35 = \$12.33$$

The basis quoted in the paper is $347.10 − $333.50 = $13.60. Because the basis you determine for yourself is lower than the prevailing market basis, you can take advantage of the situation. To do so, here are the steps you would take:

1. borrow money at 7%;
2. buy gold at the spot price of $333.50;
3. sell June futures at $347.10;
4. pay storage costs of $0.30 per ounce over six months;
5. deliver your stored gold in fulfillment of the futures contract and pay $0.35 per ounce in shipping costs.

These steps would yield you an arbitrage profit of $1.27 per ounce, or $127 per contract.

SILVER

Like gold, silver is used in coins, jewelry, and industry, with the latter category accounting for over 90 percent of total world production. Its resistance to corrosion and its high electrical conductivity make it a logical component in products ranging from photographic film to computer circuitry and metal alloys. Photographic film and copying machines comprise the largest U.S. market for silver.

Photographic film and copying machines comprise the largest U.S. demand for silver.

Supply

Approximately 70 percent of world production occurs in the Western Hemisphere, with Canada, Peru, Mexico, and the United States the principal suppliers. Figure 16-9 shows recent worldwide production figures. U.S. mines are located principally in Idaho, Arizona, Montana, and Utah. Hecla

Figure 16-9 World Silver Production, 1992
(millions of troy ounces)
Source: *Metal Statistics* 1992

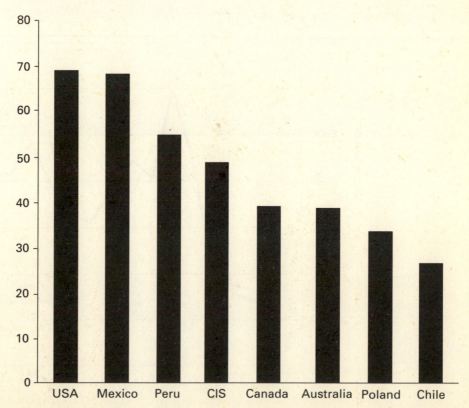

Mining and Sunshine Mining (HL and SSC, respectively, on the New York Stock Exchange) are major U.S. producers.

The Hunt Brothers' "Silver Corner"

An aspect of the silver market that will probably become a permanent part of market folklore is the activity associated with the Hunt brothers in late 1979 and 1980. This Texas oil family, worth billions of dollars, was accused of attempting to "corner the market" in silver. A **corner** is an illegal attempt to manipulate the price of a commodity.

The Hunt brothers acquired an extraordinary quantity of silver in the cash market and had simultaneously gone long in the futures market. Had they gone short, this would have been a hedge. But a long position is bullish, and the Hunt brothers apparently intended to take delivery of the silver.

Figure 16-10 Silver Prices

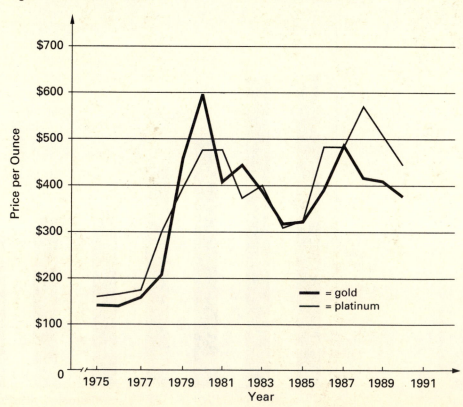

By late December of 1979, the Hunt family was estimated to control 60 million ounces of silver. During the delivery month, the short sellers discovered that there was very little silver available on the cash market: the Hunt brothers already held most of it. This caused the price of the remaining silver to skyrocket as short sellers "bid the market" to cover their shorts. Under special rules, the Chicago Board of Trade and the COMEX declared emergency conditions, which caused the price of silver to drop. The Hunt Brothers were unable to meet massive margin calls as a consequence of the falling prices; they lost huge sums of money, and federal charges of price manipulation were subsequently filed against them. Figure 16-10 shows the dramatic swing in the price of silver during this period.

Spreading

There is a popular futures spread known as the **gold/silver ratio spread.** This involves buying futures in one of these metals and selling futures in the other, with the dollar amounts on both sides approximately equal. One reason this spread is attractive to speculators is the low margin: a GSR spread can be established with a good faith deposit of about $300.

The GSR does not force traders to predict price changes in either metal. Rather, the spread provides a convenient means of speculating on changes in the relative value of the two metals. If, for instance, you believe that gold prices will rise faster than silver, a spreader could buy gold and sell silver.

Some people follow the GSR as a market indicator. If, over some period of time, the price of gold averaged 50 times the price of silver, a sudden drop in this statistic might indicate that gold had become cheap or that silver had become expensive. Either way, a long gold/short silver GSR spread would be profitable if prices returned to their "normal" relationship.

STRATEGIC METALS

While gold and silver attract the most investor attention, these metals are not the only game in town. Futures contracts trade on platinum and palladium, two metals for which there are both hedging and speculative interests. The remainder of the platinum group and other strategic metals are briefly discussed for the sake of completeness.

The Platinum Group

The **platinum group** consists of six related metals: platinum, palladium, iridium, osmium, rhodium, and ruthenium. Futures contracts are traded on

TABLE 16-2   THE CHEMISTRY OF THE PRECIOUS METALS

				The Coinage Metals
	The Iron Triad			
Element	Iron	Cobalt	Nickel	Copper
Symbol	Fe	Co	Ni	Cu
Atomic Number	26	27	28	29
	The Light Platinum Triad			
Element	Ruthenium	Rhodium	Palladium	Silver
Symbol	Tu	Rh	Pd	Ag
Atomic Number	44	45	46	47
	The Heavy Platinum Triad			
Element	Osmium	Iridium	Platinum	Gold
Symbol	Os	Ir	Pt	Au
Atomic Number	76	77	78	79

the first two of these. These two metals comprise 31 and 64 percent, respectively, of the mining of the platinum group. Table 16-2 is an extract of the Periodic Table of the Elements showing the chemical relationship of these elements.

Platinum (Pt)   Platinum and gold share many investment characteristics. Their prices change in tandem with world events; Figure 16-11 shows the positive correlation. It is rare for platinum to trade at a discount to gold. This has only happened twice in the past decade, in 1983 and 1985. According to William O'Neill, futures strategist at Merrill Lynch, "There is no inherent reason why [platinum] should trade at a premium other than history."[6]

Platinum is the rarest of the precious metals; unlike gold, it is not well understood by the public.

Despite our habit of associating platinum just with jewelry, only about 2 percent is used for this purpose. Platinum's most important application is as a high-technology metal. It is much harder than gold and has a higher melting point. Measured on the Vickers Hardness scale, platinum scores 41, compared to gold at 20 and silver at 26. Like gold, platinum does not tarnish and is very resistant to acid corrosion.

---

[6]Reported in "Platinum Trading at Discount to Gold Is Rare, But Some Analysts Say It's Likely to Happen Soon," by Elyse Tanouye, *Wall Street Journal* (January 30, 1991).

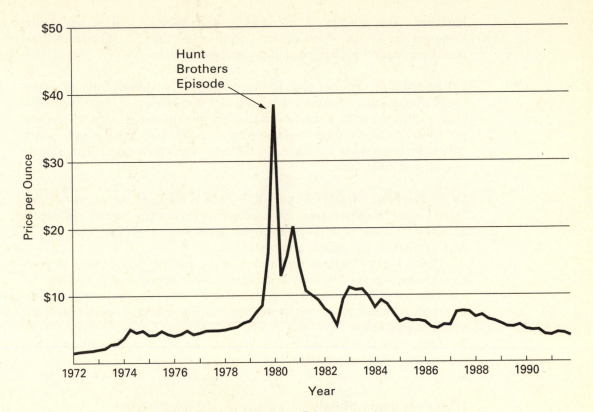

Figure 16-11 Gold and Platinum Prices
Source: *Metal Statistics*, published by American Metal Market

Platinum also is an important catalyst; it can cause chemical reactions in other materials without itself being altered in the process. A well-known application is in the catalytic converter of an automobile's exhaust system. Almost three-fourths of U.S. use of platinum is for this purpose.

Other industrial applications of platinum include the manufacture of razor blades, explosives, high-octane gasoline, fertilizer, laser rubies, optical glass, fiberglas, and heart pacemakers. The U.S. Department of Defense has about 453,000 ounces of platinum in the strategic stockpile. Public utilities in New York and Tokyo are experimenting with electromechanical fuel cells to generate electricity as a means of providing electricity to their city power grids. Platinum serves as a catalytic electrode coating in these cells.

Another increasingly important use of platinum is in cancer research. Johnson Matthey, a Canadian firm, produces a platinum-based drug called Cisplatin, which is effective in attacking the DNA in a cancer cell. This drug is used worldwide in the treatment of testicular and ovarian cancer.

Approximately 95 percent of all platinum is mined in South Africa and the former Soviet Union. The remainder comes principally from Canada and Columbia. A certain amount is also recovered from catalytic converters at the junkyard. The principal U.S. miner is the Montana Stillwater Mining Company, which has a peak annual output of less than 50,000 ounces. Total world production is nearly 1 million ounces per year.

Palladium (Pd)   Futures contracts are traded on palladium. This important metal shares many physical properties with platinum, but costs much less. Like platinum, it is a useful catalyst in the hydrogenation of refined petroleum products and is used in electrical circuits and dental alloys. In fact, palladium is often used in place of platinum. White gold is usually a mixture of gold and palladium.

Other Platinum Metals   *Iridium (Ir)* Iridium is the most corrosion-resistant metal known. For this reason, it is used widely in the manufacture of compass bearings. Iridium is also used in the manufacture of pen tips and of high-temperature crucibles and tools.

Osmium (Os) Osmium has a very high melting point: 3045 degrees Centigrade. It is used in the manufacture of some phonograph needles.

Rhodium (Rh) This metal is combined with platinum in electrical instruments and also is used in jewelry and mirrors. Some aircraft spark plugs have rhodium electrodes.

Ruthenium (Ru) Ruthenium is used as an alloy with platinum and palladium to harden jewelry.

Other Strategic Metals

Strategic metals get their name from the fact that the world's primary sources of these metals are in politically unstable or communist countries. While profits can be made via speculation in these commodities, they suffer a major trading disadvantage: they are not traded on a commodity exchange. Consequently, the speculator in strategic metals finds it difficult to get in and out of the market quickly at a fair price. Also, prices are not easily discovered, as the financial press devotes little if any space to these commodities.

Strategic metals come primarily from countries with unstable governments.

Another disadvantage to investing in any commodity that lacks a futures exchange is the requirement to pay cash rather than post a good faith deposit. There is no leverage involved with strategic metal investing; you must put up the entire purchase price of the metal you buy.

For reasons described above, few investors ever own non-platinum group strategic metals directly. But many people do own shares in companies that would suffer if the supply of these metals were interrupted. Therefore, it may

TABLE 16-3 OTHER STRATEGIC METALS

Element	Chemical Symbol	Use
Antimony	Sb	Flame-retardant in plastics and textiles
Bismuth	Bi	Pharmaceuticals
Cadmium	Cd	Electroplating and batteries
Germanium	Ge	Optics
Indium	In	Nuclear reactor control rods
Manganese	Mn	Essential for steel production
Mercury	Hg	Precision instruments
Molybdenum	Mo	Aerospace alloy
Selenium	Se	Electronic components
Tellurium	Te	Catalyst for the manufacture of glass
Titanium	Ti	Aerospace alloy
Vanadium	V	Iron and steel alloys

make sense to know something about the principal use of these unusual elements. Table 16-3 is a summary of the remaining strategic metals.

SUMMARY

Gold is an example of a commodity that is usually a pure speculative asset. It is sufficiently important in the world financial markets to warrant discussion in the study of speculative markets.

Gold is an extremely popular investment asset in Europe. In times of trouble, gold has held its value much better than national currencies or securities. The French people have suffered more than their share of war and political disruption, and the French people hold about one-third of all the gold in private hands.

The supply of gold is not as important a factor in the pricing of gold as the demand. Gold serves as a haven for those who are concerned about weakening currencies, inflation, or international uncertainty.

There are six principal means by which individuals might invest in gold. If they have the money, they can buy bullion, but this earns no interest, provides no leverage, and is expensive to store and insure. Rather than hold the bullion directly, investors can buy gold certificates, which represent an interest in gold bullion held in a bank vault. Mining shares provide a convenient, marketable way to invest in gold. Gold coins allow for the purchase of small standardized quantities that can be quickly sold if necessary. Gold futures or futures options provide leverage for the speculator and a hedging vehicle for the mining company or the jewelry manufacturer. Gold futures are always priced in a contango market.

Silver and platinum share many of the investment features of gold. Futures contracts are available on each. Strategic metals get their name from the fact that most of them are mined in areas that are politically unstable. There are no standardized contracts for the trading of these metals, and they are consequently questionable investments for anyone who is not extremely well diversified and well capitalized. The absence of futures contracts means that investments in strategic metals must be paid for in full and that there is no leverage available.

QUESTIONS

1. Gold sometimes appears to have a negative beta, much like other commodity futures contracts. What implications does this have for portfolio management?

2. Conventional wisdom states that "Wall Street does not like uncertainty." Suppose the political situation in the Mideast deteriorates. What effect would you expect this development to have on the stock of Homestake Mining?

3. What advantages and disadvantages do you see to investing in gold certificates rather than investing in gold bullion or gold coins?

4. Suppose a cost-effective method for extracting gold from the ocean were discovered. What impact would you expect this to have on the price of gold?

5. Comment on the following statement: "Gold futures contracts are inherently speculative, because there are so few people who can use them as a hedge."

6. If market interest rates rise, would you expect gold futures prices to rise or fall? Why?

7. Look at the COMEX gold futures prices in Figure 16-8 (p. 376). As expected, the futures price is higher for the more distant delivery dates. Why is the price difference between adjacent delivery months not exactly the same? Give at least three reasons.

8. The quotation in the chapter indicates that there is no "inherent reason" platinum should sell for more than gold. If the markets are efficient, how can it continue to do so?

9. Would it make sense to establish a futures spread between platinum and palladium?

10. Suppose an exchange submits a proposal to begin futures trading on a portfolio consisting of 25 ounces of each of the strategic metals. What difficulties do you foresee with such a contract?

PROBLEMS

1. Suppose it would cost you 40 cents per ounce to ship gold. Using a current futures contract, estimate your basis in the commodity.

2. Using reference material from the library, what impact does each dollar per ounce change in the price of gold likely have on Homestake Mining?

3. Go to a current edition of the *Wall Street Journal* and calculate the current value of the gold/silver ratio spread.

4. Investigate the price behavior of silver during the Hunt brothers episode in 1979. During this time, what percentage profit could have been made by buying at the low and selling at the top?

17 Conclusion: Hedging and Speculating in the Real World

*T*he hardest trip we ever make is across a strange threshold.

James L. Haddix

This book covers many unusual assets and investment activities: covered calls, protective puts, straddles, strangles, combinations, debit spreads, wheat futures, cash prices, futures options, warrant hedges, when-issued stock, gold Canadian Maple Leafs, strategic metals, etc. Because these are unusual in no way makes them inappropriate.

Speculators should learn as much as they possibly can about the investment alternatives they consider. I hope this book has piqued your interest about some entries from the list above, and if you have read the previous sixteen chapters you know far more about finance than most people. Now the fun part begins: your education in "real world" phenomena.

THEORY VERSUS PRACTICE

The Efficient Market Hypothesis

The efficient market hypothesis (EMH) is a central paradigm of finance. There are few free lunches on Wall Street, in Chicago, or in any other well-developed marketplace. As new information arrives, market participants analyze the information and take actions that cause market prices to adjust to a new level. According to the theory, all investment vehicles routinely show the proper relationship between risk and expected return.

If you are applying for an investments position and the interviewer asks if you believe the markets are efficient, "yes" is the wrong answer; so is "no." You have to waffle on this one. We do know from a plethora of evidence that the markets are very efficient, but not perfectly so. Arbitrage situations do not last long, but they routinely appear. This does not in itself violate the EMH; it is the activity of arbitrageurs that helps keep the market efficient. Security analysts are hired to look for ways to exploit deviations from "proper pricing"; they are not hired to put up their heels and pronounce everything hunky-dory.

> Don't gamble: buy some good stock, hold it till it goes up, and then sell it. If it doesn't go up, don't buy it.
>
> Will Rogers

In this book I have occasionally used an analogy based on the low likelihood of finding a five-dollar bill on the sidewalk. I once used such an example in class, and two minutes after the period ended an ecstatic student, armed with three witnesses, triumphantly returned to show me what he found outside the classroom building: a five-dollar bill. The theory of finance does not say five-dollar bills will be absent from a busy sidewalk; it proposes that it is unlikely that *you* will find one.

Consider the concept of implied volatility. In one respect, such an idea seems to go against market efficiency. Given the variables needed for the Black-Scholes option pricing model, we can solve for the theoretical value of a call option. Perhaps it is $2.33. On the exchange, however, we find that this option is actually selling for $2.75. How do we reconcile fact with theory here? It makes no sense to say that the actual, current price is wrong. What we can say is that market expectations are such that the implied volatility is higher than the historical volatility. Perhaps people expect unusual volatility in the underlying security before the option expires. They expect the future behavior of the underlying security to be significantly different from its past behavior.

This does not mean that you, armed with your calculator and the BSOPM, can quickly identify free lunches and leave your colleagues in awe. Because you understand something about option pricing, though, you can recognize the relationship between the two measures of volatility and then use this information in your decision making. Do you feel the level of implied volatility is reasonable? If so, then as far as you are concerned, the option is fairly (read *efficiently*) priced. If not, then you have concluded the option is overpriced and you might consider writing it, naked, covered, or as part of a spread. Differences of opinion are what make horse races, and although there are very valuable economic functions fulfilled by these markets, the action in the trading pit sometimes resembles a horse race even to those who know what is going on.

Another fun-to-tell story about market efficiency lies in the portfolio insurance saga from the Crash of 1987. Any portfolio insurance strategy works like a charm if the markets behave as they are "supposed to." As we have seen, the markets did not cooperate on October 19th and 20th, 1987. The huge discounts in the S&P 500 futures contract "should not" have occurred; to the efficient market Samurai, it means arbitrage was present. The fact remains that the negative basis prevailed for an extended period, and trading strategies predicated on well-functioning, efficient markets failed.

Every time the stock market takes a tumble, another class graduates from the School of Experience.

Anonymous

The point is the efficient market hypothesis is a very accurate description of day-to-day activity in the marketplace; but don't bet your house on it.

Similarly, the rules of the game sometimes change. As I am writing this, the futures industry is closely watching a legal dispute between the Internal Revenue Service and the Federal National Mortgage Association. Dubbed

"Arkansas Best,"[1] the 1988 case is before the U.S. Supreme Court. The issue is the tax status of certain long hedges.

At issue is basic tax perspective. There are two kinds of income: ordinary and capital. While ordinary losses are fully deductible, capital losses are often only deductible against capital gains. Hedgers seek to reduce their risk, as with the insurance analogy used repeatedly in this book. Therefore, it should seem that the profits or losses in the hedge should offset losses or profits in the asset being hedged, and that the tax laws should follow this economic reasoning, with the taxpayer reporting the net gain or loss. The IRS, in fact, has held since 1932 that hedges were insurance and generated ordinary income or losses, not capital income or losses. Section 1221 of the Internal Revenue Code defines a capital asset as "property held by the taxpayer." There are five exceptions, one of which is inventory.

The IRS says, "It is possible for a long forward or futures position to be part of an inventory acquisition system and a substitute for inventory." If futures are inventory hedges, the IRS argues they generate ordinary income or losses. This leaves open the possibility that the hedger could be left with an unusable capital loss and a tax liability from the ordinary income on the other side of the hedge.

It seems unlikely that the IRS will successfully argue that most business hedges result in capital gains or losses; insurance policies do not, and they are used for the same purpose. Numerous members of Congress have complained to the Secretary of the Treasury about the unreasonableness of the IRS position. If the IRS position is upheld, it will drastically affect the futures industry.

Not only does the IRS interpretation of Arkansas Best expose business to greater financial risk . . . but it threatens to rip the heart out of the futures industry.

Patrick H. Arbor
Chairman, CBOT

Performance Measurement

Academics are fond of discussing the direct relationship between risk and expected return. Riskier securities, over the long term, should yield higher returns than safer securities. Yet this relationship does not always hold; if it did, there would be no risk.

---

[1]Formally, Arkansas Best v. Commissioner.

If riskier securities always earned higher returns, there would be no risk.

There continues to be active research into the ways in which options, futures, or futures options alter the return characteristics of a portfolio. We know there are trade-offs. A person who writes a covered call, for instance, foregoes the possibility of large returns for added safety and current income.

There also is evidence that portfolio managers are evaluated largely on their realized return, without regard to the risk they took in achieving it. A few years ago I conducted a nationwide survey[2] of finance professionals and finance educators. One question asked about the extent to which respondents agreed with the following statement:

> Portfolio managers are hired and fired largely on the basis of realized investment returns with little regard to risk taken in achieving the returns.

[2]Strong, Robert A. "A Behavioral Investigation of Three Paradigms in Finance," *Northeast Journal of Business and Economics* (Spring/Summer 1988).

Three-fourths of the respondents could not disagree with this statement. We should know that risk is important; why do we seem to sweep it under the rug?

Writing puts is theoretically equivalent to writing covered calls. Still, there are horror stories of individual investors who, during the 1987 Crash, lost more than 100 percent of their investment portfolio by writing puts. The huge market decline led to massive margin calls that left some accounts with negative equity.

People who had written covered calls, however, fared much better than people who held an identical portfolio without having written options against it. The point is that while the two strategies may be theoretically equivalent, the presence of position risk (a negative position gamma) makes for extraordinary circumstances. This is a story that we are not yet fluent in telling.

Technical Analysis

Technical analysis refers to any technique for predicting futures prices by using past price data (charts) or other versions of the crystal ball. If the markets are efficient, technical analysis shouldn't work.

Any reader of the financial press will find the pages replete with advertisements for various charting services, telephone hotlines, or other advisory services. If these services are of no value, why do thousands of subscribers pay big bucks for them? This is another aspect of finance that we do not yet completely understand. It is probably not a good idea to dismiss all technical analysis with a wave of the hand. Academic researchers do not have all the answers, particularly in this mysterious dimension of the investment trade.

> Chartism isn't a science, in spite of calling itself technical analysis; [it's] more a form of impressionist art.
>
> Anthony Harris
> Financial Times in London

TAKING THE FIRST STEP: THE NEED FOR AN "OVERT ACT"

The Right Way

It is very, very easy to put off investment decisions. As trite as it sounds, the way to start is *to start*. The criminal act of conspiracy requires an overt act as a necessary ingredient. For instance, if you sit with a friend in a coffee shop and decide to burn down a building, you have not committed a crime until you do something to show your intent to carry through with your plans. You might go fill a few gallon jugs with gasoline. This is an overt act, and you are now guilty of conspiracy to commit arson.

Similarly, you can talk about futures, options, and gold coins all day, but talk is cheap in the investment world. You need an overt act, too, to complete your initiation. The individual investor might open an options trading account and try some simple call bull spreads. A would-be speculator might buy a ten-ounce bar of silver bullion from a *Wall Street Journal* advertisement.

Talk is cheap in the investment world.

If you are a portfolio manager, or if you already have a portfolio in place, write a covered call. The next time you decide to sell a security and are in no hurry to do so, improve on the market by writing a deep-in-the-money call on it. If you want to buy stock, write an in-the-money put. See what happens. You will probably get a rise out of your broker if nothing else.

Portfolio managers also should consider opening a futures account. Start small; go short an S&P 500 futures contract against your existing portfolio and see how deteriorating basis works in practice. It is good practice for portfolio managers to avoid the "S Word."[3] Derivative assets serve hedging and income generation purposes in a portfolio, and this is the usage that should be stressed. Regulators, boards of trustees, and beneficiaries are uncomfortable with the S Word.

The Wrong Way

The "Spend a Little on Options" Plan   The wrong way to take your first step into these previously uncharted waters is also the most common: buying cheap, out-of-the-money call options. These usually expire worthless, and while there is a lesson in this, it may not be the best way to start.

There was a time when a fool and his money were soon parted, but now it happens to everybody.

Adlai Stevenson II

The other thing that can happen is that these options make you a ton of money. This circumstance might even be worse. It is analogous to the golfer

---

[3]Speculation.

who hooks his ball into the trees. The "smart" shot is usually a pitch out to the fairway. Most golfers, though, can always find a narrow corridor through the trees to the green that requires a perfect, low punch shot. If you miss, you will ricochet off the trees even deeper into the jungle, losing your ball, and incurring a two-stroke penalty. If you make it, you will hear cries of "great shot" from your playing partners, and you will get all pumped up and cocky. The problem is that you will try that same shot the next dozen times you are in the woods, and you won't make any of them. Remember the admonitions above about risk and return. Is the punch shot really worth the risk? Also, you can ignore the lost ball penalty on the golf course if you so choose, but you cannot ignore lost money in the market.

If you make money on your out-of-the-money options, you are going to buy them next time, too. They have their uses, as we have seen. As a first venture into the options market, they probably aren't the best way to go. Covered calls or well-conceived spreads are much better.

The "Casino Syndrome"   Most people who visit a casino lose money. The reason they do is because they planned to lose right from the start. You hear folks say, "We are going to quit when we have lost $200." This is a remarkable game plan, when you think about it. Anybody can accomplish this goal. Otherwise intelligent people who are afflicted with this syndrome might initially win $200, but their nature makes it difficult for them to cash in their chips and go home. They can't quit because they haven't lost their $200 yet. So they keep playing until they do.

The same thing happens with options. People say, "I am going to put $500 into the options market. When I lose it, I'm quitting." This is the casino syndrome, and it obviously doesn't make any sense.

My marketing person hates when I say this, but I tell potential clients I will lose all their money for them but will do it in a responsible, professional manner.

A tongue-in-cheek comment from a commodity trading advisor.

CONTINUING EDUCATION

The speculative markets are dynamic; changes are rapidly occurring. You need to keep up with them. As a minimum, I think the serious player should read *Futures* magazine, published monthly at low cost. This is an excellent source of current topics in both futures and options.

The exchanges provide an extraordinary amount of information of varying levels of complexity. You can request a catalog of educational material from each of them. Your brokerage firm may publish its own material, and probably has guest speakers periodically who give evening presentations about some of these topics.

> In Wall Street the bulls sometimes make it and the bears sometimes make it, but the hogs never do.
>
> Anonymous

For the investment professional and academician, the annual Derivatives Colloquium at the American Stock Exchange is well worth attending. Rubbing shoulders with your counterparts at other firms and with leading researchers in the field is invaluable. Write to the AMEX for information.

Finally, the CBOE and the Chicago Board of Trade conduct annual "futures and options" seminars, similar in format to the AMEX Colloquium. You cannot leave one of these without a handful of new ideas to explore when you get home.

Glossary

Acapulco trade   An unusually large trade by someone who normally trades just a few contracts at a time.

accounting exposure   The chance of loss associated with having to convert a foreign-currency denominated asset into the home currency.

accrued interest   Interest that has been earned on a bond, but that has not yet been paid.

American option   An option that can be exercised anytime prior to its expiration.

Americus Trust   A legal entity that held a portfolio of stock and divided the shares into ''units'' composed of ''PRIMES'' and ''SCORES,'' which could be sold separately.

arbitrage   This term has evolved into a generic word for the existence of a riskless profit. In the *International Encyclopedia of the Social Sciences*, Paul Cootner defines arbitrage as the ''simultaneous purchase and sale of equivalent assets at prices which guarantee a fixed profit at the time of the transactions, although the life of the assets, and, hence, the consummation of the profit may be delayed until some future date.''

arbitrageur   A person who actively seeks arbitrage situations, and by exploiting them helps keep the marketplace efficient.

ask discount   The discount from par value associated with the current asking price for a U.S. treasury bill.

asked price   The lowest price at which anyone has expressed a willingness to sell a security.

assignment   The notice received by an option writer that the option holder intends to exercise the option.

at-the-money   An option where the striking price equals the current market price of the underlying security or other asset.

away from the market   A price that is far away from the current trading range.

backspread   A vertical option spread where extra options are written such that the spread often generates a credit to your account.

bank immunization   A risk-reduction technique used by financial institutions in which the dollar-weighted duration of its rate-sensitive assets is made equal to the dollar-weighted duration of its rate-sensitive liabilities.

basis   The difference between the futures price of a commodity and the current cash price at a specific location.

basis convergence   The phenomenon with stock index futures contracts that causes the futures price to equal the stock index itself at delivery date. At this point, the basis equals zero.

basis point   One one-hundredth of a percent.

basis point value   The change in the price of a bond for a one basis point change in the yield to maturity of the bond.

bear   Someone who believes the price of a particular commodity will move lower.

bearspread   A spread that becomes valuable as prices of the underlying asset decline.

beta   A measure of the systematic risk of an asset. The average beta is one; securities with a beta more than this are more risky than average, and vice-versa.

bid price   The highest price at which anyone has expressed a willingness to buy.

Black Monday   The colloquial term given to October 19, 1987 (the day the stock market crashed).

Black-Scholes Option Pricing Model   One of the most significant developments in the history of finance. This model provides an analytical framework for the evaluation of securities that provide a claim on other assets.

bond equivalent yield   A method of determining the yield on a U.S. treasury bill so as to account for a 365 day year and for the fact that the security is purchased at a discount.

Brady Report   A study conducted following Black Monday to determine the implications of the Crash of 1987.

broker   A person in the pit who works for a member of the exchange.

bucket trading   A fraudulent practice in which a client is charged more than necessary and two brokers split the difference.

bull   Someone who believes the price of an asset will increase.

bullet immunization   A technique appropriate for a client who has an initial sum of money to invest and wants to accumulate a predetermined sum by a specific future date; the technique involves assembling a basket of bonds whose collective holding period returns will match that of a hypothetical zero coupon bond.

bullion   Unworked gold, usually in bar form.

bullspread   An option spread that becomes valuable as the price of the underlying asset rises.

butterfly spread   A spread involving three option positions. There are various ways to construct such a spread, but all involve writing two options and then buying one with a higher striking price and one with a lower striking price.

buying hedge   When a hedger goes long to protect some economic interest; also known as a long hedge.

buy/write   Buying stock and writing a covered call.

calendar spread   A simultaneous long and short position in options, where the options are chosen horizontally from the financial listing. Also called a *time spread.*

call a stock   The act of exercising one's prerogative as the owner of a call option. If you buy a call option and subsequently "call the stock," it means you want the writer of the call option to deliver the stock to you in exchange for your payment of the striking price.

call option   The owner of a call option has purchased the right to *buy* a set number of shares of common stock (normally 100) at a set price (the striking, or exercise, price) from a specified person (the option writer) anytime prior to a specified date (the expiration date).

call ratio spread   A call bull spread is transformed into a call ratio spread by writing more than one call at the higher striking price.

cap price   With a CAP option, the option striking price plus (with calls) or minus (with puts) the cap interval.

CAPS   An exchange-traded option package similar to a spread.

carrying cost   The cost of actually holding a commodity, including insurance costs, storage costs, interest charges, etc.

cash dividend   A payment to shareholders of a portion of the firm's earnings.

cash market   Any market in which cash is exchanged for current delivery of an asset.

cash price   The current price of an asset, particularly an asset on which futures contracts trade. Also called the *spot price.*

cash secured put   See *fiduciary put.*

cash settlement   The settlement procedure used with stock index futures and options. No delivery of the underlying asset occurs with these securities.

cheapest to deliver   The specific financial instrument that is most advantageous to use in delivery against a Treasury bond or Treasury note futures contract. The term originated with the now-inactive GNMA futures contract.

churning   An illegal activity in which a broker makes, or advises a client to make, unnecessary trades in an account for the purpose of generating excess commissions.

circuit breaker   A system to temporarily halt trading in the markets in the event of a major change in price levels.

class   All options on the same underlying asset.

Clearing Corporation   A mechanism designed to eliminate uncertainty in the futures and options markets. It does this by interposing itself between buyers and sellers. All trades are actually sales to or purchases from the clearing corporation.

clearinghouse   An agency associated with a futures or options exchange where trade reports are matched and any outtrades are identified.

closing price   The price that is actually paid when a previously established option position is eliminated, or closed. The last price of the day (or the settlement price) for a particular commodity.

closing transaction   An option trade in which an investor eliminates a previously established option position. For the purchaser of an option, a closing transaction would be a sale of the option. For an option writer, a closing transaction is a purchase of the option or receiving an exercise notice from the option holder.

combination   An option strategy in which you are simultaneously long or short puts and calls.

combined call writing   Writing calls at more than one striking price.

commission   A fee paid to a broker for executing a trade.

Commodity Futures Trading Commission   A five-member U.S. government agency charged with supervising and regulating the futures exchanges.

condor   A less risky version of the strangle that involves *four* different striking prices.

contango market   The typical relationship with most futures contracts, in which the futures price exceeds the cash price.

contingent immunization   The essence of contingent immunization is the provision of a "floor value" below which the value of the portfolio will not fall or the establishment of a minimum rate of return for the portfolio; it "leaves the upside open" while limiting downside risk.

continuous compounding   The most advantageous form of calculating interest for a saver. Continuous compounding uses natural logarithms and uses continuous time rather than discrete time intervals.

contract   The unit of trading for a futures transaction.

contract month   See *delivery month.*

conversion factor   An adjustment factor used to convert U.S. treasury bonds into 8 percent equivalents.

convexity   For a given interest rate change, convexity is the difference between the actual price change in a bond and that predicted by the duration statistic.

corner   Any system for interrupting the supply of a commodity in the marketplace in an attempt to manipulate prices.

coupon rate   The stated interest rate that determines the dollar amount of interest the bond pays.

cover The process of eliminating an existing investment position by taking an offsetting trade.

cover a short The elimination of a short position by buying securities identical to those sold short.

covered call A call option that an investor has written against common stock that he or she owns. A call option is also considered covered if it is held in the same portfolio as a call option with the same expiration date but a lower striking price, or with a call option of the same striking price but a later expiration date.

covered futures option A written futures option in which the writer holds a corresponding futures position on the other side of the market.

covered put An ambiguous term which usually refers to a fiduciary put. Also sometimes used to refer to a combination of a short put and a short stock position.

covered write See *covered call*.

crack A crude oil/heating oil/gasoline counterpart to the soybean/soybean meal/soybean oil "crush."

crawling stop A stop order used to protect a profit by continually raising the stop price behind a rising stock.

credit An option transaction that results into a cash inflow into the investor's account.

credit risk See *default risk*.

cross company spread A non-standard spread using securities on more than one company.

cross trading The illegal practice of switching customer orders and those for one's personal account.

crowd The colloquial term used for the people in a trading pit.

crush A hedging activity used by soybean processors in which soybean futures are purchased and soybean oil and meal futures are sold. By "putting on a crush," the processor can lock in a certain profit margin.

current yield The annual income generated by a security divided by its current price.

daily price limit An exchange-imposed restriction on how much the price of a particular futures contract is allowed to move in a single trading day. Contracts are said to be "limit up" or "limit down" when the daily price limit is reached.

day trading Opening security positions or futures contracts and closing them on the same day.

debit An option position that requires a cash outflow from an investor's brokerage account.

deck The collection of cards on which a futures or options trader has recorded the day's transactions.

deep-in-the-money This subjective description applies to any option that has "substantial" intrinsic value.

default risk A measure of the likelihood that a borrower will be unable to repay principal and interest as agreed.

deflation The situation when the general price level is declining; negative inflation.

deliverable bond A bond that satisfies the delivery requirements of the U.S. Treasury bond futures contract. A deliverable bond has at least 15 years until maturity, and, if callable, at least 15 years of call protection.

delivery day The day that a commodity or financial instrument is actually delivered against a futures contract.

delivery month The month during which a commodity is due to be delivered in a futures contract.

delivery notice The written notice that a futures seller gives, indicating a desire to make delivery of the commodity underlying the futures contract.

delta The change in option premium expected from a small change in the stock price.

delta exposure The sum of the deltas in a portfolio.

delta management A method of risk management in which the manager seeks to maintain position delta at a particular value within a certain range.

delta neutrality The situation in which the delta exposure of a position is zero.

derivative asset An asset whose value is primarily determined by the value of another asset.

diagonal spread A spread in which the options are selected from different expiration months and where the options have different striking prices.

directional market One's outlook for the overall market: bullish, bearish, or neutral.

discount brokerage firm A firm that offers substantially reduced commission costs, usually at the expense of reduced services such as investment advice or research.

discount factor The interest rate used to equate present values and futures values. The discount factor may include a risk factor in addition to a pure interest rate.

discrete compounding The periodic computation of interest. Periods are defined in finite time intervals.

Dow Jones Industrial Average A popular measure of stock market activity based on the closing prices of the common stock of 30 large firms.

DOT The Designated Order Turnaround system at the New York Stock

Exchange; also called *SuperDOT*. This system allows trades of less than 2100 shares to be placed directly with the specialist via electronic means.

dual trading   The contemporary phenomenon in which a specific commodity trades simultaneously on two or more exchanges, and where the contracts are fungible across the exchanges.

due bill   A document received during the processing of a stock split. Holders of due bills are entitled to new shares when the shares are issued.

duration   A measure of interest rate risk. Duration is a weighted average of the length of time required for cash flows to be received from a fixed-income security.

duration matching   A form of portfolio dedication or immunization in which a basket of assets is assembled such that its present value and its duration match that of a liability or stream of liabilities.

duration shifting   An interest rate reduction strategy in which the duration of a portfolio is altered in anticipation of changing market interest rates.

dynamic hedging   A portfolio insurance technique that requires frequent revision of a hedge, using stock index futures or options.

economic exposure   This type of exposure measures the risk that the value of a security will decline due to an unexpected change in relative foreign exchange rates.

effective rate   The realized compound yield on an investment. The effective rate considers the effects of compounding.

efficient   In the marketplace, the prompt and accurate processing of new information into security prices.

efficient market hypothesis   The theory that publicly available information is rapidly and accurately reflected in the price of securities, and that over the long run realized returns will be consistent with their level of undiversifiable risk.

equity option   An option in which common stock is the underlying security.

Eurodollars   A U.S. dollar-denominated account located outside the United States.

European option   An option that can be exercised only at expiration.

ex-dividend date   The date established by the brokerage community to eliminate uncertainty about who is entitled to dividends when trades are made near the date of record. The ex-dividend date is four business days prior to the date of record. Investors must buy stock before the ex-dividend date to be entitled to the next dividend.

exercise   The act by which an option holder expresses an interest to sell shares to the option writer at the specified price (with puts) or to buy shares from the option writer at the specified price (with calls).

exercise price   The agreed-upon price for the exchange of common stock (or the other appropriate underlying asset) in the terms of a put or call option; synonymous with the term *striking price.*

expectations hypothesis The theory that the futures price for a commodity is what the marketplace expects the cash price to be when the delivery month arrives.

expected value The weighted average of all possible outcomes from a distribution, where the weights reflect the probability of the various outcomes.

expiration date The last date of an option's life.

exposure The extent to which a loss is possible because of adverse changes in foreign exchange rates.

fair premium A term used with stock index futures to reflect the value that the index futures contract should sell for in the absence of arbitrage.

fiat value Value arbitrarily established by a government authority. Currency has value because the government says it does, not because of intrinsic value.

fiduciary A person or institution who is responsible for the management of someone else's money.

fiduciary put A short put option in which the put writer deposits the striking price of the put into an interest bearing account. Also called a *cash-secured put.*

financial asset An asset for which there is a corresponding liability somewhere.

financial engineering The construction of asset portfolios with predetermined technical characteristics, particularly when those characteristics are not available in an exchange-traded product.

financial futures A generic term for futures contracts on debt instruments, stock indexes, and foreign currencies.

financial risk The variation of returns that are a function of the extent to which borrowed funds are used in the generation of the returns.

first notice day Generally, the first business day prior to the first day of the delivery month.

floor broker A member of an exchange who, for a fee, executes orders for other members.

floor trader See *local.*

foreign currency option A listed option giving the holder the right to buy or sell a specified quantity of foreign currency. These are distinct from foreign currency futures options.

foreign exchange risk The chance of loss due to adverse fluctuations in exchange rates between national currencies.

forward rate A contractual rate between a commercial bank and a client for the future delivery of a specified quantity of foreign currency; normally quoted on the basis of one, two, three, six, and twelve months.

forward split   A stock split in which shareholders receive additional shares and are left with a greater number of shares than before the split.

full carrying charge market   A futures market for a particular commodity in which the basis for successive delivery months reflects the cost of storing (of holding, in the case of financial futures) the commodity or financial instrument.

fundamental analyst   A person who studies earnings and relative value in determining the intrinsic value of a security.

funds gap   The difference between a bank's rate sensitive assets and its rate sensitive liabilities.

fungibility   The ability of participants in the futures and options markets to reverse their position by making an offsetting trade. This occurs because the individual contracts are standardized and interchangeable.

futures commission merchant (FCM)   A broker in commodity futures.

futures contract   A legal, transferable, standardized contract that represents a promise to buy or sell a quantity of a standardized commodity by a predetermined delivery date.

futures option   A type of option that gives the holder of a call the right to assume a long position in a futures contract, while the holder of a futures put has the right to go short a futures contract.

gamma   The sensitivity of delta to changes in the stock price.

GLOBEX   A world-wide computerized trading system developed by the Chicago Mercantile Exchange, the Chicago Board of Trade, and Reuters Limited.

going long   When a speculator "goes long" in the futures market, he is making a promise to pay for a commodity at a future date.

going short   When a speculator "goes short" in the futures market, he is making a promise to deliver a commodity at a future date.

gold certificate   A document that represents ownership of gold bullion that is kept by someone else on your behalf.

gold/silver ratio spread   Buying futures in one type of metal and selling futures in the other; dollar amounts on both sides are approximately equal.

good delivery bar   A 400-troy ounce bar of gold that is at least 99.6 percent pure. Good delivery bars may be delivered against a short futures position.

good faith deposit   The initial equity requirement that must be deposited with an opening transaction in a futures contract. This is often called *margin,* although no money is borrowed.

hedge   The purchase and sale of two assets whose values are expected to move opposite to each other.

hedger   A person who faces some type of economic risk and chooses to eliminate or reduce it by some type of offsetting transaction.

hedge ratio   A calculated value that indicates the quantity of an asset that must be acquired or sold to completely eliminate a certain type of risk with an investment position.

hedge wrapper   The simultaneous writing of a covered call *and* buying a protective put.

historical volatility   The volatility that is determined from a past series of prices.

holding period return   A comparison of the ending value of an investment with its original cost. The holding period return is insensitive to the length of the period.

horizontal spread   See *calendar spread.*

house out   An outtrade where the clearing members do not match.

immunization   The process of removing interest rate risk by adjusting the duration of assets and liabilities via the futures market or with portfolio rebalancing.

implied volatility   The annual volatility that, when input into an option pricing model, will cause the model to predict the current market price with no error. Implied volatility is sometimes thought to be the market's estimate of future volatility.

improving on the market   The practice of writing deep-in-the-money covered calls to sell stock at a slightly above-market price, or writing in-the-money puts to acquire stock at a below-market price.

index   A calculated measure of market activity, such as the S&P 500 stock index.

indexing   The practice of continually adjusting a portfolio so that its characteristics match as nearly as possible those of some market index.

index option   An option to buy or sell a hypothetical basket of securities whose value is determined by a market index. Index options are settled in cash; there is no delivery mechanism.

inflation premium   Reflects the rapidity with which prices are rising; it measures how rapidly the money standard is losing its purchasing power.

informational efficiency   The aspect of the market considered by the efficient market hypothesis. Informational efficiency means that the market quickly and accurately reacts to the arrival of new information.

inside information   Privately held news which, when released to the public, is likely to have an impact on the price of securities. Trading on the basis of inside information is illegal.

intercommodity spread   In the futures market, taking a long and a short position in two related commodities.

interest rate parity   The fact that differences in national interest rates are reflected in the currency forward market.

interest rate sensitivity   The extent to which an asset's value is affected by changing interest rates.

intermarket spread   Taking opposite positions in the same commodity on two different markets.

internal rate of return   The discount rate that will cause a series of future cash flows to have a present value equal to the cost of acquiring the future cash flows.

intention day   The day following the date by which a "Long Position Report" must be filed. On this day the Clearing Corporation may assign delivery to the member with the oldest long position in the particular commodity.

intercommodity spread   This type of spread involves a long and short position in two related commodities.

in-the-money   An option is in-the-money if it has intrinsic value based on the stock price and striking price. Calls are in-the-money when the striking price is less than the stock price; vice-versa for puts.

intracommodity spread   Also called an *intermonth spread;* involves taking different positions in different delivery months.

intrinsic value   An option has intrinsic value determined by the degree to which it is "in-the-money."

inverted market   When a futures price is less than the cash price.

investment grade   Bonds rated BBB or higher by Standard & Poors.

investment horizon   The period of time a particular investment is expected to be held.

invoice price   The amount that the buyer of a interest rate futures contract must pay when the securities underlying the futures contract are delivered.

issuer   The organization which created a particular debt or equity security.

Itô's lemma   A mathematical relationship used to improve the forecasting ability of a first-order differential equation.

junk bond   Historically, a junk bond is any bond rated BB or below by Standard and Poors.

kappa   Another name for *vega.*

karat   A measure of the purity of gold. 24 karat gold is 99.9 percent pure.

lambda   See *gamma.*

last trading day   The final day in which trading occurs for a particular futures or options contract.

law of one price   The fundamental finance principle that requires equivalent assets to sell for the same price.

LEAPS   An exchange traded long-term option.

LED spread   An interest rate spread involving the LIBOR and Eurodollar futures contracts.

LIBOR   The London Interbank Offer Rate, an important money market interest rate.

limit order   An order to buy or sell securities or other assets in which the client has specified the time for which the order is to be kept open and the minimum price acceptable for the trade.

limit price   On a standing order, the highest price the buyer will pay or the lowest price a seller will accept.

liquidity   The extent to which something can be quickly converted into cash at approximately its market value.

liquidity risk   The potential for loss because of an inability to convert an asset to cash at a reasonable price.

listed option   An option that trades on an exchange.

locals   Members of an exchange who trade for their own account. They are not employees of another firm.

London fix   The price of gold determined twice a day in London by a group of bankers who seek to match buy and sell orders until equilibrium is found.

long hedge   A transaction in which an asset is purchased as a hedge.

long position   The common investment position in which an asset is held as opposed to borrowed or written.

Long Position Report   This document provides a summary of all clearing members' long positions and their dates of purchase.

Macauley duration   The traditional measure of duration. Duration is a measure of interest rate risk and a weighted average of the time it takes to recover the cost of a security.

maintenance margin   The minimum equity requirement that must be maintained with a particular investment position before a margin call is received and more money must be deposited into your account.

margin   A deposit of funds required to provide collateral for an investment position.

margin call   The requirement to add equity to an investment account because of adverse price movements or new transactions.

margin requirement   See *margin.*

mark to the market   The practice in the futures markets of transferring funds from one account to another each day on the basis of unrealized (or paper) gains and losses.

marketmaker   One of a number of people who compete against each other for the public's business, thereby helping to ensure that the public receives a market-determined price for their options.

marketmaker system   The trading system used at the futures exchanges, at the Chicago Board Options Exchange, and at the Pacific Stock Exchange.

market order The simplest type of order. It instructs a broker to execute a client's order at the best possible price at the earliest opportunity.

market risk The chance of loss due to adverse movements in the level of the stock market.

market variation call When the President of the Clearing Corporation calls on a member to deposit more funds into his account during the day because of adverse price movements. Market variation calls must be met within one hour of the time they are received.

matching trades The act of processing one's deck through a clearing corporation.

MOB spread An interest rate spread using municipal bonds and government bonds.

naked call A short call option in which the writer does not own or have a claim to the underlying security or asset.

naked option This term properly is given only to the writing of an uncovered call option. To the writer of an uncovered call, potential losses are theoretically unlimited.

naked put Usually means a short put by itself.

near-the-money An option where the striking price and the price of the underlying asset are approximately equal.

NOB spread An interest rate futures spread in which opposite positions are established using U.S. Treasury bond futures and U.S. Treasury note futures.

nominal rate Stated interest rate.

normal backwardation The theory of futures pricing that predicts the futures price is downward biased in order to provide a risk premium to the speculators, who normally have a net long position.

numismatic value The value of a coin that is determined by its collector or investor appeal, rather than its intrinsic value.

odd-lot A quantity of stock which is not evenly divisible by 100 shares.

odd-lot generating split A stock split that is not in a whole number ratio like two- or four-to-one. For instance in a three-for-two split, the holder of 100 shares would have 150 after the split. One hundred fifty shares is an odd lot.

OEX The Standard & Poors 100 stock index. This term is particularly used with options on this index.

offer price See *asked price.*

open, the The initial price of a trading day.

opening transaction The establishment of an investment position. This position may be long or short.

open interest A measure of how many futures contracts in a given commodity exist at a particular point in time.

open outcry The trading method used at the futures exchanges and at some of the options exchanges. Trades are made verbally among members of a trading "crowd," rather than through a single specialist.

option A contract that gives the holder the choice to buy or sell a certain security at a set price, on or before a given date.

option beta An option's elasticity multiplied by the beta of the underlying asset.

option clearing corporation (OCC) An organization that acts as a guarantor of all option trades between buyers and sellers. The OCC also regulates the trading activities of members of option exchanges.

option elasticity An option's delta multiplied by the ratio of the underlying asset price and the option premium.

order book A book that is kept by a specialist in which he or she keeps standing orders from all over the country to ensure that the market in these securities is maintained in a fair and orderly fashion.

order book official The exchange employee responsible for maintaining the order book at an options exchange.

out-of-the-money An option which has no intrinsic value.

outtrades When a Clearing Corporation's computer is not able to exactly match all trades, the mismatches are called "out trades."

overriding See *overwriting*.

overwriting The practice of writing options against an existing portfolio.

percent of par The pricing convention for debt instruments. If a security has a par value of $100,000, a price of 78⁶⁄₃₂ means the price is 78⁶⁄₃₂ "percent of par" or $78,187.50.

PERCS A "Preferred Equity Redemption Cumulative Stock"; an exchange-traded security that is similar to a PRIME.

pit Refers to the sunken trading arena of a futures or options exchange where members of that exchange engage in trades.

platinum group The section of the periodic table of the elements that contains platinum, palladium, iridium, osmium, rhodium, and ruthenium.

portfolio insurance A quasi-insurance activity that seeks to provide a floor value below which a portfolio will not fall, or a minimum level of income.

Position Day The date that the "Long Position Report" is required.

position delta The sum of the deltas in a portfolio.

position gamma The sum of the gammas in a portfolio.

position risk The possible loss associated with extreme market movements.

position theta The sum of the thetas in a portfolio.

position trader A speculator who routinely maintains futures positions overnight and sometimes keeps a contract open for weeks.

precious metals   The term is applied to the platinum group metals, to gold, and to silver.

premium   With options, the actual amount that is paid for an option. With futures, the situation in which a particular futures price is higher than some other price.

present value   The value of an asset in today's dollars.

price discovery   The function of the futures markets that produces a "best estimate" of the future spot price of a commodity; a function of the futures market which helps indicate the market's consensus about likely future prices for a commodity.

price out   An outtrade where the prices differ.

price risk   The chance of loss due to an adverse future price; the risk of loss because of an uncertain future price for a commodity or a financial asset.

PRIME   "Prescribed Right to Income and Maximum Equity"; one part of an Americus Trust unit. PRIMES are like covered call positions.

Priority Trading Rule   An exchange's policy that ensures that public orders of ten options or less are quickly executed at a fair price.

processor   A participant in the soybean market who buys soybeans and crushes them into soy oil and soy meal.

program trading   A generic term used for any activity that involves the trading of portfolios via computers, where the decision to make a trade is also computer generated.

protective put   A long position in a put option held simultaneously with a long position in the same common stock. A protective put is a hedge.

purchasing power parity   The phenomenon in international finance whereby relative exchange rates reflect differences in the relative purchasing power of a currency in the two countries.

put/call parity   The theory that call prices should exceed put prices by about the riskless rate of interest when the options are at-the-money and the stock pays no dividends.

put option   The owner of a put option has purchased the right to sell a set number of shares of common stock (normally 100) for a set price (the striking, or exercise price) to a specified person (the option writer) anytime prior to a specified date (the expiration date).

put ratio spread   A bear spread with puts becomes a put ratio backspread by the addition of extra short put positions.

putting on a crush   The activity of a soybean processor that involves buying soybean futures and selling soybean oil and soybean meal futures. A processor puts on a crush to lock in an acceptable profit margin.

quality option   The right of the holder of a short position in Treasury bond futures contracts to deliver any eligible bond against the contract.

quantity out   An outtrade where the number of contracts in a particular trade is in dispute.

rate sensitivity   See *interest rate sensitivity.*

ratio backspread   The opposite of ratio spreads. Backspreads generate a *credit* to one's account.

ratio spread   A spread with an unequal number of long and short options.

real asset   An asset for which there is no corresponding liability.

realized compound yield   The effective rate of interest actually earned on an investment over a period of time, including the reinvestment of intermediate cash flows.

real rate   A theoretical interest rate representing the cost people charge for deferring consumption.

reinvestment rate risk   The chance of loss due to uncertainty about the rate at which cash proceeds to be received in the futures will be reinvested.

rho   The sensitivity of an option premium to changes in the interest rate.

riskless rate of interest   A theoretical value representing the price of deferring consumption from one period to the next. The riskless interest rate is usually proxied by the rate on a 30-day U.S. Treasury bill.

risk premium   The component of interest rates that is toughest to measure; the magnitude of the risk premium is a function of how much risk the security carries.

round lot   The purchase or sale of shares of stock in multiples of 100 shares.

round-turn   The convention for commissions on commodity futures. A single commission is paid, which provides for both the establishment of a position and its subsequent closing by delivery or an offsetting trade.

scalper   See *local.*

SCORE   A "Special Claim on Residual Equity"; one part of an American Trust unit. Owning a SCORE is like owning a long-term call option.

serial expiration   Options on a particular futures contract that have multiple expiration months.

settlement price   Analogous to the closing price with stock, the settlement price represents the "ending" price for a futures contract at the close of trading. The settlement price may be an average of prices during the last few minutes of trading.

short call   A written call.

short position   1. In the futures market, a promise to deliver; 2. in the options market, writing an option; 3. in the stock market, borrowing shares and selling them in the hope of buying them back later at a lower price.

short put   A written put.

short sale   Short sellers borrow stock from their broker, sell it, and hope to buy similar shares in the future at a lower price to replace those borrowed.

sides out   An outtrade where both cards indicate the same side of the market, i.e., both indicate buy, or both indicate sell.

specialist   An individual at the American and New York Stock Exchanges through whom all orders to buy or sell a particular security must pass. The specialist is charged with maintaining a fair and orderly market.

specialist system   A market trading system using specialists rather than marketmakers.

speculator   In the futures market a speculator is a person who, for a price, is willing to bear the risk that the hedger does not want.

speed market   The aspect of the market measured by gamma; the extent to which a position benefits from rapid or slow changes in market prices.

spot market   See *cash market.*

spot price   See *cash price.*

spot rate   1. The current exchange rate for two currencies; 2. the cash price for a commodity.

spread   The simultaneous purchase and sale of futures or options contracts, where there is an anticipated relation between the assets underlying the futures or options.

stock index   A measure of the general level of stock market prices.

stock index arbitrage   A type of program trading that seeks to take advantage of discrepancies in the relative pricing of stock index futures contracts and the level of the stock index itself.

stock split   Recapitalization of a firm's equity by increasing or decreasing the number of shares outstanding.

stop loss order   A special type of limit order that becomes a market order if the stop price is touched.

stop order   See *stop loss order.*

stop price   The "trigger" price with a stop order, causing the order to be executed.

S&P 500 Stock Index   A standard against which portfolio managers and investment advisors might be judged. It is currently one of the Commerce Department's leading indicators.

straddle   Holding a put and a call with the same striking price, expiration date, and on the same underlying security, is being *long* a straddle. If one is short these options, they have *written* a straddle.

strangle   Similar to a straddle, except that the puts and calls have different striking prices.

strategic metal   Any metal whose primary source is in a communist or other politically unstable country.

strike out   An outtrade primarily with futures options, where the traders are inconsistent in the striking price they record on their trading cards.

striking price   Synonymous with *exercise price*, but striking price is generally used when describing options.

synthetic index portfolio   A combination of futures contracts and Treasury bills that yields a position equivalent to an equity portfolio.

synthetic option   A portfolio of security positions that is equivalent to a particular option position.

synthetic purchase   The combination of a short position in a put option, a long position in a call option, and a long position in Treasury bills, such that the resulting portfolio has investment characteristics nearly identical to a long position in the common stock of the same company.

systematic factors   Factors that influence the stock market as a whole, including market interest rates, economic indicators, the political climate, regulatory policy, and fiscal or monetary policy.

Tapioca City   A colloquial name for the destination of traders who lose their trading capital.

TED spread   An interest rate futures spread using U.S. Treasury bill futures and Eurodollar futures.

termination claim   The "strike price" of an Americus Trust PRIME or SCORE.

Terrible Tuesday   October 20, 1987, the day after the Crash of 1987.

theta   A measure of the sensitivity of a call option to the time remaining until its expiration.

thin trading   Sparse volume.

tick   The minimum allowable price change in a futures or options position.

time decay   The phenomenon whereby the value of an option declines as time passes if the price of the underlying asset does not change.

time spread   See *calendar spread.*

time out   An outtrade when the delivery month or expiration is in dispute.

time value   The amount by which the market price of an option exceeds its intrinsic value.

timing option   The right of someone with a short position in T bond futures to choose when to deliver.

transaction exposure   According to the Financial Accounting Standards Board: "A transaction involving purchase or sale of goods or services with the price stated in foreign currency is incomplete until the amount in dollars necessary to liquidate the related payable or receivable is determined."

translation exposure   This type of exposure stems from the holding of foreign assets and liabilities that are denominated in currencies other than the U.S. dollars

trend   The general direction of the market for a particular commodity.

triple witching hour   Occurs on four days each year when stock index futures, stock index options, and equity options all expire. These dates are the third Fridays of March, June, September, and December.

troy ounce   The standard for gold weight. A troy ounce weighs 9.7 percent more than the standard ounce.

type of option   There are two types of options: puts and calls.

uncirculated coin   A coin that is in the same condition as when it left the mint. It doesn't matter how many have owned it.

uncovered option (or call)   This term is normally used as an alternative to *naked call*. The term *uncovered put* has no unambiguous meaning.

underlying security   The common stock or other asset that an option allows its holder to buy or sell.

unit   The combination of an Americus Trust PRIME and a SCORE.

Unmatched Trade Notice   A notice informing clearing members of the existence of outtrades with their accounts.

unsystematic factors   Factors unique to a specific company or industry, including earnings reports, technological developments, labor negotiations, cost of materials, and merger or acquisition activity.

vega   The sensitivity of an option premium to changes in the volatility of the underlying asset.

vertical spread   A spread in which the options have the same expiration but different striking prices.

volatility   The extent to which an asset changes in price with the passage of time. In option pricing, volatility is measured as the annualized standard deviation of returns.

volume   The quantity of futures or options contracts traded during a given period of time.

warehouse receipt   A document representing the ownership of a specific quantity and quality of a commodity. Warehouse receipts are sometimes called depository receipts, especially with gold.

warrant   Essentially a long-term call option issued by a company rather than written by an individual.

warrant hedge   A strategy that appears unusually profitable, in which shares are purchased and warrants on the same company are sold short.

wasting asset   A property of an option that, when everything else remains equal (i.e., the stock price does not change), the value of the option will decline over time.

when-issued stock   A curious, short-lived security that is issued in conjunction with a stock split.

wild card option   The right of someone with a short position in T bond futures to choose to deliver based upon a settlement price determined earlier in the day.

writing   The act of selling options as an opening transaction.

yield curve inversion   The phenomenon whereby long-term interest rates are lower than short-term rates.

yield to maturity   The true rate of return that will be earned on a debt instrument if the security is held until its maturity and all interest and principal is repaid as agreed. The calculation of yield to maturity assumes that it is possible to reinvest coupon returns at the yield to maturity.

 **Selected References**

CHAPTER 2 BASIC PRINCIPLES OF STOCK OPTIONS

Books

Gastineau, Gary. (1988). *The Options Manual* (3rd ed.). New York: McGraw-Hill. This classic book is a part of the library of most option traders. It provides a very good introduction to options, as well as a good insight into more advanced strategies.

Goldstone, Nancy Bazelon. (1988). *Trading Up.* New York: Dutton. This entertaining book describes a bank employee's unlikely rise to chief of the options trading desk at a large commercial bank in New York. Her experiences with people who do not understand options are useful case studies. Students enjoy this light reading.

Malkiel, Burton, and Richard Quandt. (1960). *Strategies and Rational Decisions in the Securities Options Markets.* Cambridge, MA: MIT Press, 1969.

Ritchken, Peter. (1987). *Options: Theory, Strategy, and Applications.* Glenview, IL: Scott, Foresman.

Articles

Black, F. (1975, July/August). Fact and Fantasy in the Use of Options. *Financial Analysts Journal*, pp. 36–72.

Bookstaber, Richard. (1985, Summer). The Use of Options in Performance Structuring. *Journal of Portfolio Management*, pp. 36–50.

Degler, W. (1986, April). How to Survive the First Few Months of Options Trading. *Futures*, pp. 52–53.

Gladstein, M., Robert Merton, and Myron Scholes. (1982, January). The Returns and Risks of Alternative Put Option Portfolio Investment Strategies. *Journal of Business*, pp. 1–55.

Merton, Robert. (1973, Spring). Theory of Rational Option Pricing. *Bell Journal of Economics and Management Science*, pp. 141–83.

Stoll, Hans. (1969, December). The Relationship Between Put and Call Option Prices. *Journal of Finance*, pp. 801–24.

CHAPTER 3   BASIC OPTION STRATEGIES

Books

Malkiel, B., and R. Quandt. (1969). *Strategies and Rational Decisions in the Securities Options Market.* Cambridge, MA: MIT Press. This book was one of the first exhaustive studies of what kinds of activity make sense in the option marketplace. Although now somewhat outdated, it is a classic. Readers will still find it interesting, particularly with regard to the attitude toward puts before the advent of listed options.

McMillan, L. (1980). *Options as a Strategic Investment.* New York: New York Institute of Finance. This well-known book has been read by thousands of option traders. It sits on the bookshelf of amateur and expert alike.

Yates, J. (1987). *The Options Strategy Spectrum.* Homewood, IL: Dow Jones-Irwin. This well-known book provides a good summary of the development of options markets. Although the book is not particularly rigorous, it provides a good discussion of the relative risk of various options strategies.

Articles

Bookstaber, R. (1985, Summer). The Use of Options in Performance Structuring. *Journal of Portfolio Management,* pp. 36–50.

Dawson, F. (1978, Winter). Risks and Returns in Continuous Option Writing. *Journal of Portfolio Management,* 58–63.

Gastineau, G., and A. Mandansky. (1979, September/October). Simulation is No Guide to Option Strategies. *Financial Analysts Journal.*

Gladstein, M., R. Merton, and M. Scholes. (1982, January). The Returns and Risks of Alternate Put Option Portfolio Investment Strategies. *Journal of Business,* pp. 1–55.

Manaster, S., and R. Rendleman. (1982, September). Option Prices as Predictors of Equilibrium Stock Prices. *Journal of Finance,* pp. 1043–57.

Merton, R., M. Scholes, and M. Gladstein. (1978, April). The Return and Risk of Alternative Call Option Portfolio Investment Strategies. *Journal of Portfolio Management,* pp. 31–42.

Pounds, H. (1977, Winter). Covered Call Writing: Strategies and Results. *Journal of Portfolio Management,* pp. 31–42.

Pozen, R. (1978, July/August). The Purchase of Protective Puts by Financial Institutions. *Financial Analysts Journal,* pp. 47–60.

Yates, J., and R. Kopprasch. (1980, Fall). Writing Covered Call Options: Profits and Risks. *Journal of Portfolio Management,* pp. 74–77.

CHAPTER 4 OPTION COMBINATIONS AND SPREADS

Articles

Frankfurter, G., R. Stevenson, and A. Young. (1979, Spring). Option Spreading: Theory and an Illustration. *Journal of Portfolio Management,* pp. 59–63.

Heston, J. Clark. (1986, October). Option Calendar Spreads: A Good Bet Over Time. *Futures,* pp. 60–62.

Raphael, Ken. (1985, October). Using Option Pricing Models in Neutral Spread Strategies. *Futures,* p. 64.

Ritchken, P., and H. Salkin. (1983, Spring). Safety First Selection Techniques for Option Spreads. *Journal of Portfolio Management,* pp. 61–67.

Slivka, R. (1981, Spring). Call Option Spreading. *Journal of Portfolio Management,* pp. 71–76.

CHAPTER 5 OPTION PRICING

Books

Bookstaber, Richard. (1981). *Option Pricing and Strategies in Investing.* Reading, MA: Addison-Wesley. This well-known book provides an intermediate discussion of options pricing and other arbitrage relationships.

Brenner, M. (1983). *Option Pricing.* Lexington, MA: Lexington Books. This technical book is a collection of papers presented at an options conference sponsored by Salomon Brothers in 1982. The book includes papers on commodity option pricing and option pricing applied to bank debt portfolios.

Cox, J., and M. Rubenstein. (1985). *Options Markets.* Englewood Cliffs, NJ: Prentice-Hall. This is perhaps the best available book on option pricing. While quite mathematical, it provides good intuition into the arbitrage issues that surround option pricing. It is an excellent reference source.

Jarrow, Robert A., and Andrew Rudd. (1983). *Option Pricing.* Homewood, IL: Richard D. Irwin. This is a rather mathematical treatise on option pricing; an understanding of calculus is necessary to follow much of the discussion. The book provides a very thorough discussion of alternative option pricing models.

Ritchken, P. (1987). *Options: Theory, Strategy, and Applications.* Glenview, IL: Scott Foresman. This is an excellent treatise on the theory and application of options. While much of it is heavy with mathematics, it is an excellent reference source. It provides good intuition into some complicated theoretical issues regarding option pricing.

Articles

Beckers, S. (1981, September). Standard Deviations Implied in Option Prices as Predictors of Future Stock Price Variability. *Journal of Banking and Finance,* pp. 363–82.

Black, F., and M. Scholes. (1973, May). The Pricing of Options and Corporate Liabilities. *Journal of Political Economics,* pp. 637–59.

Boness, A. J. (1964). Elements of a Theory of Stock Option Value. *Journal of Political Economy,* 72, pp. 163–75.

Brennan, M., and E. Schwartz. (1977, May). The Valuation of American Put Options. *Journal of Finance,* pp. 449–62.

Dimson, E. (1977, November/December). Option Valuation Nomograms. *Financial Analysts Journal,* pp. 71–74.

Gould, J., and D. Galai. (1974, July). Transactions Costs and the Relationship Between Put and Call Prices. *Journal of Financial Economics,* pp. 105–30.

Klemkosky, R., and T. Maness. (1974, Winter). The Impact of Options on the Underlying Securities. *Journal of Portfolio Management,* pp. 12–18.

——————, and B. Resnick. (1979, December). Put-Call Parity and Market Efficiency. *Journal of Finance,* pp. 1141–46.

Latane, H., and R. Rendleman. (1980, January). Standard Deviations of Stock Price Ratios Implied in Option Prices. *Journal of Finance,* pp. 67–78.

Merton, R. (1973, Spring). Theory of Rational Option Pricing. *Bell Journal of Economics and Management Science,* pp. 141–83.

Parkinson, M. (1977, January). Option Pricing: The American Put. *Journal of Business,* pp. 21–36.

Rogalski, R. (1977, Winter). Variances and Option Prices in Theory and Practice. *Journal of Portfolio Management,* pp. 43–51.

Stoll. H. (1969, December). The Relationship Between Put and Call Option Prices. *Journal of Finance,* pp. 801–24.

Sullivan, Edward J., and Timothy M. Weithers. (1991, Spring). Louis Bachelier: The Father of Modern Option Pricing Theory. *Journal of Economic Education,* pp. 165–71.

CHAPTER 6 DELTA, GAMMA, AND THETA

Articles

Chambers, Donald R., and Nelson J. Lacey. (1990). More Generalized Hedging Models for Options. In *Managing Institutional Assets,* ed. Frank J. Fabozzi. New York: Harper & Row, pp. 585–602.

Conine, Thomas E., and Maurry Tamarkin. (1984, November). A Pedagogic Note on the Derivation of the Comparative Statics of the Option Pricing Model. In *Financial Review,* pp. 397–400.

Strong, Robert A., and Amy Dickinson. Forecasting Better OEX Hedge Ratios. *Financial Analysts Journal,* forthcoming.

CHAPTER 7   STOCK INDEX OPTIONS AND OVERWRITING STRATEGIES

Books

Fabozzi, Frank H., and Gregory M. Kipnes, eds. (1989). *The Handbook of Stock Index Futures and Options.* Homewood, IL: Dow Jones-Irwin. This is a collection of twenty-six chapters on various applications of stock index futures and option contracts. It is a handy reference tool.

Articles

Clark, Stephen E. (1990, November). Portfolio Strategy: Overwriting Options. *Institutional Investor,* pp. 22–26.

Dawson, F. (1978, Winter). Risks and Returns in Continuous Option Writing. *Journal of Portfolio Management,* pp. 58–63.

Evnine, Jeremy, and Andrew Rudd. (1985, July). Index Options: The Early Evidence. *Journal of Finance,* pp. 743–56.

Hardy, Steve. (1986, October). Index Options Versus Stock Options. *Intermarket,* pp. 70–71.

Pounds, H. (1977, Winter). Covered Call Writing: Strategies and Results. *Journal of Portfolio Management,* pp. 331–42.

Szala, Ginger. (1986, January). Overwriting Options to Boost Portfolio Returns. *Futures,* pp. 60–61.

CHAPTER 8   FUNDAMENTALS ON THE FUTURES MARKET

Books

Kolb, Robert. (1988). *Understanding Futures Markets.* Glenview, IL: Scott Foresman. This is a good, all-purpose exposition of the futures market. Non-mathematical, it is within reach of anyone who has a basic understanding of the security markets.

Seidel, Andrew D., and Philip M. Ginsberg. (1983). *Commodities Trading.* Chicago: Chicago Board of Trade. This is an important reference tool that provides an interesting discussion of the development of the marketplace and a concise explanation of hedging and speculating. I find its primary value in the detailed description of the futures contracts, to include position limits, trading hours, contract size, etc. The book covers all U.S. futures exchanges in addition to the Chicago Board of Trade.

Tamarkin, Bob. (1985). *The New Gatsbys.* New York: Quill. This book is to the futures market what *A Random Walk Down Wall Street* is to the stock market. Extremely easy and enjoyable to read, the book offers many informative vignettes of rags to riches stories, and vice-versa! The reader gets a feel for the development of the exchanges and for the life of a scalper. This book should be required reading for anyone studying the pits.

Teweles, Richard, Charles Harlow, and Herbert Stone. (1977). *The Commodity Futures Game: Who Wins? Who Loses? Why?* New York: McGraw-Hill. This classic book has been used in a great many settings as an introduction to the futures market. It is not written as a textbook, and at times is wordy and lacking in organization. But it contains many interesting ideas and perspectives. The serious student of the futures market will find it useful.

Articles

Black, F. (1976, January/March). The Pricing of Commodity Contracts. *Journal of Financial Economics,* pp. 167–79.

Carlton, D. (1984, Fall). Futures Markets: Their Purpose, Their History, Their Successes and Failures. *Journal of Futures Markets,* pp. 237–71.

Cootner, Paul. (1967). Speculation and Hedging. *Food Research Institute Studies,* Sup 7, pp. 369–92.

Edwards, R. (1983, Winter). The Clearing Association in Futures Markets: Grantor and Regulator. *Journal of Futures Markets,* pp. 369–92.

Gregory-Williams, E. (1987, October). Selling What Isn't Yours to Sell . . . Sort Of. *Futures,* pp. 88, 90.

Kamara, A. (1984, July/August). The Behavior of Futures Prices: A Review of Theory and Evidence. *Financial Analysts Journal,* pp. 68–75.

Raynaud, J., and J. Tessier. (1984, Summer). Risk Premiums in Futures Markets: An Empirical Investigation. *Journal of Futures Markets,* pp. 189–211.

Rockwell, Charles. (1967). Normal Backwardation, Forecasting, and the Returns to Commodity Futures Traders. *Food Research Institute Studies,* Sup 7, pp. 107–30.

Silber, G. (1987, October). How to Break a Losing Streak. *Futures,* pp. 80–81.

Working, Holbrook. (1949, December). The Theory of Price of Storage. *American Economic Review,* p. 1262.

_____. (1953, June). Futures Trading and Hedging. *American Economic Review,* pp. 314–41.

CHAPTER 9 STOCK INDEX FUTURES

Books

Ansbacher, M. (1983). *The New Stock Index Market.* This is a better-than-average "how-to" book on stock index futures.

Fabozzi, F., and G. Kipnis, eds. (1984). *Stock Index Futures.* Homewood, IL: Dow Jones-Irwin. This is a well-done collection of articles by preeminent authors on numerous aspects of stock index futures.

Figlewski, Stephen. (1986). *Hedging with Financial Futures for Institutional Investors.* Cambridge, MA: Ballinger. Stephen Figlewski is a respected figure in both academics and on the street. This is a "cookbook" that does a nice job of moving from theory to practice. It is useful for the person interested in the relationship between portfolio management and the futures management.

Loosigan, Allen. (1985). *Stock Index Futures.* Reading, MA: Addison-Wesley. This is a rather basic book that is quite easy to read. It probably accomplishes its purpose of acquainting the reader with stock index futures but will leave many questions unanswered for the more intellectual reader.

Luskin, Donald L. (1987). *Index Options and Futures.* New York: John Wiley & Sons. This is a useful, up-to-date book that provides a generally easy to read description of index options and futures and their uses. The first section of the book is titled "Nuts and Bolts" and provides an excellent overview of the marketplace. Chapter 3 describes the world of the floor trader at the CBOE and CBT in lucid, fascinating detail.

Schwartz, Edward, Joanne Hill, and Thomas Schneeweis. (1986). *Financial Futures.* Homewood, IL: Irwin. This book is much longer than it needs to be, and the reader must search to find specific points. There is some excellent material here, and it is unfortunate that the text is often cryptic.

Articles

Figlewski, S. (1985, Summer). Hedging with Stock Index Futures: Theory and Application in a New Market. *Journal of Futures Markets*, pp. 183–99.

Gastineau, G., and A. Mandansky. (1983, November/December). S&P 500 Index Futures Evaluation Tables. *Financial Analysts Journal.*

Junkus, J. (1986, Fall). Weekend and Day of the Week Effects in Returns on Stock Index Futures. *Journal of Futures Markets*, pp. 397–408.

Modest, D. (1984, Summer). On the Pricing of Stock Index Futures. *Journal of Portfolio Management*, pp. 51–57.

Nordhauser, F. (1984, Spring). Using Stock Index Futures to Reduce Market Risk. *Journal of Portfolio Management*, pp. 56–62.

Roevs, Alden, and David P. Jacob. (1986, Spring). Futures and Alternative Hedge Ratio Methodologies. *Journal of Portfolio Management*, pp. 60–70.

CHAPTER 10 FOREIGN EXCHANGE FUTURES

Articles

Black, Fischer. (1990, July). Equilibrium Exchange Rate Hedging. *Journal of Finance*, pp. 899–907.

Celebuski, Matthew J., Joanne Hill, and John Kilgannon. (1990, January/February). Managing Currency Exposures in International Portfolios. *Financial Analysts Journal*, pp. 16–22.

Eaker, Mark R., and Dwight M. Grant. (1990, Fall). Currency Hedging Strategies for Internationally Diversified Equity Portfolios. *Journal of Portfolio Management*, pp. 74–80.

Hammer, Jerry A. (1990, Winter). Hedging Performance and Hedging Objectives: Tests of New Performance Measure in the Foreign Currency Market. *Journal of Financial Research*, pp. 307–23.

Hill, Joanne M., and Thomas Schneeweis. (1981, Winter). A Note on the Hedging Effectiveness of Foreign Currency Futures. *Journal of Futures Markets*, pp. 659–64.

Hilley, J., C. Beidleman, and J. Greenleaf. (1979, Winter). Does Covered Interest Arbitrage Dominate in Foreign Exchange Markets? *Columbia Journal of World Business*, pp. 99–107.

CHAPTER 11   INTEREST RATE FUTURES

Books

Not in TX

Burghardt, Belaton, Lane, Luce, & McVey. (1991). *Eurodollar Futures and Options.* Chicago: Probus. This book is aptly subtitled "Controlling Money Market Risk." Swaps, caps, collars, etc. are covered in its 500 pages.

Kolb, Robert (1982). *Interest Rate Futures.* Richmond, VA: Robert F. Dame. This is a useful, although somewhat out-of-date, discussion of financial futures. Many of the numerical examples of hedging and speculating are quite instructive. It contains a particularly useful discussion of immunization of fixed income portfolios.

Articles

Bacon, P., and R. Williams. (1978, Spring). Interest Rate Futures: New Tools for the Financial Manager. *Financial Management,* pp. 32–38.

Bortz, G. (1984, Spring). Does the Treasury Bond Futures Market Destabilize the Treasury Bond Cash Market? *Journal of Futures Markets,* pp. 25–38.

Gay, G., and R. Kolb. (1983, Fall). The Management of Interest Rate Risk. *Journal of Portfolio Management,* pp. 65–70.

Hemler, Michael L. (1990, December). The Quality Delivery Option in Treasury Bond Futures Contracts. *Journal of Finance,* pp. 1565–86.

Hill, J., and T. Schneeweis. (1984, November/December). Reducing Volatility with Financial Futures. *Financial Analysts Journal,* pp. 34–40.

Livingston, M. (1984, Summer). The Cheapest Deliverable Bond of the CBT Treasury Bond Futures Contract. *Journal of Futures Markets,* pp. 161–72.

Poole, William. (1978, Spring). Using T-Bill Futures to Gauge Interest Rate Expectations. *Federal Reserve Bank of San Francisco Economic Review,* pp. 7–19.

CHAPTER 12 IMMUNIZATION AND SPREADING STRATEGIES

Articles

Arak, Marcelle, Philip Fischer, Laurie Goodman, and Raj Daryanani. (1987, August). The Municipal-Treasury Futures Spread. *Journal of Futures Markets,* pp. 173–87.

Bierwag, G. O. (1979, April). Dynamic Portfolio Immunization Policies. *Journal of Banking and Finance,* pp. 23–41.

_____. (1977, December). Immunization, Duration, and the Term Structure of Interest Rates. *Journal of Financial and Quantitative Analysis,* pp. 725–42.

Chambers, Donald R. (1984, Summer). An Immunization Strategy for Futures Contracts on Government Securities. *Journal of Futures Markets,* pp. 173–87.

Chance, D. (1982, Fall). An Immunized-Hedge Procedure for Bond Futures. *Journal of Futures Markets,* pp. 231–42.

_____. (1986, March). Futures Contracts and Immunization. Review of Research in Futures Markets, pp. 124–40.

Labuzewski, John W. (1989, May). Examining Duration, "Hedge Ratio," and Basis Risk to Hedge Securities. *Futures,* pp. 50–51.

Little, Patricia Knain. (1986, Spring). Financial Futures and Immunization. *Journal of Financial Research,* pp. 1–12.

Miller, Robert. (1990, October). Putting on the TED Spread. *Futures and Options World,* pp. 38–39.

Slentz, James W. (1992, August/September). The Kringle Crinkle: A Year-End LED Spread. *Trade Market Perspectives,* pp. 1–2.

Veit, E., and W. Reiff. (1983, Fall). Commercial Banks and Interest Rate Futures: A Hedging Survey. *Journal of Futures Markets,* pp. 283–93.

CHAPTER 13 FUTURES OPTIONS AND OTHER DERIVATIVE ASSETS

Books

Editors of *Futures. Ag Options.* This soft-cover book is a step-by-step introduction to options on agricultural futures.

Labuszewski, J., and J. Sinquefield. (1985). *Inside the Commodity Options Markets.* This is a substantially above average practitioner's guide to commodity option strategies. The book does a particularly thorough job of discussing option pricing.

Mayer, T. *Commodity Options.* A basic guide to speculating and hedging with futures options. The book gives extensive detail to strategies, delta neutral positions, and intrinsic value calculation.

Thorp, E., and S. Kassouf. (1967). *Beat the Market.* New York: Random House. Despite its immodest title, this book has become a classic. It deals with a real-world application of warrant hedging and describes the success of this strategy over a period of time.

Articles

Burghardt, Glaen, and Morton Lane. (1990, Winter). How to Tell if Options Are Cheap. *Journal of Portfolio Management,* pp. 72–78.

Chance, Don M. (1990, Summer). Option Volume and Stock Market Performance. *Journal of Portfolio Management,* pp. 42–51.

Chang, K., and L. Shanker. (1986, Summer). Hedging Effectiveness of

Currency Options and Currency Futures. *Journal of Futures Markets*, pp. 289–306.

Goodman, L., S. Ross, and F. Schmidt. (1985, Fall). Are Foreign Currency Options Overvalued? The Early Experience of the Philadelphia Stock Exchange. *Journal of Futures Markets*, pp. 349–59.

Hauser, R., and D. Neff. (1985, Winter). Pricing Options on Agricultural Futures: Departures from Traditional Theory. *Journal of Futures Markets*, pp. 65–68.

Oldfield, G., and D. Siefel. (1984, Winter). Futures Contract Options. *Journal of Futures Markets*, pp. 479–90.

Shastri, K., and K. Tandon. (1986, Spring). On the Use of European Models to Price American Options. *Journal of Futures Markets*, pp. 93–108.

Thomas, L. (1985, Fall). A Winning Strategy for Currency-Futures Speculation. *Journal of Portfolio Management*, pp. 65–69.

Whaley, R. (1986, May/June). On Valuing American Futures Options. *Financial Analysts Journal*, pp. 49–59.

Wolf, Avner. (1984, Winter). Options on Futures: Pricing and the Effects of an Anticipated Price Change. *Journal of Futures Markets*, pp. 491–512.

CHAPTER 14   RISK MANAGEMENT

Books

Gastineau, Gary L. (1992). *Dictionary of Financial Risk Management*. Chicago: Probus. This is an excellent reference book containing a very complete listing of terms that have been spawned by the growth of risk management applications.

Articles

Moriarty, E., S. Phillips, and P. Tosini. (1981, January/February). A Comparison of Options and Futures in the Management of Portfolio Risk. *Financial Analysts Journal*, pp. 61–67.

Nusbaum, David. (1992, July). Where No Trading System Has Gone Before. *Futures*, pp. 46–50.

CHAPTER 15 FINANCIAL ENGINEERING, GLOBEX, AND PROGRAM TRADING

Books

Smith, Clifford W., and Charles W. Smithson, eds. (1990). *The Handbook of Financial Engineering*. New York: Harper & Row. This is a collection of thirty-two chapters on various aspects of financial engineering, each written by a prominent researcher or investment professional. It is a useful reference volume.

Articles

Finnerty, John D. (1988, Winter). Financial Engineering in Corporate Finance: An Overview. *Financial Management*, pp. 14–33.

Furbush, Dean. (1989, Autumn). Program Trading and Price Movement: Evidence from the October 1987 Market Crash. *Financial Management*, pp. 68–83.

Gould, F. J. "Stock Index Futures: The Arbitrage Cycle and Portfolio Insurance. *Financial Analysts Journal*, pp. 48–62.

Grant, James L. (1990, Winter). Stock Return Volatility During the Crash of 1987. *Journal of Portfolio Management*, pp. 69–71.

Harris, Lawrence. (1989, March). The October 1987 S&P 500 Stock-Futures Basis. *Journal of Finance*, pp. 77–100.

Heston, C. (1987, March). Buying and Selling Insurance in the Futures and Options Markets. *Futures*, pp. 60–61.

Hill, Joanne M., and Frank J. Jones. (1988, July/August). Equity Trading, Program Trading, Portfolio Insurance, Computer Trading, and All That. *Financial Analysts Journal*, pp. 29–38.

Jarrow, Robert A., and Maureen O'Hara. (1989, December). Primes and Scores: An Essay on Market Imperfections. *Journal of Finance*, pp. 1263–88.

Keane, Simon M. (1988, January/February). October 1987 and the Efficient Market. *Financial Analysts Journal*, pp. 6–7.

Kritzman, M. (1986, Fall). What's Wrong with Portfolio Insurance. *Journal of Portfolio Management*, pp. 13–17.

Leland, H. (1980, May). Who Buys Portfolio Insurance? *Journal of Finance*, pp. 581–94.

Levinson, M. (1987, March). Program Trading May Help the Small Investor. *Futures*, p. 12.

Pratt, Tom. (1992, January 13). Percs After Market Trading Seen as Red Flag for Street. *Investment Dealers' Digest*, p. 15.

Rubenstein, Mark. (1988, January/February). Portfolio Insurance and the Market Crash. *Financial Analysts Journal*, pp. 38–47.

Singleton, J., and R. Grieves. (F1984, Spring). Synthetic Puts and Portfolio Insurance Strategies. *Journal of Portfolio Management*, pp. 63–69.

Stoll, Hans R. (1988, August). Index Futures, Program Trading, and Stock Market Procedures. *Journal of Futures Markets*, pp. 391–412.

Strong, Robert A. (1991, June). Engineering a Long-Term Put. *Futures*, pp. 32–34.

Szala, G. (1987, April). How Pension Fund Managers Look at "Insurance" Tools. *Futures*, pp. 48–49.

CHAPTER 16   PRECIOUS METALS

Books

Sherman, E. (1986). *Gold Investment Theory and Application.* New York: New York Institute of Finance/Prentice Hall. This book contains numerous statistics on gold production and use. Chapter 6 provides a comparison of gold prices, stocks, bonds, and the money market in six countries over the period 1963–83.

Articles

Brauer, G., and R. Ravichandran. (1986, Summer). How Sweet Is Silver? *Journal of Portfolio Management*, pp. 33–42.

Carter, J., J. Allfeck-Graves, and A. Money. (1983, Fall). Are Gold Shares Better than Gold for Diversification? *Journal of Portfolio Management*, pp. 52–55.

Followill, Richard A., and Billy P. Helms. (1990, August), Put-Call-Futures Parity and Arbitrage Opportunity in the Market for Options on Gold Futures Contracts. *Journal of Futures Markets*, pp. 999–1021.

Ma, C. (1986, Fall). A Further Investigation of the Day of the Week Effects in the Gold Market. *Journal of Futures Markets*, pp. 409–20.

_____. (1985, Winter). Spreading Between the Gold and Silver Markets: Is There a Parity? *Journal of Futures Markets*, pp. 579–94.

McDonald, J., and B. Solnik. (1977, Spring). Valuation and Strategy for Gold Stocks. *Journal of Portfolio Management,* pp. 23–33.

Monroe, M., and R. Cohn. (1986, Fall). The Relative Efficiency of the Gold and Treasury Bill Futures Markets. *Journal of Futures Markets,* pp. 477–94.

Poitras, Geoffrey. (1990, December). The Distribution of Gold Futures Spreads. *Journal of Futures Markets,* pp. 643–59.

Renshaw, A., and E. Renshaw. (1982, Spring). Does Gold Have a Place in Investment Portfolios? *Journal of Portfolio Management,* pp. 28–31.

Sherman, E. (Spring, 1983). A Gold Pricing Model. *Journal of Portfolio Management,* pp. 68–70.

_____. Gold: A Conservative, Prudent Diversifier. *Journal of Portfolio Management,* pp. 21–27.

Shisko, I. (1977, Spring). Why Gold? *Journal of Portfolio Management,* pp. 34–40.

Tauber, R. (1981, Fall). Is Gold a Prudent Investment Under Erisa? *Journal of Portfolio Management,* pp. 29–31.

IMPORTANT ADDRESSES

Exchanges

American Stock Exchange
Derivative Securities
86 Trinity Place
New York, NY 10006
(212) 306-1000

Australian Stock Exchange
20 Bond Street
Sydney, NSW 2000
Australia
61-2-227-0000

Baltic Futures Exchange
24/28 St. Mary Axe
London, England EC3A 8EP
44-1-283-5146

Brazilian Futures Exchange
Rua do Mercado 11-6 Andar
20010 Rio de Janiero
Brazil
55-21-271-1088

Chicago Board of Trade
141 W. Jackson Blvd.
Chicago, IL 60604
(312) 435-3620

Chicago Board Options Exchange
400 S. LaSalle Street
Chicago, IL 60605
(312) 786-5600

Chicago Rice & Cotton Exchange
141 W. Jackson Blvd.
Chicago, IL 60604
(312) 341-3078

Coffee, Sugar & Cocoa Exchange, Inc.
4 World Trade Center
New York, NY 10048
(212) 938-2800

Commodity Exchange, Inc. (COMEX)
4 World Trade Center
New York, NY 10048
(212) 938-2900

European Options Exchange
Rokin 65, 1012 KK Amsterdam
The Netherlands
31-20-550-4550

Financiele Termijnmarkt Amsterdam N. V.
Nes 49, 1012 KK Amsterdam
The Netherlands
31-20-550-4555

International Futures Exchange (Bermuda) Ltd.
P. O. Box HM579, The Perry Bldg.
40 Church Street
Hamilton, Bermuda HMCX
(212) 809-7070

International Petroleum Exchange of
    London, Ltd.
International House
1 St. Katherine's Way
London, England E1 9UN
44-71-481-0843

International Stock Exchange
Old Broad Street
London, England EC2N 1HP
44-1-588-2355

Hong Kong Futures Exchange, Ltd.
5/F Asia Pacific Finance Tower
Citibank Plaza
3 Garden Way
Hong Kong
852-842-9333

Kansas City Board of Trade
4800 Main Street, Suite 303
Kansas City, MO 64112
(816) 753-7500

Kuala Lumpur Commodity Exchange
Fourth Floor, City Point
Komplex Dayabumi
Jalan Sultan Hishamuddin
P. O. Box 11260
50740 Kuala Lumpur, Malaysia
60-3-2936822

London Commodity Exchange, Ltd.
Cereal House, 58 Mark Lane
London, England EC3R 7NE
01-480-2080

London Futures and Options Exchange
1 Commodity Quay
St. Katherine Docks
London, England E1 9AX
44-1-481-2080

London International Financial Futures
    and Options Exchange
Cannon Bridge
London, England EC4R 3XX
44-71-623-0444

London Metal Exchange
Plantation House, Fenchurch Street
London, England EC3M 3AP
44-1-626-3311

Marche a Terme des Instruments Financiers
    de Paris
108 rue de Richelieu
Paris, France 75002
33-1-40-15-21-21

MidAmerica Commodity Exchange
141 W. Jackson Boulevard
Chicago, IL 60604
(312) 341-3000

Midwest Stock Exchange
440 S. LaSalle Street
Chicago, IL 60605
(312) 663-2222

Minneapolis Grain Exchange
400 S. Fourth Street
Minneapolis, MN 55415
(612) 338-6212

Montreal Exchange
The Stock Exchange Tower, C. P. 61
800 Square Victoria
Montreal, Que.
Canada H4Z 1A9
(514) 871-2424

New York Cotton Exchange
4 World Trade Center
New York, NY 10048
(212) 938-2702

New York Futures Exchange
20 Broad Street
New York, NY 10005
(212) 656-4949
(800) 221-7722

New York Mercantile Exchange
4 World Trade Center
New York, NY 10048
(212) 938-2222

New York Stock Exchange
11 Wall Street
New York, NY 10005
(212) 656-8533

New Zealand Futures Exchange Ltd.
P. O. Box 6734, Wellesley Street
Auckland, New Zealand
64-9-309-8308

Osaka Securities Exchange
8-16, Kitahama, 1-Chome, Chuo-ku
Osaka, 541, Japan
81-6-229-8643

Pacific Stock Exchange
301 Pine Street
San Francisco, CA 94104
(415) 393-4000

Paris Futures Exchange
Bourse do Commerce
2 rue de Viarmes
75001 Paris, France
33-1-45-08-82-50

Philadelphia Board of Trade
1900 Market Street
Philadelphia, PA 19103
(215) 496-5000

Philadelphia Stock Exchange
1900 Market Street
Philadelphia, PA 19103
(215) 496-5000

Sao Paulo Commodities Exchange
Rua Libero Badaro, 471 Fourth Floor
Sao Paulo, Brazil 01009
55-11-32-3101

Singapore International Monetary Exchange
1 Raffles Place, No 07-00
World Trade Centre, Singapore 0409
65-535-7382

Stockholm Options Market
Box 16305
S-10326 Stockholm, Sweden
46-8-700-0600

Swedish Options and Futures Exchange
P. O. Box 7267
Stockholm, Sweden 103 87
46-8-791-4080

Swiss Options and Financial Futures Exchange
Neumattstrasse 7
CH-8953 Dietikon
Switzerland
41-1-740-3020

Sydney Futures Exchange, Ltd.
30-32 Grosvenor St.
Sydney, N. S. W. 2000
Australia
61-2-256-0555

Toronto Futures Exchange
2 First Canadian Place
The Exchange Tower, Toronto, Ont.
Canada M5X 1J2
(416) 947-4487

Toronto Stock Exchange
2 First Canadian Place
The Exchange Tower, Toronto, Ont.
Canada M5X 1J2
(416) 947-4700

Vancouver Stock Exchange
609 Granville Street
Stock Exchange Tower
Vancouver, B. C.
Canada V7Y 1H1
(604) 689-3334

Winnipeg Commodity Exchange
500 Commodity Exchange Tower
360 Main Street
Winnipeg, Manitoba
Canada R3C 3Z4
(204) 949-0495

Clearinghouses

Board of Trade Clearing Corporation
141 W. Jackson Blvd., Suite 1460
Chicago, IL 60604
(312) 786-5700

Chambre de Compensation des Instruments
    Financiers de Paris
15, rue de la Banque
Paris, France 75002
33-1-42-96-53-65

Chicago Mercantile Exchange Clearinghouse
30 S. Wacker Drive
Chicago, IL 60606
(312) 930-3170

COMEX Clearing Association
4 World Trade Center, Suite 7300-D
New York, NY 10048

Commodity Clearing Corporation
4 World Trade Center, Suite 7300-C
New York, NY 10048
(212) 775-0190

CSC Clearing Corporation
4 World Trade Center, Suite 7300-A
New York, NY 10048
(212) 775-0900

European Stock Options Clearing Corporation
Rokin 65, Amsterdam
1012 KK The Netherlands
31-20-550-4511

International Commodities Clearing House, Ltd.
Roman Wall House, 1-2 Crutched
Friars, London, England EC3N 2AN
44-1-488-3200

KCBT Clearing Corporation
4800 Main St., Suite 270
Kansas City, MO 64112
(816) 931-8964

Minneapolis Grain Exchange Clearinghouse
400 S. Fourth, Rm. 150
Minneapolis, MN 55415
(612) 333-1623

NYMEX Clearinghouse
4 World Trade Center, Suite 744
New York, NY 10048
(212) 938-2206

Options Clearing Corporation
440 S. LaSalle St., Suite 908
Chicago, IL 60605
(312) 322-6200

Trans-Canada Options Corporation
The Exchange Tower
First Canadian Place
Toronto, Canada M5X 1B1

Regulatory Agencies

National Association of Securities Dealers
1735 K Street, NW
Washington, D. C. 20006
(202) 728-8955

Securities and Exchange Commission
450 Fifth Street, NW
Washington, D. C. 20549
(202) 272-3100

Commodity Futures Trading Commission
2033 K Street, NW
Washington, D. C. 20581
(202) 254-6387

Professional Associations

American Association of Individual Investors
612 N. Michigan Avenue
Chicago, IL 60611
(312) 280-0170

Financial Analysts Federation
1633 Broadway, 14th Floor
New York, NY 10019
(212) 957-2860

Futures Industry Association
2001 Pennsylvania Avenue, NW Suite 600
Washington, D. C. 20006
(202) 466-5460

National Futures Association
200 W. Madison Street, Suite 1600
Chicago, IL 60606-3447
(312) 781-1300
(800) 572-9400

Security Industry Association
120 Broadway, 35th Floor
New York, NY 10271
(212) 608-1500

Other Groups

Gold Information Center
900 Third Avenue
New York, NY 10022

Industry Council for Tangible Assets
214 Massachusetts Avenue, N. E. Suite 560
Washington, D. C. 20002
(202) 544-1101

International Precious Metals Institute
Government Building, ABE Airport
Allentown, PA 18103
(215) 266-1570

ACKNOWLEDGMENTS

Table 4-13 From "How to Survive the First Few Months of Options Trading," by William Degler, *Futures*, 219 Parkade, Cedar Falls, Iowa 50613, August 1986, pp. 52–53.

Figure 7-4 Reprinted by permission of the Options Clearing Corporation, 440 S. La Salle Street, Chicago, IL 60605.

Figure 8-1, 8-2 Source: Chicago Mercantile Exchange; Figure 8-3 Reprinted from *Futures*, June 1987, 219 Parkade, Cedar Falls, Iowa 50613; Figure 8-4 Source: Chicago Mercantile Exchange; Figure 8-6 Reprinted from *Futures*, December 1986, 219 Parkade, Cedar Falls, Iowa 50613; Figure 8-8 By Brenda Burbank, reprinted by permission of THE ROTARIAN.

Table 10-2 Reprinted with permission from *Treasury*, spring 1993, p. 19. All Rights Reserved.

Box 15.1 Reprinted from *Futures*, October 1992, 219 Parkade, Cedar Falls, Iowa 50613; Table 15A-1, Figure 15A-6 Reprinted from *Futures*, December 1987, 219 Parkade, Cedar Falls, Iowa 50613.

Box 16.1 Reprinted from *Futures*, November 1988, 219 Parkade, Cedar Falls, Iowa 50613; Figure 16-2 Reprinted by permission of the Chicago Board of Trade. All Rights Reserved.

Index